W9-CJZ-280

GUIDE TO

Grantseeking on the Web

THE
FOUNDATION
CENTER'S

GUIDE TO

Grantseeking on the Web

CONTRIBUTING STAFF

The operation of the Foundation Center's Web site is truly a team effort. Similarly, this book is the result of the hard work of the following staff, as well as their considerable experience with the World Wide Web.

Kathleen Collins	Beverly McGrath
Sarah Collins	David Mitchum
Elizabeth Cuccaro	Mitchell Nauffts
Jeffrey Falkenstein	Ellen Przybyla
Andrea Feld	Frederick Schoff
Susanne Leigh Goddeau	Amanda Spielman
Rebecca Kopf	Renée Westmoreland
Cheryl Loe	

The Foundation Center also thanks the Fund for the City of New York <http://www.fcny.org> for generously contributing the material in Appendix B, "How to Connect to the Internet." The appendix is based on material presented in training offered through the Fund's Internet Academy. The full range of offerings of the Internet Academy can be viewed at <http://www.fcny.org> within the "Technology and Information" section.

Library of Congress Cataloging-in-Publication Data
The Foundation Center's guide to grantseeking on the web.
     p.   cm.
    Includes bibliographical references.
    ISBN 0-87954-800-2
    1. Fund raising—Computer network resources—Directories.
2. Endowments—Computer network resources—Directories. 3. Web sites—Directories. I. Foundation Center. II. Title: Guide to grant seeking on the web. III. Title: Guide to grant seeking on the web.
HV41.2.F68   1998
025.06´65815224—dc21   98-33151
                               CIP

TABLE OF CONTENTS

FOREWORD

The World Wide Web is building community in the nonprofit field in an unprecedented way. Because of the number of us who now actively use the World Wide Web, we are able to witness this development as it unfolds. Where initially we marvelled at the "culture of the Web" as we tried to adapt to it, we are now perhaps more often awed by the "web of our networked culture." In many visible ways, the culture of the nonprofit sector is forming around and being formed by the concepts, practices, predictions, and, yes, the risks that are being taken within the Internet environment.

Like other important new popular media of this century, in particular the telephone and the television, the Internet demonstrates great power not only as a communication tool but also as a reshaper of culture. The World Wide Web is both a reflection and a cornerstone of our increasingly global society. Earlier in this decade, we heard dire warnings that this new medium would be captured by commercial, for-profit, .com ("dot com") interests, that the communal, sharing ethos and culture of the Internet would be destroyed. It has now become clear that the very technology of the Web would not permit outright monopolization. (See Appendix A for a discussion of the technology underlying the Internet.) While large commercial interests do have the resources to be the most visible players, any community of interest can find a place on the Web so long as it has conviction, energy, and the most basic resources needed to place itself there. In fact, the culture of the Web seems ideally suited to embrace and serve the nonprofit community.

Web observers are now heralding the "virtual communities" being formed in cyberspace. With our own Web site and with publication of this print volume, the Foundation Center is both documenting and contributing to the creation of a fully networked philanthropic community. We have created Your Gateway to Philanthropy on the World Wide Web. We hope it opens doorways for you as you pursue your goals.

Sara Engelhardt
October 1998

INTRODUCTION

The Foundation Center: Your Gateway to Philanthropy on the World Wide Web

The goal of this book is to save you time, to help you use the World Wide Web for finding information relevant to grantseeking. The Foundation Center decided to produce this print work to help people seek grants on the Web simply because, for all its wonders, the World Wide Web will chew up an extraordinary amount of your time. Using this book to become familiar with the Web resources available to grantseekers will help you make the most of your time spent online.

Foundation Center staff have been scanning the Web since 1994, when Netscape Navigator 1.0 was released and the Center launched its own Web site <www.fdncenter.org>. A primary goal of the Web site is to fulfill our organizational mission of fostering public understanding of the foundation field by collecting, organizing, analyzing, and disseminating information on foundations, corporate giving, and related subjects. However, in addition to helping describe and quantify the contributions of U.S. foundations to society, our Web site has given us the ability to provide grantseekers direct access to a tremendous variety of available Web resources, to be Your Gateway to Philanthropy on the World Wide Web.

Since 1994, Foundation Center staff have been cataloging Web sites of potential value to grantseekers interested in any and all potential sources of support—whether foundation funding, corporate giving programs, government grant and aid programs, or wealthy individuals identified through what is known as prospect research—and putting links to these sites on our Web site.

This book presents in linear print form the results of our continuous scanning of the Web. In many ways the presentation tracks the organization of our Web site.

Be forewarned. We fully expect that there will be some "broken links" in this print version of Your Gateway to Philanthropy on the World Wide Web (broken links are Web addresses that are no longer accurate). These only reflect the incredible dynamism of this new medium. A print version can only be a snapshot of the Web at a particular moment in time. Links change for any number of reasons. Sometimes individuals or small organizations cannot sustain the effort required to maintain a vital Web site. Some Web addresses will change because what was once a small effort hosted on someone else's computer has grown into a full-fledged site that is moved to a larger or dedicated host computer. In preparing this volume, we were excited to see the stability and indeed growth of sites concerned with philanthropy and the nonprofit world. As we discuss below, the development of the Web has observers talking about its potential for community building, and the energy and dynamism of the nonprofit world is plainly visible on the Web.

With our Web site and this book, the Foundation Center has created what is known in current Web parlance as a "portal," a concept we discuss more below. In short, a portal is a Web site organized to serve as an entrance point to the World Wide Web at large. In our case, we have created a specialty portal for grantseekers and others interested in philanthropy.

We continue to develop and expand the offerings of this gateway, trying to keep pace with the burgeoning Web. Once you have become familiar with the Web resources available in your areas of interest, we invite you to log onto <www.fdncenter.org> and follow the paths that open up to you.

Appendix A reviews the history of the Internet and the World Wide Web from a technology perspective. However, below we present a brief overview of how people's ability to access and interact with the World Wide Web has evolved in just a few short years. Our hope is that it serves to demonstrate for those new to the Web some of the trends driving the composition of Web services being offered as of late 1998.

From Surfing to Searching, From Portals to Community Building

COWABUNGA: WE ALL HIT THE SURF

When the Web was young, proprietary networks like Prodigy, Compuserve, America Online, and the Microsoft Network offered a collection of specific content modules they created and designed for you, in addition to Internet e-mail services. Many people first got on the Internet through these few proprietary doors. However, with the arrival of easy-to-use "browsers" (see Chapter 1), users soon opted for plain vanilla Internet access that allowed them to surf the Web on their own. Going through a proprietary network to get to the Web had become unnecessary. In response, the various proprietary networks began offering direct Internet access as an additional service in order to compete with a growing number of Internet Service Providers (ISPs), those companies that connect individual customers to the Internet.

Soon after, the proprietary networks began offering unlimited-use pricing (doing away with charging for time online) so that they could continue to compete with the ISPs. As further illustration of this trend, by the summer of 1998 the MSN Premier service of the Microsoft Network, deemed a failure as a proprietary network when compared to America Online, was renamed MSN Internet Access. According to a Microsoft spokesperson, "Internet access has become a distinct, and very important, service for customers, as many services that used to be tied to an ISP have evolved into free services on the Web. Today key differentiators for ISPs are great call success rates, fast login times, and high modem connection speeds."

SEARCH ENGINES

With easy-to-use browsers and direct access to the Web, people could "surf" the Web to their heart's content, or at least to the limits of their patience. The appearance of search engines available to anyone through a standard Web address was a great advance. Digital's AltaVista search engine was perhaps the most visible early entry. People could begin to actively seek out the information available on the Web themselves, rather than rely only on hyperlinks or word-of-mouth referrals to particular Web sites. The power and speed of AltaVista in particular was a real eye-opener. However, using a simple search engine across something as large and diverse as the Web has its drawbacks. Users were thrilled that they could surf the Web on their own, but they found themselves sifting through long search results lists that contained a lot of irrelevant material. As the Web expanded rapidly, containing more and more information, much of it frivolous, this problem grew worse. Hybrid search services arose that let users search the Web, but across indexes that had been prepared through editorial research, human beings reviewing and classifying Web sites. Yahoo! is probably the best known and most successful example.

Some observers insist that the vast, ever-expanding territory of the World Wide Web is still largely uncharted. For instance, the *Wall Street Journal* paraphrased a study published in the journal *Science*, saying that, "Even the most thorough search engine manages to find only about a third of the pages on the Web. . . . And other popular search sites cover 10% or less of the electronic universe." ("Web's Vastness Foils Even Best Search Engines," *Wall Street Journal*, Friday, April 3, 1998, p. B1.) The study was challenged by some of the leading search site companies, and indeed the percentages of coverage by various popular services listed in the study were estimates, but many people assert that it is impossible to index the entire Web, which grows daily. (Interestingly, that study did not even include Yahoo! The authors of the study did not consider it a search engine at all.)

Whatever their limitations, stand-alone search engines were a great boon to Web users. However, Web evolution proceeds rapidly, and many service providers, including various search engine sites, began aggregating a number of Internet services in order to create and/or maintain high traffic rates for their sites. These full-service sites were dubbed "portals." The term describes a Web page offering a variety of Web services, which people can use as a home base for all of their Web explorations, the page they choose as the first page they see when they log onto the Web and open their browser.

THE ARRIVAL OF "PORTALS"

Historically, the various search services worked differently, but that changed by mid-1998. Search capability became a commodity, with the various search software technologies homogenized by corporate acquisitions and licensing/co-branding agreements among the major players. For example, AT&T signed deals with Lycos, Excite, and Infoseek, three well-known search services. Excite paid handsomely to become the technology behind Netscape's search service. Microsoft licensed search technology from Inktomi (shortly after they had purchased the Hotmail e-mail service). As this evolution was taking place, search service providers began offering a cluster of Web services as a way to compete for Web traffic, the basis for advertising revenue, the primary successful online revenue model at that time.

Now when you visit various traditional "search sites," you will see that many of them offer, surrounding a basic "search" box, free e-mail services as well as the ability to customize your own search site "home page," creating your own personalized portal. Local weather, specific stock market quotations, particular news or sports feeds, and individual horoscopes can all greet you when you open up these search site pages (in addition to the advertisements that support their existence). They look very much like the customizable "start" page that was offered by Microsoft through Internet Explorer 4, which itself contained links to several search services.

Even those slow to get into the act moved into this full-service direction. For instance, AltaVista began to offer more at its site when its relative popularity dipped following the initial wonderment at the speed and scope of its search engine and the arrival of more competitors. In discussing Netscape's new portal, known as Netcenter, *Business Week* described their late entrance into this arena by saying "(Netscape) failed to spot the potential for turning the Netscape Web site into a marketplace of content and services to rival the popularity of Yahoo! Inc. and America Online Inc. It wasn't until October 1997 that they launched Netcenter, their content-oriented Web site." The article goes on to quote Marc Andreessen, who said, "Our biggest mistake was we didn't think of this two years ago." ("The Education of Marc Andreessen," *Business Week*, April 13, 1998).

The fact is, there are now many portal sites offering the same combination of services and links, even though they may have started out providing individual services quite distinct from each other. The blurring of distinctions between the operation of different search engines made search capability a commodity. There are even services, such as Metacrawler and Inference Find, that query several search services simultaneously.

Because the Web is a vast and ever-expanding territory, learning how to explore it on your own may come in handy, as well as further your understanding of the Web and how it works. On any of the Web portals that survive the millenium, you will have ready access to a variety of search engines. However, learning to use a search engine is not required in order to do funding research on the Web. Using a specialty portal like <www.fdncenter.org> will save you considerable time.

BEYOND PORTALS TO COMMUNITIES

User preferences and behavior evolve rapidly as the population becomes more sophisticated about the Web. With portals themselves rapidly becoming an undifferentiated commodity, some analysts have speculated that the anticipated advertising revenue required to support them may not be forthcoming. By late 1998, Excite, Yahoo!, Infoseek, Lycos, America Online, and others were trying to create "portal loyalty" by offering the ability for people with common interests to create their own private networks within their suite of services. The goal is to retain users, create loyalty to their portals, to support the advertising revenue model by capitalizing on the relationships that already exist in the real—as opposed to the virtual—world.

While not supported by advertising, the Foundation Center's Web site fills this role for its particular community by serving and indeed strengthening the relationships that exist within philanthropy. Since 1956 the Foundation Center has helped build effective bridges between grantseekers and grantmakers by providing information that can help people identify their common goals and interests and by educating grantseekers about the need to build relationships with grantmakers. In this way the Center's World Wide Web site is a powerful tool with which to further this goal of connecting the vital and important ideas of the nonprofit world with the resources that can help advance them.

Arrangement of the Book

Chapter 1 briefly discusses the genesis and development of Web "browsers," the software tools whose arrival fueled the tremendous growth of the Web and accelerated its evolution. After this brief discussion, this chapter presents the features and operation of a fully developed browser product, using Netscape Navigator 4.0 as a leading example. Those people new to Web, or those who may be upgrading their browser versions, can get a survey of the full set of tools these software products offer.

In Chapter 2 we discuss various approaches that independent private foundations have taken in using the World Wide Web within their operations. From simply providing basic information to actively championing the use of new communication technologies, foundations are increasingly getting involved with the Web. As in many chapters of this book, we list the many links to foundations that can be found at <www.fdncenter.org>, along with brief abstracts of what can be found at these foundation sites. This print version cannot, of course, offer the ability to search the text of these abstracts that we offer at our Web site, but readers can familarize themselves with the world of foundations on the Web prior to going online, as well as learn about the programs of individual foundations.

The Foundation Center takes pains to accurately present a picture of U.S. philanthropy, to define the field. In doing so we stress the legal distinctions between private foundations and public charities, sometimes known as "public foundations." In Chapter 3 we present separately the U.S. public charities on the Web we have identified as having grantmaking programs. This group includes community foundations, a growing segment of U.S. philanthropy. As we did with foundations in Chapter 2, we present the many links to grantmaking public charities to be found at <www.fdncenter.org> as well as the abstracts to these we have prepared. (We write abstracts continually, so check the "Grantmaker Information" area of <www.fdncenter.org> for the latest listings.) Tracking grantmaking public charities beyond community foundations is a relatively new effort of the Foundation Center. Information is not as systematically available for the great variety of public charities as it is for foundations, so it is our hope that highlighting grant-making public charities in this way will stimulate more of them to provide us with detailed information about their grantmaking activities. In this chapter, we list grantmaking public charities alphabetically by name, but we present all community foundations in a separate listing by individual states.

Chapter 4 surveys the field of corporate philanthropy, in addition to reviewing strategies for finding corporate funding information on the Web. Corporations present their giving programs in a variety of ways and to varying degrees, so creativity and persistence come into play when doing corporate giving research. This chapter stresses the need to consider the different motivations and goals of corporate givers, and how this can affect your funding approach. The annotated list of links in this chapter combines those of corporate foundations and of direct giving programs. Similar to the situation with community foundations versus other grantmaking public charities, you will often find more detailed information for corporate foundations than you will for direct company giving programs.

There is a tremendous amount of government information on the World Wide Web. Chapter 5 attempts to make sense of this vast amount of information by pointing you to those sites, at many levels of governement, that describe assistance programs. Researching government sources of support is different than researching corporations, described in Chapter 4, where you may need to sift through general company information to find information specifically about giving programs. Since historically one of the major activities of government has been to provide assistance, there is a wealth of information. People both within and without government have tried to organize this information for you. This chapter reviews the many sites describing specific support programs, as well as sites that can lead you to more specific information. Reviewing these sites can help you understand how government agencies and programs are organized and can be revealing of their relationship to the nonprofit sector.

Chapter 6 has a functional focus, in recognition that the World Wide Web distributes interactive software capability as well as information and hyperlinks. This chapter surveys a variety of sites—housed in a variety of settings—that offer searchable databases which may help Web users identify potential sources of assistance or general information. We have divided the world of searchable databases into the two major categories of "for-free" and "for-fee," although some blurring of the line between them is occurring as older Web services evolve and newer ones are created. There is some overlap of this chapter with others in the book because these databases are offered within corporate, government, and nonprofit organization—including foundation—settings.

Chapter 7 chronicles Web sites, many of them housed at nonprofit organizations, that Foundation Center staff have found to be the most useful and descriptive of the nonprofit sector and philanthropy, including some sites concerned with philanthropy in other countries. Many of the sites in this chapter can, like <www.fdncenter.org>, provide you with links to other resources you may find useful. We survey some of our staff's picks in detail. The full listing of sites is organized under the various subject categories used at the Center's Web site to provide ready access to this growing number of resources.

Chapter 8 is a comprehensive listing of online publications (with abstracts for each) concerned with philanthropy and the nonprofit sector. Included are many field-specific newsletters and other online publications that can provide the current trends and policy context for nonprofit activities. Use this chapter to identify the online publications that will keep you up-to-date with your field and your interests.

Chapter 9 illustrates how two-way communication is used to build community on the World Wide Web. The simple but powerful interactivity of Internet e-mail and electronic mailing lists and bulletin boards allows communities of Web users to define themselves online, and to create dialogs and conversations, both private and public, which can advance their work or inform their interests. This chapter surveys a number of the community-building services available for grantseekers and other nonprofit practitioners, as well as provides tips on how to begin participating in these various forums.

Chapter 10 is a survey of the range of information and services available at <www.fdncenter.org>, the Foundation Center's Web site. We reorganized and redesigned our Web site in late 1998 (our second major redesign) to accommodate the growing amount of information and number of services provided, and to make navigating through the site easier for both first-time and repeat visitors. Especially for first-time visitors, reviewing this chapter may make navigating our site even easier than we have tried to make it. And remember, the Web is vast; if you get lost following a trail of links, you can always return to <www.fdncenter.org>, Your Gateway to Philanthropy on the World Wide Web, and pick up the trail afresh.

Appendix A provides a brief overview of the technical underpinnings of the Internet. It then tracks the software developments that spurred the initial phenomenal growth of the World Wide Web and that continue to offer a seemingly unlimited potential for the Web to knit together various global communities. The apparent promise of Web technology to break down barriers to communication and to distribute computing resources around the world is truly astounding. The development of software, and as important, the adoption of universally recognized software standards, is an ongoing process and will only accelerate.

Appendix B contains practical information and advice about how to connect to the Internet. This piece was generously provided by the Fund for the City of New York, whose Internet Academy classes have been linking nonprofits to the Internet resources available to them for several years.

Appendix C is a bibliography of titles about the Internet that may be of interest to nonprofit practitioners. It is a compilation drawn from the Foundation Center's Literature of the Nonprofit Sector database, a bibliograpic database you can search for free yourself by visiting <http://fdncenter.org/lnps/index.html>. (Please note that to reach the Center's Web site you can drop the "www." and just use <fdncenter.org>.)

Appendix D is a glossary concerning the World Wide Web, pulled down from the Web itself.

The Foundation Center's Web site, described in detail in Chapter 10, is a specialty portal that we call "Your Gateway to Philanthropy on the World Wide Web." It has been designed for those interested in the nonprofit world, particularly the world of U.S. grantmakers. This book is in one sense a print version of this specialty portal. It is full of specific information about where to find Web sites that may be useful in your grantseeking efforts. We invite you to use both formats of Your Gateway to Philanthropy on the World Wide Web as a way to get your Web funding research off to a flying start.

CHAPTER ONE

The Web Browser: Your Cyberspace Viewer

Birth of the Browser

Around 1993, while a staff member of the National Center for Supercomputing Applications (NCSA) at the University of Illinois, a fellow named Marc Andreessen created a software program called Mosaic. It was the first true graphical user interface (GUI) to the World Wide Web, making access to the World Wide Web much simpler. A GUI providing ready access to the Web was dubbed a "browser." This one development is arguably the single biggest factor in the subsequent phenomenal growth of the Web. Several versions of Mosaic were released, but along the way Marc Andreessen and others involved in its original development left NCSA to join Jim Clark and form Mosaic Communications Corp., which soon changed its name to Netscape Communications. A *Wall Street Journal* article described the situation in May of 1994 this way:

> But his new company will have to move fast to provide added features and functions that will separate its product from a horde of similar offerings. Many companies are seeking licenses to develop commercial versions of Mosaic, or are developing knockoffs of the concept. . . . Most of the companies are developing products that will facilitate initial access to the Internet as well as provide a Mosaic-like look and feel. . . . "There's lots of competition," notes Marc Porat, chief executive officer of General Magic Inc., a software consortium based in Mountain View, Calif. Eventually, he says, software giant Microsoft Corp., could join the fray, bundling an Internet navigator with its best-selling Windows operating system "and undermining everyone."
> *("Silicon Graphics' Clark Sets Up Firm to Provide Internet Operating System," Wall Street Journal, Monday May 9, 1994, page B2)*

A couple of these were truly prophetic comments. But generally, in the same way GUIs had made personal computing accessible to millions of people, GUI access to the Web brought the global connectivity offered by the Internet to millions of people around the world. Also, in the same way that GUIs had made it possible for personal computer users to be ignorant of operating system file structures and specialized computer languages, GUI access to the Web rendered some of the basic, ground-breaking functionality of the original Internet quaint, if not obsolete, particularly as these earlier developments work more transparently within browsers (see Appendix A for a summary of pre-browser Internet development). With an internet connection established, browser installed, and mouse in hand, all it took for millions of people to enter cyberspace was the ability to type a Web address knows as a URL.

What Is a URL?

URL stands for "Uniform Resource Locator." It is the standard form for specifying an address on the Internet, such as a file, newsgroup, or Web site home page or document. URLs look like this:

- file://wuarchive.wustl.edu/doc/gutenberg/standard.new
- ftp://wuarchive.wustl.edu/graphics/mirrors/avalon/ITIndex.zip
- http://www.w3.org:80/Consortium/
- news://alt.hypertext
- telnet://dra.com

The first part of the URL, before the colon, specifies the access method and indicates the type of file represented by the address. In general, two slashes after the colon indicate that a machine name (or "port") follows. The domain name, including the appropriate domain suffix, is often used here. It used to be necessary to precede that with "www" to indicate a hypertext Web document, but that is often assumed now (given the "http" designation, which stands for "hypertext transfer protocol") and can be omitted. Additional address information after the domain name refers to specific Web pages or files on a particular Web server. URLs are either typed into browser address boxes or operate behind the scenes when the user clicks on a hyperlink.

Browser Development

Netscape Navigator 1.0 shipped in December 1994, just as the Foundation Center put its first home page on the Web. The arrival of a Web browser used easily by anyone with a mouse brought a Star-Trek-like capability to a tremendous number of desktops. Since that time, browser development and the acceptance of developing standards have allowed more and different kinds of content to be provided on the Web. At various times, key browser enhancements have altered the mix of available Web content, and spurred the continued evolution of the culture of the Web. Netscape Communications played a key role in the development of the Web. According to a company profile published in 1997 by Jones Digital Century (http://www.jii.com):

By replacing NCSA Mosaic as the browser of choice for millions of users, Netscape's browser became a de facto Internet standard. . . . At the same time that Netscape established itself as a de facto Internet standard, the company established a system of open standards for Internet software. . . . Prior to Netscape's entry into the Web market, other browsers, including NCSA Mosaic, had adhered to an accepted standard version of hypertext markup language (HTML), the language with which Web sites are written, organized, and linked to each other. Although there exists a semi-official body, the World Wide Web Consortium (W3C), that designs, promotes and sanctions standards for the Web, Netscape has consistently refused to wait for W3C. Instead, the company has added its own enhancements and features to HTML, and has released them on the Web. Because Netscape's enhancements display text and graphics in unique and sophisticated ways, millions of Web users have adopted Navigator as their browser of choice, and the authors of thousands of Web sites have adopted Netscape's enhancements. The vast majority of Web sites are presently optimized for Netscape's browser and thousands of companies have developed plug-ins, or downloadable application programs, for Netscape. While some have criticized Netscape for taking the standard-setting process into its own hands, the facts remain that the company's standards and innovations have been consistently excellent, and that many of Netscape's de facto standards are now part of W3C's official standard. . . . Although Netscape has established Internet standards that are likely to persevere, any player can copy, embrace and enhance upon those standards. Any browser can, and therefore will, quickly adopt the best features of its competitors. . . .

The "Browser War"

Adopt features already available in Netscape Navigator is certainly what Microsoft did. In December 1994, in order to issue a browser of its own that could compete with Netscape, Microsoft licensed Spyglass Mosaic, added some features to it, and released a new browser named Microsoft Explorer. The so-called "browser war" had officially begun. Although it is well known that for quite a while the various releases of Netscape Navigator were more technically advanced than Microsoft's browser offerings, the gap had narrowed considerably by the time they each had released their 3.0 versions. Now you will find people as opinionated about the respective merits of the 4.0 versions of these two browsers as people are about their Macs or PCs, but you also will find knowledgeable people who say browsers are a commodity, that they all do basically the same things. Each person can and will make up their own mind.

Whatever the outcome of the browser war, in 1997, Jones Digitial Century explained the future of browsers this way:

> As a result of [Netscape's] technological and business innovations, virtually all players in the Internet software industry now envision a future of "distributed computing resources," within which people will use the Internet in ways analogous to their present use of computer hard drives. Perhaps even more importantly, as more and more information becomes digitalized, stored in enormous databases, and made available on the Internet or on closed

networks, the browser will become an increasingly important tool for the organization, access, and preservation of the world's knowledge.

It is possible to get as deeply involved with the Web and its various technologies as it is (for any enthusiast) to become absorbed in the details of any particular passion. However, the focus of this book is the content available via the Web that is useful for grantseekers. Our goal is to help those grantseekers fairly new to the Web get past the technology involved, to bring them closer to the information of value to them. The latest versions of both the Netscape and Microsoft browsers now include additional features that go beyond basic browser functioning. Below we reference these added features briefly so that you will know what they are and can recognize them on your screen, but the browser function is your true window onto the World Wide Web. E-mail is the other function essential to doing research on the Web (see Chapter 9 in particular), and its use is now closely integrated with routine browser operation.

Browser Suites

The leading creators of browser software envision a future where all of your desktop computing—whether you are creating a personal document or spreadsheet, working collaboratively in a networked workplace environment, or communicating throughout the world via the Web—takes place in a single screen window on your computer. Netscape Communications paved the way for this by creating the Netscape Communicator 4.0 suite. Microsoft followed suit by adding a clustered suite of tools to its Internet Explorer 4.0 browser.

NETSCAPE COMMUNICATOR 4.0

This software suite contains the following functions:

Navigator 4.0 Browser
This works very much like Navigator 3.0, although certain menu items were rearranged to work in conjunction with the full Communicator suite.

Netcaster
This feature is used to create "channels" to your computer, through which various information providers "push" regularly updated information to your desktop. This is a fairly new technology, and information providers are now moving to take advantage of it. You will need both time and hard-drive space to spare to explore this feature.

Messenger
This is your Internet e-mail capability. (In Navigator 3.0, the e-mail function was accessible from the Window Menu; in Navigator 4.0, it's accessible from the Component Bar or the Communicator Menu. See below.)

Collabra Discussion Groups
This feature lets you participate in Web newsgroups and forums or in private discussion groups within a workplace setting.

Composer

This feature lets you create your own HTML documents.

Conference

This feature lets you make phone calls and conduct online chats.

When you first click on the Communicator icon on your desktop, the Navigator browser window opens as the default. If you are connected to the Internet you will be taken to Netscape's homepage, called Netcenter.

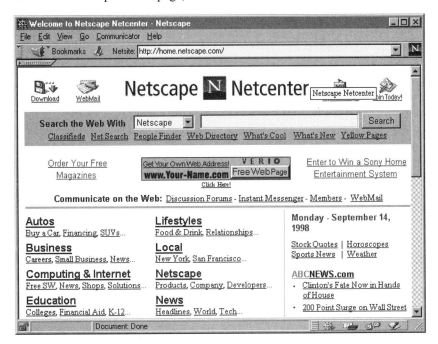

You can use the option available under "Preferences" (see more on Preferences further on in this chapter) to choose any Web page as your default, to appear any time you launch the browser.

Most of the functions in the Communicator suite are accessible from the Component Bar (shown below), which can stay on your desktop or be minimized to appear in the "status line" at the bottom of the Navigator window.

The Netcaster and Conference functions can be opened from the drop-down Communicator Menu on the Menu Bar.

MICROSOFT INTERNET EXPLORER 4.0

This suite contains the following software functions:

Internet Explorer 4.0 Browser (IE4)

The ability to subscribe to "channels" is integrated with the basic browser function. Through the "Settings" area on the "Start Menu" of the Windows 95 operating system, you will be able to choose the "active desktop," the more Web-integrated way of computing.

Outlook Express

This integrated mail program gives you access to Internet e-mail and newsgroups.

Microsoft Chat

This feature gives you access to the Internet Relay Chat (IRC) capability.

Microsoft Netmeeting

This lets you participate in audio- and video-conferencing as well as online bulletin boards/discussion groups.

FrontPage Express

This is the Web-page authoring tool that is integrated into the Internet Explorer suite.

When you first click on the IE4 icon on your desktop, the Internet Explorer browser window opens as the default.

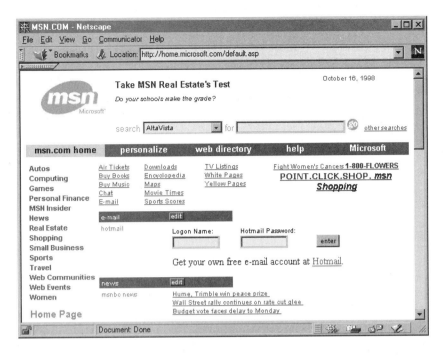

IE4 lets you customize your own "start" page, which you can then choose as your default. Or, as in Navigator, you can choose any Web page as your default, so that it appears automatically any time you launch the browser.

"A Browser Is a Browser"

Analogous features can be found in Netscape Navigator 4.0 and Internet Explorer 4.0 (IE4), confirming one pundit's general statement that "a browser is a browser." This is particularly true if you are doing specific Web-based research, instead of looking to be entertained or intrigued by evolving Web technology. That the two leading browsers now offer more or less the same functionality is testimony to the progress made by Microsoft since Bill Gates' famous Pearl Harbor Day speech in 1995 when, in one of the more visible corporate course corrections in history, he put the helm hard over and steered Microsoft's ship directly at the Internet.

At this point in time, whether the tighter integration of IE4 with the Windows desktop, and indeed the continuing integration of all Microsoft software with the Web, is useful for the end user is a matter of opinion. Because Netscape Communications does not distribute general PC software applications or its own proprietary operating system, to some there are issues in choosing a browser that go beyond the issue of basic browser functionality. Microsoft, because it provides a full line of software applications, is more visibly preparing for the day when all desktop computing takes place in a single screen window.

Basic Browser Operation

Netscape Navigator was the browser to choose in December 1994 when the Foundation Center launched its original Web site. While we try to ensure that the pages we post at our Web site display correctly in other browsers, in the course of our work, we use Navigator (3.0 and 4.0 versions) as our primary browser. Statistics from our own Web site reveal that, as of spring 1998, versions of Netscape were being used over versions of Internet Explorer by a more than a two-to-one margin. That ratio is changing, but our brief discussion of browser functionality will use Navigator 4.0 as its example. In addition, throughout the book, all graphic examples of Web pages will be shown within the Netscape Navigator 4.0 browser window. Although Netscape 3.0 may still be quite popular, we are assuming that more and more users will migrate to Navigator 4.0, whether or not they make use of the full Communicator software suite. We will alert you to cases where a particularly useful Navigator feature or menu item appears in a different location in version 4.0 than in version 3.0.

LAUNCHING NAVIGATOR 4.0

Netscape revamped its own home page by creating Netcenter, admitting that they were slow to provide a multi-service home base for Navigator users (*Business Week*, April 1998). Before this makeover, the Netscape home page looked primarily like a place to buy software. Now Netscape is trying to be a more active partner in your Internet experience. However, if you want to cut right to the chase you will be on most often, changing your default home page is very easy. Click "Edit" on the Menu Bar, then click on "Preferences," the last item in the drop-down list. You will see the following window:

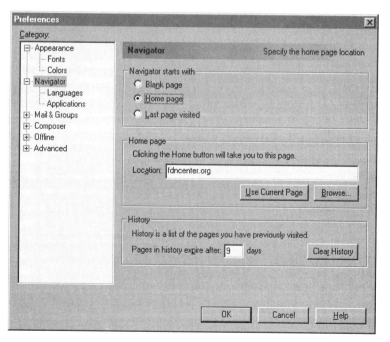

Click on "Navigator" in the topic list displayed in the window (if it isn't already the default). There is a box labeled "Location" on the right-hand side of the window in which you can type the URL of your choice. Click "OK" and, unless you change it at another time, whenever Navigator opens, it will take you to that Web page. (You can also use the "Browse" feature to locate an HTML file on your local drive to use as your default home page.)

"Preferences" is a useful place to remember, and we will talk about it more fully later. In Navigator 3.0, "Preferences" was under "Options" on the Menu Bar. In the Communicator suite, there are fewer separate pull-down menus than in Navigator 3.0. Other items from the old "Options," "Directory," and "Window" menus are now part of the new "Communicator" menu. Putting "Preferences" on the Edit Menu may seem like a strange choice for those who associate "Edit" with the basic cut, copy, and paste functions offered in Windows. When you first begin using Navigator 4.0, it may be handy to think in terms of "editing your preferences" as a reminder of the new location for "Preferences."

TOOLBARS

We will review the most important of the various pull-down menus later, but the various toolbars available in Navigator 4.0 are the most useful tools for browsing the Web. There are three of them: the Navigation Toolbar, the Location Toolbar, and the Personal Toolbar. We will discuss them all, but before you make any of them disappear by accident, we'll show you how to customize their arrangement in the blank Navigator window shown below. (To get a blank window, just open Navigator without connecting to the Internet.)

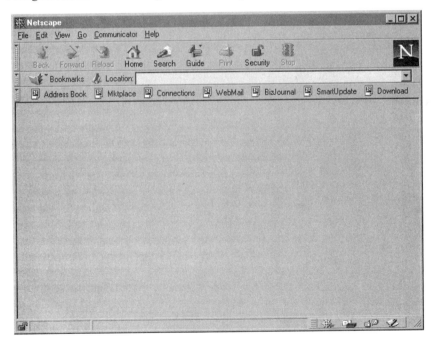

The three toolbars are stacked one on top of the other in the above order: Navigation, Location, Personal. Note the narrow vertical bars containing little triangle arrows that appear at the left of each of these toolbar areas. Click on one of them to see how that toolbar is now hidden. You can hide all of them if you wish at any time during your Web browsing. To restore them, simply click on the narrow bars again (which are horizontal when the toolbars are hidden). You can also change the "stacking" order of the toolbars. Just click (and hold) on one of the narrow bars and drag that toolbar past the others to put it where you prefer. For instance, you might want to have the Location Toolbar up top. In any case, we are going to discuss that one first, because getting to the home pages containing the information you seek is likely to be your top priority.

Location Toolbar

The Location Toolbar is the one containing the long box into which you type URL (Uniform Resource Locator) addresses. A URL is text used for identifying and addressing an item in a computer network. A URL provides location information, and Navigator displays it in the location field. Most often you don't need to know a page's URL because the location information is included automatically as part of a highlighted link or a toolbar link. However, if you have learned of a URL from some other source than surfing the Web itself (getting such a tip is often the best way to learn of something really useful), you will have to type it into the Location Box on the Location Toolbar. After you type in a URL and before you hit "Enter," the word "Location" changes to "Go to" in the Location Toolbar. If you are viewing a page that comes from a Netscape server, the word "Location" changes to "Netsite."

With a URL address typed into this box, just press "Enter" to bring that particular Web page to your Navigator window. (You will soon discover that even one incorrectly typed character in a URL address will prevent your browser from finding that Web resource.) Once you bring up any page that has blue hyperlinks on it, you can be off and surfing the Web simply by clicking on the links provided. However, you can start over again at any time by typing in a different URL or by clicking on a URL already stored within any of several places within Navigator.

One of the places to store URLs you want to remember (and therefore won't have to type again) is your "Bookmarks" function, the link to which appears directly to the left of the Location Box on this toolbar. Creating your own list of URLs to remember and never type again is a very useful capability, and we will discuss creating your own list of "bookmarks" more thoroughly later. For now, while viewing the blank Netscape Navigator page offline, click on the Bookmark icon on the Location Toolbar to see a list of default categories that Netscape has provided. Pick a category and put your cursor on it. Another list will appear containing the names of specific Web pages in that category. These names each represent an Internet URL address. When you click on a name in one of these lists, behind the scenes the URL for the Web page it represents is inserted automatically into the address box in the Location Toolbar, and Navigator takes you to that page (if you are connected to the Internet, that is, and not just learning browser functions while offline).

One other interesting capability on the Location Toolbar: if you click on the "drop-down arrow" at the right-hand side of the address box, you will see a drop-down list of those URL addresses you visited recently by typing them directly into the address box. This is another place where Navigator stores URLs which you can click on to revisit frequently viewed Web pages. The important thing to remember about this particular list is that it only contains URLs that were *typed* in recently. It won't store the URLs you chose by clicking on links or that you have stored as bookmarks.

Navigation Toolbar

This is the toolbar to use for navigation and page control. The buttons described below provide quick access to the most commonly used Web-surfing features.

Back. Click on this button to display the page you were viewing just previously. Holding down the button will display a window containing a history list, which we will discuss more later.

Forward. If you have used the "Back" button (or made use of its history list), clicking on this button will bring you to what you were viewing before. It will be "grayed out" (i.e., disabled) if you have returned to the most recently viewed page.

Reload. Click this button to redisplay the current Navigator page, reflecting any changes made since the original loading. To reload, Navigator checks the network server to see if any change to the page has occurred. If no change has occurred, the original page is retrieved from the cache (see more about caching later in this chapter). If there has been a change, the updated page is retrieved from the server. If you hold down the Shift key and then press the Reload button, Navigator will retrieve the page from the server, bypassing the cache.

Home. Click this button to display the home page designated in the "Navigator" panel in "Preferences" (under "Edit" on the Menu Bar). If you haven't designated a particular home page to use as your default, clicking on Home will take you to the Netscape home page.

Search. Click on "Search" to visit a Netscape server and retrieve a Web page that offers access to a number of ways to explore the Web. On this page you will find a list of direct links to what people initially called "search engines." However, as discussed in the Introduction, with the further development of these Web services, that terminology has become too limited. So, on the Netscape "Search" page you will find links to some of the major search services displayed prominently. You will also find sub-menus listing some search service links under the heading "Search the Web," while others are listed under the heading "Explore by Topic." The fact is, the major Web search services take different approaches, both technical and philosophical, trying to "index" the contents of the World Wide Web.

Guide. Clicking this button takes you to the Netcenter portal launched in mid-1998 (see the Introduction for more on the advent of "portals"). Netcenter contains a menu of category links which will in turn take you to pages with more specific links that help you find information in those categories.

Images. This button is available on the Navigation Toolbar only if you have turned off the "Automatically load images" option found within the "Advanced" panel of the "Preferences" section (found in the Edit Menu). If you had turned off automatic image loading, clicking on this button will load the images for the page you are viewing.

Print. Just as you would expect, clicking on this button takes you to a dialog box that lets you select printing characteristics.

Security. The options available concerning Internet security are numerous, and we won't go into them in this book. Briefly, clicking on this button takes you to a page where you can establish encryption status, personal and site certificates, passwords, and other security-related applications.

Stop. Clicking this button halts any ongoing transfer of page information. It is often used to stop downloading a particular page that seems to be taking too long. Clicking "Stop" and then "Reload" can sometimes bring down the page you are seeking more quickly.

The Personal Toolbar

The Personal Toolbar isn't really a toolbar in the way the Navigation Toolbar is. Basically, the Personal Toobar displays icons of your favorite bookmarks. We will discuss how to customize it when we talk more about Navigator's Bookmarks feature. When you first install Navigator, you will see that, as a default, Netscape has placed some potentially useful bookmarks within easy reach on your Personal Toolbar.

THE BROWSER WINDOW

Page Content Area

The content area contains the current page corresponding to the most recently requested URL. Vertical and horizontal scroll bars should be present if the page is larger than the screen area. The title bar at the very top of the browser window shows the title of the currently loaded page. You can open multiple Navigator windows to view multiple pages of information. You might want to do this, for instance, if you are doing specific research and have found different Web sites that you wish to compare. You can open separate windows to look at them side by side. Also, if a page you are trying to load is for some reason loading very slowly, you can continue to surf while you wait for it to appear in its own window.

Web pages can contain a lot of text which requires scrolling to view them in their entirety. However, it is easy to search Web pages for particular words and phrases. You can click on "Edit" on the Menu Bar and then click on the "Find in Page" menu item. This opens a "Find" dialog box that lets you type the string of characters you wish to find on a Web page. Within this dialog box you can choose to search up or down. You can access this dialog box in an even easier way: simply hit "Control-F" on your keyboard.

A Word about Frames

Some pages are designed to be a patchwork of separate pages called "frames." Each frame is a smaller page within the larger page. (Together, a group of frames forms a top-level page called a frameset.) Individual frames may have different characteristics. Each frame may contain a scroll bar to let you view more information within that frame. Individual frames can be resized by positioning your cursor in the border between frames and dragging them to the desired size. Generally, toolbar and menu items affect the top-level page. However, some menu items, such as printing or saving, might apply only to individual frames. Many people have been surprised after clicking "Print" and then receiving only a portion of the full Web page on their screen.

Status Message

The status message area is located at the bottom of the browser window. It contains text describing a page's location. When you position your cursor over highlighted words serving as a link to a page, the status message will show the URL that will be used to bring that page to the screen. When you position your cursor over an image with "hotspots" (active links within an image area), the status message will show a description for the active area. When you click on a link, the status message will tell you what is happening: whether Navigator made a connection with the server, what percentage of a file has been downloaded, etc. It's always nice to (finally) get the "Document: Done" message, which shows that the complete file has been downloaded.

Progress Bar

Also located at the bottom of the browser window, the Progress Bar animates to show the progress of the current operation. It displays graphically the percentage done as a page loads. When the amount of time necessary to load a page cannot be estimated accurately, a segment of the Progress Bar "bounces" between its boundaries.

Component Bar

If you have closed the Communicator Component Bar we showed earlier, it will appear in minimized form in the status line at the bottom right-hand side of the browser window. You can click any of the icons to access other Communicator features, such as e-mail. Click the Mailbox icon to display the mail Inbox folder and retrieve new messages. The Mailbox icon will show a question mark (?) if Communicator cannot automatically check the mail server for new messages (for example, if you have not yet supplied your password to access messages). The Mailbox icon will include a down-arrow if the mail server has new messages for you.

Security Indicator

At the bottom left-hand side of the status line a padlock icon indicates security information. A closed padlock shows that a page is encrypted. An open padlock shows that a page isn't encrypted. Clicking the padlock icon displays the same security information window accessible by clicking the Security button on the Navigation Toolbar.

LINKS AND IMAGES

It's usually easy to tell what's a link. When using the default "Appearance" settings (found in "Preferences," which of course you will recall is under the Edit Menu), text links are underlined and appear in blue. When you put your cursor on a link, your cursor arrow will change to a friendly pointing hand and the status line will show you the URL for that link. After you follow a link, when you return to the page you linked from, that link appears in purple to show that you've already visited there. (You can always use the link again; the change in color is just a reminder for you.) "Hotspots," mentioned earlier, are just like links except that they are embedded within graphic displays. Hotspots perform an action when you click on them. Sometimes hotspots are small, or "thumbnail," versions of larger graphic images that you can download or view. Hotspots are often used as graphic menu items that take you to a different part of a site.

RIGHT-CLICKING THE MOUSE

In general, desktop software has gotten sophisticated enough that "right-clicking" the mouse should become a new habit. The right mouse button is often used now to provide additional information or access to additional functions on your desktop. Navigator 4.0 takes advantage of the right mouse button. By right-clicking on the links and images you encounter on Web pages, you have access to a wide range of functions concerning those items. As an example, go to the Netscape home page at <home.netscape.com>. Right-click while your cursor is on any of the many links on the Netcenter page. A menu will display, as shown.

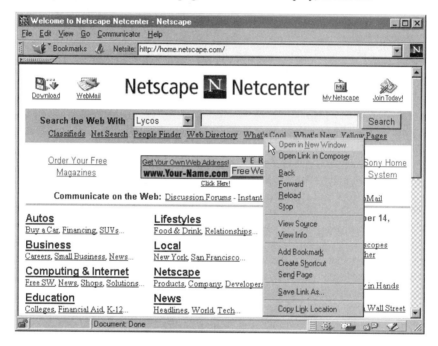

The "Back," "Forward," "Reload," and "Stop" commands on this menu work just like their counterpart buttons on the Navigation Toolbar. However, there are a number of other things you can do from this pop-up menu.

Open in New Window. This opens a new browser window that displays the document specified in the link. Your original window stays open.

Open Link in Composer. This opens the linked page in Netscape Composer so that you can modify the document contents.

View Source. Click here to see the HTML code for the current document.

View Info. Click here to view information about the current document, including the various graphic components and when it was created.

Add Bookmark. More about bookmarks later, but by clicking here you can add the link to your bookmark list without visiting the actual page. You can look at it later.

Create Shortcut. Similar to adding a bookmark, without having to visit the page, you can add an icon to your desktop that will link you directly to this page.

Send Page. When you click on this item, a New Message window appears so that you can address an e-mail to any recipient. The e-mail message will automatically include the currently displayed document as an attachment.

Save Link As. This lets you save the HTML file for the currently displayed page on your hard drive or a network drive.

Copy Link Location. This copies the link to your Windows clipboard.

When you right-click on an image hotspot or a graphic, you will see many of the menu items listed above, plus a few similar ones that are more pertinent to image files.

MENU BAR

We've mentioned various "menu items" a number of times so far in our tour of Navigator 4.0. While the toolbars let you do most of what you need to do to simply browse the Web, there are a few specific menu items that may be helpful during your Web research. In this section we will briefly describe some of the most useful. (We will skip entirely the ones that are self-evident or that are familiar as standard computing functions.)

File Menu

New. Click here and you get a sub-menu which lets you open a new Navigator window, open the e-mail message composition window, or perform actions in Composer.

Open Page. This feature lets you type a URL or select a file using the "Choose File" button to display a page in the content area, either in the Navigator or Composer window. With this feature you can view HTML documents within your browser that are stored on your local hard drive or network.

Save (Frame) As. In the File Menu, one of the most useful functions is called "Save As." The "Save Frame As" feature does the same thing, except for an individual frame rather than a top-level page. Clicking here will open a standard window that lets you choose where on your hard drive or network to save the frame you are viewing. Simply specify the location where you want the document saved and then choose whether to save the document as an HTML file (for viewing in your browser at a future time) or as an ASCII text file. As you search the Web and find documents useful for your work, you'll find yourself making good use of this feature to save valuable documents to view offline later.

Send Page (or *Send Frame* if you are within a frame). This feature lets you create and send an e-mail message with the page you are currently viewing as an attachment. When you click on this feature, the message composition window is displayed with the current page's URL automatically inserted into the message area. You can add more text to the message. The window doesn't display the page you are sending, but the recipient will see your additional message followed by a display of the attached page.

Edit Page/Edit Frame. This feature lets you modify the underlying HTML source text that determines the page's/frame's content and display.

Edit Menu

Preferences. The Edit Menu contains the "Find in Page" utility already mentioned (don't forget the Control+F shortcut to this utility) and the "Search Internet" and "Search Directory" features, which take you to lists of different services to do those very things. Explore these at your leisure. In this brief overview, the only feature in the Edit Menu that needs emphasizing is the aforementioned "Preferences" feature. (In Navigator 3.0, "Preferences" was found under "Options.")

Preferences panels. Click on "Preferences" in the Edit Menu to display a dialog box containing a list of separate preference panels. There are six main panels: Appearance, Navigator, Mail & Groups, Composer, Offline, and Advanced. These have additional sub-panels listed under them. Click on the plus sign ("+") next to these main category names to see the complete list of preference panels available. The default settings in most of these panels are just fine unless you want to customize Navigator, so we recommend experimenting with them at your leisure. However, there are a couple of panels you should be familiar with because they have a direct influence on the performance of your browsing and Internet e-mail functions.

Mail & Groups. E-mail is becoming more and more integrated with browser functioning and the Web pages you will be visiting. Underneath the Mail & Groups main preference panel are a number of sub-panels. Two of these sub-panels need to be filled out correctly for Internet e-mail to work for you as it should: "Identity" and "Mail Server." Click on the "Identity" sub-panel under Mail & Groups. Your e-mail address needs to be in the appropriate box. Next, click on the "Mail Server" sub-panel. Your e-mail account name (your e-mail address minus the @_____ part) needs to be in the "Mail server user name" box. There may already be a default called "mail" in the boxes for both "Outgoing mail (SMTP) Server" and "Incoming mail server." These won't necessarily work and you won't be able to send or receive Internet e-mail until you specify your own server names, which in most cases will be the same. You may need to know the exact name of the mail server used at your e-mail service provider, as well as the protocols it uses. Chances are it is using POP3 (Post Office Protocol, version 3). IMAP (Internet Message Access Protocol) is becoming more prevalent. If your service provider offers a choice between these two, choose IMAP. In this sub-panel you can elect to have your POP3 messages left on the server if that is allowed. That way you can retrieve them again later or access them from a different computer if you sometimes travel or work from home.

Advanced. The Advanced preference panel has three additional sub-panels, entitled "Cache," "Proxies," and "Disk Space." The Cache panel can possibly be of help to you in optimizing your computer for Web use.

Caching

Each time your computer has to connect to a remote server to pull down a Web page, you are entering the packet-switching maelstrom which is the Internet. Especially if the pages you wish to view have graphic elements or are large files for other reasons, you are competing with all the other file transfer traffic on the Internet. The concept of caching was developed to artificially improve the performance in this environment. With caching, the files that compose Web pages viewed recently within your browser window are stored on your local computer, either in memory or on your hard drive. If you revisit those pages, your browser first checks the remote server to see if the requested pages have changed at all since you last viewed them. If they haven't, the browser pulls the files down from the local source, thereby obviating the need to connect again to the remote server. Each page file pulled down from your own computer will be visible within your browser window faster than if it is sent anew over the Internet. (When you use the "Back" button or choose an item from its history list, Navigator does not check the network to see if the page has changed. It will automatically look to see if a cached version of the page is still available. Click the "Reload" button to make sure you are using the most recent version of a Web page.)

In the "Cache" sub-panel of the Advanced preferences panel you can increase or decrease the size of the memory cache and the disk (hard-drive) cache on your computer. Navigator retrieves a page from the memory cache more quickly than from the disk cache, but retrieving from the disk cache is still faster than retrieving a page from a remote server. Another difference: the memory cache is cleared each time you exit Communicator. The disk cache is maintained between sessions (and so takes up space on your hard drive). Click on "Cache" and you will see the following sub-panel.

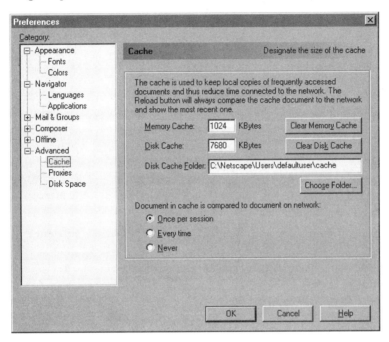

The default for the memory cache is probably set at 1024K. The default for the disk cache is probably set at 7680. These are simple to change; just type in new numbers. A larger cache may increase performance, although allocating too much space will constrict other applications. Netscape recommends increasing your memory cache conservatively, to whatever units of memory your system routinely doesn't use. Depending on the amount of space left unused on your hard drive, allocating more megabytes for the disk cache is less problematic. However, you may find that a large disk cache increases the time required to quit Communicator. If cache maintenance is causing noticeable delay when exiting the program, consider reducing the size of the disk cache.

View Menu

Items in the View Menu are mainly redundant with toolbar functioning or are self-evident. For the curious, however, clicking "Page Source" will display a window showing the current page in HTML format. This HTML source text includes all the commands used to create the content of the page as you see it. Clicking "Page Info" will display a window with details about the current page's structure and composition, including (if available) the title, location (URL), MIME type, source, local cache file, date of last modification, content length, expiration, character-set encoding, and security status. Pages with security features will also show the type of encryption used and certificate information. Is this more than you want to know? Probably.

Go Menu

The Go Menu contains the same "Back," "Forward," and "Home" commands readily available on the Navigation Toolbar. However, it has one other interesting feature: a history list slightly different than the one you can pull down from the Location Toolbar. Whereas that one showed only the URLs you had typed directly into the Location Box recently, the history list that is accessible from the Go Menu shows all the URLs you have used in your current session, whether you visited those pages by typing in the URLs or by clicking on links. For that reason, it may prove more useful to you.

Communicator Menu

The Communicator Menu lets you access all the components of the Communicator suite. Assuming that, besides the Navigator browser itself, you most often will use the e-mail component that is available on the minimized Component Bar (in the status line at the bottom of the browser window), you won't need to use this menu very often. However, it does give access to yet another level of your Web-browsing history. Click on "History" on the Communicator Menu and you will see a window displayed like this one:

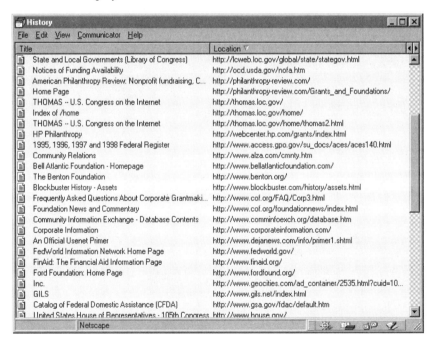

This history list contains all the URLs you have visited in the current as well as all earlier sessions, going back as many days as is indicated in the main Navigator preference panel (Remember that? Click on "Preferences" in the Edit Menu and then highlight "Navigator"). At the bottom of this panel you can set the number of days' activity that you want this comprehensive history list to remember for you. Or you can wipe out the entire list and start again by choosing the "Clear History" button.

BOOKMARKS

So far we have described three different places where Navigator 4.0 remembers Web pages you have visited recently. These various history lists can be very useful for the active user who becomes familiar with them. But perhaps one of the most useful features of Navigator is Bookmarks. This function lets you *selectively* store and then organize the history of your Web travels, remembering those sites you never want to forget until you choose to. The Bookmarks feature is available from the Communicator Menu, but it is so useful that Netscape put an icon for it (the Bookmarks QuickFile icon) right on the Location Toolbar, just to the left of the Location Box.

The Bookmarks feature offers an easy way to retrieve pages you want to visit over and over again. You store bookmarks in a list that's saved on your hard drive. Clicking on them sends the URL to your browser, which automatically goes out and retrieves that page. Try clicking on one of the default bookmark categories that Netscape includes with the initial installation of Navigator 4.

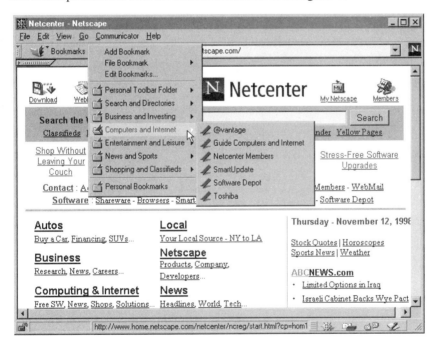

Simply put your cursor on one of these default categories and then click on one of the links appearing in the list of bookmarks displayed for that category. Navigator goes out and retrieves that page and places the URL associated with that bookmark into the Location Box on the Location Toolbar.

Adding Bookmarks to Your Lists

There are a number of ways to add bookmarks of your choosing to your list. You can click on the Bookmarks QuickFile icon on the Location Toolbar and then click "Add Bookmark" from the menu that appears. A name for the page you are viewing will be added to your list, identified behind the scenes with the appropriate URL. You can also right-click while your cursor is on the page you are viewing and choose the same "Add Bookmark" command in the menu that appears. You can also hit "Control+D" and the bookmark for the page you are viewing gets added to your list behind the scenes. It is important to note that when using any of these three methods, the new bookmark is simply added to the bottom of your list of bookmarks. This is fine when you have just a short list stored, but your list will get unwieldy very quickly when you start bookmarking all the good pages you find.

Filing Bookmarks

You can actually file your new bookmarks right when you first create them. When you find a page you will want to return to often, click on the Bookmarks QuickFile icon on the Location Toolbar and then put your cursor on "File Bookmark," rather than clicking on "Add Bookmark." Your list of bookmark categories will appear. Just select the category in which you want to put your new bookmark and it will be added to the bottom of the list within that specific category. You can perform this same operation in another way. When viewing a page you wish to bookmark, put your cursor on the Page icon just to the left of the Location Box on the Location Toolbar. (If you look closely the Page icon looks like an open book with a bookmark lying on it.) When you do this your cursor changes into a little hand. Now click and drag the Page icon to the Bookmark QuickFile icon directly to the left. The same list of bookmark categories will appear, and you can drag your cursor to the appropriate category and drop your new bookmark there. This method takes a little more dexterity, but with either of these two methods you can file a new bookmark in the appropriate place at the same time that you initially save it.

Note that if you file a bookmark in your Personal Toolbar Folder, that bookmark becomes an icon displayed on your Personal Toolbar whenever you have it activated.

Once you add a bookmark to your list, unlike the automatic history lists, it stays there until you remove it (or change lists). The permanence and accessibility of bookmarks make them a tremendous resource for customizing your Web-browsing experience.

Bookmark Window

Even if you file all your new bookmarks conscientiously when you first create them, pretty soon you will want to edit them even more, delete ones that weren't as valuable as you thought, rename them so that even your over-worked, multi-tasked brain can remember what they are—whatever rethinking is generated by your continued Web-browsing experience. When you feel the need to further refine your list of bookmarks, click on the Bookmark QuickFile icon and select "Edit Bookmarks." The Bookmark Window will appear in a slightly different format (see below). Once again we show the default list of bookmarks loaded with the initial installation of Netscape Navigator 4.0. You can see that Netscape thoughtfully included a category called "My Stuff" at the very bottom of the bookmark list, so that even if you thoughtlessly add bookmarks without filing them, they will clutter up only your own catch-all category.

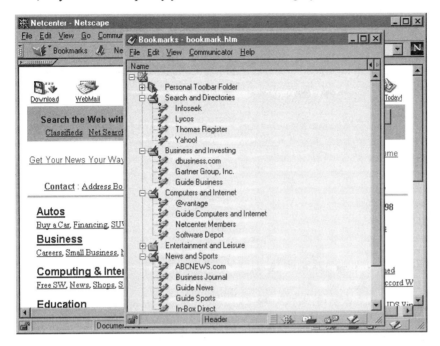

This Bookmark Window offers a full set of menu items to help you organize the list by creating your own hierarchical menus, different menu displays, even multiple bookmark files. You can drag and drop bookmark icons or use the menu items provided in the window to arrange the display of your bookmarks and folders. These menus work a lot like the standard Windows menus you see elsewhere, so we won't review their functioning. However, one very useful function again depends on that new habit, right-clicking.

Highlight a specific bookmark folder or an individual bookmark and right-click. A menu will appear that duplicates some of the menu functions available on the Bookmark Window's own menu. However, the last item on the list is called "Bookmark Properties." Click on this and you will come to the panel that lets you rename a bookmark or bookmark folder as well as type in a description of what it is. This proves a handy feature when that clever mnemonic device you chose as a bookmark name six months ago doesn't ring a bell.

The Bookmark Window is worth exploring and experimenting with as a way to enhance your research work on the World Wide Web. You can download additional software applications that soup up your bookmark editing capabilities, but the capabilities provided in Navigator itself will help you remember and locate again the most useful Web sites you find in the course of your browsing. By the way, if you decide to install IE4 in addition to Netscape, IE4 will copy your Netscape "bookmarks" into its listing of "favorites."

Like Riding a Bike

To get close to the information on the Web you find valuable for your work, using your browser of choice should become automatic, something you don't have to think about. The newer versions of the leading browsers come with a lot of functionality. This can appear daunting if you try to learn it all at once. The good news is that you can begin browsing the Web very quickly, without understanding all the capabilities right at the beginning. We hope that this admittedly selective tour of Navigator 4.0 helps you discover the wide world that awaits you on the Web.

CHAPTER TWO

Independent Foundations on the Web

The world of foundation philanthropy in the United States has grown considerably since its beginnings. Philanthropy in general has been in the news more and more in recent years, with stories of high-profile gifts such as Ted Turner's pledge to the United Nations. However, the field of *foundation* philanthropy has not always taken clear shape for the general public, for several reasons. The fact is, the word "foundation" is used in the names of many organizations, including those that are not technically private foundations, although in some cases they make grants to other organizations. These organizations aren't recognized as foundations by the Internal Revenue Service. Similarly, many organizations legally defined as foundations use different words in their names, such as "fund," "trust," or "endowment," rather than "foundation." These different terms do not indicate legal or operational differences. The terminology can be confusing, but the significant distinction is that those nonprofits classified by the IRS as private foundations must be organized and operated under specific regulations.

Foundations are usually created and organized as corporations or charitable trusts under state laws and receive their federal tax-exempt status under the Internal Revenue Code. The Tax Reform Act of 1969, the first major legislation dealing with foundations, used the term "private foundation" and defined the phrase only by the exclusion of other nonprofit organizations. David Freeman, former president of the Council on Foundations, explains the code in his book, *The Handbook of Private Foundations*:

> Starting with the universe of voluntary organizations described in Section 501(c)(3), the code excludes broad groups such as churches, schools,

hospitals, government, and publicly supported charities and their affiliates. (Publicly supported charities derive much of their support from the general public and reach out in other ways to a public constituency.) The code refers to all of the above kinds of excluded organizations as *public charities*. Section 501(c)(3) organizations remaining after these exclusions are considered private foundations.

Within the category of private foundations, the 1969 Tax Reform Act distinguishes between operating foundations—that is, foundations established primarily to operate specific research, social welfare, or other charitable programs—and nonoperating foundations. The category of nonoperating private foundation includes independent grantmaking foundations, company-sponsored foundations, and a variety of nongrantmaking organizations that function much like operating foundations or "public charities" but do not meet the legal criteria established by the Internal Revenue Code to qualify as either.

The ability to describe and study the field of philanthropy depends on maintaining definitional consistency. Annually, the Foundation Center produces *Foundation Giving*, a statistical snapshot of the "foundation universe" which is used by the general public, legislators, the media, and other audiences interested in learning more about foundation philanthropy. In truth, many grantseekers may not be interested in the technical legal category within which a particular grantmaker falls. Properly, they are focused on garnering the resources they need to pursue their worthwhle goals. However, the World Wide Web has the potential to bring a large new audience into contact with the world of foundation philanthropy, and so it is important to present the definition of a foundation for this potential new audience.

Rather than rely on the "exclusionary definition" detailed earlier, the Foundation Center defines a private foundation as *a nongovernmental, nonprofit organization that has a principal fund managed by its own trustees and directors and that maintains or aids charitable, educational, religious, or other activities serving the public good, primarily by making grants to other nonprofit organizations.*

The Foundation Center emphasizes definitional distinctions between grantmaking organizations, not only to enable it to present a picture of the field, but also because definitions can have an effect on the application requirements involved in seeking support. They also determine the amount of information available with which to research grantmakers. For example, private foundations are required to file Form 990-PF with the IRS, and these tax returns are publicly available in several ways. Clearly, as will be seen in the rest of this chapter, good information about foundations and their giving is becoming more readily available through the World Wide Web. However, it may be that for some time to come the publicly available tax return will remain a primary source of information. Non-foundation charitable organizations are required to file Form 990. These tax returns also are available for public inspection, but the information on them does not relate as specifically to grantmaking activities as that on Form 990-PF.

For decades the Foundation Center has been defining the field of foundation philanthropy, drawing a circle around the universe of U.S. private foundations, tracking foundation funding activities, providing ready access to the world of foundation funding, and educating the public about the information resources available and how to use them. The World Wide Web has created an unprecedented opportunity for the field to be defined, and to define itself, for a broad audience. We invite you to explore the tremendous amount of information available at the foundation Web sites described in this chapter. The full listing of links to independent foundation Web sites included at the end of this chapter can be found at the Center's own site <fdncenter.org>.

One more clarification before we embark on our tour of foundation information on the Web: community foundations are technically public charities, and therefore not required to file Form 990-PF (see Chapter 3 for more on the definition of a "public charity"). However, the Foundation Center traditionally has included community foundations in its statistical analyses of the foundation universe because their primary activity is grantmaking. Their more formal grantmaking and grant-reporting operations allow them to be represented logically and systematically within the foundation group. In this book, for definitional clarity we include the links to and abstracts describing community foundations in Chapter 3, "Grantmaking Public Charities on the Web," following the organization of the Center's *National Guide to Grantmaking Public Charities*. Similarly, you will find the links to and descriptions of corporate foundations (also known as company-sponsored foundations) in Chapter 4, "Corporate Giving Information on the Web."

Foundation Approaches to the Web

The Internet, an ever-expanding electronic clearinghouse of information, gives individuals and organizations an opportunity to transmit and receive information with increased efficiency and reduced cost. Because the medium is inherently dynamic, it can be an invaluable source of accurate and timely information. These qualities of efficiency and timeliness can be especially useful to foundations, which continuously need to respond to a large number of inquiries. Not only can they distribute widely basic information about themselves and answer frequently asked questions (FAQs), but they can instantly convey policy or procedural changes of interest to their audiences.

Because Web technology is continually developing, the infrastructure has limitations and therefore operational constraints. It is an industry attempting simultaneously to build a car and learn how to drive, resulting at best in an awkward relationship between theoretical and applied science. But as new developmental tools emerge and conceptualizations of the medium and information architecture evolve, design strategies are unfolding that strive to bridge the chasm between the visionaries and the pragmatists.

For instance, Web designers are constantly bombarded with news of new techniques that will revolutionize the medium. The designer must decide if the new gadgetry is a "must have," an interesting prospect, or simply an overrated nuisance. Animation, javascript, and frames are examples of potentially useful design tools that, in some instances, hinder the user's experience rather than enhance it. This is especially true for those users who have slow Internet connections or older browsers. It's also true for users who really "just want the facts" and don't care about fancy presentation. While browser upgrades are freely available to all users, Internet connection speed depends in part on hardware investment. Therefore, those working in the nonprofit sector must reconcile the desire to design for design's sake and the need to design democratically, so that audiences have equal access to the information.

For this reason, some grantmaking organizations have chosen deliberately to design simply, using straightforward presentations. Others have chosen to embrace the medium differently, creating more dynamic interfaces. In this chapter we use examples to show how certain foundations have chosen to present their organizations and activities on the World Wide Web. As more and more foundations take advantage of the Web technology available to them, the possibility exists for individual foundation philanthropy, as well as the *field* of foundation philanthropy, to be better known and understood.

The reasons grantmakers give for being "on the Net" are as varied as the grantmaking community itself. Their goals include electronic messaging, access to the information riches of the Web, community building, and increased accountability and visibility for the nonprofit sector. For most grantmakers, however, the decision is motivated by a desire to present mission-critical information efficiently and inexpensively to a larger audience. And the Web, in just a few years, has proven itself to be the best medium in history for achieving that end. The Web's relatively low barriers to entry, both financial and technological, allow even small foundations to put their informational materials online, where any one of the estimated (at the time of this writing) 60 million people with Internet access can find them.

PRESENTING BASIC INFORMATION

For many foundations, the decision to join the online arena stems from this basic goal of efficiently reaching a larger audience. However, a foundation may not have the resources to support on-going Web development. (There is a lot of evidence to indicate that maintaining a Web site for a year costs more than starting one up.) And the foundation may not have sufficient staff to respond directly to online requests or queries. For these and other reasons, a foundation's online goals may not extend to participating in online community-building, acting as a gateway to a broader array of research material, or using the Internet to fulfill its own information-gathering needs. In these cases, the Internet serves the primary purpose of disseminating basic information about the foundation. The design remains fairly simple, giving users a straightforward presentation.

The contents of a basic informational site might include a short history of the foundation and/or the original donor, brief statements about giving interests, and some form of contact information. In most instances, the design remains simple and straightforward. The following examples illustrate this approach:

Carnegie Corporation of New York <http://www.carnegie.org>
This is a simple menu-driven interface, with few graphic elements and minimal formatting to ensure maximum compatability across browsers and platforms.

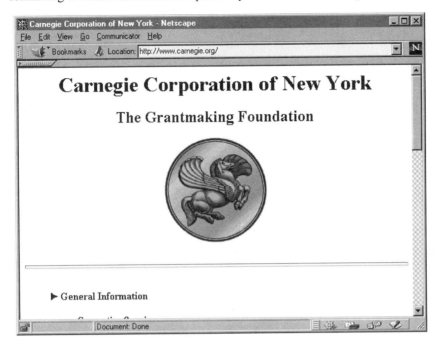

No e-mail addresses are provided. Only telephone and mail communications regarding proposals or information requests are accepted by the foundation. There are no interactive functions—no search engines, databases, or documents created "on the fly," that is, in immediate response to an action by the visitor to the site. Carnegie Corporation still maintains a gopher site. The Corporation has published many reports that it wants to disseminate widely and so simplicity of presentation ensures their availability, including internationally where hardware limitations may be more of a factor. (For a full list of the contents of this and hundreds of other foundation Web sites, see the collection of foundation site abstracts from the Center's Web site reproduced later in the chapter.)

In short, this site provides a lot of information presented in static documents with minimal "eye candy" and programming. One of the first foundation Web sites, it is easy to maintain and serves the Corporation's purposes well.

The four main program areas of the Corporation are: education and healthy development of children and youth; preventing deadly conflict; strengthening human resources in developing countries; and special projects. "Although a grant-making foundation, Carnegie Corporation also carries out its work by means of study groups and programs managed by the officers through appropriations from the grants budget. From 1986 to 1994, five such operating programs were established, based either at the Corporation's headquarters or in Washington, D.C." They were/are: Carnegie Commission on Preventing Deadly Conflict; Carnegie Task Force on Learning in the Primary Grades; Carnegie Task Force on Meeting the Needs of Young Children; Carnegie Council on Adolescent Development; Carnegie Commission on Science, Technology, and Government. Information about these programs can be found at the Corporation's Web site, along with grant restrictions and proposal guidelines, recent grants, recent publications, press releases, and links to other Internet resources.

Do Right Foundation <http://www.doright.org>

The broadly stated mission of the Do Right Foundation is to "address some of the current obstacles to a more joyful and rewarding society," and the Foundation's Web site is devoted to explaining this philosophy as it relates to the grantseeking process.

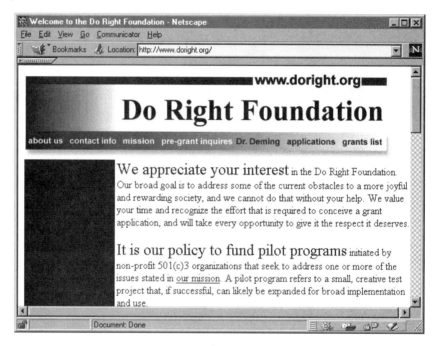

The Foundation gives priority to grantseekers who focus on the application of new and improved management theories. Visitors to the site will find a biography of W. Edwards Deming, upon whose management concepts the Foundation's philosophies are based. Also available are grants lists, a downloadable grant application, and contact information. Grantseekers are encouraged to submit a pre-grant inquiry by e-mail before applying formally.

The Do Right Foundation also has a straightforward approach to the design of its site. The Foundation does not use a frame element, but it does include various graphics to add color and dimension. Although it has chosen to use graphics, the information still very much forms the presentation. The graphical content does not distract from text and it gives the site a more polished appearance. In addition, the Foundation elected to limit the amount of textual content, including only basic facts about the Foundation and its mission.

The Abell Foundation <http://www.abell.org/abell>

The mission of the Baltimore-based Abell Foundation is "to effect positive change on the region's societal problems, with a strong focus on programs promoting educational reform, job creation and tourism; strengthening families; reducing drug addiction; and alleviating hunger and homelessness." The Foundation is committed to being an agent of change; working creatively to define issues; providing a forum to exchange ideas about them; and taking its place in the community's efforts to improve and enrich the quality of life in Maryland, and specifically in the Baltimore area.

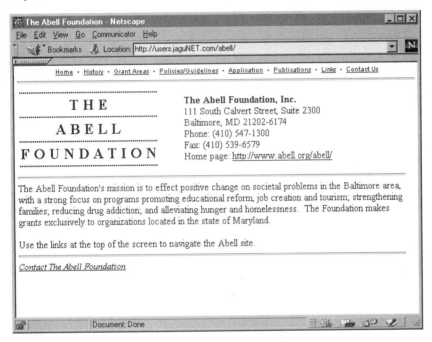

Visitors to the Foundation's Web site will find a brief history of the Foundation, general program descriptions, information about its grant policies and application procedures, a downloadable grant application form, and a number of links to other organizations of interest. The coherent and accessible presentation of this Web site is unobtrusive, giving you an immediate sense of the site's contents. In this example, the frame layout (supported by Netscape 2.0 and above and similar browsers) is a useful incorporation of frames. The stationary navigation bar, contained in the top frame, keeps you anchored as you move through the site. Notably, the foundation does not use graphics, making its pages "lightweight" in terms of file size, a key determinant of page-loading performance. On this site you will not have to wait long to receive the information.

The Heinz Endowments <http://www.heinz.org/>

This is an example of a solid informational site with a neat twist: through the use of a simple two-frame architecture, the entire site can be navigated from the opening page.

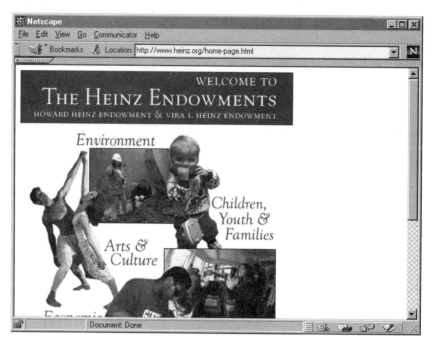

The Pittsburgh-based Heinz Endowments support the efforts of nonprofit organizations active in the areas of arts and culture, education, health and human services, economic opportunity, and the environment, with an emphasis on programs either in southwestern Pennsylvania or of clear benefit to the region. A model of functional design, the Endowments' Web site offers a range of information, including broad and program-specific statements of philosophy; information about goals, grants, projects, and staff in each program area; application guidelines; FAQs; news; and brief biographies of Howard Heinz and Vira I. Heinz as well as various program officers and directors.

Soros Foundations Network <http://www.soros.org>

This is a sophisticated example of a basic informational site. Because primary audiences for this information reside in the developing world, the site is designed for maximum compatibility with LCD (lowest-common demoninator) Internet connections.

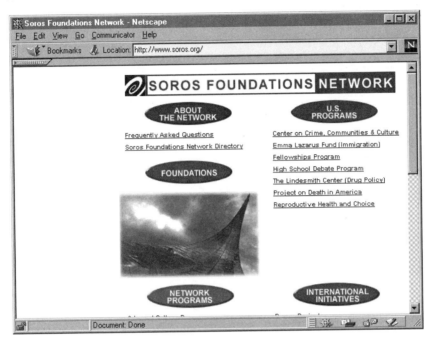

The site structure, and how it reflects the mission of the Soros philanthropies, has been explained by the Soros Foundation Network:

"Because information is such an important part of an open society, we have created a host to serve the broadest possible constituency. This includes those with only e-mail access as well as those with a WWW connection. Our WWW site is limited in its use of graphics to insure that those in the developing world with low-speed Internet connections also have an easy time accessing it. We are trying to insure that the entities who generate information for this server have the ability to update the data themselves as well.

"To achieve our stated goals, we designed our site in a rather interesting way using a mix of Internet tools. . . . We used a Gopher server as a primary engine to store data. This allows users with graphics or character-based WWW access as well as basic Gopher users to view information on our site. More significantly, we use Gopher mail to facilitate access to our data for those who only use e-mail. Our information is therefore available via multiple types of access."

INTERACTIVE INTERFACES

Some foundations have increased user interactivity by providing links to additional resources, including online communities, search engines, or additional original content. In response to emerging communications technologies, some foundations have forged ahead in order to address specifically the social implications of new media. These grantmaking organizations' philanthropic activities focus specifically on the "medium as the message," and seek to ensure an equal access Internet environment. The following foundations demonstrate a variety of approaches to interactivity, each contributing to the evolution of electronic information collection and design.

W.K. Kellogg Foundation <http://www.wkkf.org>

The mission of the W.K. Kellogg Foundation is to "help people help themselves through the practical application of knowledge and resources to improve their quality of life and that of future generations." The Foundation awards grants in three primary global regions: the United States; five southern African countries, including Botswana, Lesotho, South Africa, Swaziland, and Zimbabwe; and Latin America and the Caribbean.

In addition to thorough program descriptions, application guidelines, and the Foundation's annual report, the Foundation's sophisticated Web site offers a variety of useful features, including a state-of-the-art searchable grants database (see Chapter 6 for more details on this database); an electronic version of the International Journal of the W.K. Kellogg Foundation; and individual listings of resources of interest in the Foundation's various program areas.

Charles Stewart Mott Foundation <http://www.mott.org>

This is a good example of basic informational site with an additional layer of interactivity. Design incorporates more graphics than the typical informational site and allows visitors to interact in a variety of ways with the information on the site.

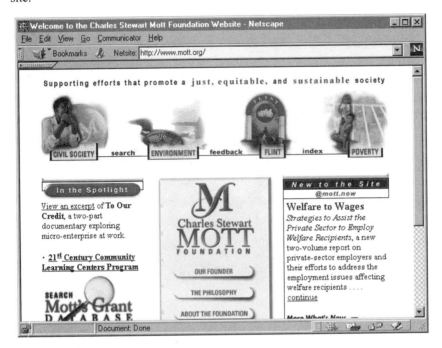

Interactive features include a site-wide search engine; a grants database that provides detailed fact sheets on all grants made from 1995 to 1998, searchable by keyword and specific fields (see Chapter 6 for more on this database); occasional use of forms as a navigation device; an electronic publications order form, which can be used to order multiple copies (the user has the option to specify quantity) of some 30 foundation-sponsored publications; and a feedback feature that allows Web site visitors to submit their comments about the site, Mott programs, etc. electronically.

Ford Foundation <http://www.fordfound.org>
This is another good example of an informational site with an interactive layer. The mission of the Ford Foundation is to serve as "a resource for innovative people and institutions worldwide. Its main goals are to strengthen democratic values, reduce poverty and injustice, promote international cooperation, and advance human achievement."

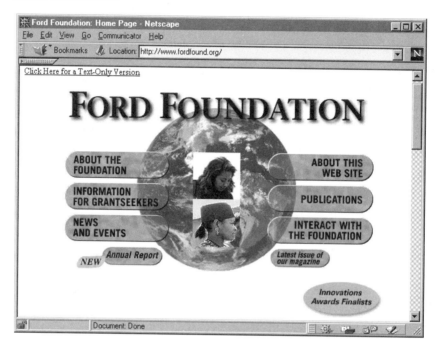

Basic information includes guidelines for grantseekers; program descriptions; answers to frequently asked questions; listings of trustees, officers, and staff; archived versions of Ford's annual reports; complete text of fifteen Ford Foundation Reports (3 each for '93, '94, '95, '96, and '97; articles can also be accessed by program); recent grants by program area; full text versions of two Susan Berresford speeches and one article written by program staff. Interactive features include a guestbook, a user survey, a publications order form, and a site-wide search engine.

Robert Wood Johnson Foundation <http://www.rwjf.org>

The mission of the Robert Wood Johnson Foundation is to improve the health and health care of all Americans. The Foundation's main funding goals are to assure that all Americans have access to basic health care at reasonable cost; to improve the way services are organized and provided to people with chronic health conditions; and to reduce the harm caused by substance abuse—tobacco, alcohol, and illicit drugs.

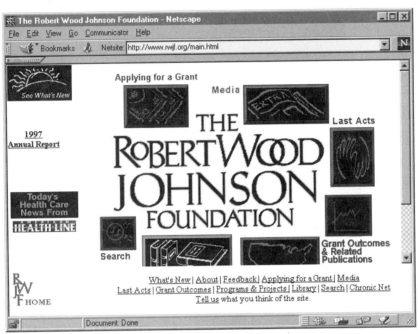

The Foundation's comprehensive Web site is a guide to its programs and activities but it is also a substantial resource for the health care field. Visitors will find detailed program descriptions and application guidelines, comprehensive grants lists, links to grantee Web/gopher sites (as well as the Foundation's own gopher site), several FAQs, and a list of its current requests for proposals (RFPs). This last feature, useful for those foundations who proactively seek specific proposals, makes great use of the Web's ability to reach a wide audience easily and quickly. Visitors to this site can also access bulletins from American Health Line, a service providing daily briefings on health care politics and policy; excerpts from the Foundation's recent annual reports; and complete text versions of "Advances," the Foundation's newsletter.

Whitaker Foundation <http://www.whitaker.org>

The Whitaker Foundation primarily supports research and education in biomedical engineering. Since its inception in 1975, the Foundation has awarded approximately $250 million to colleges and universities for faculty research, graduate fellowships and program development. In the field of biomedical engineering, the Foundation funds research grants, graduate fellowships, development awards, special opportunity awards, a teaching materials program, industrial internships, leadership awards, and conference awards.

Visitors to the Foundation's searchable Web site will find detailed program announcements and application guidelines with downloadable applications presented as .PDF (Portable Document Format) files, which are readable using the Acrobat Reader software available free from Adobe <www.adobe.com/prodindex/acrobat/adobepdf.html>. Also available on the site are annual reports going back to 1993, including lists of grantees; research grants program abstracts for 1996–97; and news from the Foundation.

As an early adopter of Internet technology, the Whitaker Foundation has utilized the medium to maximize its constituency's connectivity. The Foundation funded an initiative to develop an electronic network for biomedical engineers, including grantees. The result: *BMEnet: The Biomedical Engineering Network,* maintained at Purdue University. *BMEnet* provides links to searchable databases, professional societies, conference schedules, and various other resources. In providing this service, the foundation has participated in virtual community building, thereby furthering its mission; it gives those in the field of biomedical engineering a reference point from which they can cultivate contacts, learn about academic programs, place or review job notices, and peruse journal abstracts.

Benton Foundation <http://www.benton.org>

The Benton Foundation promotes public interest values and noncommercial services for the National Information Infrastructure through research, policy analysis, outreach to nonprofits and foundations, and print, video, and online publishing. Through its Communications Policy & Practice arm, the Foundation supports nonprofits using communications to solve social problems and strengthen social bonds.

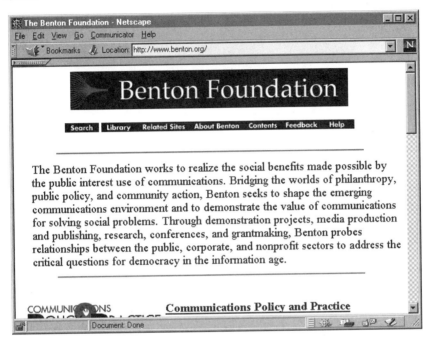

The Foundation has created the Universal Service and Universal Access Virtual Library, which supplies dozens of papers and policy documents online. Visitors to the site will find useful communications technology "best practices"; the Benton Foundation Library; nearly 200 annotated links to nonprofit and telecommunications resources on the Internet; and a listing of the Foundation's board members and staff. Other projects of the Foundation are KidsCampaigns, an online resource for "helping Americans act on behalf of children"; Open Studio: the Arts Online, which provides community access to the arts on the Internet; Destination Democracy, dedicated to campaign finance reform; and the Funders' Committee on Citizen Participation (FCCP), a group of grantmakers committed to enhancing democratic involvement in civic life.

The Bell Atlantic Foundation <http://www.bellatlanticfoundation.com>
Though we provide our comprehensive list of links and abstracts for corporate foundations in Chapter 3, the Bell Atlantic Foundation's Web site is a good example of a sophisticated, interactive site, as you would expect from a foundation whose program interests include communications technology.

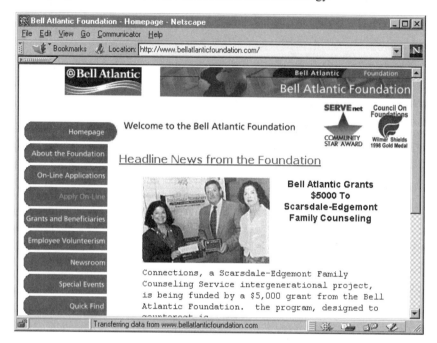

The merger of Bell Atlantic and NYNEX, announced August 14, 1997, joined the two corporations' foundations to create a new Bell Atlantic Foundation. The Foundation provides "opportunities for non-profit organizations to apply new technology to the programs and services they offer," focusing its efforts on the communities from Maine to Virginia served by Bell Atlantic, particularly those communities' children and young people. Most of the Foundation's support aims to make technology more available to students, teachers, service organizations, and cultural institutions with youth programs. Priority is given to activities in education, health and human services, arts and humanities, and community service that facilitate collaborations through network solutions and enhanced communications systems.

The Foundation's sophisticated Web site comes in Java and non-Java versions (see the Glossary in Appendix D for a description of the Java programming language). Visitors to the Web site will find summaries of giving by state, grants lists by state going back to 1994, an overview of the Foundation, grant guidelines, detailed program descriptions, contact information (here e-mail is the preferred form of communication), news, and a list of the Foundation's board of directors. Grantseekers can locate the local community relations manager by entering their zip code in a form on the Web site, and the Foundation encourages online submission of grant applications, guaranteeing a response within 48 hours.

The Foundation Center's Online Project: Tracking and Expanding Grantmaker Web Presence

THE CENTER'S "FOUNDATION FOLDER" INITIATIVE

Through its "Foundation Folder" initiative, the Foundation Center provides an opportunity for any grantmaking independent, community, or company-sponsored foundation in the U.S. to establish a Web presence. Not only does the initiative seek to provide individual foundations with an immediate Web presence, it puts more foundation information in front of a wider audience. The Center does this by offering space on its Web site to any eligible foundation interested in seeing its program descriptions and guidelines, application information, grants lists, RFPs, and newsletters on the World Wide Web. Funders interested in having their informational materials hosted by the Center are assigned their own "folder"—the universally recognized organizing metaphor of the desktop computing environment—in the Grantmaker Information section of the Center's Web site. Foundation Folders act as virtual Web sites. (Because the folders do not have a unique domain name and exist within the framework of the Center's site, they are not considered actual Web sites.) The hot links to Foundation Folders are listed on the Center's Web site along with those of foundation Web sites hosted elsewhere. The folder information design is modular and at this time does not incorporate more advanced interactive tools. The efficiencies gained by staying with a modular approach will allow for broader participation in this free service.

LINKED GRANTMAKER ANNOTATIONS

The Foundation Center's Web site offers annotations of and links to hundreds of grantmaker sites. The online grantmaker directory divides the annotations into searchable areas: independent foundations, community foundations and other grantmaking public charities, and corporate foundations and giving programs. (The list of links and abstracts for these sites are included in Chapters 2, 3, and 4, respectively.) The Foundation Center's grantmaker search engine enables you to query the online annotations by subject and geographic area (the community foundation section is organized by state), making it possible for you to assemble lists of funders on the Web that may address your specific needs. Each annotation links to the funder's Web site or Foundation Folder. Although the Center's online directory represents the most complete compilation of annotated foundation material online, the list is restricted to those grantmakers that have a Web presence. You should note that, unlike the Foundation Center's database-driven print directories and *FC Search* CD-ROM, the comprehensiveness of the annotations depends solely on the availability and breadth of the online resources themselves. As more foundations join the online citizenry, the Center will continue to expand its list of searchable site annotations.

USING THE GRANTMAKER SEARCH ENGINE

The independent foundation, corporate grantmaker, community foundation and other grantmaking public charities subdirectories all contain unique search engines that will yield results based on user-directed keyword input.

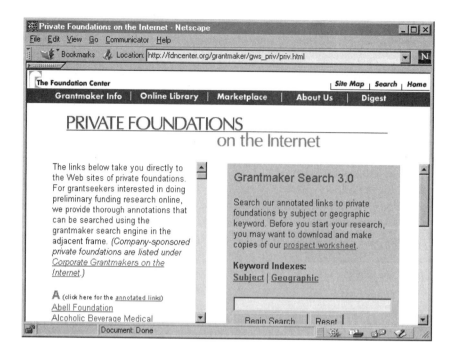

To begin your search, determine which type of grantmaker you would like to locate. To execute a query, go to the appropriate subdirectory and enter either a subject or geographic keyword into the Foundation Center's Grantmaker Search Engine. The Center has compiled keyword indexes for each each category (see the graphic below) so that you can cross reference your own keywords with those that the Center has determined to be most useful.

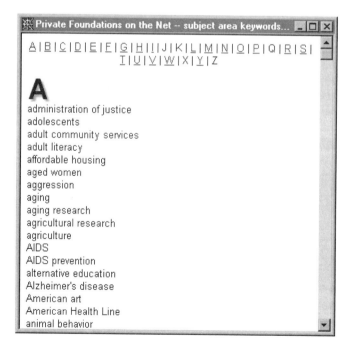

Although you do not have to use the keywords provided in the indexes, using them will often target your search more effectively; the keyword listings are based on the most commonly used words in the annotations, therefore they will reference the annotations more precisely. Once the results appear on the screen, you can link directly to the annotation. The keyword you selected will appear in bold in the text and the foundation name at the top of the page will link you directly to the grantmaker site.

If the foundation appears to support projects that match your organizational or individual needs, link to the grantmaker's site. Once you have reached the site of interest, you have entered the grantmaker's own domain (i.e., you are outside of the Foundation Center's Web site). You can easily link back to the Foundation Center by using your browser's 'Back' or 'Go' buttons. The Back button will take you to the page most recently visited, while the Go button contains a more elaborate page history (see Chapter 1 for a description of the "history lists" stored within your browser functioning). As you explore individual foundation sites, you may want to "bookmark" any page that gives you relevent information. (See Chapter 1 for a description of this browser function.) The URLs for the bookmarked pages will be stored within your browser and are extremely useful in cataloging potentially useful areas of the Web that you may wish to visit again.

Links and Abstracts of "Independent" Private Foundation Web Sites

Below are the independent private foundations that were on the Web at the time of writing. Check <fdncenter.org/grantmaker/priv.html> for the latest listing. (See Chapter 3 for the links/abstracts for grantmaking public charities and Chapter 4 for the links/abstracts for corporate foundations and giving programs.)

The Abell Foundation <http://www.abell.org/abell>
The mission of the Baltimore-based Abell Foundation is "to effect positive change on the region's societal problems, with a strong focus on programs promoting educational reform, job creation and tourism; strengthening families; reducing drug addiction; and alleviating hunger and homelessness." The Foundation is committed to being an agent of change; working creatively to define issues; providing a forum to exchange ideas about them; and taking its place in the community's efforts to improve and enrich the quality of life in Maryland, and specifically in the Baltimore area. Visitors to the Foundation's Web site will find a brief history of the Foundation, general program descriptions, information about its grant policies and application procedures, a downloadable grant application form, and a number of links to other organizations of interest.

Alcoholic Beverage Medical Research Foundation <http://www.abmrf.org/>

The Paul G. Allen Charitable Foundation
<http://www.paulallen.com/foundations/>
The purpose of the Bellevue, Washington-based Paul G. Allen Charitable Foundation is to "improve the quality of life in the Pacific Northwest through programs designed to create new opportunities for community service." To that end, the Foundation funds projects in whole or in part in the areas of education,

environmental research, youth services, social services, and aid to the disabled and disadvantaged. Ordinarily, the Foundation does not consider grant requests for operating, administrative or overhead expenses; for contributions to general fund drives, annual appeals or federated campaigns; for the benefit of specific individuals; for conduit organizations; to institutions "whose policy or practice unfairly discriminates against race, ethnic origin, sex, creed or sexual orientation"; to sectarian or religious organizations; or to organizations currently funded by any other Paul G. Allen foundation. In addition to a fair amount of biographical information about Microsoft co-founder Allen, "The Wired World of Paul Allen" Web site provides examples of recent grants and projects supported by the Foundation, grant application guidelines, a description of the application process, and a downloadable application form.

The Paul G. Allen Foundation for Medical Research
<http://www.paulallen.com/foundations/>

The purpose of the Bellevue, Washington-based Paul G. Allen Foundation for Medical Research is to "promote innovative medical research in a variety of fields, including biochemistry, biomedical engineering, virology, immunology, cell and molecular biology, pharmacology and genetics." Projects that "develop new insights into the prevention or successful treatment of cancer" are of special interest. Ordinarily, the Foundation does not consider grant requests for operating, administrative or overhead expenses; for contributions to general fund drives, annual appeals or federated campaigns; for the benefit of specific individuals; for conduit organizations; to institutions "whose policy or practice unfairly discriminates against race, ethnic origin, sex, creed or sexual orientation"; to sectarian or religious organizations; or to organizations currently funded by any other Paul G. Allen foundation. In addition to a fair amount of biographical information about Microsoft co-founder Allen, "The Wired World of Paul Allen" Web site provides examples of recent grants and projects supported by the Foundation, grant application guidelines, a description of the application process, and a downloadable application form.

The Allen Foundation for the Arts <http://www.paulallen.com/foundations/>

The purpose of the Bellevue, Washington-based Allen Foundation for the Arts is to "promote a creative and flourishing arts community in the Pacific Northwest." The Foundation, which is especially interested in the performing and visual arts, also supports entities that sustain artists and art organizations. Ordinarily, the Foundation does not consider grant requests for operating, administrative or overhead expenses; for contributions to general fund drives, annual appeals or federated campaigns; for the benefit of specific individuals; for conduit organizations; to institutions "whose policy or practice unfairly discriminates against race, ethnic origin, sex, creed or sexual orientation"; to sectarian or religious organizations; or to organizations currently funded by any other Paul G. Allen foundation. In addition to a fair amount of biographical information about Microsoft co-founder Allen, "The Wired World of Paul Allen" Web site provides examples of recent grants and projects supported by the Foundation, grant application guidelines, a description of the application process, and a downloadable application form.

The Paul G. Allen Forest Protection Foundation
<http://www.paulallen.com/foundations/>

The purpose of the Bellevue, Washington-based Paul G. Allen Forest Protection Foundation—the newest Allen foundation—is to assist in "the acquisition and conservation of forest land in order to preserve needed wildlife habitat and, where possible, to provide public recreational access." Rather than directly acquiring and preserving properties, the Foundation works with established conservancies (e.g.,. the Wilderness Society, the Nature Conservancy) to leverage, through its contributions, the expertise of these organizations to implement programs consistent with the Foundation's purpose. Ordinarily, the Foundation does not consider grant requests for operating, administrative or overhead expenses; for contributions to general fund drives, annual appeals or federated campaigns; for the benefit of specific individuals; for conduit organizations; to institutions "whose policy or practice unfairly discriminates against race, ethnic origin, sex, creed or sexual orientation"; to sectarian or religious organizations; or to organizations currently funded by any other Paul G. Allen foundation. In addition to a fair amount of biographical information about Microsoft co-founder Allen, "The Wired World of Paul Allen" Web site provides examples of recent grants and projects supported by the Foundation, grant application guidelines, a description of the application process, and a downloadable application form.

Allen Foundation, Inc. <http://http.tamu.edu/baum/allen.html>

Established in 1975 by agricultural chemist William Webster Allen, the Michigan-based Allen Foundation makes grants to projects that benefit human nutrition in the areas of education, training, and research. Visitors to the Foundation's Web site will find a brief biography of Mr. Allen, a listing of the Foundation's board of trustees, a downloadable grant application form, and links to other nutrition and food science sites on the Internet. Visitors may also access the Foundation's annual reports from 1990 through 1997.

Alliance Healthcare Foundation <http://www.alliancehf.org/>

The San Diego-based Alliance Healthcare Foundation funds healthcare programs for medically indigent and underserved populations in Southern California, primarily in San Diego County. Priority is given to programs that address the issues of restricted access to healthcare, substance abuse, communicable diseases, violence, mental health, and environmental and community health problems. The Foundation also performs fundraising, advocacy, and public education campaigns to benefit the healthcare field. The Foundation's brand-new Web site provides general program descriptions; detailed application guidelines, rules, and procedures; links to related organizations and resources in the healthcare field; board and staff listings; a brief "News" section; and contact information.

Amateur Athletic Foundation of Los Angeles <http://www.aafla.com>

The Amateur Athletic Foundation of Los Angeles was established to manage Southern California's share of the surplus funds generated by the 1984 Olympic Games. The Foundation focuses its grantmaking activities on sports programs for youth in Southern California's eight counties: Imperial, Los Angeles, Orange, Riverside, San Bernardino, San Diego, Santa Barbara, and Ventura. At the same time, the Foundation gives special attention to women, minorities, the physically challenged or developmentally disabled, and youth in areas where the risk of involvement in delinquency is particularly high. Visitors to the Foundation's Web site will find detailed grant guidelines and application criteria, a list of the Foundation's board of directors, and links to other sports sites. The site also offers information on the Foundation's own youth sports program, historic sports art and artifact collection, sports research library, and special events.

Amy Foundation <http://www.amyfound.org/index.html>

The Annenberg Foundation <http://www.whannenberg.org/>

The principal grantmaking focus of the Pennsylvania-based Annenberg Foundation is on pre-collegiate education and public school restructuring and reform, grades K through 12. Within these broad areas, the Foundation is particularly interested in early childhood education in relation to public education at the primary level, and in child development and youth services. Visitors to the Foundation's no-frills Web site will find a brief biography of founder/donor and former *TV Guide* publisher Walter H. Annenberg; an overview of the Foundation's K–12 Challenge Grant program and contact information for 15 challenge grant sites and initiatives; general information about three independent Foundation-sponsored programs (the Annenberg/CPB math and Science Project, the Annenberg Washington Program in Communications Policy Studies at the University of Pennsylvania, and the Annenberg Institute for School Reform); a short list of sample grants; application procedures and proposal guidelines; and basic fiscal information for the year ended 6/97.

The Arca Foundation <http://fdncenter.org/grantmaker/arca/index.html>

Established in 1952 as the Nancy Reynolds Bagley Foundation, the Arca Foundation received its present name in 1968. Domestically, the Foundation's primary concern is "the overwhelming influence of private money in politics and its effect on who runs for public office, who wins, and in whose interest they govern." Arca's funding emphasizes "educational efforts to expose this legal form of corruption and suggest effective remedies at the state and national level." It also funds projects "that address the imbalance of power in society more generally, emphasizing issues of economic equity and labor rights at home and abroad." In the foreign policy field, Arca's grantmaking "reflects a focus on issues that are particularly influenced by U.S. policy in the Western Hemisphere. U.S. policy toward Cuba and Central America continues to be a central concern, alongside the human consequences of globalized production." The Foundation's "folder" on the Center's Web site provides a brief history of the Foundation, grantmaking guidelines and a 1996 grants list organized by area of interest, and contact information.

Mary Reynolds Babcock Foundation
<http://fdncenter.org/grantmaker/babcock/index.html>

Based in Winston-Salem, North Carolina, the Mary Reynolds Babcock Foundation concentrates its activities on community-building initiatives in the southeastern United States, placing a special emphasis on activities that seek to assure the well-being of children, youth, and families; bridge the faultlines of race and class; and invest in communities' human and natural resources over the long term. The Foundation addresses its interests through three specific programs: the Community Problem Solving Program, which aims to support coalitions working on local community issues in ways that "build lasting capacity in their communities to solve problems"; the Organizational Development Program, the purpose of which is to help 75–100 Southeastern organizations over the next five years "to clarify their missions, increase their effectiveness, and sustain their work"; and the Opportunity Fund, which provides core support to emerging organizations. The Foundation's "folder" on the Center's Web site provides a statement of purpose and values, general program descriptions, listings of the Foundation's board and staff, and contact information.

Helen Bader Foundation <http://www.hbf.org/>
The Milwaukee-based Helen Bader Foundation supports innovative programs that advance the well-being of people and promote succesful relationships with their families and communities. The Foundation concentrates its grantmaking in five areas: Alzheimer's disease and dementia (geographic focus: national, with priority given to Milwaukee and Wisconsin), children and youth in Israel (geographic focus: Israel), economic development (geographic focus: Milwaukee), education (geographic focus: Milwaukee), and Jewish life and learning (geographic focus: Milwaukee and Delaware River Valley area). In addition to background information, press releases, and a biography of founder Helen Bader, the Foundation's elegant, easy-to-navigate Web site provides general program information; application guidelines and online and downloadable application forms; 1997 grants, grant summaries by program area, and profiles of featured grantees; and contact information.

Lee & Ramona Bass Foundation <http://www.sidrichardson.org/lrbf.htm>

The Arnold and Mabel Beckman Foundation
<http://www.beckman-foundation.com/>
The Arnold and Mabel Beckman Foundation makes grants "to promote research in chemistry and the life sciences, broadly interpreted, and particularly to foster the invention of methods, instruments, and materials that will open up new avenues of research in science." The Irvine, California-based Foundation's no-frills Web site provides brief bios of Arnold and Mabel Beckman; guidelines and downloadable application forms for the Beckman Young Investigators (BYI) Program, which provides research support to promising young faculty members in the early stages of academic careers in the chemical and life sciences, and the Beckman Research Technologies Initiatives; and links to Beckman Institutes/Centers at the University of Illinois at Urbana-Champaign, the California Institute of Technology, Stanford University, the Beckman Laser Institute, and City of Hope.

Benton Foundation <http://www.benton.org/>
The Benton Foundation promotes public interest values and noncommercial services for the National Information Infrastructure through research, policy analysis, outreach to nonprofits and foundations, and print, video, and online publishing. Through its Communications Policy & Practice arm, the Foundation supports nonprofits using communications to solve social problems and strengthen social bonds. The Foundation has created the Universal Service and Universal Access Virtual Library, which supplies dozens of papers and policy documents online. Visitors to the site will find useful communications technology "best practices"; the Benton Foundation Library; nearly 200 annotated links to nonprofit and telecommunications resources on the Internet; and a listing of the Foundation's board

members and staff. Other projects of the Foundation are KidsCampaigns, an online resource for "helping Americans act on behalf of children"; Open Studio: The Arts Online, which provides community access to the arts on the Internet; Destination Democracy, dedicated to campaign finance reform; and The Funders' Committee on Citizen Participation (FCCP), a group of grantmakers committed to enhancing democratic involvement in civic life.

Frank Stanley Beveridge Foundation, Inc.
<http://www.beveridge.org/

The Florida-based Beveridge Foundation was established in Massachusetts in 1947 by Frank Stanley Beveridge, the founder of Stanley Home Products, Inc. Today the Foundation considers grant proposals in some two dozen institutional/ program activity areas, including animal related, arts and culture, civil rights, community improvement, conservation/environment, crime, disasters/safety, diseases/medical disciplines, education, employment, food and agriculture, health-general & rehabilitative, housing, human services, mental health—crisis intervention, philanthropy/voluntarism, public affairs and society benefit, recreation, religion, science, social sciences, and youth development. The stated purpose of the Foundation's Web site, however, is to determine whether potential applicants are eligible to receive grants from the Foundation. In addition to a self-administered interactive survey to help grantseekers determine whether they meet the Foundation's basic eligibility requirements, visitors to the site will find a biography of Mr. Beveridge, a 1997 grants list, a listing of the Foundation's officers and directors, and contact information.

The William Bingham Foundation
<http://fdncenter.org/grantmaker/bingham/index.html>

The William Bingham Foundation was established in 1955 by Elizabeth Bingham Blossom in memory of her brother, William Bingham II, to continue the philanthropic tradition of the family. Initially, the Foundation's grantmaking focused on educational, cultural, and health and human service organizations in the Cleveland area. Over the years, however, the Foundation's objectives have broadened to reflect the needs of the communities in which its trustees reside. Today, the Foundation contributes to a wide variety of organizations in the areas of the arts, education, and health and human services in those communities as well as nationwide. The Foundation's "folder" on the Center's Web site provides a brief history of the Foundation, its program interests and grantmaking procedures, a list of grants paid in 1997, and trustee, officer, and staff listings.

Blandin Foundation <http://www.blandinfoundation.org/>

The mission of the Blandin Foundation is to strengthen rural Minnesota communities, with a special focus on the Grand Rapids community and Itasca County. To that end, the Foundation sponsors conferences and leadership programs and provides approximately $12 million to Minnesota organizations annually. Outside of Itasca County, Blandin grants are restricted to the focus areas established by the Foundation's board of trustees: education, cultural opportunities, community leadership training, environmental stewardship, safe communities, economic opportunity, and "convening." The trustees commit most of the Foundation's grant dollars to its major partners, who have the responsibility of administering each focus area. Potential grant applicants are encouraged to review the Foundation's current focus areas and then contact the appropriate partner organization, which can be done via e-mail through the Foundation's Web site. The site also provides program descriptions, a list of grants made through January 1998, and detailed grant restrictions.

The Arthur M. Blank Family Foundation <http://www.BlankFoundation.org/>

The Blowitz-Ridgeway Foundation
<http://fdncenter.org/grantmaker/blowitz/index.html>
Founded in 1984 with the proceeds from the sale of Chicago's Ridgeway Hospital, a psychiatric facility focusing on low-income adolescents, the Blowitz-Ridgeway Foundation continues the hospital's mission by making grants primarily for medical, psychiatric, psychological and/or residential care; and research programs in medicine, psychology, social science, and education. Preference is given to organizations operating within the state of Illinois. Visitors to the Foundation's "folder" on the Center's Web site will find application guidelines and procedures, and a listing of recent grants.

The Mary Owen Borden Foundation
<http://fdncenter.org/grantmaker/borden/index.html>
The Mary Owen Borden Foundation was founded by Bertram H. Borden in 1934 to honor his recently departed wife. In recent decades, the Foundation has limited its new funding to New Jersey's Mercer and Monmouth counties. Its current giving is focused on disadvantaged youth and their families, including needs such as health, family planning, education, counseling, childcare, substance abuse, and delinquency. Other areas of interest for the Foundation include affordable housing, conservation and the environment, and the arts. The Foundation's "folder" on the Center's Web site provides general Foundation information, application guidelines and procedures, a summary of grants made in 1996, a listing of the Foundation's officers and trustees, and contact information.

The Lynde and Harry Bradley Foundation <http://www.townhall.com/bradley/>
Established to commemorate Lynde and Harry Bradley, successful turn-of-the-century Milwaukee businessmen, the Bradley Foundation furthers the brothers' mutual interest in helping to improve the quality of life in the metropolitan Milwaukee area and to "preserving and defending the tradition of free representative government and private enterprise which has enabled the American nation . . . to flourish intellectually and economically." Like the Bradley brothers, the Foundation is "devoted to strengthening American democratic capitalism and the institutions, principles and values which sustain and nurture it. Its programs support limited, competent government; a dynamic marketplace for economic, intellectual, and cultural activity; and a vigorous defense at home and abroad of American ideas and institutions." Recognizing that "responsible self-government depends on enlightened citizens and informed public opinion," the Bradley Foundation also supports scholarly studies and academic achievement. The Foundation's Web site provides passionate descriptions of the Foundation's mission and driving philosophy; general information about its current program interests and grantmaking policies; and listings of the Foundation's board, officers, and staff.

The Brainerd Foundation <http://www.brainerd.org/>

The Brainerd Foundation is dedicated to protecting the environmental quality of the Pacific Northwest—Alaska, Idaho, Montana, Oregon, Washington, and the Canadian province of British Columbia by supporting "grassroots-oriented projects that motivate citizens to get involved in efforts to protect the environment." The majority of the foundation's grants are awarded within one of three program areas: endangered ecosystems, toxic pollution, and communication strategies. The Foundation also makes what it calls Emergency Grants, which range from $250 to $2,000 and are given to "organizations that are confronted with an opportunity to carry out important work in a hurry." Visitors to the Foundation's Web site will find detailed program guidelines and limitations, application procedures, lists of 1995, 1996, 1997 and 1998 grant recipients, biographies of the Foundation's directors and staff, and a handful of links to community resources in the Pacific Northwest.

Otto Bremer Foundation
<http://fdncenter.org/grantmaker/bremer/index.html>

The mission of the St. Paul-based Otto Bremer Foundation is "to be an accessible and responsible financial resource to aid in the development and cohesion of communities within the states of Minnesota, North Dakota, Wisconsin, and Montana, with preference given to those communities served by the affiliates of Bremer Financial Corporation." Within its geographic focus, the Foundation makes grants in the areas of racism, rural poverty, community affairs, education, health, human services, and religion. Visitors to the Foundation's "folder" on the Center's Web site will find program and application guidelines, a summary of the Foundation's 1996 grantmaking activities, and comprehensive grants lists in each program area.

James Graham Brown Foundation, Inc. <http://www.brownfoundation.com/>

Established under a trust agreement in 1943 and formally incorporated in 1954, the James Graham Brown Foundation is dedicated to fostering the well-being, quality of life, and image of Louisville (i.e., Jefferson County) and Kentucky. The Foundation does this by actively supporting and funding projects in the fields of civic and economic development, education, youth, and health and general welfare. Since the death of its benefactor, James Graham Brown, in 1969, the Foundation has awarded approximately 2,100 grants totaling more than $200 million. mainly in Kentucky, with a small percentage awarded in other parts of the Southeast. Visitors to the Foundation's Web site will find information about its proposal requirements and application procedures, a list of 1997 grant recipients organized by program area, and contact information.

Kathleen Price Bryan Family Fund
<http://fdncenter.org/grantmaker/kpbryan/index.html>

Established in 1955, the Kathleen Price Bryan Family Fund serves North Carolinians in building strong and healthy communities. To that end, the Fund is interested in the development of tangible, sustainable results in North Carolina in the following areas: human resources (education, health, safety); economic resources (affordable housing, business development, asset generation and development, income and economic self-reliance); natural resources (environmental concerns); North Carolina cultural resources (preserving distinctive arts, customs, and cultures); public interest; and societal issues. In addition, the Fund takes a special interest "in community-based organizations working to build their own capacities through projects which expand local resources for local concerns, create results that have long-term effects, and link individual, family and community interests," as well as organizations "working to build collaborative action and approaches to statewide issues through public/private partnerships, prevention programs, and advocacy on key issues." Visitors to the Fund's "folder" on the Center's Web site will find a brief history of the Fund, detailed statements of the Fund's grantmaking policies and interests, answers to FAQs, a 1997 grants list, and contact information.

Burroughs Wellcome Fund <http://www.bwfund.org/index.html>
Established in 1955 to advance the medical sciences by supporting research and other scientific and educational activities, the Burroughs Wellcome Fund today emphasizes "career development of outstanding scientists and . . . advancing areas in the basic medical sciences that are underfunded or that have a shortage of qualified researchers." Ninety percent of the Fund's resources are distributed through seven competitive award programs, and the majority of those programs are open to scientists who are citizens or permanent residents of the United States and Canada. BWF's straightforward Web site offers complete descriptions of the Fund's programs; award eligibility requirements and guidelines; application deadlines; a listing of the Fund's board of directors, officers, and staff; a fast-loading version of its 1997 annual report; and recent issues of Focus, the Fund's newsletter.

Edyth Bush Charitable Foundation
<http://fdncenter.org/grantmaker/bush/index.html>
The mission of the Edyth Bush Charitable Foundation is to "help relieve human suffering and help underprivileged and needy people improve themselves." To that end, the Foundation supports programs that "enable people to increase their self-sufficiency and improve their capabilities to make a better community." The Foundation makes grants to nonprofit organizations exclusively located and/or operating within a 100-mile radius of Winter Park, Florida, with special emphasis in Orange, Seminole, Osceola, and Lake counties. The Foundation, which was founded by the widow of Archibald G. Bush, a director and principal shareholder of the Minnesota Mining & Manufacturing Company, also has broad interests in human service, education, and health care, and a limited interest in the arts. Visitors to the Foundation's "folder" on the Foundation Center's Web site will find a detailed account of the Foundation's application policies and procedures, as well as 1997 and 1998 grants lists by subject area.

Morris and Gwendolyn Cafritz Foundation
<http://members.aol.com/grantscoor/cafritzfdn/home.htm>

California HealthCare Foundation <http://www.chcf.org/>
The California HealthCare Foundation was established in May 1996 as a result of the conversion of Blue Cross of California from a nonprofit health plan to WellPoint Health Networks, a for-profit corporation. The Foundation is one of two philanthropies created by the conversion—the other is the California Endowment—and is charged with responsibility for gradually divesting the Foundation of WellPoint stock and transferring 80 percent of the proceeds to the Endowment,

and for developing the Foundation's own independent grantmaking program with the remaining 20 percent of the funds. The Foundation's grantmaking is statewide and focuses initially on five program areas: managed care and special populations, California's uninsured, California health policy, consumer health information and education, and public health. CHCF's well-organized Web site provides general program information, grant guidelines and limitations, a list of recent grants, RFPs (in MS Word and .PDF format), an electronic form for ordering Foundation publications, a comprehensive set of links to health-related Web sites, a message from Foundation president Mark D. Smith, listings of the board and staff, and contact information.

The California Wellness Foundation <http://www.tcwf.org/>
The mission of the California Wellness Foundation is to improve the health and well-being of the people of California through health promotion and disease prevention programs. The Foundation concentrates its grantmaking activities in five areas—community health, population health improvement, teenage pregnancy prevention, violence prevention, and work and health—and while it generally supports organizations located in California or projects that directly benefit California residents, national organizations providing services in California are also considered. In addition to information about its general grants program and descriptions of strategic initiatives in each of its five focus areas, the Foundation's Web site provides a listing of 1997 grants, links to related Web sites, and the Foundation's newsletter, downloadable as a .PDF file.

Iris & B. Gerald Cantor Foundation <http://www.cantorfoundation.com/>

Canyon Research <http://www.jcdowning.org/canyon/canyonresearch.htm>

CarEth Foundation <http://www.funder.org/careth/>
The CarEth Foundation seeks to promote "a compassionate world of enduring peace, with justice, and with social, economic, and political equality for all." In support of its mission, the Foundation is currently funding programs that promote the creation of a global community of peace and justice, a genuine democracy in the United States, and peaceful conflict resolution. The Foundation is also currently interested in projects involving today's youth. Visitors to CarEth's Web site will find general descriptions of program goals, application procedures and limitations, and a list of 1996–1997 grantees with links to all recipient organizations with Web sites.

Carlisle Foudation <http://www.carlislefoundation.org>

Carnegie Corporation of New York <http://www.carnegie.org/>
In addition to a brief history of Andrew Carnegie and his philanthropies and information about the Foundation itself, the Web site of the Carnegie Corporation of New York gives visitors general information about the Foundation's four currently supported program areas: education and the healthy development of children and youth, preventing deadly conflict, strengthening human resources in developing countries, and special projects. The last affords the Foundation an opportunity to make grants and appropriations outside its three defined program areas. Available as well are application guidelines and grant restrictions; a

description of the Foundation's six special initiatives; full-text online versions of selected Carnegie publications; a listing of Foundation officers and trustees; links to other foundation and nonprofit resources on the Internet; and contact information.

Carnegie Endowment for International Peace <http://www.ceip.org/>

Carnegie Hero Fund Commission <http://trfn.clpgh.org/carnegiehero/>

The Annie E. Casey Foundation <http://www.aecf.org/>
Established in 1948 by Jim Casey, one of the founders of United Parcel Service, and his siblings, the Annie E. Casey Foundation is dedicated to fostering "public policies, human-service reforms, and community supports that more effectively meet the needs of today's vulnerable children and families." In general, the grant-making of the Baltimore-based Foundation is limited to "initiatives that have significant potential to demonstrate innovative policy, service delivery, and community supports for children and families." Most grantees have been invited by the Foundation to participate in these projects. The Foundation does not make grants to individuals, nor does it support capital projects that are not an integral part of a Foundation-sponsored initiative. The Foundation's new Web site is organized into four broad areas: Kid's Count, a national and state-by-state effort to track the educational, economic, social, and physical well-being of children in the United States; Foundation Initiatives; Foundation News; and a listing of Foundation publications.

The Casey Family Program <http://www.casey.org>

Samuel N. & Mary Castle Foundation
<http://fdncenter.org/grantmaker/castle/index.html>
For more than a century, the Samuel N. and Mary Castle Foundation and its precursor, the Samuel N. Castle Memorial Trust, have served the needs of the people of Hawai'i. Over the years, the Foundation's grantmaking has focused primarily on the support of early education and child care, private education (elementary and high schools as well as colleges and universities), Protestant churches, and arts and cultural organizations with ties to the Castle family. In addition, through the Henry and Dorothy Castle Memorial Fund, the Foundation supports the health and human services sector, concentrating its funds on agencies directly providing services to young children and their families. Because Hawaii's population is concentrated on O'ahu, preference is given to organizations whose programs are O'ahu-based. The Foundation's "folder" on the Center's Web site provides a history of the Foundation and brief biographies of Samuel N. and Mary Tenney Castle, messages from the Foundation's president and executive director, a rundown of its grantmaking policies and application procedures, a list of grants awarded in 1997, and contact information.

Chiesman Foundation for Democracy <http://www.chiesman.org>

Edna McConnell Clark Foundation
<http://fdncenter.org/grantmaker/emclark/index.html>
The Edna McConnell Clark Foundation seeks to improve conditions and opportunities for people who live in poor and disadvantaged communities. Through its grantmaking, the Foundation "assists nonprofit organizations and public agencies committed to advancing practices and policies that better the lives of children and families, [while supporting] initiatives that promise to help systems and institutions become more responsive to the needs of the people they serve." The current interests of the Foundation fall into four separate program areas, each with specific goals, strategies, and grantmaking priorities: the Program for Children, the Program for New York Neighborhoods, the Program for Student Achievement, and the Program for Tropical Disease Research. Applicants may want to read the Foundation's latest annual report to ensure that their projects fit within the above programs' very specific, site-based grantmaking strategies. Visitors to the Foundation's "folder" on the Center's Web site will find detailed program descriptions, application guidelines, a 1997 grants list organized by program area, a report from Foundation president Michael A. Bailin, a list of Foundation-sponsored publications that can be obtained free of charge, board and staff listings, and contact information.

Robert Sterling Clark Foundation
<http://fdncenter.org/grantmaker/rsclark/index.html>
Incorporated in 1952, the Robert Sterling Clark Foundation has provided financial assistance to a wide variety of charitable organizations over the years. At present, it is concentrating its resources in the following fields: improving the performance of public institutions in New York City and State, strengthening the management of New York cultural institutions, and ensuring access to family planning practices. While most of its support will be allocated for these purposes, the Foundation has also begun to make funds available to protect artistic freedom and to educate the public about the importance of the arts in our society. Visitors to the Foundation's "folder" on the Center's Web site will find program guidelines, application procedures, and contact information.

Clipper Ship Foundation <http://www.agmconnect.org/clipper1.html>

The Coleman Foundation, Inc. <http://www.colemanfoundation.org/>

Colorado Trust <http://www.coltrust.org/>
The mission of the Colorado Trust is to promote the health and well-being of the people of Colorado through the support of accessible and affordable health care programs and the strengthening of families. The Trust employs an initiative framework in which it identifies objectives, establishes workable approaches, and recruits interested organizations to implement programs. Visitors to the Trust's easy-to-navigate Web site will find descriptions of its initiatives in each of Colorado's counties as well as information about its approaches to grantmaking. Special features of the site include a funding opportunities mailing list and a program evaluation section entitled "Lessons Learned at the Colorado Trust."

Columbia Foundation <http://www.columbia.org/>

The Commonwealth Fund <http://www.cmwf.org/>

The Commonwealth Fund, a national New York City-based foundation, under-takes independent research on health and social issues. Its programs focus on improving health care services, bettering the health of minority Americans, advancing the well being of elderly people, and developing the capacities of children and young people. The Fund's Web site provides a history of the organization, descriptions of its most recent initiatives and related publications, grant guidelines, a listing of its board and staff, and a financial summary.

Conservation, Food & Health Foundation
<http://fdncenter.org/grantmaker/cf&hf/index.html>

The primary purpose of the Massachusetts-based Conservation, Food & Health Foundation is "to assist in the conservation of natural resources, the production and distribution of food, and the improvement and promotion of health in the developing world." The Foundation is especially interested in supporting projects that lead to the transfer of responsibility to the citizens of developing countries for managing and solving their own problems and in supporting self-help initiatives. Preference is given to organizations located in developing countries or to developed country organizations whose activities are of direct and immediate benefit to developing countries. The Foundation does not consider the states of the former Soviet Union or former eastern bloc countries as within its geographic focus, however. Visitors to the Foundation's "folder" on the Center's Web site will find detailed application guidelines and eligibility requirements, a 1996 grants list, a form for submitting a concept paper to the Foundation (in advance of a final proposal), and contact information.

Cooper Foundation <http://www.cooperfoundation.org>

The Nebraska-based Cooper Foundation restricts it support to organizations within its home state, primarily in Lincoln and Lancaster County. The Foundation's mission is to support innovative ideas that "promise substantial impact and encourage others to make similar or larger grants." To that end, it funds programs in education, human services, the arts, and the humanities. It does not fund individuals, endowments, private foundations, businesses, health or religious issues, travel, or organizations outside of Nebraska, and most of its grants are for program funding rather than general operating support. In addition, the Foundation accepts formal applications only from organizations that have already communicated with them and been asked to complete an application form. Visitors to the Foundation's Web site will find a brief history of the foundation, an equally brief description of program priorities, and contact information.

Jessie B. Cox Charitable Trust <http://www.agmconnect.org/cox.html>

Crail-Johnson Foundation <http://www.crail-johnson.org/>

The Crail-Johnson Foundation of San Pedro, California, is committed to "promot[ing] the well being of children in need, through the effective application of human and financial resources." Although national organizations may apply for Foundation support, priority is given to organizations and projects within California and more specifically within the greater Los Angeles area. In addition to awarding cash grants, the Foundation also provides technical assistance to select community-based projects benefiting children and families. No grants are made directly to individuals, or for programs and projects benefiting religious purposes, university-level graduate and post-graduate education, research, cultural programs, sporting events, political causes, or programs attempting to influence legislation. Visitors to the CJF Web site can access the Foundation's 1996 annual report, which provides detailed grant application guidelines and limitations, a financial statement, information on selected grants, and a listing of officers and staff. The Web site also provides links to other grantmakers online, detailed descriptions of special Foundation projects, and contact information.

Charles E. Culpeper Foundation <http://www.culpeper.org/>
The Charles E. Culpeper Foundation awards grants in four primary program areas: health, specifically research, clinical services, and medical education; education, with a focus on foreign language training, environmental studies, and the application of information technologies in the classroom; arts and culture, with a focus on educational programming and outreach across all artistic and cultural fields; and administration of justice, with a focus on problems within the criminal justice system. The Foundation's Web site provides visitors with a brief history of the Foundation, detailed program descriptions and guidelines, application procedures, a board and staff listings, highlights from the Foundation's 1997 annual report, and recent grants and other announcements.

Nathan Cummings Foundation <http://www.ncf.org/>
Established by noted philanthropist and founder of the Sara Lee Corporation, Nathan Cummings, the Nathan Cummings Foundation is "rooted in the Jewish tradition and committed to democratic values, including fairness, diversity, and community. [The Foundation seeks] to build a society that values nature and protects ecological balance for future generations; promotes humane health care; and fosters arts to enrich communities." To that end, the Foundation focuses its grantmaking activities in five program areas: arts, environment, health, Jewish life, and "interprogram," which reinforces connections among the Foundations core areas. Visitors to the Foundation's Web site will find detailed guidelines, grant lists for each program area, and links to grantee Web sites; application procedures; staff and trustee listings; and various reports and publications, including the Foundation's 1997 annual report.

The Charles A. Dana Foundation <http://www.dana.org/>
The Charles A. Dana Foundation is a private philanthropic foundation with principle interests in brain research and public-education initiatives. The Foundation's Web site includes a statement of the Foundation's grantmaking policies and procedures; detailed application and program information, including recent major grants; information about the Charles A. Dana Awards, which honor innovators in neuroscience and education reform; the Dana Alliance for Brain initiatives, a nonprofit dedicated to educating the public about the benefits of brain research; a publications archive (including the Foundation's 1994 and 1996 annual reports); Dana BrainWeb (annotated links to Web sites devoted to specific brain disorders, general health, and neuroscience); a listing of the Foundation's directors, officers, and staff; and press and contact information.

Arthur Vining Davis Foundations <http://www.jvm.com/davis/>

The Arthur Davis Vining Foundations provide support nationally for five primary program areas: private higher education, secondary education, religion (graduate theological education), health care (caring attitudes), and public television. The Foundations do not make grants to individuals; institutions or programs outside the United States and its possessions; publicly governed colleges, universities, and other entities that are supported primarily by government funds (except in health care and secondary education programs); or projects incurring obligations extending over several years. Visitors to the Foundation's Web site will find descriptions of each program area, a recent grants list organized by program area, application procedures, a brief FAQ, and contact information.

The Dekko Foundation <http://www.dekkofoundation.org/>

Gladys Krieble Delmas Foundation <http://www.delmas.org/>

The Gladys Krieble Delmas Foundation promotes "the advancement and perpetuation of humanistic inquiry and artistic creativity by encouraging excellence in scholarship and in the performing arts, and by supporting research libraries and other institutions that preserve the resources which transmit this cultural heritage." The Foundation sponsors four distinct grantmaking programs: in the humanities, in the performing arts, for research libraries, and for Venetian research. Foundation trustees may also award discretionary grants outside of these specific programs. Visitors to the Foundation's Web site will find descriptions and 1992–1994 grants lists for each program area, as well as a 1997–1998 list of grants for Independent Research in Venice and the Veneto; application procedures and eligibility requirements; and a listing of the Foundation's trustees, staff, and advisory board members.

The Geraldine R. Dodge Foundation <http://www.grdodge.org>

The Geraldine R. Dodge Foundation makes grants in five major areas: 1) elementary and secondary education; 2) arts, with a primary focus on New Jersey and on programs that seek to establish and improve education in the arts, foster conditions that promote public access to the arts, recognize the critical role of the individual artist, enable developing institutions to gain stability, and help major institutions realize long-term goals; 3) welfare of animals, especially projects with national implications that encourage a more humane ethic and lower the violence in the way we treat animals; 4) public issues, with a particular interest in New Jersey and the Northeast and focusing on ecosystems preservation, energy conservation, pollution prevention and reduction, education and communication efforts that lead to enlightened environmental policy, and projects that address population growth and family planning; and 5) local projects in Morris County, New Jersey. The Foundation's elegant Web site (frames-enabled browsers a must) provides concise program descriptions, application guidelines, a brief history of the Foundation, and contact information.

The William H. Donner Foundation <http://www.donner.org/>

The main focus of the William H. Donner Foundation, a small, professionally staffed family foundation based in New York City, is on three wide-ranging program areas: U.S.-Canadian relations, especially projects that, while recognizing the fundamental affinities between Canada and the United States, attempt to clarify, analyze, and assess the effects of the often differing approaches they bring to key issues (the Foundation also has an interest in projects that relate to Canada, the U.S., and Mexico); education, especially projects aimed at improving what is taught in formal educational settings, as well as activities that bring to the general public informed and balanced perspectives on important foreign and domestic issues; and human capital development, in particular projects that will help people who are out of the social and economic mainstream to enter or reenter it. The Foundation's Web site provides a good deal of information about the Foundation and its grantmaking philosophy, a brief bio of William H. Donner, general program descriptions, a current grants list, litsings of the Foundation's officers, trustees, and staff, and contact information.

The Do Right Foundation <http://www.doright.org/>

The broadly stated mission of the Do Right Foundation is to "address some of the current obstacles to a more joyful and rewarding society," and the Foundation's Web site is devoted to explaining this philosophy as it relates to the grantseeking process. The Foundation gives priority to grantseekers who focus on the application of new and improved management theories. Visitors to the site will find a biography of Dr. W. Edwards Deming, upon whose management concepts the Foundation's philosophies are based. Grants lists, a downloadable application, and contact information are also available. Prospectors are encouraged to submit a pre-grant inquiry by e-mail before applying formally.

The J.C. Downing Foundation <http://www.jcdowning.org/jcdf/jcdowning.htm>

The San Diego-based J.C. Downing Foundation supports innovative efforts and original projects in five program areas: science and technology, sports and athletics, education and child development, wildlife research and preservation, and environmental research and economics. The Foundation awards grants to qualified nonprofit organizations with explicit, identifiable needs, and does not place geographic or dollar restrictions on its grants (although the typical award falls between $5,000 and $50,000). The Foundation's Web site provides grantmaking guidelines and areas of exclusion, application procedures, a list of selected grants the Foundation has made since 1990, and a "Resource" section, which includes information about the grantseeeking process, a recommended reading list, and links to Web sites of interest.

The Camille and Henry Dreyfus Foundation <http://www.dreyfus.org/>

The principal aim of the Camille and Henry Dreyfus Foundation is to "advance the science of chemistry, chemical engineering and related sciences as a means of improving human relations and circumstances around the world." To that end, the Foundation makes grant awards to academic and other eligible institutions for the purposes of sponsoring qualified applicants in their education and research. The Foundation's Web site provides detailed descriptions of the Foundation's various programs, including eligibility requirements and application and nomination procedures, and a listing of recent grantees. As an added convenience, requests for nomination forms can be submitted through the Foundation's Web site.

Peter F. Drucker Foundation for Nonprofit Management
<http://www.pfdf.org/>

The Duke Endowment <http://www.dukeendowment.org/>

The Duke Endowment, a charitable trust established in 1924 by North Carolina industrialist James Buchanan Duke, continues its founder's philanthropic legacy of giving to "educate students and teachers, to heal minds and bodies, to nurture children, and to strengthen the human spirit." As a trust, the Duke Endowment differs from a private foundation in that its principle donor named specific organizations or individuals eligible to receive funding. In the case of the Endowment, these are: not-for-profit health care organizations in North and South Carolina; not-for-profit child care institutions in North and South Carolina; rural United Methodist churches and retired ministers in North Carolina; and Duke, Furman, and Johnson C. Smith universities, and Davidson College. The Endowment's Web site provides general program descriptions and application procedures, a 1996 grants list organized by area of interest, a searchable online catalog of library materials (the Endowmment's library houses a Foundation Center Cooperating Collection), financial statements, a listing of Endowment trustees and staff, and contact information.

The Jessie Ball duPont Fund <http://www.dupontfund.org/index.html>

The Jessie Ball duPont Fund, a national foundation having a special, though not exclusive, interest in issues affecting the South, makes grants "to a defined universe of eligible institutions"—that is, any institution that received a contribution from Mrs. duPont between January 1, 1960, and December 31, 1964 (approximately 350 in total). Proof of eligibility is determined by the Fund from examination of Mrs. duPont's personal or tax records or by the applicant presenting written verifiable evidence of having received a contribution during the eligibility period. The Fund's mission, "to address broad-based issues of communities and of the larger society that have regional, national, and international relevance," is achieved through programs in arts and culture, education, health, historic preservation, human services, and religion. Visitors to the Fund's Web site will find detailed program information and eligibility guidelines, a statement of the Fund's mission and core values, a biography of Mrs. DuPont, and contact information. The Fund also plans to post to excerpts from Notes from the Field, its publication devoted to philanthropic "best practices," in the following areas: access to health care, affordable housing for low-income families, inclusiveness in institutions of higher education, taking action and seeking justice, and creating healthy outcomes for children.

Echoing Green Foundation <http://www.echoinggreen.org/>

El Pomar Foundation <http://www.elpomar.org/>

Founded in 1937 by copper mining magnate Spencer Penrose, El Pomar Foundation today has assets in excess of $350 million, making it one of the largest and oldest foundations in the Rocky Mountain West. The Foundation makes grants throughout the state of Colorado in the areas of human services, community development, the arts, health care, amateur athletics, and education. In addition to grant application guidelines and summary financial information for the year ended December 31, 1996, visitors to the Foundation's Web site will find general information about the Foundation and its many operating programs: Fellowship in Community Service, a program designed to develop future leaders among recent college graduates; El Pomar Youth in Community Service (EPYCS); El

Pomar Awards for Excellence, which reward outstanding nonprofit organizations in Colorado; the Foundation's Education Initiative; and El Pomar Center, which is dedicated to the recognition and promotion of excellence within the nonprofit community.

Lois and Richard England Family Foundation
<http://fdncenter.org/grantmaker/england/index.html>

Created in 1994, the Lois and Richard England Family Foundation is "committed to improving the lives of those in need in the Washington metropolitan area." Toward that end, the Foundation's grantmaking focuses on local human services, education, and arts and culture. The Foundation also supports programs to strengthen Jewish life and institutions locally, nationally, and in Israel. In addition to mission and goal statements, the Foundation's "folder" on the Center's Web site provides grant guidelines, '96 and '97 grants lists, a listing of the Foundation's trustees, and contact information.

The Energy Foundation <http://www.ef.org/>

Created in 1991 under the auspices of the MacArthur Foundation, The Pew Charitable Trusts, and the Rockefeller Foundation, the mission of the Energy Foundation is "to assist in the nation's transition to a sustainable energy future by promoting energy efficiency and renewable energy." Visitors to the Foundation's Web site will find program descriptions, application guidelines, lists of recent grant recipients, and downloadable application forms for each of the Foundation's five program areas: utilities, buildings, transportation, renewable energy, and integrated issues. Also available online are essays devoted to the realities surrounding the Foundation's mission, a section for special Foundation reports, and a list of annotated links to energy-related Web sites.

Esquel Group Foundation <http://www.esquel.org/>

The Flinn Foundation <http://aspin.asu.edu/flinn/index.html>

The Phoenix-based Flinn Foundation focuses its grantmaking activities in three fields: health, education, and the arts. The Foundation, which limits its activities to Arizona, does not award grants for general operating expenses, capital campaigns, advocacy, or projects of sectarian or religious organizations that principally benefit the members of those organizations. In addition to brief biographies of Foundation founders Dr. Robert Flinn and his wife, Irene Pierce Flinn, visitors to the Foundation's Web site will find program descriptions in its areas of interest, grant application procedures, and a listing of the Foundation's trustees and staff.

The Ford Foundation <http://www.fordfound.org/>

Founded in 1936 by Henry and Edsel Ford and operated as a local philanthropy in the state of Michigan until 1950, the Ford Foundation has since expanded to become a leading force in the world of national and international philanthropy. The Foundation's broadly stated goals are to "strengthen democratic values, reduce poverty and injustice, promote international cooperation, and advance human achievement." To better realize its goals, the Foundation implemented a new program and organizational structure in October 1996 that, among other things, consolidated its grantmaking into three program areas: asset building and community development; education, media, arts, and culture; and peace and social justice. In addition to providing visitors with program guidelines, application procedures, a listing of recent grants, and worldwide contact information, the Foundation's comprehensive Web site also contains the full text of the its 1993–1996 annual reports as well as every issue of the quarterly Ford Foundation REPORT dating back to 1993.

Thomas B. Fordham Foundation <http://www.edexcellence.net/>

The Foundation for Microbiology <http://www.tiac.net/users/waksman/>
The purpose of the New York City-based Foundation for Microbiology is "to promote, encourage, and aid scientific research in microbiology; [and] to provide and assist in providing the funds and facilities by which scientific discoveries, inventions, and processes in microbiology may be developed." The Foundation does not offer conventional research, fellowship, or travel grants. Instead, its funds are used "for the support of lectureships, prizes, or courses related to the field of microbiology, as well as for unusual publications or other activities in this field poorly supported by the usual Government agencies." To qualify for support, any of these activities must be expected to address a national or an international audience. Innovative educational programs dealing with microbiological topics and making use of contemporary communication techniques are a special focus of interest, as are programs concerned with enhancing public awareness of science, including K–12 teaching programs that make use of microorganisms. Visitors to the Foundation's Web site will find financial information for fiscal year 1997; concise application guidelines and limitations; a list of grants and contributions made by the Foundation in 1997; and a directory of officers and trustees (complete with phone, fax, and e-mail info).

The Foundation for Seacoast Health <http://www.nh.ultranet.com/~ffsh/>
The mission of the Foundation for Seacoast Health, the largest private charitable foundation in the State of New Hampshire, is to support and promote health care in the New Hampshire/Maine Seacoast area, which includes Portsmouth, Rye, New Castle, Greenland, Newington, and North Hampton, New Hampshire; and Kittery, Eliot, and York, Maine. The Foundation awards grants to nonprofit agencies and public entities addressing the health-related needs of persons residing in the Seacoast communities. It also offers annual scholarships ranging from $1,000 to $10,000 to assist qualified students who are residents of the Seacoast area and are pursuing health-related fields of study. Visitors to the Foundation's Web site will find general background and contact information, and grant application guidelines with time tables for both general grants and individual scholarships.

The Freedom Forum <http://www.freedomforum.org/>
Dedicated to "free press, free speech and free spirit for all people," the mission of the Freedom Forum is to help the public and the news media understand one another better. Primary areas of interest include First Amendment rights, journalism education, newsroom diversity, professional development of journalists, media studies and research, and international journalism programs. The Forum does not accept unsolicited grant applications and only makes limited grants in connection with its programs. Its Web site offers a range of information and features, including detailed descriptions of the Forum's programs and history; articles drawn from various Freedom Forum publications; links to the Gannett Center

for Media Studies as well as dozens of related online resources; an online version of the Forum's 1997 annual report, with grant "highlights" organized by month; and a listing of the Foundation's trustees and officers.

Frey Foundation <http://www.freyfdn.org/>

Friedman-Klarreich Family Foundation <http://home.att.net/~klarff/>
Established in 1992 by Susan Friedman Klarreich and her four daughters, Karin, Betsy, Kathie, and Beth, the Los Altos, California-based Friedman-Klarreich Family Foundation awards grants of up to $5,000 to innovative nonprofit organizations or properly qualified individuals dedicated to achieving educational and economic equality for girls and women and/or to enhancing the stability of families. The Foundation's simple Web site provides application guidelines and requirements, a listing of grants awarded to date, links to related sites of interest, and contact information.

The Fuller Foundation, Inc. <http://www.agmconnect.org/fuller1.html>

Fund for the City of New York <http://www.fcny.org/>
The Fund is an independent private operating foundation whose mandate is "to respond to the opportunities and problems of New York City; to improve the performance of the city's government and the quality of life of its citizens." The Fund's five primary grantmaking areas are children and youth, AIDS, community development and housing, the urban environment, and government and technology, but it also makes a limited number of grants that do not fall neatly into any of the above categories. Grants awarded are generally between $5,000 and $10,000, and the Fund provides both general and project support. It also operates the Cash Flow Loan Program, the Nonprofit Computer Exchange, and the Management Initiative, all of which address "the importance of this type of funding to maintain the management infrastructure needed to support an agency's programs." Visitors to the Fund's Web site will find detailed information on all of the Fund's programs and initiatives, as well as contact information.

Gates Library Foundation <http://www.glf.org/>
Established in June 1997 by Microsoft founder Bill Gates and his wife, Melinda French Gates, the Gates Library Foundation is "dedicated to partnering with U.S. and Canadian public libraries to bring computers and digital information to the communities they serve." The Foundation has two initiatives that will guide its activities and funding decisions over the next five years: One, to work with underserved public libraries in low-income areas to provide the hardware and software required for community access to digital information; and two, to support and train library staffs to access and manage digital information to maintain and expand their systems as their patrons and communities require. The Foundation's Web site offers a helpful FAQ section, brief biographies of the Foundation's staff and board, a press release or two and limited number of links to related Web sites, and background and contact information. The Foundation's grantmaking guidelines were due to be posted to the site in the fall of 1998.

Gebbie Foundation <http://www.gebbie.org/>

The Gebbie Foundation was established in 1964 by the daughters of Frank and Harriett Louise Gebbie as a memorial to their parents. Since its inception, the Foundation has paid out more than $55 million in grants to support its "focus on children, education, the arts, cultural activities, family welfare, health care and medical research to alleviate human suffering." The Foundation primarily supports activities in the Jamestown/Chautauqua County region of New York State but will consider making grants elsewhere, provided the requests meet the broad criteria outlined in the Foundation's mission. Grants are not made to individuals or to sectarian or religious organizations, and funds are not usually available for general support, endowment purposes, or national appeals. Visitors to the Foundation's Web site will find biographies of the Gebbies and their daughters, brief descriptions of the Foundation's policies and guidelines, application procedures, and contact information.

Carl Gellert and Celia Berta Gellert Foundation
<http://fdncenter.org/grantmaker/gellert/index.html>

Based in San Francisco, the Gellert Foundation promotes religious, charitable, scientific, literary, and educational activities in the nine counties of the greater San Francisco Bay Area (i.e., Alameda, Contra Costa, Marin, Napa, San Francisco, San Mateo, Santa Clara, Solano, and Sonoma counties). Visitors to the Foundation's "folder" on the Center's Web site will find a mission statement, application guidelines, a list of grants and contributions made in the fiscal year ending November 30, 1997, and contact information.

The Wallace Alexander Gerbode Foundation
<http://fdncenter.org/grantmaker/gerbode/index.html>

The Wallace Alexander Gerbode Foundation supports programs in the San Francisco Bay Area and Hawaii in the areas of arts and culture, environment, population, reproductive rights, citizen participation/building communities/inclusiveness, and strength of the philanthropic process and the nonprofit sector. The Foundation generally does not support direct services, deficit budgets, general operating funds, building or equipment funds, general fundraising campaigns, religious purposes, private schools, publications, scholarships, or grants to individuals. In addition to general application and fiscal information, the Foundation's "folder" on the Center's Web site provides 1995 and 1996 grants lists by program area.

J. Paul Getty Trust <http://www.getty.edu/grant/>

The J. Paul Getty Trust, a private operating foundation dedicated to the visual arts and humanities, comprises a museum, five institutes, and a grant program. The purpose of the latter is to strengthen the fields in which the Trust is active by funding exceptional projects throughout the world that promote research in the history of art and related fields, advancement of the understanding of art, and conservation of cultural heritage. Grants may fund conceptual projects that take intellectual risks, or they may support more basic resources and activities. Funded projects include a wide variety of methodologies and subject matter, ranging through all historical periods and geographic regions. The Trust's Web site provides a general overview of the Trust's grantmaking activities, extensive program information and guidelines, a list of grants recently awarded, and application and contact information.

Glenn Foundation for Medical Research <http://www.glenn.deco.net/>

The purpose of the Glenn Foundation is "to extend the healthful productive years of life through research on the mechanisms of biological aging." The Foundation neither solicits nor accepts charitable contributions, and it does not consider unsolicited grant applications or fellowship nominations. Its Web site, which was developed as a resource and point-of-access for scientists whose primary interest is the biology of aging, offers brief descriptions of the Foundation's programs, conferences, and workshops, as well as numerous links to other organizations involved in aging research.

Gould Family Foundation <http://members.aol.com/gouldfound/index.html>

William T. Grant Foundation
<http://fdncenter.org/grantmaker/wtgrant/index.html>

Established in 1936 to "assist research, education, and training through the sciences," the William T. Grant Foundation has pursued that goal over the years through its support of postdoctoral research projects on the development of children, adolescents, and youth, and for service projects in the New York City area. Prospective applicants should note that the Foundation does not support or make contributions to conferences and meetings; fellowships and scholarships; building funds; fund-raising drives; operating budgets of ongoing service agencies or educational institutions; or endowments. The Foundation's "folder" on the Center's Web site offers a good deal of general information about the Foundation and its programs; detailed application procedures; a downloadable cover sheet for letters of inquiry; a list of grants awarded in 1996; officer, staff, and trustee listings; and an online version of the Foundation's 1995 annual report.

William Caspar Graustein Memorial Fund <http://www.pcnet.com/~wcgmf/>

The Green Mountain Fund for Popular Struggle
<http://homepages.together.net/~gmfps/>

The Harry Frank Guggenheim Foundation <http://www.hfg.org/>

The Harry Frank Guggenheim Foundation sponsors scholarly research on problems of violence, aggression, and dominance and encourages related research projects in neuroscience, genetics, animal behavior, the social sciences, history, criminology, and the humanities. The Foundation also awards research grants to established scholars and dissertation fellowships to graduate students. (Institutions, programs, and pure interventions are not supported.) Visitors to the Foundation's Web site will find a section on its research priorities, detailed application guidelines and procedures, a comprehensive listing of recent Foundation grants and fellowships, and an interactive form for requesting written application guidelines and/or the Foundation's 1995 annual report.

John Simon Guggenheim Memorial Foundation <http://www.gf.org/>

The John Simon Guggenheim Memorial Foundation awards fellowships for advanced professionals in all areas of the natural sciences, social sciences, humanities, and creative arts (except the performing arts). The Foundation selects its Fellows on the basis of two separate competitions, one for the United States and Canada, the other for Latin America and the Caribbean. Only professional individuals are eligible for awards; the Foundation does not support students, organizations, or institutions. The Foundation's straightforward Web site provides general information about its programs, fellowship eligibility requirements, and application deadlines in English, Spanish, and Portuguese. Also available in English only is a listing of recent Guggenheim Fellows, a helpful FAQ, an interactive form for ordering application forms, a listing of Foundation officers and trustees, and contact information.

The George Gund Foundation <http://www.gundfdn.org/>

The George Gund Foundation was created in 1952 by Cleveland banker and businessman George Gund, who believed the private foundation structure provided the most positive, far-sighted vehicle for intelligent underwriting of creative solutions to social ills in a manner which would not be limited to his own lifetime. Today, the Foundation makes grants quarterly in the areas of education, economic development and community revitalization, human services, arts, environment and civic affairs. The Foundation's Web site offers a biography of George Gund, program descriptions, grant application instructions and grant restrictions, contact information, and links to a handful of related Web sites.

The Gunk Foundation <http://www1.mhv.net/~gunk/welcome.html>

The Gunk Foundation is a charitable operating foundation established in 1994 "to provide a counterbalance to the recent, disturbing trends in funding for intellectual endeavors. . . . " It does this by supporting two types of projects—public arts projects, which are funded through the Foundation itself, and scholarly/artistic publications, which are funded through Critical Press, the Foundation's publishing arm. Grant amounts are small and usually fall in a range between $1,000 and $5,000. Visitors to "GunkWeb" will find grant application guidelines (for the Foundation), proposal guidelines (for Critical Press), and a grant archive. A component with links to public arts related resources is under construction.

The Luke B. Hancock Foundation
<http://fdncenter.org/grantmaker/hancock/index.html>

Established in 1948 with a donation from pioneering oilman Luke B. Hancock, the Hancock Foundation received its principal assets from his estate in 1963 and later changed its name to the Luke B. Hancock Foundation in order to recognize its founder and first president. Because of limited resources and the large number of requests it receives, the Foundation focuses its support on the Bay Area of Northern California, in particular San Jose, and on grassroots neighborhood initiatives that benefit youth as well as the entire community. Historically, the Foundation has considered some cultural grants and special projects, but these are primarily initiated by the Foundation itself. In addition to a 1996/97 grants list and financial statements, the Foundation's "folder" on the Center's Web site provides application guidelines, a look at three community organizations funded by the Foundation that are "changing their world," a brief biography of Luke Hancock, board and staff listings, and contact information.

The John A. Hartford Foundation, Inc. <http://www.jhartfound.com/>
Established in 1929 by John A. and George L. Hartford, former chief executives
of the Great Atlantic and Pacific Tea Company (A&P), the John A. Hartford
Foundation is concerned with the improvement of health care in America. The
Foundation focuses its grantmaking activities in the areas of aging and health and
healthcare cost and quality, and generally makes grants by invitation. Grantseekers are encouraged to familiarize themselves with the Foundation's program areas
and guidelines—detailed information about which can be found at its Web site
before submitting a letter of inquiry in writing. The Web site also provides the
Foundation's 1996 finances, a report from the chairman, Foundation trustees and
staff, and contact information.

Charles Hayden Foundation
<http://fdncenter.org/grantmaker/hayden/index.html>
The New York City-based Hayden Foundation seeks to promote the mental,
moral, and physical development of school-aged youth in the New York and
Boston metropolitan areas—the former defined as New York City and Nassau
County, the southern portion of Westchester County and, in New Jersey, all of
Hudson and Essex Counties and the contiguous urban portions of Union, Passaic,
and Bergen counties, the latter as the City of Boston and adjacent municipalities
located on the east side of an arc from Salem to Quincy that is roughly delineated
by Route 128. Priority is given to institutions and programs serving youth most at
risk of not reaching their full potential, especially youth in low-income communities, and that continuously provide opportunities and supports over many years.
Visitors to the Foundation's "folder" on the Center's Web site will find a mission statement, recent grants lists, detailed application guidelines, and contact
information.

The John Randolph Haynes and Dora Haynes Foundation
<http://www.usc.edu/Library/Haynes/>
Established in 1926, the Haynes Foundation supports study and research in political science, economics, public policy, history, social psychology, and sociology,
favoring projects with specific application to California and, more particularly,
the Los Angeles region. The Foundation also provides undergraduate scholarships, graduate fellowships, and faculty research fellowships in the social sciences
to colleges and universities in the greater Los Angeles area. All support is made
directly to institutions; no grants are awarded to individuals. A searchable bibliography of publications resulting from 70 years of Foundation support is available at
the Foundation's Web site, along with detailed program information, application
guidelines, a listing of the Foundation's board of trustees, and a history of the
Foundation and the Haynes family.

Healthcare Foundation of New Jersey
<http://fdncenter.org/grantmaker/hfnj/index.html/>
Created to fulfill the obligations of its Jewish heritage by embodying the ideal of
Tzedakah, or social justice, the Healthcare Foundation of New Jersey (formerly
the NBI Healthcare Foundation) seeks to alleviate the suffering and safeguard the
healthcare needs of the most vulnerable members of the community it serves—
historically, the MetroWest Jewish comunity and individuals and families in Newark's South Ward. Recently, in conjunction with the name change, the Foundation

has expanded its grantmaking to include Essex County and the State of New Jersey, while maintaining its interest in medical education and training, including opportunities for disadvantaged youth in Newark to become healthcare professionals, and clinical medical research, especially at the Newark Beth Israel Medical Center. The Foundation's "folder" on the Center's Web site provides a history of the Foundation and its objectives, a description of its grantmaking priorities, a list of '97 grants, application procedures, financial statements, and contact information.

The William Randolph Hearst Foundations
<http://fdncenter.org/grantmaker/hearst/index.html>
The Hearst Foundation, Inc., was founded in 1945 by publisher and philanthropist William Randolph Hearst. In 1948, Hearst established the California Charities Foundation, the name of which was changed to the William Randolph Hearst Foundation after Mr. Hearst's death in 1951. The charitable goals of the two Foundations are essentially the same, reflecting the philanthropic interests of William Randolph Hearst—education, health, social service, and culture. The Foundations' proposal evaluation process is divided geographically: organizations east of the Mississippi River must apply to the Foundations' New York offices, while organizations west of the Mississippi are asked to apply through the Foundations' San Francisco offices. In addition to their grantmaking activities in the four program areas mentioned above, the Hearst Foundations make grants to students through the Hearst Journalism Awards Program and the United States Senate Youth Program. Visitors to the Foundations' "folder" on the Center's Web site will find program guidelines, funding policies and limitations, application procedures, and descriptions of both awards programs.

Heathcote Art Foundation, Inc.
<http://www.artswire.org/ArtsWire/heathcote/index.html>

The Heinz Endowments <http://www.heinz.org/>
The Pittsburgh-based Heinz Endowments support the efforts of nonprofit organizations active in the areas of arts and culture, education, health and human services, economic opportunity, and the environment, with an emphasis on programs either in southwestern Pennsylvania or of clear benefit to the region. A model of functional design, the Endowments' Web site offers a range of information, including broad and program-specific statements of philosophy; information about goals, grants, projects, and staff in each program area; application guidelines; FAQs; news; and brief biographies of Howard Heinz and Vira I. Heinz as well as various program officers and directors.

The Hershey Foundation
<http://fdncenter.org/grantmaker/hershey/index.html>
The Hershey Foundation is dedicated to providing Northeast Ohio children from all socioeconomic and cultural backgrounds with opportunities for personal growth, development, and a brighter future by improving their quality of life, building self esteem, enhancing learning, increasing exposure to other cultures and ideas, and encouraging the development of independent thinking and problem-solving skills. The trustees have extended the philanthropic goals established by Jo Hershey Selden, who began the Foundation in 1986 in honor of her

husband, Al. Montessori education remains a funding focus, as do other innovative education programs, especially those embodying Maria Montessori's child-
centered approach to learning. Maintaining opportunities for all children to be
engaged in the arts and stimulated by the sciences also remains a priority. Visitors
to the Foundation's "folder" on the Center's Web site will find a mission statement and a brief history of the Foundation, application guidelines and procedures,
a 1996 grants list, financial statements, and a listing of the Foundation's trustees.

Fannie and John Hertz Foundation <http://www.hertzfndn.org/>

The William and Flora Hewlett Foundation <http://www.hewlett.org/>
The broadly stated mission of the Hewlett Foundation, established by Palo Alto
industrialist William R. Hewlett (of Hewlett-Packard fame), his late wife, Flora
Lamson Hewlett, and their eldest son, Walter B. Hewlett in 1966, is "to promote
the well-being of mankind by supporting selected activities of a charitable nature,
as well as organizations or institutions engaged in such activities." The Foundation concentrates its resources on activities in the areas of education, performing
arts, population, environment, conflict resolution, family and community development, and U.S.-Latin American relations, the latter an outgrowth of the Foundation's long-standing interest in U.S.-Mexico relations. The Foundation's Web
site provides program descriptions and application guidelines, a list of 1998 grant
authorizations organized by program area, an online version of the Foundation's
1996 annual report, and contact information.

The Hoglund Foundation <http://www.dallas.net/~hogfdtn/home.html>

The Houston Endowment <http://www.hou-endow.org/>
Founded in 1937 by Jesse H. Jones and Mary Gibbs Jones, and today the largest
private philanthropic foundation in Texas, the Houston Endowment is dedicated
to the support of charitable undertakings serving the people of the greater Houston
area and the state of Texas, and contributes to a broad spectrum of programs in
education, health care, human services, cultural arts, and other areas. An endowment valued in excess of $1 billion at the end of 1995 allows annual giving of
approximately $45 million. In addition to general information about the founda-
tion and its founders, visitors to the Web site will find descriptions of the Foundation's programs and grant eligibility criteria; application procedures; online versions of the Foundation's 1994, 1995 and 1996 annual reports; 1997 and 1998
grants lists; board and staff listings; and contact information.

The "I Have a Dream" Foundation <http://www.ihad.org/>

International Science Foundation <http://www.isf.ru/index-isf.html>

The James Irvine Foundation <http://www.irvine.org/>
The San Francisco-based Irvine Foundation was established in 1937 as trustee of
the charitable trust of James Irvine, a California agricultural pioneer, to promote
the general welfare of the people of California. Today, it is dedicated "to enhancing the social, economic, and physical quality of life throughout California, and to
enriching the State's intellectual and cultural environment." Within this broad
mandate, the Foundation makes grants in seven program areas: the arts; children,

youth and families; civic culture; health; higher education; sustainable communities; and workforce development. Visitors to the Foundation's Web site will find detailed program information, including priority goals and recent grants in each funding area; application guidelines; board and staff listings; numerous links to grantee organizations; an interesting feedback area; and contact information.

Irvine Health Foundation <http://www.ihf.org/>
Established in 1985, the Irvine Health Foundation provides support for prevention, service, research, and policy activities related to the health and wellness of the Orange County, California community. The Foundation's feature-rich Web site offers a mission statement, a listing of directors and staff, FAQs, press releases, grant "highlights" from the past decade, a "Topic of the Month" feature, highlights from the IHF lecture series, grant application procedures, and links to numerous related sites. Visitors can also access the complete text of the Foundation's 10th Anniversary Report, the Condition of Children report along with annual reports from 1996 and 1997.

Martha Holden Jennings Foundation
<http://fdncenter.org/grantmaker/jennings/index.html>

Jerome Foundation <http://www.jeromefdn.org/>
The St. Paul-based Jerome Foundation promotes the careers and work of emerging artists in Minnesota and New York City through its support of programs in dance, literature, media arts, music, theater, performance art, visual arts, multidisciplinary work, and arts criticism. The Foundation places the emerging creative artist at the center of its grantmaking and gives funding priority to programs and projects that are artist-driven. The Foundation's Web site comes in two versions, Java-flavored and Java-free, and provides program guidelines; application requirements and procedures; full descriptions of every grant awarded in 1996–1997 arranged alphabetically, by program area, or by date; answers to frequently asked questions; financial statements; contact information; and enough multimedia bits to keep you busy for hours.

The Johnson Foundation <http://www.johnsonfdn.org/index.html>
The primary activity of the Wisconsin-based Johnson Foundation is planning and co-sponsoring conferences of public interest at Wingspread, its Frank Lloyd Wright-designed headquarters and conference center in Racine. The Foundation encourages conference proposals from nonprofit organizations in six areas of interest:supporting sustainable development; enhancing learning productivity at all educational levels; building civil and civic community; encouraging constructive adult engagement in the lives of children and youth; Keland Endowment conferences on the arts, the environment, and persons with disabilities; and southeastern Wisconsin. The Foundation does not award grants; fund programs; sponsor retreats or fundraisers; or rent its facilities. Visitors to the Foundation's elegant, earth-toned Web site will find a brief history of the Foundation and its mission; general descriptions of its program interests; a searchable "Virtual Library" with online versions of recent annual reports and conference proceedings, articles (both HTML and .PDF versions) from back issues of the Wingspread Journal, and dozens of links organized by program interest; an Online Discussion area with

both "open" and "closed" discussions; and detailed information about proposing a conference.

Robert Wood Johnson Foundation <http://www.rwjf.org/>

The mission of the Robert Wood Johnson Foundation is to improve the health and health care of all Americans. The Foundation's main funding goals are to assure that all Americans have access to basic health care at reasonable cost; to improve the way services are organized and provided to people with chronic health conditions; and to reduce the harm caused by substance abuse—tobacco, alcohol, and elicit drugs. The Foundation's comprehensive Web site is a guide to its programs and activities and a substantial resource for the health care field. Visitors will find detailed program descriptions and application guidelines, comprehensive grants lists, links to grantee Web/gopher sites (as well as the Foundation's own gopher site), several FAQs, and a list of current calls for proposals. Visitors can also access bulletins from American Health Line, a service providing daily briefings on health care politics and policy; excerpts from the Foundation's recent annual reports; and complete text versions of "Advances," the Foundation's newsletter.

The Walter S. Johnson Foundation <http://www.wsjf.org/>

The Walter S. Johnson Foundation supports programs in Northern California and Washoe County, Nevada, that "help children and youth meet their full potential and rise to the challenges of our diverse and changing society." The Foundation's grants program is focused on three primary goals: ensuring the well-being of children and youth, strengthening public education, and assisting young people in the transition to adulthood. Within these broad goals, the majority of grants are likely to focus on positive youth development, the professional development of educators, or the transition from school to career. Grants are also made for families in crisis, and for integrated services, family support, and neighborhood development. The Foundation's straightforward Web site provides grantmaking guidelines and grants lists for each program area, as well as application procedures and a listing of the Foundation's trustees and staff.

W. Alton Jones Foundation <http://www.wajones.org/>

Established in 1944 by millionaire oilman "Pete" Jones, the W. Alton Jones Foundation "focuses on global environmental protection and the prevention of nuclear war [or disaster]." At present, the Foundation concentrates its efforts in two main areas: a Sustainable World Program, which "supports efforts that will ensure that human activities do not undermine the quality of life of future generations"; and a Secure World Program, which "seeks to build a secure world, free from the nuclear threat." The Foundation's Web site combines a smartly efficient architecture with an array of features and content, including program descriptions; grants lists and links to grantee Web sites; a grants "almanac" for the 1990–1996 period; application procedures; a listing of trustees, officers, and staff; and extensive e-mail contact information.

The Henry J. Kaiser Family Foundation <http://www.kff.org/homepage/>

The Kaiser Family Foundation is an independent health care philanthropy whose work is focused on four main areas: health policy, reproductive health, HIV policy, and health and development in South Africa. In addition to an extensive listing of Foundation-sponsored surveys and reports on a range of health-related issues, Kaiser's Web site provides application guidelines, a message from the president, a helpful FAQ that lists the Foundation's board members, press and contact information, as well as annotated links to other resources related to Kaiser's research concentrations. The Foundation's site also has useful reports for downloading and state Medicaid information.

Kansas Health Foundation <http://www.kansashealth.org/>

Established with the proceeds from the sale of the Wesley Medical Center in 1985, and with an endowment of more than $200 million, the Kansas Health Foundation makes grants to health organizations throughout the state aimed at improving the quality of health in Kansas. Although the majority of the Foundation's activity centers around Foundation-initiated partnerships and programs, it does provide $500,000 in funding each year through its Recognition Grant program "to support grass-roots organizations doing creative and innovative work to improve the health of Kansans." Recognition Grants fall into five primary categories: primary care education, rural health, health promotion and disease prevention, public health, and health policy and research. In addition to general information about the Foundation and its programs, visitors to the Foundation's Web site will find Recognition Grant program descriptions and funding guidelines.

Ewing Marion Kauffman Foundation <http://www.emkf.org/>

The Kansas City-based Kauffman Foundation is an operating and grantmaking foundation with a special interest in entrepreneurial leadership and youth development. In making grants, the foundation aims to support "sustainable programs and projects that will lead to individual, organizational and community self-sufficiency." The Foundation accepts direct inquiries but does not seek unsolicited proposals. Features of its Web site include program descriptions and application criteria, grant guidelines, contact information, and a brief biography of Ewing Kauffman.

The W.M. Keck Foundation <http://www.wmkeck.org/>

Established in 1954 by William Myron Keck, founder of the Superior Oil Company, the W.M. Keck Foundation focuses its grantmaking on the areas of medical research, science, and engineering. The Foundation also maintains a program for liberal arts colleges and a Southern California Grant Program that provides support in the areas of civic and community services, health care and hospitals, precollegiate education, and the arts. According to the Foundation's guidelines, eligible institutions in the fields of science, engineering, medical research, and liberal arts are "accredited universities, colleges, medical schools, and major, independent medical research institutions." In the Southern California program, "only organizations located in and serving the population of Southern California are eligible for consideration." Visitors to the Foundation's Web site will find general program descriptions, application criteria and guidelines, excerpts from the Foundation's 1997 annual report, 1996 and 1997 grants lists organized by program area (no dollar amounts), a page devoted to the W.M. Keck Observatory on Hawaii's Mauna Kea volcano, and contact information.

W.K. Kellogg Foundation <http://www.wkkf.org/>

The mission of the W.K. Kellogg Foundation is to "help people help themselves through the practical application of knowledge and resources to improve their quality of life and that of future generations." The Foundation awards grants in three primary global regions: the United States; five southern Africa countries, including Botswana, Lesotho, South Africa, Swaziland, and Zimbabwe; and Latin America and the Caribbean. In addition to thorough program descriptions, application guidelines, and the Foundation's 1997 annual report, the Foundation's sophisticated Web site offers a variety of useful features, including a state-of-the-art searchable grants database; an electronic version of the International Journal of the W.K. Kellogg Foundation; and individual listings of resources of interest in the Foundation's various program areas.

The Joseph P. Kennedy, Jr. Foundation
<http://www.familyvillage.wisc.edu/jpkf/>

The Joseph P. Kennedy, Jr. Foundation has two major objectives: "to improve the way society deals with its citizens who have mental retardation, and to help identify and disseminate ways to prevent the causes of mental retardation." To that end, the Foundation provides seed funding that encourages new methods of service and supports, and through the use of its influence to promote public awareness of the needs of persons with mental retardation and their families. The Foundation does not participate in capital costs or costs of equipment for projects, or pay for ongoing support or operations of existing programs. Visitors to the Foundation's Web site will find information on the Foundation's various funding and award programs, detailed application guidelines, and an extensive listing of links to other online resources for mental retardation.

The Kentucky Foundation for Women <http://www.kfw.org/>

The mission of the Kentucky Foundation for Women is "to change the lives of women by supporting feminist expression in the arts in Kentucky." The primary goal of the Foundation's grants program is to support the work of individual artists who live or work in Kentucky and "whose work embodies a feminist consciousness." Grants may also be awarded to organizations and for special collaborative projects that share the Foundation's goals. In addition to general Foundation information, application guidelines and procedures, and a list of 1997 and 1998 grant recipients, visitors to the KFW Web site can learn about the Foundation's literary journal, The American Voice, and Hopscotch House, its rural retreat for women.

Kettering Foundation <http://www.kettering.org/>

Established in 1927 by inventor Charles F. Kettering, the Kettering Foundation's objective is "to understand the way bodies politic . . . function or fail to function." The Foundation does not make grants, but rather sponsors its own programs and participates in collaborative research efforts with other organizations to address the roles of politics and institutional structures as a dimension of everyday life. The results of the Foundation's research are published in study guides, community workbooks, and other exercises to help the public act responsibly and effectively on its problems. In addition to general information about the Foundation's activities and publications, a listing of Foundation trustees, and e-mail and contact information, visitors to the Foundation's Web site site can access a searchable database of more than 2,000 non-evaluative summaries of books and articles in the subject areas of governing, community, education, international, science, policy, and political philosophy.

John S. and James L. Knight Foundation <http://www.knightfdn.org/>

Established in 1950, the John S. and James L. Knight Foundation focuses its grantmaking activities on journalism, education, and arts and culture. The Foundation also supports organizations in 27 communities where the communications company founded by the Knight brothers publishes newspapers, and it "remains flexible enough to respond to unique challenges, ideas and projects that lie beyond its identified program areas, yet would fulfill the broad vision of its founders." Visitors to the site can access an array of information about the Foundation and its programs; application guidelines and restrictions, including a sample proposal and proposal cover sheet (in Adobe Acrobat format); Foundation news, including the most recent annual report; a listing of recent grants by program area; and an informative FAQ section.

Samuel H. Kress Foundation <http://www.users.interport.net/~kress/>

Kronkosky Charitable Foundation <http://www.kronkosky.org/>

Albert & Mary Lasker Foundation <http://www.laskerfoundation.com>

The Edward Lowe Foundation <http://www.lowe.org/>

The focus of the Edward Lowe Foundation, a private operating foundation, is "on encouraging entrepreneurship throughout the United States." The Foundation does not make awards, grants, or loans to individual entrepreneurs or their businesses, nor does it consider unsolicited grant proposals or publish grant guidelines. In addition to its mission statement and a listing of officers and directors, the Foundation's Web site offers a history of its grants, detailed program information, and a number of electronic information services related to its mission.

The George Lucas Educational Foundation <http://glef.org/>

The George Lucas Educational Foundation uses various media, including its Web site, to promote and share the latest strategies to change the K–12 educational system, especially those that integrate technology with teaching or learning. Those strategies are based on the filmmaker's belief that "education is the most important investment we can make to secure the future of our democracy." Visitors to the site can access Edutopia, the Foundation's newsletter and "Learn & Live," the Foundation's educational resource guide. Although the Foundation is a private operating entity and does not make grants, visitors are encouraged to contact the Foundation if they know of a program or resource that can advance the Foundation's mission.

The Henry Luce Foundation <http://www.hluce.org/>

Established in 1936 by the late Henry R. Luce, co-founder and editor-in-chief of Time Inc., the New York City-based Henry Luce Foundation today focuses its activities on the interdisciplinary exploration of higher education; increased understanding between Asia and the United States; the study of religion and theology; scholarship in American art; opportunities for women in science and engineering; and contributions to youth and public policy programs. Higher education has been a persistent theme for most of the Foundation's programs, with an emphasis on innovation and scholarship. The Foundation's elegant, bandwidth-friendly Web site provides detailed information about a range of programs, including the Luce Fund in American Art, the American Collections Enhancement Initiative, the Clare Booth Luce Program, the Henry R. Luce Professorships, the Luce Scholars Program, the United States-China Cooperative Research Program, and the Asia Project; general application guidelines, guidelines for specific programs, and grant restrictions; recent grants list organized by program area; a helpful FAQ; listings of the Foundation's board and staff; and contact information.

The Christopher Ludwick Foundation
<http://www.libertynet.org/athena/ludwick.html>

The Lumpkin Foundation
<http://fdncenter.org/grantmaker/lumpkin/index.html>
The mission of the Illinois-based Lumpkin Foundation is "to provide leadership, individually and collectively, both locally and globally, to enrich [family members'] respective communities and in so doing preserve the tradition and goals of the [Lumpkin] family." The Foundation is dedicated to supporting education, preserving and protecting the environment, and fostering opportunities for leadership, and gives special consideration to its heritage in East Central Illinois. In addition to a mission statement and officer and committee listings, the Foundation's "folder" on the Center's Web site provides grant application procedures and restrictions, a letter of conditions (for grant recipients), downloadable versions of its grant application cover sheet and post-evaluation grant report, and contact information.

John D. and Catherine T. MacArthur Foundation <http://www.macfdn.org/>
The Chicago-based MacArthur Foundation recently revised most of its programs and guidelines, and unveiled a redesigned Web site to help get the message out. With a broad goal of fostering lasting improvement in the human condition, the Foundation seeks the development of healthy individuals and effective communities; peace within and among nations; responsible choices about human reproduction; and a global ecosystem capable of supporting healthy human societies. The Foundation makes grants through two major integrated programs—Human and Community Development and Global Security and Sustainability—and two special programs. The former supports national research and policy work and—in Chicago and Palm Beach County, Florida—direct local efforts. The program on Global Security and Sustainability focuses on arms reduction and security policy, ecosystems conservation, and population, and on three cross-cutting themes: concepts of security and sustainability; new partnerships and institutions; and education about United States interests and responsibilities.

The Foundation's two special programs are the General Program, which undertakes special initiatives and supports projects that promote excellence and diversity in the media, and the MacArthur Fellows Program, which awards fellowships to exceptionally creative individuals, regardless of field of endeavor. Visitors to the Foundation's well-organized, bandwidth-friendly Web site will find a great deal of information, including brief biographies of John D. and Catherine T. MacArthur, detailed program descriptions and application guidelines, financial statements, links to philanthropy resources, contact information, and a variety of other materials.

A. L. Mailman Family Foundation <http://www.mailman.org/>

Headquartered in White Plains, New York, the A. L. Mailman Family Foundation focuses its grantmaking activities on children and families, with a special emphasis on early childhood. The Foundation's current program is focused in the following areas: early care and education, family support, and moral education and social responsibility. Foundation grants generally range from $30,000 to $35,000, but are not awarded for ongoing direct services, general operating expenses, individuals, capital expenditures, endowment campaigns, or for local services or programs. Visitors to the Foundation's Web site will find general information and 1997 grant lists for each program area; grant application guidelines; a listing of directors, officer and staff; and contact information.

Manitou Foundation <http://www.manitou.org/mf_homepage.html>

The Manitou Foundation offers land grants in the Crestone/Baca area of Colorado to qualified U.S. nonprofit organizations in the following categories: religious organizations and spiritual projects, ecological and environmental sustainability projects, and related educational endeavors (youth and adult). The Foundation also administers a land preservation program and seeks to network with individuals and organizations locally, nationally, and internationally to facilitate its mission objectives. The Land Preservation Program component of the Foundation's Web site includes links to involved religious and spiritual projects. Visitors will also find program guidelines and application procedures for the program, information on its Solitary Retreat Hermitage Building Project, and contact information with e-mail addresses.

Marion Foundation (http://www.marion.org)

Established in 1993 by Marion Sue Kauffman, the Marion Foundation "strives to improve communications and relationships among youth and parents by implementing innovative programs that address the social, emotional and educational issues of our ever changing society." Among other activities, the Arizona-based operating foundation lends financial support to teachers and schools, operates a peer counseling phone line, and sponsors a number of youth-related activities in the Phoenix metropolitan area. The Foundation's stylish Web site provides general information about Raising Today's Teens, a Foundation-sponsored phone and Internet peer-counseling service, as well as two recently concluded projects: the School House Project, which helped supply selected schools in Maricopa County with basic educational materials, and Project A.C.E. ("Arizona Classroom Enhancement"), which was designed to provide teachers who lacked basic educational tools the opportunity to enhance their classroom capabilities.

The John and Mary R. Markle Foundation <http://www.markle.org/>

The John and Mary R. Markle Foundation was established in 1927 "to promote the advancement and diffusion of knowledge . . . and the general good of mankind." Today the Foundation focuses its activities on developing and using "the technologies of communication and information to enhance lifelong learning and to promote an informed citizenry." The Foundation currently supports projects within three program areas: media and political participation, interactive communications technologies, and communications policy. In these areas, the Foundation initiates and supports research, analysis, programming, and the development of innovative communications products and services. Visitors to the Foundation's user-friendly Web site will find lots of general information about the Foundation, including financial information for 1996 and 1997, recent press releases, and board and staff listings; a listing of Foundation grants complete with detailed project descriptions; application guidelines and limitations; and electronic mailing list and contact information. Additional components of the site include a news and opinion section, a media map with links to "the best media information on the Web," and a site-wide search engine.

Mayday Fund <http://fdncenter.org/grantmaker/mayday/index.html>

Edmund F. Maxwell Foundation <http://www.maxwell.org/>

McCarthy Family Foundation
<http://fdncenter.org/grantmaker/mccarthy/index.html>
The San Diego-based McCarthy Family Foundation makes grants in five primary program areas: secondary school science education; AIDS research, education and support; assistance to homeless people; support for children and families in need; and environmental protection. The Foundation makes grants exclusively within California, with the typical grant award between $5,000 and $15,000. The Foundation does not make grants for individuals, scholarship funds, sectarian religious activities, general fundraising drives, or programs supporting political candidates or to influence legislation. The Foundation's "folder" on the Center's Web site provides visitors with program guidelines, application instructions, and a complete 1997 grants list.

Robert R. McCormick Tribune Foundation <http://www.rrmtf.org>
The Robert R. McCormick Tribune Foundation was established as a charitable trust in 1955 upon the death of Colonel Robert R. McCormick, longtime editor and publisher of the Chicago Tribune, and was restructured as a foundation in 1991 with an emphasis on four grantmaking areas: communities, journalism, education, and citizenship. Because each program has its own guidelines, geographic restrictions, and application procedures, grantseekers are encouraged to read carefully all information pertaining to their particular program of interest. The Web site provides summaries of grants paid. In addition to the four program areas mentioned above, the Foundation also provides annual support to Cantigny, the Colonel's former estate in Wheaton, Illinois, which is now operated as a park for the "education, instruction and welfare of the people of Illinois."

James S. McDonnell Foundation <http://www.jsmf.org/>
The McDonnell Foundation was established in 1950 "to explore methods for developing a stable world order and lasting peace." Today the foundation awards $11 million in grants annually, primarily in the areas of biomedical and behavioral sciences and research and innovation in education. The Foundation's Web site provides program information, application guidelines, a listing of grants and awards made by the Foundation since January 1, 1995, current Foundation financial reports for the years ending December 31, 1995 and 1996, and contact information.

R.J. McElroy Trust <http://www.cedarnet.org/mcelroy/index.html>

McGregor Fund <http://comnet.org/mcgregor/>

Founded in 1925 by Michigan philanthropists Tracy and Katherine Whitney McGregor, the McGregor Fund was established to "relieve the misfortunes and promote the well being of mankind." The Fund presently awards grants in the areas of human services, education, health care, arts and culture, and public benefit. Only organizations located in the metropolitan Detroit area, or projects which significantly benefit that area, are eligible for support. The Fund does not award grants for individuals or student scholarships and generally does not support travel, conferences, seminars or workshops, film or video projects, or disease specific organizations. Visitors to the Fund's Web site will find brief descriptions of each program area, application procedures and guidelines, a FY 1997 grants list organized by program area, complete financial statements through 1997, a listing of Fund trustees and staff, and contact information.

The Meadows Foundation <http://www.mfi.org/>

The Meadows Foundation was established in 1948 by Algur H. and Virginia Meadows to benefit the people of Texas by "working toward the elimination of ignorance, hopelessness and suffering, protecting the environment, providing cultural enrichment, encouraging excellence and promoting understanding and cooperation among people." The Foundation provides grants in the areas of art and culture, civic and public affairs, education, health, and human services. In addition to examples of grants awarded in each area of giving, visitors to the Foundation's Web site can access grant guidelines (in Spanish and English), the Foundation's financial information, a listing of officers, directors, and staff, and links to local and national nonprofit organizations. The site also describes the Foundation's Wilson Historic District housing restoration project as well as its Awards for Charitable School project, which supports youth voluntarism.

The Medina Foundation <http://www.medfdn.org/>

The Medina Foundation seeks to "aid in improving the human condition in the greater Puget Sound community by fostering positive change, growth and the improvement of people." The Foundation makes grants to qualified charitable organizations, particularly those offering direct service delivery. No grants are made to individuals. The Foundation's Web site includes program and financial guidelines; funding parameters and geographical restrictions; application procedures; an overview of the Foundation's Management Excellence Awards Program; FAQs; and contact information.

The Andrew W. Mellon Foundation <http://www.mellon.org/>

Under its broad charter, the New York City-based Andrew W. Mellon Foundation currently makes grants on a selective basis in the following areas of interest: higher education; cultural affairs and the performing arts; population; conservation and the environment; and public affairs. Although the Foundation reviews proposals on a rolling basis throughout the year, "prospective applicants are encouraged to explore their ideas informally with Foundation staff (preferably in writing) before submitting formal proposals." The Foundation does not make grants to individuals or to primarily local organizations. In addition to a range of general information, visitors to the Foundation's no-frills Web site will find program descriptions, a list of Foundation trustees and staff, and online versions of some two dozen Foundation reports from 1989–1997.

Joyce Mertz-Gilmore Foundation <http://www.jmgf.org/>

The Joyce Mertz-Gilmore Foundation makes grants to nonprofit organizations active in the areas of the environment, human rights, peace and security, and New York City civic and cultural life. The Foundation currently sponsors five grant-making programs: environment/energy, human rights, peace and security, New York City human and built environment, and arts in New York City. The Foundation does not typically make grants for endowments or annual fund appeals; capital projects; political activities such as lobbying; conferences or workshops; sectarian religious concerns; individual scholarships, research, fellowships, loans, or travel; film or media projects; or publications. Visitors to the Foundation's Web site will find program guidelines and restrictions, a listing of selected grants by program area, 1996 and 1997 financial statements, application instructions, and a listing of the Foundation's staff and board of directors.

Meru Foundation <http://www.meru.org/>

Meyer Memorial Trust <http://www.mmt.org/>

Founded by retail-store magnate Fred G. Meyer, the Portland-based Meyer Memorial Trust operates three grantmaking programs—General Purpose Grants, Small Grants, and Support for Teacher Initiatives—to benefit qualified tax-exempt applicants in Oregon and Clark County, Washington. The Trust does not provide grants, loans, or scholarships to individuals, nor does it provide assistance to for-profit businesses. Visitors to the Trust's Web site will find application guidelines, restrictions, and cover sheets (in .PDF format) for each of its programs; grants lists by subject area for 1995–96, 1996–97, and 1997–98; a listing of trustees and staff; a brief biography of Trust founder Fred Meyer; and a short list of links to other online resources.

Milbank Memorial Fund <http://www.milbank.org/>

Milken Family Foundation <http://www.mff.org/index.html>

Established in 1982 by Lowell and Michael Milken, the California-based Milken Family Foundation advances its mission of "helping people help themselves and those around them to lead productive and satisfying lives" by focusing its activities on education and medicine (specifically prostate cancer and epilepsy). The Foundation's Web site comes in Shockwave Flash and non-Shockwave versions. It has a number of interactive features and a good deal of information about the Foundation's areas of interest and programs. Among the latter are the American Epilepsy Society/Milken Family Foundation Epilepsy Research Award Grants and Fellowship Program, recognizing outstanding physicians and scientists working to improve the lives of people with epilepsy; Mike's Math Club, a mentoring program for fifth- and sixth-graders; and the Milken Family Jewish Educator Awards, offering financial recognition to outstanding educators in schools affiliated with the Bureau of Jewish Education of Greater Los Angeles.

Morino Foundation/Institute <http://www.morino.org/welcome2.html>

Founded by business leader and "social entrepreneur" Mario Marino, the Morino Foundation/Institute is dedicated to "opening the doors of opportunity—economic, civic, health and education—and empowering people to improve their lives and communities in the communications age." Grants are normally made from the Morino Foundation, on behalf of the Institute, in support of initiatives or focus areas in which the Institute is actively engaged—youth advocacy and services, entrepreneurship, social networking, and community services. In all of its grantmaking activities, the Institute, which does not accept unsolicited proposals, emphasizes the emerging medium of electronic communications and how it can be applied to further positive social change and community improvement. The Institute's elegant Web site offers a good deal of interesting information about the Institute's core beliefs and funding philosophy, general program and grant information, links to a variety of Institute-sponsored projects and partners, and contact information.

Charles Stewart Mott Foundation <http://www.mott.org/>

Established in 1926 by industrialist Charles Stewart Mott, the Flint, Michigan-based Mott foundation makes grants in the United States and, on a limited geographic basis, internationally, in four broad program areas: civil society, the environment, Flint, and poverty. These programs, in turn, are divided into more specific areas: the civil society program focuses on the United States, South Africa, Central/Eastern Europe, Russia, and the newly created Republics; the environment program is devoted to reform of international lending and trade policies, prevention of toxic pollution, protection of the Great Lakes ecosystem, and special initiatives; the Flint program concentrates on institutional capacity building, arts and recreation, economic and community development, and education; and the poverty program focuses on building communities, strengthening families, improving education, economic opportunity, and cross-cutting initiatives. In addition to detailed application guidelines and a biography of Charles Stewart Mott, the Foundation's well-organized Web site offers a searchable grants database, dozens of links to grantee Web sites, a list of publications available through the Foundation (many downloadable in part or full), and related stories in each broad program area.

M.J. Murdock Charitable Trust <http://www.murdock-trust.org/>

The Murdock Charitable Trust was created by the will of the late Melvin J. (Jack) Murdock, a co-founder of Tektronix, Inc. of Beaverton, Oregon, in 1975. Today, with assets approaching $400 million, it is the second largest private foundation in the Pacific Northwest and among the hundred largest private foundations in the nation. In the two decades since its establishment, the Trust has focused its grant-making efforts in the areas of education, scientific research, and, more recently, arts and culture and health and human services, with an emphasis on the five states of the Pacific Northwest—Alaska, Idaho, Montana, Oregon, and Washington. In addition, it operates five formal grants programs, all of which are open to applicants only upon invitation or by special arrangements initiated by the Trust: the Murdock College Science Research Program, the Murdock College Research Program for Life Sciences, the Exceptional Opportunity Grants Program, the Partners in Science Program, and the Program to Strengthen the Contemporary American Family. Still under construction, the Foundation's no-frills Web site provides general program information, grant application guidelines and procedures (including guidelines for the initial letter of inquiry), a downloadable grant application form, brief bios of the staff, and contact information.

The Murray Foundation, Inc. <http://www.murrayfoundation.org/>

The Needmor Fund <http://fdncenter.org/grantmaker/needmor/index.html>

Established in Toledo, Ohio, in 1956, the Colorado-based Needmor Fund today works to change the social, economic, and political conditions that bar access to participation in a democratic society. The Fund is committed to the idea that "citizens should be free and equal to determine the actions of government and the terms of public policy" and thus assure their right to justice, political liberty, the basic necessities of life, an education that enables them to be contributing members of society, and the opportunity to secure productive work with just wages and benefits and decent working conditions. Visitors to the Fund's "folder" on the Center's Web site will find a statement of the Fund's mission and values, detailed application guidelines and restrictions, and a list of recent grants made.

New England Biolabs Foundation <http://www.nebf.org/>

Established in 1982, NEBF supports grassroots organizations working in the areas of the environment, social change, the arts, elementary education, and limited scientific research. Ordinarily, NEBF limits its domestic grantmaking to the greater Boston/North Shore area. But the Foundation does encourage proposals from or about developing countries with an emphasis on assisting community organizations in their endeavors. Due to its size, it restricts these activities to specific countries. Visitors to the NEBF site will find detailed application guidelines and reporting requirements, proposal tips from the Foundation's director, a list of awards made in 1996, and contact information. NEBF accepts the common grant application form sponsored by the National Network of Grantmakers.

The Samuel Roberts Noble Foundation <http://www.noble.org/>

Established in 1945 by oil industrialist Lloyd Noble in honor of his father, the Samuel Roberts Noble Foundation seeks "to assist humanity in reaching its maximum usefulness." To that end, the Ardmore, Oklahoma-based Foundation focuses on basic plant biology and agricultural research, consultation, and demonstration projects that enable farmers and ranchers to achieve their goals, enhancing plant productivity through fundamental research and applied biotechnology and assisting community, health, and educational organizations through grants and employee involvement. Among other offerings, the Foundation's Web site provides grant guidelines and procedures; an overview of activities in the Foundation's Plant Biology and Agricultural divisions; links to a variety of local, regional, and Internet resources; and contact information.

Nord Family Foundation <http://www.kellnet.com/nordf/>

Norman Foundation <http://www.normanfdn.org/>

The New York-based Norman Foundation is committed to a strategy of seeking and supporting grassroots efforts that strengthen the ability of communities to determine their economic, environmental and civic well-being; promote community-based economic development efforts that are trying out new ownership structures and financing mechanisms; work to prevent the use of toxics and their disposal into the environment; build bridges across issues and constituencies and organize to counter the "radical right" in all its forms; promote civil rights by fighting discrimination and violence and working for ethnic, religious, and sexual equity and for reproductive freedom; challenge the power of money over our political process; and/or seek to improve governments' and businesses' accountability to the public and especially to those affected by their actions. The Foundation also seeks to address "the profound civic disengagement in society," and is particularly interested in strategies "on how to engage more Americans in their civic lives and how to increase their faith and involvement in community institutions." The Foundation's Web site provides a description of the application process, grant guidelines and restrictions, basic financial information, a list of the grants the Foundation awarded in 1996 and 1997, listings of the Foundation's officers, directors, and staff, and contact information.

Northwest Area Foundation <http://www.nwaf.org/>
The Northwest Area Foundation was established in 1934 by Louis W. Hill, son of James J. Hill, the founder of the Great Northern Railroad, and renamed in 1975 to reflect its "commitment to the region that provided its original resources and its growth beyond the scope of the traditional family foundation." Recently, it announced a new mission: to help communities most in need in an eight-state area—Minnesota, Iowa, North Dakota, South Dakota, Montana, Idaho, Washington, and Oregon—create positive futures—economically, ecologically, and socially. To implement that mission, the Foundation will help communities "work toward a balanced and sustainable system that will reduce poverty; stimulate economic growth; sustain the natural environment; and develop effective institutions, relationships, and individuals." In addition to contact information, a brief history of the Foundation, and staff and trustee listings, the Foundation's new Web site provides an overview of its new direction and the decision-making process that led to it.

Northwest Fund for the Environment <http://www.wolfenet.com/~nwfund/>

Jessie Smith Noyes Foundation <http://www.noyes.org/>

John M. Olin Foundation, Inc. <http://www.jmof.org/>
The John M. Olin Foundation was established in 1953 by the industrialist John Merrill Olin (1892–1982). Mr. Olin was committed to "the preservation of the principles of political and economic liberty as they have been expressed in American thought, institutions and practice." Accordingly, the purpose of the John M. Olin Foundation is to provide support for projects that "reflect or are intended to strengthen the economic, political and cultural institutions upon which the American heritage of constitutional government and private enterprise is based." Within this context, the Foundation has authorized grants in the areas of American institutions, law and the legal system, public policy research, and strategic and international studies. In each of these areas, it attempts to advance its objectives through support of research, institutional support, fellowships, professorships, lectures and lectures series, books, scholarly journals, journals of opinion, conferences and seminars, and, on occasion, television and radio programs. The Foundation's straightforward Web site provides general information about its programs, grant-making policies, and application procedures; a schedule of the Foundation's 1996 grants; listings of the Foundation's trustees and staff; and contact information.

Onan Family Foundation <http://www.onanfamily.org/foundation.htm>

Ottinger Foundation <http://www.funder.org/ottinger/>

The Ottinger Foundation, a private family foundation based in Amherst, Massachusetts, supports organizations that promote "democratic participation, economic justice, environmental preservation, and energy conservation." The Foundation encourages the "submission of innovative proposals that address causes rather than symptoms of problems," and it supports the common grant application form sponsored by the National Network of Grantmakers. Most of the projects funded by the Foundation include a strong component of grassroots activism and have national significance. In addition to basic contact information, visitors to the Foundation's straightforward Web site will find concise application guidelines and procedures, a list of grants awarded by the Foundation in 1997, and its Funders' Handbook on Money in Politics.

The David and Lucile Packard Foundation <http://www.packfound.org/>

The David and Lucile Packard Foundation strives to improve the quality of life in the United States by supporting programs that foster scientific knowledge and/or improve education, health, the environment, culture, and employment opportunities. The Foundation's Web site offers program guidelines for more than a dozen areas, grant application information, a checklist of what a proposal should include, the Foundation's 1997 annual report (available in standard HTML text and Adobe Acrobat .PDF formats), recent awards lists by program area, program guidelines for the Foundation's 1998 scholarship and fellowship programs, information about the Foundation supported Center for the Future of Children, and a listing of officers and trustees.

The William Penn Foundation
<http://fdncenter.org/grantmaker/wmpenn/index.html>

The William Penn Foundation, a private grantmaking organization created in 1945 by Otto Haas and his wife, Phoebe, strives to improve the quality of life in the greater Philadelphia area, particularly for its neediest residents. The Foundation makes grants ranging from a few thousand dollars to several million dollars in four main categories: Children, Youth and Families; Communities; Arts and Culture; and the Natural Environment. Within the first three categories, the Foundation's grantmaking is limited to the six-county Philadelphia area (Bucks, Chester, Delaware, Montgomery, and Philadelphia counties in Pennsylvania and Camden County, especially the City of Camden, in New Jersey) unless initiated by the Foundation. Grants for school-based programs in Philadelphia are generally limited to the Martin Luther King, Jr. and West Philadelphia clusters. Grants in the Natural Environment category are awarded throughout a larger region extending from the Delaware Water Gap southeast along the northern border of Warren, Hunterdon, Mercer, and Ocean counties in New Jersey to the Atlantic coast at Manasquan; south along the coast to the mouth of the Delaware Bay; west along the C & D Canal and the Susquehanna River to the Appalachian trail; and north along the trail to the Delaware Water Gap. The Foundation's "folder" on the Center's Web site provides detailed program descriptions, application guidelines and restrictions, a complete 1996 grants list, statements of the Foundation's mission and grantmaking values, a history of the Foundation, board and staff listings, and contact information.

The Pew Charitable Trusts <http://www.pewtrusts.com/>
The Philadelphia-based Pew Trusts are a group of seven individual charitable funds established by the children of Sun Oil Company founder Joseph N. Pew and his wife, Mary Anderson Pew. Each year, the Trusts make grants of about $180 million to between 400 and 500 nonprofit organizations in the areas of culture, education, the environment, health and human services, public policy, religion, and interdisciplinary programs. In addition to a strong national giving program, the Trusts maintain a particular commitment to their local community. The Trusts' well-organized Web site provides visitors with program guidelines and limitations, application procedures, a searchable grants database, links to recipient organizations when available, and a complete staff list with phone numbers and e-mail addresses. The site also incorporates a number of interactive features, allowing visitors to make inquiries, offer feedback, and order publications.

Plan for Social Excellence, Inc. <http://www.netsurftech.com/pfse/>

The Pollock-Krasner Foundation, Inc. <http://www.pkf.org/>
Established by Lee Krasner, widow of the painter Jackson Pollock and a celebrated artist in her own right, the Pollock-Krasner Foundation's mission is "to aid, internationally, those individuals who have worked as professional artists over a significant period of time." Potential grant recipients must demonstrate a combination of recognizable artistic merit and financial need, relating to either work, living, or medical expenses. The Foundation provides support exclusively to visual artists—painters, sculptors, and artists who work on paper, including printmakers—and will not accept applications from commercial artists, photographers, video artists, performance artists, filmmakers, crafts-makers, or any artist whose work primarily falls into one of these categories. Nor does the Foundation fund academic study or make grants to pay for past debts, legal fees, the purchase of real estate, relocation to another city, or the costs of installations, commissions, or projects ordered by others. The Foundation's Web site provides visitors with a brief history of the Foundation, application and selection procedures, a listing of officers and staff, and contact information.

Pickett & Hatcher Educational Fund, Inc.
<http://www.pickettandhatcher.org/>

Public Welfare Foundation <http://www.publicwelfare.org/>
Established and incorporated in Texas in 1947 and reincorporated in Washington, D.C., in 1960, the Public Welfare Foundation is dedicated "to supporting organizations that provide services to disadvantaged populations and work for lasting improvements in the delivery of services that meet basic human needs." The Foundation's wide-ranging interests include community support (homelessness, low-income housing, low-income community and economic development, global security, countering hate-motivated activity and discrimination, immigration and refugees, international human rights, technical assistance to grassroots community development efforts); criminal justice (community-based correctional options, institutional programming, legal representation of low-income persons, violence prevention); the disadvantaged elderly (community-based long-term care), disadvantaged youth (early intervention; employment, training, and alternative education; teen parents and their children; violence prevention; youth

empowerment and leadership development); the environment (global climate change, sustainable development, direct support and technical assistance to grassroots organizations); health (health advocacy and reform, hunger and nutrition, mental health advocacy and services, occupational health and safety, preventive and primary services); and population and reproductive health (AIDS prevention, education, and advocacy; international family planning; reproductive rights; reproductive health for teens; emerging issues). A model of uncluttered, functional design, the Foundation's Web site provides a short history of the Foundation, answers to frequently asked questions, detailed program information, financial statements, application procedures, grants lists organized by specific funding area, contact information, and more. And in 1998, PWF planned to launch bulletin boards and interactive forums for online workgroups, discussion, conferences, and evaluation.

A.C. Ratshesky Foundation <http://www.agmconnect.org/ratshes1.html>

Michael Reese Health Trust
<http://fdncenter.org/grantmaker/health/index.html>
The Michael Reese Health Trust seeks to improve the health of people in Chicago's metropolitan communities through effective grantmaking in health care, health education, and health research. The Trust, which funds exclusively in metropolitan Chicago, with an emphasis on the city of Chicago, seeks to address the needs of the most vulnerable in society, particularly programs that serve the medically indigent and underserved, immigrants, refugees, the elderly, mentally and physically disabled, children and youth. To emphasize the Trust's Jewish heritage, special consideration will be given to programs that serve those in the Jewish community who fall within these populations. The Trust does not fund programs operating outside of metropolitan Chicago; capital needs (such as buildings, vehicles, and equipment); endowment; fundraising events; debt reduction; individuals; or scholarships. The Trust's "folder" on the Center's Web site includes a mission statement, program guidelines, application procedures, a 1996/1997 grantee list and contact information.

Research Corporation <http://www.rescorp.org/>
Established in New York in 1912, making it one of the first private foundations in the United States, the Research Corporation is the only domestic foundation wholly devoted to the advancement of science and technology. Its unique philanthropic mission is to make inventions and patent rights "more available and effective in the useful arts and manufactures," and to devote any new resources therefrom "to provide means for the advancement and extension of technical and scientific investigation, research and experimentation" at scholarly institutions. The Foundation makes between 200 and 300 awards annually for original research in chemistry, physics, and astronomy at colleges and universities throughout the U.S. and Canada. Visitors to the Web site will find guidelines for seven Foundation-supported programs (Cottrell College Science Awards, Cottrell Scholars, Partners in Science, Research Opportunity Awards, Research Innovation Awards, Department Development Program, and General Foundation Awards); recent news releases; contact information; and the current issue of the Research Corporation Bulletin in Adobe Acrobat (.PDF) format.

The Retirement Research Foundation
<http://fdncenter.org/grantmaker/rrf/index.html>
The Chicago-based Retirement Research Foundation is the nation's largest private foundation exclusively devoted to aging and retirement issues. Founded by the late John D. MacArthur, it makes approximately $8 million in grants each year to nonprofit and educational organizations to support programs, research, and public policy studies to improve the quality of life of older Americans. The Foundation operates a general grants program, two award programs (ENCORE and the Congregation Connection Program) open to Chicago-area nonprofits only, and the National Media Owl Awards, a national film and video competition. Visitors to RRF's "folder" on the Foundation Center's Web site will find a variety of materials, including an overview of the Foundation and its funding interests, program descriptions, a 1996 grants list, program-related FAQs, application information, and a number of press releases.

Z. Smith Reynolds Foundation <http://www.zsr.org/>
Created almost 60 years ago to serve the people of North Carolina, the Z. Smith Reynolds Foundation is the country's largest general purpose foundation with a mandate to make grants within a single state. The Foundation focuses its activities in the areas of pre-collegiate education, community economic development, environmental interests, minority issues, and women's issues, but will consider proposals that fall outside these areas as long as they are consistent with the foundation's mission. The Foundation's Web site provides general information about the Foundation, detailed grant application procedures, information on special publications and programs, a helpful FAQ section, a list of grants awarded since 1994, and links to grantee Web sites.

Sid W. Richardson Foundation <http://www.sidrichardson.org/>

Fannie E. Rippel Foundation
<http://fdncenter.org/grantmaker/rippel/index.html>
The Fannie E. Rippel Foundation's objectives are to support the relief and care of aged women, the erection and maintenance of hospitals, and the treatment of and/or research concerning heart disease and cancer. Although strict geographic limitations are not imposed, emphasis is given to institutions located in New Jersey and the greater New York metropolitan area, the general Northeast, and the Middle Atlantic Seaboard. The Foundation's "folder" on the Center's Web site serves as an online version of the Foundation's FYE 1997 annual report, offering application guidelines, messages from the Foundation's president and chairman, 1997 grants listings, statements of financial position and activities, and a listing of its trustees and staff.

Rockefeller Brothers Fund <http://www.rbf.org/>
Since 1984, the main part of the Rockefeller Brother Fund's grantmaking program has been organized around the theme of One World, with two major components: sustainable resource use and world security. The Fund expects to adopt new guidelines in early 1998 for its World Security program. In the interim, new grants are not being made under the program that is being phased out. The Fund's other program interests are promoting and sustaining a vital nonprofit sector, both nationally and internationally; strengthening the numbers and quality of teachers

in public education in the United States; and improving the quality and accessibility of basic education for children and adults in South Africa. Visitors to the Fund's Web site will find program guidelines and comprehensive lists of recent grants going back to 1993; application procedures and grant restrictions; a list of Fund publications (available upon e-mailed request); a listing of trustees and officers; and links to the Fund's non-grantmaking programs and affiliations.

Rockefeller Foundation <http://www.rockfound.org/>

Endowed by John D. Rockefeller and chartered in 1913 for "the well-being of people throughout the world," the Rockefeller Foundation is one of America's oldest private foundations and one of the few with strong international interests. The Foundation focuses its activities in three principal areas: the arts and humanities, equal opportunity and school reform, and international science-based development, which encompasses the agricultural, health, and population sciences, global environment, and several special African initiatives, including female education. The balance of the Foundation's grant and fellowship programs "supports work in international security, international philanthropy, and other special interests and initiatives." Visitors to the Foundation's comprehensive Web site will find information about the Foundation's programs, funding priorities, fellowships, and recent grants, along with a capsule version of the Foundation's 1997 financial report, a listing of the Foundation's trustees, and a letter from Foundation president Peter C. Goldmark, Jr.

Rosenberg Foundation <http://www.rosenbergfdn.org/>

The Rosenberg Foundation was established in 1935 by relatives and associates of Max L. Rosenberg, a San Francisco businessman and philanthropist. Since the 1940s, the Foundation has emphasized the health, education, and recreation of California's children and communities. Today, the Foundation accepts grant requests in three priority areas: the Changing Population of California, which includes activities that "promote the full social, economic, and cultural integration of immigrants and minorities into a pluralistic society"; Children and their Families in Poverty, which includes activities that "reduce dependency, promote self-help, create access to the economic mainstream, or address the causes of poverty among children and families"; and Child Support Reform, a multi-year initiative aimed at increasing "economic security for children, particularly children in low-income families, through the development of a public system that is effective in establishing paternity, fair in awarding support, efficient and effective in collecting and distributing payments, and build[s] toward a national program of child support assurance." Visitors to the Foundation's user-friendly Web site will find thorough program descriptions and recent grants lists by program area; application guidelines and procedures; current financial information; a brief history of the Foundation; and contact information.

Russell Sage Foundation <http://www.epn.org/sage.html>

The Russell Sage Foundation is dedicated "to strengthening the methods, data, and theoretical core of the social sciences as a means of improving social policies." It does this by conducting a Visiting Scholars program and by funding studies by scholars at other academic and research institutions. The Foundation currently is focusing on four areas: the future of work, immigration, literacy and disadvantaged children, and the psychology of cultural contact. Offerings on its

Web site include brief biographies of the Foundation's Visiting Scholars for academic years 1994–1995 through 1997–1998; examples of recent project awards; general application and proposal guidelines; and brief excerpts from recent Foundation-sponsored publications.

Arthur B. Schultz Foundation <http://www.absfoundation.org>

The Self Family Foundation <http://www.selffoundation.greenwood.net/>

Harry Singer Foundation <http://www.singerfoundation.org/>
The California-based Harry Singer Foundation focuses on promoting "responsibility and involv[ing] people more fully in public policy." As a private operating foundation, it supports and administers active programs but does not make grants. Current programs focus on government spending, personal responsibility, values, and emotional intelligence. The Foundation's Web site provides information about a range of Foundation programs, including current and past essay contests, a teacher's mentor program, a workbook series, and offers an electronic lending library. The site's archives have an interactive feature called "Match Maker," an electronic bulletin board designed to match worthy grantseekers with sponsors.

The Skillman Foundation <http://www.skillman.org/>
Founded in December 1960 by Rose P. Skillman, widow of 3M vice president and director Robert H. Skillman, the Skillman Foundation seeks to improve the well-being of residents of Southeastern Michigan and, in particular, the Metropolitan Detroit area (Wayne, Oakland, and Macomb counties). Developing children and youth to their maximum potential is the Foundation's primary goal, and to that end it makes grants in the areas of child and family welfare, child and family health, education, juvenile justice, youth development, basic human needs, culture and the arts, and strengthening community and civic institutions. The Foundation's nicely laid out, no-frills Web site provides information about the Foundation's grantmaking policies and procedures, a list of 1996, 1997, and 1998 grants organized by subject area, online versions of its most recent newsletter and reports and publications (under construction), an evaluation guide, a listing of the Foundation's trustees and staff, and contact information.

Alfred P. Sloan Foundation <http://www.sloan.org/>
Established in 1934 by longtime General Motors chairman and CEO Alfred P. Sloan, the New York City-based Sloan Foundation today concentrates its activities in four main areas: science and technology; standard of living, competitiveness, and economics; education and careers in science and technology; and selected national issues. Visitors to the Foundation's Web site will find detailed program descriptions, application procedures, a directory of Foundation officers and staff, and a brief biography of founder Alfred P. Sloan, Jr.

Christopher D. Smithers Foundation <http://aaw.com/smithers/>

Sobrato Family Foundation <http://www.sobrato.com/foundation/>

Soros Foundations Network <http://www.soros.org/>

Supported by financier-turned-philanthropist George Soros, the Soros Foundations Network comprises 26 national foundations located in the countries of Central and Eastern Europe, the former Soviet Union, South Africa, and Haiti; and the Open Society Institute, which promotes connections and cooperation among the various Soros-sponsored foundations. The SFN's member organizations "help build the infrastructure and institutions necessary for open societies" by supporting programs for education, children and youth, media and communications, civil society, human rights and humanitarian aid, science and medicine, arts and culture, and economic restructuring. SFN's Web site, which serves as the information clearinghouse for the network, offers a wide range of information, including general program categories and application guidelines, annotated bibliographies, newsletters, press releases, and contact info. Also of interest is the manner in which the SFN site integrates a Web interface with a central gopher database to allow for meaningful access by the broadest possible online constituency.

The Spencer Foundation <http://www.spencer.org/>

Established by Lyle M. Spencer, founder of the educational publishing firm Science Research Associates Inc., the Spencer Foundation investigates "ways in which education, broadly conceived, can be improved around the world." To this end, the Foundation supports "high quality investigation of education through its research programs . . . [and] strengthens and renews the educational research community through fellowship programs and related activities." Since 1968, the Foundation has made grants totaling approximately $180 million. Visitors to the Foundation's Web site will find descriptions, eligibility guidelines, and application instructions or contact information for each research grant program. The Foundation's annual reports for 1996 and 1997 (in Adobe .PDF format) and a listing of its directors, advisors, and staff are also available.

The Stanley Foundation <http://www.stanleyfdn.org/>

Stern Family Fund <http://www.essential.org/stern/>

The Arlington, Virginia-based Stern Family Fund "supports policy oriented government and corporate accountability projects. . . . [T]he Fund is committed to aiding citizens striving to guarantee the responsiveness of public and private institutions that wield substantial power over their lives." The Stern Fund seeks to achieve these goals through two distinct grant programs: the Public Interest Pioneer Program, which provides large seed grants ($50,000 to $100,000) to spark the creation of new organizations; and Strategic Support Grants, which are awarded to projects or organizations "at critical junctures in their development. . . ." With the exception of campaign finance reform proposals, the Fund generally limits its grants to organizations with annual operating budgets of less than $500,000. The Fund's Web site provides detailed program information, a list of grantees (with grant descriptions and amounts) going back to 1995, application guidelines and procedures, questions and answers on the Stern Grant Program, and a listing of the Fund's board members.

Sudbury Foundation <http://www.agmconnect.org/sudbury1.html>

Surdna Foundation, Inc. <http://www.surdna.org/surdna/>
Established in 1917 by businessman John E. Andrus, the New York City-based
Surdna Foundation concentrates its grantmaking activities in four programmatic
areas: the environment, community revitalization, effective citizenry, and "a small
program in the arts" (which is not accepting applications at this time). The Foundation's Web site offers general information about the Foundation and its
approach to grantmaking, as well as detailed program information, application
guidelines, and grant restrictions.

Stuart Foundation <www.stuartfoundation.org/>

The John Templeton Foundation <http://www.templeton.org/>
The Templeton Foundation was established in 1987 by international investment
manager John Templeton "to explore and encourage the relationship between science and religion." The Foundation's programs, which are primarily operating in
nature, focus on five areas: spiritual information through science, spirituality and
health, free enterprise, character development, and the John Templeton Prize for
Progress in Religion. In addition to general program and contact information, the
Foundation's Web site offers visitors a listing of the Foundation's officers and
trustees; winners of the Templeton Prizes for Progress in Religion; information
about other awards given by the Foundation; a list of recent grants; and a Request
for Proposals for scientific studies in the area of forgiveness, with RFP application
packets available for downloading as.PDF or Word for Windows files.

The Tinker Foundation <http://fdncenter.org/grantmaker/tinker/index.html>
Created in 1956 by Dr. Edward Larocque Tinker, the Tinker Foundation has long
focused its grantmaking activities on Latin America, Spain, and Portugal. More
recently, it has included in its mandate the support of projects concerning
Antarctica, "a region of significant interest on an international scale." The Foundation has two main programs: Institutional Grants are awarded to organizations
and institutions "that promote the interchange and exchange of information within
the community of those concerned with the affairs of Spain, Portugal, Ibero-
America and Antarctica." Within these parameters, the Foundation looks for innovative projects in the areas of environmental policy, governance, or economic policy that have a strong public policy component. The Foundation also awards Field
Research Grants to recognized institutes of Ibero-American or Latin American
Studies with graduate doctoral programs at accredited United States universities.
The Foundation's "folder" on the Center's Web site offers descriptions of both
programs; application instructions, reporting requirements, and a downloadable
proposal cover sheet; a selected 1997 grants list for the Institutional Grants program; and a listing of Foundation officers and staff.

Turner Foundation, Inc. <http://www.turnerfoundation.org/>
The Turner Foundation supports activities directed toward preservation of the
environment, conservation of natural resources, protection of wildlife, and sound
population policies. The Foundation supports organizations that "provide education and activism on preservation activities and seek to instill in all citizens a sense
of common responsibility for the fate of life on Earth." It does not customarily
provide support for buildings, land acquisition, endowments or startup funds. Nor
does it normally fund films, books, magazines, or other specific media projects.

The Foundation's Web site provides detailed program guidelines; lists of recent grants awarded in four main program areas (i.e., water/toxics, energy, forests/habitat, and population); application procedures and limitations; messages from Ted Turner and the Foundation's executive director; and an interactive form for feedback.

The Turrell Fund <http://fdncenter.org/grantmaker/turrell/index.html>

The main purpose of the New Jersey-based Turrell Fund is "to support social and educational activities that will contribute to the development of young people from families which could not afford these services without help." Programs that focus on children under the age of twelve are given highest priority; requests for capital support, while considered, are of secondary priority. The Fund supports programs in Vermont and in Essex, Hudson, Passaic, and Union counties in New Jersey. Visitors to the Fund's "folder" on the Foundation Center's Web site will find a brief description of its program interests, application instructions, a listing of officers, trustees, and staff, and a downloadable summary request form. Site features also include a list of FAQs as well as a grant distribution summary.

The Twentieth Century Fund <http://www.tcf.org/>

The Twentieth Century Fund, an operating foundation with an underlying philosophy that "regards government as an instrument, not an enemy, of the people," commissions individuals to carry out research projects that result in book-length manuscripts and shorter papers. It does not award fellowships or scholarships, support dissertation research, or make grants to individuals or institutions. Currently, it welcomes proposals in four areas: improving living standards, restoring civil society and respect for government, reinvigorating the media, and identifying new foundations for American foreign policy. In addition to information on and excerpts from current and recently completed projects, the Fund's Web site offers a mission statement, a message from the president, annual report, a catalog of publications, a listing of trustees, contact info, press releases and a calendar of Fund-related events.

United States - Japan Foundation
<http://www.japanese.com/nonprofit/foundation.html>

The principal mission of the United States - Japan Foundation, a private nonprofit grantmaking organization incorporated in 1980 in the State of New York, is "to promote greater mutual knowledge between the United States and Japan and to contribute to a strengthened understanding of important public policy issues of interest to both countries." The Foundation currently focuses its grantmaking in the areas of pre-college education and policy studies. It does not award grants as contributions to capital campaigns, endowment funds, or deficit operations, or for the construction or maintenance of buildings or for the purchase of equipment. Visitors to the Foundation's Web site will find basic program descriptions, application procedures, a limitations statement, and contact information.

The Valley Foundation <http://www.valley.org/>

Formed in 1984 from the proceeds of sale of the Community Hospital of Los Gatos, California, and Saratoga, Inc., the Valley Foundation provides funding for nonprofit organizations in Santa Clara County, with an emphasis in the medical field. Although the Foundation's primary interest is in medical services and health care for lower-income households, it also supports programs in the areas of youth, the arts, seniors, and general medical services. Visitors to the Foundation's Web site will find a listing of sample grants awarded in each of the program areas mentioned above, application procedures and limitations, a financial summary of the Foundation's activities in 1995, a listing of the Foundation's board, and, for visitors with a forms-capable browser, an electronic application form.

DeWitt Wallace-Reader's Digest Fund <http://www.dewittwallace.org/>

The mission of the DeWitt Wallace-Reader's Digest Fund, a private philanthropic foundation located in New York City, is to foster fundamental improvement in the quality of educational and career development opportunities for all school-age youth, and to increase access to these improved services for young people in low-income communities. The Fund's grantmaking activities, which are limited to nonprofit organizations in the United States, are designed to improve services to children and youth in three areas: elementary and secondary schools, youth-serving organizations, and school-community collaboration. Visitors to the Fund's Web site will find information about the Fund's mission, grantmaking strategies, and programs; application guidelines and restrictions; descriptions of grants given in 1997; and the Fund's new directions in grantmaking. The Fund's Web site also has a useful FAQ section, a newsletter focusing on one area of grant-making, and an interactive form for ordering the annual report.

Lila Wallace-Reader's Digest Fund <http://www.lilawallace.org/>

The mission of the Lila Wallace-Reader's Digest Fund, a private philanthropic foundation located in New York City, is to invest in programs that enhance the cultural life of communities and encourage people to make the arts and culture an active part of their everyday lives. The Fund's grantmaking activities, which are limited to nonprofit organizations in the United States, support leading nonprofit arts and cultural organizations, innovative adult literacy programs, and urban parks programs that encourage community involvement. Visitors to the Fund's Web site will find information about the Fund's mission, grantmaking strategies and programs; application guidelines and restrictions; descriptions of grants given in 1996 and 1997; answers to frequently asked questions about the Fund; and an online newsletter focusing on one area of grantmaking.

Andy Warhol Foundation for the Visual Arts
<http://www.warholfoundation.org/>

Weeden Foundation <http://www.weedenfdn.org/>

From its inception in 1963, the New York City-based Weeden Foundation (formerly the Frank Weeden Foundation) embraced the protection of biodiversity as its main priority. More recently, the Foundation has sought "to equalize distribution of grants between conservation and population programs in order to more fully address the factors driving biological impoverishment." The Foundation's well-organized Web site offers visitors a mission statement, application guidelines, an index to and summary of its grant awards for the FY 1993–FY 1997 period, and contact information.

Kurt Weill Foundation for Music, Inc. <http://www.kwf.org/Welcome.html>
The Kurt Weill Foundation for Music is chartered to preserve and perpetuate the legacies of composer Kurt Weill (1900–1950) and actress-singer Lotte Lenya (1898–1981). The Foundation awards grants to individuals and not-for-profit organizations "for projects related to Weill or Lenya" in the following categories: research and travel, publication assistance, dissertation fellowships, professional and regional performance and production, college and university performance and production, recording projects, and broadcasts. In addition to detailed guidelines, application information, and a listing of grants awarded by the Foundation from 1984–1997, visitors to the Web site can read about the Weill-Lenya Research Center, the Kurt Weill Edition (a collected critical edition of Weill's works), and the Kurt Weill Prize. Listings of Foundation staff and board members, information about copyright and licensing permissions, and contact information are also provided.

Weingart Foundation <http://www.weingartfnd.org/>
The Weingart Foundation focuses its grantmaking efforts on programs serving children and youth in the Southern California area, with secondary attention paid to institutions and agencies benefiting the Southern California community in general. The Foundation's Web site serves as an online version of their current annual report and offers a bio of founder Ben Weingart, financial statements for both the current and past year, brief profiles of eight grantees, grant guidelines and application procedures, downloadable application forms, and descriptions of grants $25,000 or more paid in the following categories: crisis intervention, education, health and medicine, community youth programs, higher education, culture and the arts, and adult community services. The annual reports from 1994–1995 and 1995–1996 are also provided.

The Whitaker Foundation <http://www.whitaker.org/>
The Whitaker Foundation primarily supports research and education in biomedical engineering. Since its inception in 1975, the foundation has awarded approximately $250 million to colleges and universities for faculty research, graduate fellowships and program development. In the field of biomedical engineering, the Foundation funds research grants, graduate fellowships, development awards, special opportunity awards, a teaching materials program, industrial internships, leadership awards, and conference awards. Visitors to the Foundation's Web site will find detailed program announcements and application guidelines with downloadable applications in .PDF format (Acrobat Reader); annual reports going back to 1993, including lists of grantees; research grants program abstracts for 1996–97; and news from the Foundation. The site is searchable and provides links to BMEnet, the Biomedical Engineering Network, which is maintained at Purdue University under a grant from the Foundation.

Whitehall Foundation, Inc. <http://www.whitehall.org/>

The Wilburforce Foundation <http://www.wilburforce.org/>
The Seattle-based Wilburforce Foundation awards grants in the areas of the environment and population stabilization to nonprofit organizations operating in the Pacific Northwest, Alaska, and the Canadian province of British Columbia. The Foundation's well-designed Web site offers detailed information on the types of

grants and support awarded; grant proposal guidelines and application information; a list of the Foundation's 1998 grants; a map of the Foundation's funding regions and grants made in each geographic location; and a wide variety of useful links to organizations and online news articles about the planet.

The Winston Foundation for World Peace
<http://www.crosslink.net/~wfwp/funding.htm>

Woods Charitable Fund, Inc. <http://www.4w.com/woods/index.html>
Based in Lincoln, Nebraska, the Woods Charitable Fund seeks to "strengthen the community by improving opportunities and life outcomes for all people in Lincoln. . . . " The Fund supports organizations that "are exploring creative alternatives and promoting more just, effective approaches to meet community needs." Within its limited geographic scope, the Fund's special funding interests are in the program areas of children, youth and families; education; community development and housing; and arts and humanities. In addition to a history of the Fund and the affiliated Woods Fund of Chicago, the Fund's Web site provides general information on its funding interests and limitations, a summary of grants by areas of interest, and a listing of the Fund's board of directors.

The Wray Trust <http://www.wt.org>
The Wray Trust, a small Texas-based family foundation, "focuses on environmental projects . . . including work on pollution control, natural resources protection, sustainable technologies, and population stabilization." Visitors to its Web site can access basic information on its application guidelines; lists of 1992–1996 grantees by subject area, location, and organization name; and full grant descriptions for the same period, with the amount of the grant and contact information included for each grantee.

CHAPTER THREE

Grantmaking Public Charities on the Web

What Is a Public Charity?

There are upwards of 600,000 public charities registered with the IRS under Section 501(c)(3) of the Internal Revenue Code. This is more than ten times the number of private foundations. Grantmaking public charities, often referred to as "public foundations," differ from private foundations in several ways, but primarily in the diversity of their support. As described in Chapter 2, private foundations typically draw their funds from a single source, either an individual, a family, or a company. With the exception of those that are endowed, the majority of public charities are supported by contributions from multiple sources, possibly including individuals, foundations, churches, and government agencies, augmented in some cases with income generated from charitable activities.

For a nonprofit organization to qualify as a public charity within the IRS definition, it must meet the requirements of the "public support test." This test normally requires an organization to receive *no more than* 30 percent of its support from gross investment and unrelated business income and to receive *at least* 30 percent of its income from the public in contributions, fees, and gross receipts related to the organization's exempt purpose.

Because public charities are assumed to be accountable to a broad support base, the regulations and reporting requirements are less stringent than they are for private foundations. Gifts to public charities are commonly eligible for maximum income tax deductibility, whereas those to private foundations are limited in this respect. Furthermore, public charities and private foundations follow different

93

annual IRS reporting requirements: public charities file Form 990 and Schedule A; private foundations file Form 990-PF.

The fact that the IRS uses the "exclusionary definition" of a private foundation as a 501(c)(3) organization that is not a church, school, hospital, or a government or a publicly supported charity has at times been a source of confusion: when a public charity fails the "public support test," it is listed with the IRS as a private foundation. The Foundation Center does not consider these "failed public charities" to be true private foundations and does not count them in its statistics on the foundation field. To further confuse the issue, a few formerly "private" foundations have deliberately qualified for "public charity" status. Perhaps the simplest definition of a public charity is a *publicly supported nonprofit organization that has been classified as "not a private foundation" and is not required to file a Form 990-PF tax return.*

It is important to remember that most grantmaking public charities are by definition grantseekers as well, with the full tax deductibility mentioned earlier. Another characteristic of grantmaking public charities is that their giving interests are typically very specific, addressing a narrow or single field of interest, a specific population group, or a limited geographic community, as is true for community foundations. For the public charities listed here, their grantmaking activity may be only a small part of their overall charitable program.

Community foundations are usually public charities and not required to file a Form 990-PF. Traditionally, in its statistical analyses the Foundation Center has included community foundations in its directories of private foundations because their primary activity is grantmaking, and so their more formal grantmaking operations and grant-reporting capabilities allow them to be represented logically and systematically within that group. Now that the Center is identifying and tracking other grantmaking public charities, for definitional clarity we can present community foundations as a group within the grantmaking public charity universe. This presentation follows the organization of the Center's *National Directory of Grantmaking Public Charities.* The Center's links to community foundations later in this chapter are organized by state, as most community foundations are focused principally on a specific geographic area.

In recent years, the Foundation Center has identified hundreds of public charities that have some sort of grantmaking program. In this chapter we include those that had a World Wide Web presence at the time of writing.

This chapter does not present a comprehensive picture of the public charity universe. This is largely because at this time there is no simple way to identify systematically those non-foundation charities that in fact do operate clearly defined giving programs. We hope that our continued efforts to manually gather information on grantmaking public charities will stimulate those organizations that believe they qualify to be included in such listings to contact us and forward information concerning their grantmaking programs.

Links and Abstracts of Community Foundation Web Sites

In its general charitable purposes, a community foundation is much like a private foundation; its funds, however, are derived from many donors rather than a single source, as is usually the case with private foundations. Further, community foundations are usually classified under the tax code as public charities and therefore are subject to different rules and regulations than those which govern private foundations. Community foundations represent a growing segment of the field of philanthropy. Be sure to check the "Grantmaker Information" area of <fdncenter.org> for the latest listing.

ALASKA

Alaska Conservation Foundation <http://fdncenter.org/grantmaker/alaska/index.html>

Established in 1980, the Alaska Conservation Foundation receives funds and makes grants to protect the integrity of Alaska's ecosystems and to promote sustainable livelihoods among its communities and peoples. New areas of interest for ACF include advocacy, community development, public communications, public policy, and rural affairs. The Foundation's guidelines favor approaches that convene diverse constituencies, promote citizen participation in public process, provide forums for increasing environmental awareness, and build capacity to implement sustainable futures. The Foundation's "folder" on the Center's Web site offers a mission statement, a brief history of the Foundation and facts about the state of Alaska, program descriptions, grant guidelines and application procedures, a section on ways to give to ACF, and contact information.

ARKANSAS

Foundation for the Mid South <http://www.fndmidsouth.org/>

The Foundation for the Mid South makes grants "to build the capacity of communities, organizations, and individuals" throughout the states of Arkansas, Louisiana, and Mississippi. Grants are made within the three primary program areas of economic development, education, and families and children. In addition to general information about the Foundation, visitors to the Web site will find detailed program descriptions, including types of funding provided within each program area; downloadable application forms in the .PDF format; and an interactive bulletin board through which regional grantseekers and grantmakers can communicate. Selections from the Foundation's 1995 annual report, including listings of 1994–1995 grants by program area, are also available.

CALIFORNIA

California Community Foundation <http://www.calfund.org/>

Established in 1915, the California Community Foundation was Los Angeles's first grantmaking institution and is the country's second-oldest community foundation. The Foundation makes grants to organizations serving the greater Los Angeles region in the following areas: human services, children and youth, community development, civic affairs, community health, community education, arts and culture, the environment, and animal welfare. Visitors to the Foundation's Web site will find a range of general information as well as grant guidelines and a downloadable version of the Foundation's grant application form, a list of recent grants, brief bios of selected donors, a list of Foundation-sponsored publications, and a calendar of upcoming Foundation-related events.

Community Foundation of Santa Cruz County <http://www.cfscc.org/>
The Foundation's single page on the Web provides basic contact information, including phone and fax numbers and an e-mail hot link for information requests.

Community Foundation Silicon Valley <http://www.commfdn.org/>
The Community Foundation Silicon Valley (formerly the Community Foundation of Santa Clara County) changed its name in November 1997 to better reflect the entrepreneurial spirit, creativity, and diversity of the community it serves. The Foundation supports programs that benefit the residents of Santa Clara County and southern San Mateo County in the following areas: arts and humanities, community and social services, education, the environment, and health. In addition, the Foundation's Neighborhood Grants Program promotes "the development of healthy and self-reliant neighborhoods by supporting residents to unify for action, actualize their collective power, and create community-based solutions to physical, social, and economic challenges." Low-to-middle-income neighborhoods in Santa Clara County receive priority. The Foundation's Web site provides general program information, application guidelines, a list of recent grants, an electronic form for ordering copies of the Foundation's print publications, related links, and e-mail contact information. A Foundation calendar, along with the results of the 1997 Corporate Community Involvement Study, is also posted.

Glendale Community Foundation <http://www.cwire.com/GCF/>
Founded in 1956 as part of Glendale's 50th anniversary celebration, the Glendale Community Foundation exists to improve the quality of life for the people of the greater Glendale community—Glendale, La Crescenta, La Cañada Flintridge, Montrose, and Verdugo City—by leveraging community assets. The Foundation administers gifts and grants according to donors' wishes and uses the income from unrestricted gifts to fund hard asset acquisitions (i.e., capital equipment and improvements) and programming for local charities to make them more efficient and effective. Visitors to the Foundation's Web site will find general information on community foundations, a brief history of the Foundation itself, grant application guidelines and procedures, recent issues of the Foundation's quarterly newsletter, and information on ways to give and the benefits of giving to donors.

Humboldt Area Foundation
<http://www.northcoast.com/~hafound/welcome.html>
The Humboldt Area Foundation was established in 1972 as a vehicle of and for the citizens of the North Coast of California—that is, Humboldt, Del Norte, and parts of Trinity and Siskiyou counties. In addition to general information about the Foundation itself, its Web site provides detailed grant application guidelines and an overview of the resources available to nonprofit organizations at the Foundation-operated William T. Rooney Resource Center.

Marin Community Foundation <http://midas.org/npo/mcf/mcf.html>
The mission of the Marin Community Foundation is to help improve the human condition and to enhance the quality of life of the community for generations to come. MCF's Web site includes a good deal of information about the Foundation and its programs, a list of recent grants, the names of staff and board members, a reference library and links to related sites.

North Valley Community Foundation <http://www.nvcf.org/>

NVCF serves rural communities in Northern California by operating and/or assisting a number of programs dedicated to improvements in those communities. NVCF programs include a Graffiti Eradication program (Chico and Oroville); Leadership Chico, which is dedicated to providing potential and existing community leaders with leadership training; Tomorrow's Leaders Today, which provides students in their junior year at Chico schools with leadership skills; Farm-City Celebration, a fall program dedicated to bringing agriculture and related aspects of the Ag industry to urban residents; P.A.R.T., a collaboration of many groups dedicated to increasing public knowledge of the agricultural industry; and Supporters of V.I.P.S., which provides equipment and supplies to a citizens group that assists local law enforcement. In addition to information about these and other Foundation activities, the NVCF Web site provides a good deal of general information about community foundations and the community foundation movement, a nice set of links to related organizations, and contact information.

Peninsula Community Foundation <http://www.pcf.org/>

Created by residents of the San Francisco peninsula in 1964, the Peninsula Community Foundation today provides funding for nonprofit groups in San Mateo and Santa Clara counties that address the needs of children, youth and families, or that work in the areas of education, health and human services, housing and homelessness, the arts, or civic and public benefit. During 1997, the Foundation made grants totaling $21 million, including $4 million in grants from its endowment funds and $17 million from advised funds. Through its Center for Venture Philanthropy, the Foundations is also forging partnerships of donor/investors "to make long-term, focused investments in complex programs . . . [such as] as school reform and welfare reform." In addition to information for potential donors, visitors to the PCF Web site will find general program information, current grantmaking guidelines, a list of recent grants, board and staff listings (including e-mail links), a calendar of deadline and events, a section devoted to the Foundation's "Strategic Philanthropy" initiatives (i.e., the Center for Venture Philanthropy, the Peninsula Partnership for Children, Youth and Families, Every Kid a Start-Up Fund, the Prenatal to Three Initiative, and the Neighborhood Grants program), and contact information.

San Diego Community Foundation <http://www.sdcf.org/>

The mission of the San Diego Community Foundation is "to assist donors to build and preserve enduring assets for charitable purposes in the San Diego Region; to monitor and assess changing needs and to meet those needs through financial awards and organizational support." Incorporated in 1975, the SDCF has assets of more than $175 million in some 350 separate funds. Approximately nine percent of the Foundation's endowments generate discretionary income, which is distributed through a community grants program. The Foundation also operates the Funding Information Center, a Foundation Center Cooperating Collection, which provides free access and technical assistance to anyone seeking nonprofit or educational funding. In addition to general information, visitors to the Foundation's Web site will find descriptive lists of its 1998 spring grant awards; excerpts from recent Foundation newsletters; staff and board listings; and contact information.

The San Francisco Foundation <http://www.sff.org/>

With more than $500 million in assets and annual giving in excess of $40 million, the San Francisco Foundation is one of the largest community foundations in the country. As the community foundation serving Alameda, Contra Costa, Marin, San Francisco, and San Mateo counties, it partners with diverse donors and organizations to mobilize resources in the promotion of vibrant, sustainable communities throughout the Bay Area. The Foundation, which marks its fiftieth anniversary this year, awards grants to nonprofit organizations in the fields of arts and humanities, community health, education, the environment, neighborhood and community development, social services, and philanthropy. The Foundation's easy-to-navigate Web site provides a good deal of information about Foundation activities, past and present; its grantmaking, including program priorities, selected grants in each program area, and grantee profiles; information about the Koshland Civic Unity Awards, the Foundation's Special Awards Program, and the Foundation's Community Initiative Funds; information for prospective donors; answers to frequently asked questions; a short list of Foundation publications available upon request; and contact information.

Sonoma Community Foundation <http://www.sonoma.org/>

The Sonoma Community Foundation administers and awards grants from a permanent endowment to eligible nonprofit organizations based and operating in Sonoma County, California, in the areas of health and human services, education, the environment, and the arts. The Foundation also manages and distributes monies from several individual funds established to support the specific philanthropic interests of their donors. In 1995, a single bequest increased the Foundation's assets from close to $6 million to more than $23 million. The Foundation's Web site is currently under construction and basic information—including 1998 grant guidelines, application materials and contact information—is listed.

Sonora Area Foundation <http://www.nsierra.org/gov/saf/>

The mission of the Sonora Area Foundation is "to enhance the community and the quality of life of its residents through facilitating the philanthropic intentions of donors, and the needs of the surrounding communities." The Foundation awards approximately 30 grants per year to nonprofit and public agencies throughout the Tuolumne County, California, area for projects that have the greatest affect on the largest number of people. Visitors to the Foundation's Web site will find a brief history of the Foundation, a list of 1993 and 1994 grants, descriptions of each individual fund administered by the Foundation, grant funding policies and limitations, application instructions, a listing of Foundation board members, and contact information.

CONNECTICUT

Hartford Foundation for Public Giving <http://www.hartnet.org/~hfpg1/>

Established in 1925 to serve the changing needs of Connecticut's Capitol region, the Hartford Foundation for Public Giving ranks as the ninth-largest community foundation in the country. Newly redesigned, the Foundation's Web site provides general information about the Foundation and its programs, a breakdown of its 1996 giving by category and an alphabetical listing of the Foundation's 1996 grant recipients, listings of the board and staff, an overview of financial mangement issues, and contact information. Organizations interested in applying for a grant are encouraged to call for the Foundation's guidelines and to discuss their interests with a member of the Foundation's program staff prior to planning a grant application. The site also includes a description of the 1996 grants initiative and a listing of the Foundation's publications.

FLORIDA

The Community Foundation for Palm Beach and Martin Counties
<http://www.cfpbmc.org/>
Founded in 1972 by Michael and Winsome McIntosh, "a communtiy-conscious couple from New York," the Community Foundation for Palm Beach and Martin Counties today is a thriving enterprise with a $50,000,000 endowment representing the gifts and commitments of many people. The Foundation applies the income from its assets to a wide range of community needs, including human and race relations, arts and culture, education, community development, health, human services, the environment, and the conservation and preservation of historical and cultural resources. In addition to a mission statement, a brief history of the Foundation, and listings of the Foundation's board, officers, and staff, the CFPBMC Web site provides program descriptions and information about the Foundation's Dwight Allison Fellows Program, grant guidelines and eligibility requirements, a selection of recent grants, a section on ways to give to the Foundation, and information about its Funding Resource Center.

The Community Foundation of Sarasota County
<http://www.communityfoundation.com/>
The Community Foundation of Sarasota County supports a variety of worthy causes throughout the West Coast of Florida, including the arts and culture (increasing audiences for local artistic pursuits), community development (encouraging access to and use of community-based development methods), education (early childhood development, primary education through completion of high school and preparation for employment), the environment (promoting ways to conserve resources, encourage responsible animal welfare, and protect wildlife), health (basic medical, dental, and mental health needs), and human services (families, youth, seniors, the disabled, and the disadvantaged). The Foundation also administers 14 scholarship funds designated for students in Charlotte, Manatee and Sarasota Counties, Florida. Scholarship recipients are selected on an objective, competitive basis that takes into account academic and non-academic factors plus demonstrated financial need. Visitors to the Foundation's Web site will find application guidelines, a current grants list, scholarship information, and information for donors.

GEORGIA

Atlanta Women's Fund <http://www.atlantawomensfund.org/index2.html>

ILLINOIS

The Aurora Foundation <http://fdncenter.org/grantmaker/aurora/>

Established in 1948, the Aurora Foundation provides scholarships to students and grants to nonprofit organizations in the greater Aurora, Ilinois area, including the Tri-Cities and Kendall County. The Foundation's "folder" on the Center's Web site includes a mission statement and a "letter to the community"; information on ways to give and benefits to donors; a statement of principal transactions for the fiscal year ended September 30, 1996; a summary of grants awarded in 1996; and a listing of directors, officers, and staff.

INDIANA

Central Indiana Community Foundation <http://www.cicf.org/>

The Central Indiana Community Foundation is the product of a collaborative effort between community foundations serving Marion and Hamilton Counties. The founding partners of CICF -the Hamilton County Legacy Fund and the Indianapolis Foundation—are "committed to a structure that sustains local engagement, leadership and capacity while supporting an expanded level of philanthropic service and growth for the region." In addition to assisting the community in "convening, consensus building and problem solving," the Foundation supports and coordinates a variety of special projects, including the Neighborhood Preservation Initiative, the Youth, Sport and Fitness Network, the Library Fund and Project Hi-Net, the Marion County Education Foundation Network, and the Partnership for National Service. Visitors to CICF's well-organized Web site will find a wealth of information about the Foundation's mission, donor services, programs, and initiatives, as well as links to resources of interest.

KANSAS

Greater Kansas City Community Foundation <http://www.gkccf.org/>

Established in 1978 and today comprised of more than 500 charitable funds, the Greater Kansas City Community Foundation strives "to make a positive difference in the lives and future of the people in Greater Kansas City"—Jackson, Clay, and Platte counties in Missouri and Johnson and Wyandotte counties in Kansas— "through grant making, advocacy, support of the not-for-profit sector and promotion of philanthropy for the benefit of the community." In addition to a listing of the Foundation's board and officers, contact information, and links to other sites of interest, visitors to the site will find general descriptions of the Foundation's programs, a listing of scholarships available through the Foundation, information about important Foundation initiatives in the areas of early childhood education and homelessness, application guidelines, and a section devoted to the services the Foundation provides to donors. The site also includes a listing of Foudation publications, an upcoming events calendar, grant recipient profiles and a section devoted to the Foundation's most recent annual report.

LOUISIANA

Foundation for the Mid South <http://www.fndmidsouth.org/>

The Foundation for the Mid South makes grants "to build the capacity of communities, organizations, and individuals" throughout the states of Arkansas, Louisiana, and Mississippi. Grants are made within the three primary program areas of economic development, education, and families and children. In addition to general information about the Foundation, visitors to the Web site will find detailed program descriptions, including types of funding provided within each program area; downloadable application forms in the .PDF format; and an interactive bulletin board through which regional grantseekers and grantmakers can communicate. Selections from the Foundation's 1995 annual report, including listings of 1994–1995 grants by program area, are also available.

MAINE

Community Foundation of Cape Cod <http://agmconnect.org/cfcc1.html>

Maine Community Foundation <http://www.mainecf.org/>

The Maine Community Foundation administers a variety of individual funds established to support a wide range of organizations and programs within the state of Maine. Funds may be restricted by their donors to support specific programmatic or geographic interests, while others are unrestricted and distributed at the Foundation's discretion. Discretionary grants are not made for lobbying or religious activities, and are not generally awarded for endowment purposes, equipment, annual campaigns, regular operations, or capital campaigns. The Foundation also manages scholarship funds, provides technical assistance to guide grantseekers through the fundraising process, and is involved with a number of initiatives that provide major support to address specific issues within Maine. Visitors to the MCF Web site will find general information about the Foundation, application procedures, and a staff listing. The site includes a full description of the Foundation's programs and a newly created news and events area. Visitors will also find contact information as well as links to a handful of other Maine-based philanthropic organizations.

MARYLAND

Community Foundation of the Eastern Shore
<http://www.intercom.net/npo/commfnd/>

The Community Foundation of the Eastern Shore is dedicated to improving the quality of life in Worcester, Wicomico, and Somerset counties, Maryland. The Foundation manages and distributes monies from individual funds in the areas of education, health and human services, arts and culture, community development and conservation, and historic preservation. Grants are awarded to nonprofit organizations located within or serving the three counties for three general purposes: "as seed funding for special projects that meet priority needs; as expansion funding to enable successful programs to serve broader constituencies; and to strengthen small and moderate sized nonprofit agencies that are providing exemplary services within [Foundation] areas of interest." Grants are usually not made for long-term operating support, building and endowment projects, budget deficits, sectarian programs, or direct assistance to individuals, other than through scholarship funds. Visitors to the Foundation's Web page will find general information about the Foundation, application guidelines and instructions, and contact information.

MASSACHUSSETS

Greater Lowell Community Foundation
<http://www.agmconnect.org/glcf.html>

Greater Worcester Community Foundation
<http://www.agmconnect.org/gwcf1.html>

MICHIGAN

The Community Foundation for Muskegon County <http://www.cffmc.org/>
Founded in 1961, the Community Foundation for Muskegon County is committed to improving the quality of life for the residents of Muskegon County, Michigan. In addition to managing numerous individual funds earmarked for specific philanthropic purposes, the Foundation also awards grants from a pool of discretionary income. Discretionary grants are made to support community projects in the areas of arts, education, community development, health and human services, and youth issues. The Foundation's Web site provides descriptions of Foundation-administered grant programs, scholarships, and special Foundation initiatives, as well as general application information. The site also includes a listing of recent scholarship recipients and a Foundation newsletter.

Community Foundation of Greater Flint <http://www.flint.lib.mi.us/cfflint/>
Through its support of "projects aimed at solving community problems or enhancing life in the county," the Community Foundation of Greater Flint is committed to improving the quality of life in Genesee County, Michigan. The Foundation makes grants through more than 100 funds in the fields of arts and humanities; advancing philanthropy; community services; education; conservation and the environment; and health, human, and social services. The Foundation also makes limited grants from discretionary funds, with special priority given to programs addressing issues of persistent and pervasive poverty and children under the age of ten. The Foundation does not make grants to individuals, for sectarian religious purposes, budget deficits, routine operating expenses of existing organizations, or endowments. Visitors to the Foundation's simple, straightforward Web site will find general information about the Foundation and its funding priorities, application guidelines, and information for potential donors.

The Grand Rapids Foundation <http://www.grfoundation.org/>

Greater Rochester Area Community Foundation
<http://metronet.lib.mi.us/ROCH/gracf/gracf.html>
The Greater Rochester Area Foundation makes grants to individuals for educational scholarships, and to nonprofit organizations located in or serving the

citizens of Rochester, Rochester Hills, and Oakland Township, Michigan. The Foundation manages and awards grants from more than 50 individual funds in the general areas of arts and culture, civic beautification, community development, education and scholarships, health and human concerns, recreation, science, and youth. The Foundation's Web site provides visitors with application information, a complete listing of individual funds and their specific areas of interest, and a listing of the Foundation's board of trustees.

Holland Community Foundation <http://www.macatawa.org/org/hcf/>

MINNESOTA

The Minneapolis Foundation <http://www.mplsfoundation.org/>
Created more than 80 years ago to encourage and facilitate philanthropy in the Minneapolis-St. Paul area, the Minneapolis Foundation today seeks to improve the quality of life in the Twin Cities by making program or project-specific support grants, operating support grants, and capital support grants in the following areas: children, youth and families in poverty; public policy research; neighborhood capacity building; economic development and employment; low-income senior citizens; people with disabilities; health care for low-income citizens; and medical research and services for children's chronic diseases. Program details are fully explained in the Foundation's grant guidelines, which can be ordered from the Publications area of the Foundation's Web site or through the Foundation's fax on demand system (612/672-3870). The site also offers brief descriptions of a dozen of the Foundation's programs and projects, press releases and a regional events calendar, information for prospective donors, financial statements and a copy of the Foundation's 990 form for 1996–97, listings of the Foundation's staff, board, and trustees, and contact information.

The Saint Paul Foundation <http://www.tspf.org/>
The Saint Paul Foundation was established in 1940 with a $5,000 bequest from a Lithuanian immigrant named Annie Paper. Today, it's the largest community foundation in the state of Minnesota and a major philanthropic force in the city of Saint Paul. In 1997, the Foundation approved more than 1,800 grants totaling some $24 million in eight fields of interest: arts and humanities, civic affairs, education, environment and nature, health, human services, religion, and scholarships. The Foundation's frames-driven Web site provides general information for grantseekers, scholarship seekers, and prospective donors, a separate section on its Diversity Endowment Funds initiative, and contact information.

MISSISSIPPI

Foundation for the Mid South <http://www.fndmidsouth.org/>
The Foundation for the Mid South makes grants "to build the capacity of communities, organizations, and individuals" throughout the states of Arkansas, Louisiana, and Mississippi. Grants are made within the three primary program areas of economic development, education, and families and children. In addition to general information about the Foundation, visitors to the Web site will find detailed program descriptions, including types of funding provided within each program

area; downloadable application forms in the .PDF format; and an interactive bulletin board through which regional grantseekers and grantmakers can communicate. Selections from the Foundation's 1995 annual report, including listings of 1994–1995 grants by program area, are also available.

MISSOURI

The Greater Kansas City Community Foundation <http://www.gkccf.org/

Established in 1978 and today comprised of more than 500 charitable funds, the Greater Kansas City Community Foundation strives "to make a positive difference in the lives and future of the people in Greater Kansas City"—Jackson, Clay, and Platte counties in Missouri and Johnson and Wyandotte counties in Kansas— "through grant making, advocacy, support of the not-for-profit sector and promotion of philanthropy for the benefit of the community." In addition to a listing of the Foundation's board and officers, contact information, and links to other sites of interest, visitors to the site will find general descriptions of the Foundation's programs, a listing of scholarships available through the Foundation, information about important Foundation intiatives in the areas of early childhood education and homelessness, application guidelines, and a section devoted to the services the Foundation provides to donors. The site also includes a list of Foundation publications, the 1996 annual report and an area featuring upcoming events.

MONTANA

Montana Community Foundation <http://www.mtcf.org/startpage.html>

NEBRASKA

The Grand Island Community Foundation <http://www.gicf.org/>

The Grand Island Community Foundation was established in 1960 to make a lasting difference in the quality of life for greater Hall County area citizens. The Foundation does not operate charitable programs itself, but rather, through partnering and coordination, assists in orchestrating charitable activities within the greater Hall County community. The principle vehicle for its activities in this area is the GICF "wish list," which leverages the GICF Web site and other emerging communications technologies to bring potential donors together with worthwhile charitable causes and organizations. In addition to the still-developing "wish list" and general background information, the GICF Web site provides information about a number of endowed scholarship funds established by people and organizations wanting to assist Grand Island and Hall County area students in continuing their education beyond high school.

Lincoln Community Foundation <http://www.lcf.org/>

The Lincoln Community Foundation makes grants to enrich the quality of life in Lincoln and Lancaster Counties, Nebraska. The Foundation administers and disperses monies from a permanent unrestricted endowment, responding to emerging and changing community needs and sustaining existing organizations through grants for education, arts and culture, health, social services, economic development, and civic affairs. The Foundation also manages a number of individual funds established by donors with specific philanthropic interests. Visitors to the Foundation's Web site will find general discretionary funding guidelines and restrictions, application instructions (including the common application form accepted by a number of area grantmakers), information for donors interested in establishing funds, and a staff listing. Visitors will also find a listing of 1997 grant recipients as well as excerpts from the 1997 annual report.

NEVADA

Nevada Women's Fund <http://www.jour.unr.edu/women/>

NEW JERSEY

Princeton Area Community Foundation
<http://www.princetonol.com/groups/pacf/>
The PACF was established in 1991 to bring the services of a community foundation to the greater Mercer County area. Today, the Foundation seeks "to enter into partnerships with non-profit organizations that are actively involved in developing their community," while supporting "groups working to coordinate resources and strengthen relationships between residents, businesses and institutions in a neighborhood." In addition to a brief history of the Foundation and information about the New Jersey AIDS Partnership, the PACF Web site provides application guidelines; a listing of the Foundation's various unrestricted, donor-advised, memorial, and scholarship funds; 1997 grants lists; brief trustee and associate profiles; and information for prospective donors.

NEW MEXICO

Albuquerque Community Foundation <http://www.swcp.com/~albcfdn/>
The Albuquerque Community Foundation manages a pool of charitable funds whose income is used to benefit the greater Albuquerque, New Mexico, community through grants to nonprofit organizations, educational programs, and scholarships. The general policy of the Foundation is to allocate funds to nonprofits (including educational institutions) whose purpose and continuing work is in the areas of arts and culture, education, health and human services, and environmental and historic preservation. ACF's well-organized Web site provides information about its grant policies and restrictions, detailed proposal guidelines, a section for prospective donors, board and staff listings, useful links to regional and national nonprofit resources, and contact information.

The Santa Fe Community Foundation <http://www.santafecf.org>

NEW YORK

Northern Chautauqua Community Foundation
<http://fdncenter.org/grantmaker/nccf/index.html>
The mission of the Northern Chautauqua Community Foundation is to enrich the area it serves. To that end, the Foundation, which was established in 1986, has five primary goals: to be a catalyst for the establishment of endowments to benefit the

community both now and in the future; to provide a vehicle for donors' varied interests; to promote local philanthropy; to serve as a steward of funds; and to provide leadership and resources in addressing local challenges and opportunities. The Foundation's "folder" on the Center's Web site provides lists of recent grants and scholarships awarded by the Foundation, brief descriptions of the many funds it administers, 1997 financial statements, a short section on "How to Become a Community Philanthropist," and a roster of the Foundation's board, staff, and members. (1/7/98)

Rochester Area Community Foundation <http://www.racf.org/>

Currently celebrating its 25th anniversary, the Rochester Area Community Foundation manages more than 500 funds that provide grants for a wide variety of arts, education, social service, and other civic purposes in the Genesee Valley region of upstate New York. Although the Foundation's Web site is very much under construction, visitors to the "Contact" section of the site can get a good sense of RACF's services and request a variety of information—including grant guidelines and application and request forms—through a convenient online order form.

NORTH CAROLINA

Community Foundation of Greater Greensboro <http://www.cfgg.org/>

The Community Foundation of Greater Greensboro "promotes philanthropy, builds and maintains a permanent collection of endowment funds, and serves as a trustworthy partner and leader in shaping effective responses" to issues and opportunities in the Greater Greensboro, North Carolina, community. Geared more to potential donors than grantseekers, the Foundation's attractive Web site provides general information about the various funds and endowments managed by CFGG, '96–'97 grants information organized by category (grants from unrestricted endowment funds, grants from special interest endowment funds, and permanent revolving loan funds), answers to frequently asked questions, general financial information, profiles of recent donors and grant recipients, listings of the Foundation's board and staff, and current and previous issues of Horizon, the Foundation's newsletter.

Foundation For The Carolinas <http://www.fftc.org/fftc/>

With assets in excess of $200 million and annual giving of $25 million, the 40-year-old Foundation For The Carolinas is the largest community foundation in the Carolinas. Building A Better Future, the Foundation's major grantmaking program, awards grants only to organizations located in or serving the greater Charlotte area. Other grant opportunities are available through affiliated community foundations serving the Lexington area and Blowing Rock, Cabarrus, Cleveland, Iredell, and Union counties in North Carolina, and Cherokee, Lancaster, and York counties in South Carolina. Specialized grants programs operated by FFTC include the Salisbury Community Foundation (Salibury and Rowan counties), the African American Community Endowment Fund (Charlotte-Mecklenburg and surrounding communities), the Cole Foundation Endowment (Richmond County area), HIV/AIDS Consortium Grants (13 Charlotte-area counties), and the Medical Research Grants program (North and South Carolina). In addition to a good deal of information aimed at potential donors, the Foundation's well-organized

Web site provides general program information, guidelines, and deadlines; listings of senior management and board members; an electronic form for requesting copies of the Foundation's publications; and contact information.

Triangle Community Foundation <http://www.trianglecf.org/>

The mission of the Triangle Community Foundation is to expand private philanthropy in the communities of the greater Triangle area, including Wake, Durham, and Orange Counties, North Carolina. The Foundation is comprised of more than 230 individual philanthropic funds with combined total assets currently exceeding $34 million. The Foundation also distributes discretionary monies for new initiatives or one-time special projects in cultural affairs and the arts, community development, education, environmental issues, health, social services, and other areas that benefit residents of the region. Visitors to the Foundation's Web site will find eligibility guidelines, application procedures, a recent grants list, and featured articles from its current newsletter. Visitors with Active-X enabled browsers can also download an application form in Microsoft Word 6.0 format.

OHIO

The Columbus Foundation <http://www.columbusfoundation.com/>

Established in 1943 under the guidance of Harrison M. Sayre, the Columbus Foundation today is one of the largest community foundations in the country. Dedicated to improving the lives of people in central Ohio, the Foundation addresses pressing needs in the community through grantmaking focused on four strategic areas: making sure that all children enter school physically, emotionally, and developmentally prepared to learn; helping youth make a positive transition to young adulthood; building the capacity of families to provide safe, nurturing, and economically secure living environments; and making neighborhoods positive environments for living. The Foundation also gives consideration to the following areas: arts and humanities, conservation, education, health, social services, urban affairs, and advancing philanthropy. In addition to general information about the Foundation, visitors to the Web site will find proposal guidelines and a.PDF version of the Foundation's proposal cover sheet; information about the scholarship funds it administers as well as its grantmaking strategies; a range of downloadble trust forms; the results of a 1996 community foundation survey; and an online version of Commentary, the Foundation's newsletter.

Community Foundation of Greater Lorain County
<http://www.centuryinter.net/cfglc/>

The Community Foundation of Greater Lorain County makes grants to improve the quality of life in Lorain County, Ohio, and has a special interest in programs that have a positive impact upon the most disadvantaged in the community. The Foundation manages and awards grants from more than 177 individual donor funds, and acts as a catalyst in helping to identify community problems. Through its discretionary grantmaking activities, the Foundation's major fields of interest are arts and culture, civic affairs, education, health, and social services. Visitors to the Foundation's Web site will find general information regarding the Foundation's mission and grantmaking activities, and options for donors.

Parkersburg Area Community Foundation
<http://fdncenter.org/grantmaker/pacf/index.html>
The Parkersburg Area Community Foundation is committed to serving the people of the Mid-Ohio Valley—Wood, Pleasants, Tyler, Ritchie, Doddridge, Gilmer, Wirt, Calhoun, Roane, Jackson, and Mason Counties in West Virginia and Washington County in Ohio—by linking community resources with community needs. PACF focuses its grantmaking in the following areas: arts and culture, education, health and human services, recreation, and youth and family services. To be eligible for a grant from the Foundation, an applicant must be a private, non-profit, tax-exempt organization under section 501(c)(3) of the Internal Revenue Code, or they must be a public institution. The Foundation also administers more than 40 different scholarship funds, the majority of which are designated for students in Wood County, West Virginia. The Foundation's "folder" on the Center's Web site provides general information about the Foundation, detailed application guidelines and scholarship information, and general information about becoming a donor to the Foundation.

OKLAHOMA

Oklahoma City Community Foundation
<http://connections.oklahoman.net/commfound/>

PENNSYLVANIA

The Philadelphia Foundation <http://www.phlfound.org/>
The Philadelphia Foundation serves as a vehicle and resource for philanthropy in Bucks, Chester, Delaware, Montgomery, and Philadelphia counties. It does this by developing, managing, and allocating community resources in partnership with donors and grantees, by building on community assets, and by promoting empowerment, leadership, and civic participation among underserved groups. The Foundation makes grants from over 250 individually named charitable trust funds, with assets totaling $120 million. Grant distributions are made according to the charitable interests and specifications of the individual fund donors, but the Foundation also identifies emerging needs in the community and sets policies and priorities for distributing unrestricted dollars in the areas of children and families; community organizing and advocacy; culture; education; health; housing and economic development; and social services. To be eligible for any funding through the Foundation, organizations must have 501(c)(3) tax exempt status and be based in one of the five counties of southeastern Pennsylvania. The Foundation's Web site offers application guidelines, detailed information about the various individual funds under the Foundation's auspices, the Foundation's financial management policies, and listings of recipient organizations, its Board of Managers, and staff. Vistors to the site can also access the "What's New" section and a donor information area.

Three Rivers Community Fund <http://www.fex.org/three/threeriv.html>

PUERTO RICO

Puerto Rico Community Foundation <http://www.fcpr.org/>

Through its support of self-directed development of Puerto Rican community groups, the Puerto Rico Community Foundation "seeks to contribute to the growth of a healthier community, [acting] as a catalytic agent in fostering new and innovative solutions to the Island's problems." Although the Foundation concentrates its efforts on the needs of Puerto Ricans on the island, it collaborates with Puerto Rican communities in the United States as well. Visitors to the Foundation's Web site will find descriptions of its various programs, including the general fund, the permanent fund for the arts, the community housing development organizations program, the middle school renewal initiative, and the institute for the development of philanthropy; a listing of the Foundation's board of directors and staff; and links to other philanthropic resources on the web.

RHODE ISLAND

The Rhode Island Foundation <http://www.rifoundation.org/>

SOUTH CAROLINA

The Community Foundation Serving Coastal South Carolina
<http://www.studiosite.com/tcf/>

The mission of the Community Foundation Serving Coastal South Carolina (TCF) is "to address community needs by fostering philanthropy through customized services to donors and to the community." All charitable 501(c)(3) organizations in Berkeley, Charleston, and Dorchester counties are eligible for funding through TCF's "Open Grants" program; the annual application deadline is July 15. TCF's Web site consists of two major components: "What Gives?," the Foundation's quarterly newsletter; and the Foundation's 1994–95 annual report, which provides condensed financial statements; a sample grants list; listings of donors, individual funds, board members, and staff; and information on giving opportunities through the Foundation. Detailed application guidelines may be obtained directly from the Foundation, and contact information is provided.

Foundation For The Carolinas <http://www.fftc.org/fftc/>

With assets in excess of $200 million and annual giving of $25 million, the 40-year-old Foundation For The Carolinas is the largest community foundation in the Carolinas. Building A Better Future, the Foundation's major grantmaking program, awards grants only to organizations located in or serving the greater Charlotte area. Other grant opportunities are available through affiliated community foundations serving the Lexington area and Blowing Rock, Cabarrus, Cleveland, Iredell, and Union counties in North Carolina, and Cherokee, Lancaster, and York counties in South Carolina. Specialized grants programs operated by FFTC include the Salisbury Community Foundation (Salibury and Rowan counties), the African American Community Endowment Fund (Charlotte-Mecklenburg and surrounding communities), the Cole Foundation Endowment (Richmond County area), HIV/AIDS Consortium Grants (13 Charlotte area counties), and the Medical Research Grants program (North and South Carolina). In addition to a good deal of information aimed at potential donors, the Foundation's well-organized Web site provides general program information, guidelines, and deadlines; listings of senior management and board members; an electronic form for requesting copies of the Foundation's publications; and contact information.

TEXAS

Kerrville Area Community Trust <http://www.iresources.com/kact/>

In operation since 1981, the Kerrville Area Community Trust is a collection of individual funds and resources given by local citizens and organizations to enhance and support the quality of life in the Kerrville, Texas, area. The KACT web site provides detailed information on the Trust and the community trust concept; answers to frequently asked questions about the Trust; a summary of KACT grants made since 1982; grant application guidelines, policies, deadlines, and a downloadable grant application form; information about established KACT funds; a list of KACT publications; the Trust's regional calendar of events and an area featuring nonprofit organizations and community resources in Kerr County.

Lubbock Area Foundation
<http://fdncenter.org/grantmaker/lubbock/index.html>

The Lubbock Area Foundation was created in 1981 to help Texas South Plains residents realize their long-term philanthropic goals. The Foundation manages a pool of charitable funds, the income from which is used to benefit the South Plains community through grants to 501(c)(3) nonprofit organizations, educational programs, and scholarships. Grants, the typical range for which is $500-$2,500, are made for start-up funding, general operating support, program support, and/or demonstration programs. The Foundation does not make grants to individuals, for political purposes, to retire indebtedness, or for payment of interest or taxes. The LAF "folder" on the Center's Web site offers information for grantseekers, including funding priorities and application procedures, as well as prospective donors; a list of endowed scholarship funds within LAF; general information about the Foundation's Mini-Grants for Teachers Program and its Funding Information Library (a Foundation Center Cooperating Collection); and contact information.

San Antonio Area Foundation <http://www.qvision.com/SAF/>

The mission of the San Antonio Area Foundation is to "improve the lives of the San Antonio community by: serving as a resource, broker and catalyst in the philanthropic community; responding to emerging, changing community needs; providing a variety of flexible services and opportunities to donors; [and] increasing the endowment resources available to community." To that end, the Foundation supports programs in arts and culture, community/social services, education, environment, preservation and animal services, and health care and biomedical research. Visitors to the Foundation's straightforward Web site will find application guidelines and procedures, donors information, a brief history of the Foundation, and a complete listing of its Board of Trustees.

The Waco Foundation <http://www.wacofdn.org>

WEST VIRGINIA

Parkersburg Area Community Foundation
<http://fdncenter.org/grantmaker/pacf/index.html>
The Parkersburg Area Community Foundation is committed to serving the people of the Mid-Ohio Valley—Wood, Pleasants, Tyler, Ritchie, Doddridge, Gilmer, Wirt, Calhoun, Roane, Jackson, and Mason Counties in West Virginia and Washington County in Ohio—by linking community resources with community needs. PACF focuses its grantmaking in the following areas: arts and culture, education, health and human services, recreation, and youth and family services. To be eligible for a grant from the Foundation, an applicant must be a private, non-profit, tax-exempt organization under section 501(c)(3) of the Internal Revenue Code, or they must be a public institution. The Foundation also administers more than 40 different scholarship funds, the majority of which are designated for students in Wood County, West Virginia. The Foundation's "folder" on the Center's Web site provides general information about the Foundation, detailed application guidelines and scholarship information, and general information about becoming a donor to the Foundation.

WISCONSIN

The Milwaukee Foundation <http://www.milwaukeefoundation.org/>
Established in 1915, making it one of the first community foundations in the U.S., the Milwaukee Foundation today comprises nearly 450 individual funds with a combined $235 million in assets. The Foundation makes grants in six areas—arts and culture, education, employment and training, health and human services, community economic development, and conservation and historic preservation—and limits its grantmaking "to projects that offer a significant improvement" to the lives of the people living in Milwaukee, Waukesha, Ozaukee, and Washington counties. Grants made outside this area are based upon donor recommendations. Detailed criteria in each of these funding areas is available from the Foundation upon request. In addition to general information and a history of the Foundation, visitors to the Web site will find application procedures, examples of recent grants, a variety of information for prospective donors, an electronic form for requesting guidelines and the Foundation's annual report, and contact information.

WYOMING

Community Foundation of Jackson Hole
<http://www.jacksonholenet.com/JH/CF/CF.htm>
The Community Foundation of Jackson Hole is committed to "enhance[ing] philanthropy and strengthen[ing] the sense of community in the Jackson Hole [Wyoming] area [by providing] a permanent source of funding and other support for non-profit organizations and scholarship recipients." The Foundation assists donors in maximizing the impact of their charitable giving; manages permanent endowments in response to donors' wishes; provides and monitors competitive grants; and holds workshops for local nonprofit organizations. The Foundation's Web site provides general fiscal information, comprehensive listings

(alphabetically and by subject category) of Jackson Hole-area charitable organizations, and contact information for grantmaking guidelines and application forms. The Foundation's 1997 annual report is also posted to the site.

Links and Abstracts of Web Sites of Other Grantmaking Public Charities

The Foundation Cneter continually strives to identify and describe public charities that operate grantmaking programs along with their other activities. Be sure to .check the "Grantmaker Information" area of <fdncenter.org> for the latest listings.

The Abraham Fund <http://www.coexistence.org/>

The Abraham Fund promotes constructive coexistence between Jews and Arabs within Israeli society. Named for Abraham, the common ancestor of Jews and Arabs, the Fund was founded in 1989 as a funding source for programs—cultural, educational, health related, recreational, and vocational—aimed at developing coexistence opportunities. Visitors to the Fund's Web site will find a description of the Fund and its activities, a listing of coexistence projects (grants summary and list), newsletter excerpts, a message from the chairman, contact information for the Fund in the U.S. and Israel, links to related Web sites, and a quiz.

The Academy of American Poets <http://www.poets.org/>

Aid to Artisans, Inc. <http://www.aid2artisans.org/ds12.htm>

Aid to Artisans, a nonprofit organization founded in 1976 to create economic opportunities for craftspeople around the world, offers design consultation, on-site workshops, business training, and links to markets where craft products are sold. It awards 30-40 grants, ranging from $500 to $1,500 every year to emerging artisans and craft-based associations worldwide. Grant application information is located in the "Description of Services" directory. The ATA site also offers information about ATA's direct service programs, a bulletin board of events, a description of its work and projects, and listings of its officers, directors, and staff.

Alabama Law Foundation <http://www.alabar.org/allaw/alfstup.html>

The Alabama Law Foundation was established in 1987 to be the recipient of funds generated by the Interest on Lawyers' Trust Accounts (IOLTA) program. The Foundation distributes IOLTA grants each March in support of legal aid to the poor, to help maintain public law libraries, and to provide law-related education to the public. It also administers the Cabaniss, Johnston Scholarship Fund and the Kids' Chance Scholarship Fund. The Foundation's Web site offers brief descriptions of its creation and programs.

Alaska Humanities Forum <http://www.akhf.org/>

Alzheimer's Association <http://www.alz.org/>

American Association of School Administrators
<http://www.aasa.org/Programs/Programs.htm>

American Association of University Women <http://www.aauw.org/>

American Bar Foundation <http://www.abf-sociolegal.org/>

American Cancer Society
<http://www.cancer.org/bottomresearchprogress.html>

American Council of Learned Societies <http://www.acls.org/jshome.htm>

American Digestive Health Foundation <http://www.gastro.org/adhf.html>

American Federation for Aging Research <http://www.afar.org/>

The American Federation of Riders <http://www2.eos.net/jjseta/afr.html>

American Floral Endowment <http://www.endowment.org/>

American Foundation for AIDS Research <http://www.amfar.org/>

American Heart Association
<http://www.americanheart.org/catalog/Scientific_catpage69.html>

American Hotel Foundation <http://www.ei-ahma.org/webs/ahf/ahf.htm>

American Physicians Fellowship for Medicine in Israel
<http://www.apfmed.org/>

American Psychological Association <http://www.apa.org>

**American Society of Consultant Pharmacists Research and Education
Foundation** <http://www.ascpfoundation.org/>

Aplastic Anemia Foundation of America <http://www.aplastic.org/>

Archstone Foundation <http://www2.archstone.com/Archstone/>
Established in 1985 as the FHP Foundation and renamed in 1996, the Archstone
Foundation has refocused its grantmaking activities on "contribut[ing] toward the
preparation of society in meeting the needs of an aging population." The Foundation's funding priorities for the immediate future include addressing the needs of
caregivers of the elderly, end-of-life issues, and direct delivery of services to non-
institutionalized seniors, with an emphasis on Southern California. The Foundation's Web site offers general statements about its funding priorities and restrictions, application procedures, an "Announcements" area, a list of Foundation-
sponsored publications, an online version of the Foundation's 1997 annual report,
and contact information.

Arizona Humanities Council <http://aztec.asu.edu/ahc/homepage.html>

Arkansas Humanities Council <http://www.arkhums.org/>

Arthritis National Research Foundation <http://www.curearthritis.org/>

Arthritis Foundation <http://www.arthritis.org/>

Arts Council of Greater Kalamazoo <http://www.kazooart.org/>

The Arts Council of Northwest Florida <http://www.artsnwfl.org/>

ArtServe Michigan <http://www.artservemichigan.org/index2.html>

Arts Midwest <http://www.artsmidwest.org/>
Formed in 1985 through the merger of two organizations, the Affiliated State Arts Agencies of the Upper Midwest and the Great Lakes Arts Alliance, Arts Midwest provides funding, training, publications, information services, and conferences to arts and cultural organizations, artists, art administrators, and art enthusiasts in Illinois, Indiana, Iowa, Michigan, Minnesota, North Dakota, Ohio, South Dakota, and Wisconsin. Since its inception, the organization has distributed almost $8 million to artists and arts organizations through a variety of funding and training programs. At present, it manages four funding programs: the Performing Arts Touring Fund, Meet the Composer/Midwest, Jazz Satellite Touring Fund, and the Jazz Master Awards. The latter serves individual artists in Arts Midwest's nine-state region. The other programs assist presenters in the region in bringing Midwestern artists as well as national artists to their communities. Visitors to the AM Web site will find a variety of program, application, conference, and publication information.

The Asia Foundation <http://www.asiafoundation.com/>
The Asia Foundation is a private, nonprofit, nongovernmental organization working to build leadership, improve policies, and strengthen institutions to foster greater openness and shared prosperity in the Asia-Pacific region. The Foundation currently has program priorities in four areas: State and Society, Opening Global Markets, International Initiatives, and Women in Politics. Visitors to the Foundation's Web site will find detailed information on the Foundation's programs in Bangladesh, Cambodia, China, Indonesia, Japan, Korea, Mongolia, Nepal, Pakistan, Philippines, Sri Lanka, Taiwan, Thailand, and Vietnam; as well as its U.S. administered programs, which are the Asian-American Exchange, Global Women in Politics, Books for Asia, Environmental Programs, and the Luce Program offering scholars work experience in Asia. The Web site provides contact information, including e-mail addresses for representatives in each country and the U.S.; lists of trustees, officers, and senior staff in the U.S.; and Web resources in Asia.

The Asia Society <http://www.asiasociety.org/>

ASTREA National Lesbian Action Foundation <http://www.astraea.org/>

Atlas Economic Research Foundation <http://www.atlas-fdn.org/>

Averitt Express Associates Charities
<http://www.averittexpress.com/aecares.htm>

Blue Cross Blue Shield of Michigan Foundation
<http://www.bcbsm.com/foundation.shtml>
The BCBSM Foundation seeks to improve health care in Michigan by "enhancing the quality and appropriate use of health care; improving access to appropriate health services; and controlling health care costs." Its grant programs support research and community health care solutions, acknowledge excellence in research, and support medical education. The Foundation area of the BCBSM Web site provides clear and concise information on the Foundation's primary funding programs, including its Proposal Development Award, Matching Initiative Program, Physician-Investigator Research Award, Student Award Program, Request for Proposal Program, Excellence in Research Awards, and Investigator-Initiated Program. Applications for the above programs are available at the site in .pdf format. The site also provides e-mail contact to program administrators, a select list of links, and an online version of the Foundation's most recent annual report.

Boston Adult Literacy Fund <http://www.tiac.org/users/balf/home.htm>
The Boston Adult Literacy Fund was founded in 1988 to provide access to basic education for adults in the Boston metro area and to raise awareness of the need for basic education and literacy. Grants are awarded to community-based literacy programs (ABE—Adult Basic Education, ESL—English as a Second Language, and high school credential programs—either GED or EDP). The Fund also awards scholarships to adults who have completed their basic education and wish to continue on to higher education or vocational training. In addition to descriptions of its programs, the BALF Web site provides a list of recent grant recipients, links to literacy-related Web sites, and contact information.

Broadway Cares/Equity Fights AIDS <http://www.bcefa.org/>

Bronx Council on the Arts <http://www.bronxarts.org/bronxhome.html>

The Brother's Brother Foundation <http://www.brothersbrother.com/>

California Council for the Humanities <http://www.calhum.org/>
The California Council for the Humanities is a non-governmental affiliate of the National Endowment for the Humanities, which looks for ways to make the knowledge and insights of the humanities available to all Californians. The CCH Web site offers two options for joining in humanities discussions—a "Citizenship, Culture, and the Humanities" e-mail discussion list and a Web-based "Humanities Forum"—as well as a calendar-style listing of programs funded by grants from CCH.

California HealthCare Foundation <http://www.chcf.org/>

Cancer Care, Inc. <http://www.cancercare.org/>

Cancer Research Foundation of America <http://www.preventcancer.org/>

Cancer Research Fund of the Damon Runyon Walter Winchell Foundation
<http://www.cancerresearchfund.org/>

Catholic Campaign for Human Development
<http://www.nccbuscc.org/cchd/index.htm>
Established in 1969 by the National Conference of Catholic Bishops, the Catholic Campaign for Human Development works to empower the poor and encourage their participation in the decisions and actions that affect their lives in order to move beyond poverty. It does this by supporting and funding community-controlled, self-help organizations, and economic development projects, as well as through transformative education. Guidelines for both types of projects are available on the CCHD Web site, as is a list of currently funded projects organized by state, local contact information (also by state), and a form for requesting more information.

Harry Chapin Foundation <http://www.harrysfriends.com/hcf/>

Child Health Foundation <http://www.childhealthfoundation.org/>

The Children's Charities Foundation, Inc. <http://www.ccfdc.org/>

Children's Scholarship Fund <http://www.orgitecture.com/csf/>

The Club Foundation <http://www.clubfoundation.org/>

Coalition for the Advancement of Jewish Education <http://www.caje.org/>

Coca-Cola Scholars Foundation <http://www.coca-cola.com/scholars/>

College Art Association <http://www.collegeart.org/caa/>

The Conservation Alliance <http://www.outdoorlink.com/consall/>

Cooper Foundation <http://www.cooperfdn.org/>

Common Counsel Foundation <http://www.commoncounsel.org>

Cottonwood Foundation <http://www.pressenter.com/~cottonwd/>
The Cottonwood Foundation is "dedicated to promoting empowerment of people, protection of the environment, and respect for cultural diversity." The Foundation focuses its modest grantmaking activities on "committed, grass roots organizations that rely strongly on volunteer efforts and where foundation support will make a significant difference." The Foundation typically awards grants in the $500 to $1,000 range to organizations in the United States and internationally that protect the environment, promote cultural diversity, empower people to meet their basic needs, and rely on volunteer efforts. In addition to general information about its activities, the Foundation's Web site provides grant guidelines, a downloadable grant application form, a list of 1997 grant recipients, and the Foundation's 1997 annual report.

Council of Independent Colleges <http://www.cic.edu/>

Delaware Humanities Forum <http://www.dhf.org/>
The Delaware Humanities Forum, an adjunct of the Delaware Humanities Council, supports educational programs in the humanities through its own programs and sponsorship of a range of activities, including lectures, conferences, radio and television broadcasts, interpretive exhibits, and book and film discussions. Descriptions of the Forum's programs, which include a Speakers Bureau, a Visiting Scholars Program, an Annual Lecture, and Workplace Programs are available on the Forum's Web site, along with information about grant eligibility requirements and deadlines, frequently asked questions, and downloadable guidelines and application forms in .pdf format. Visitors will also find a calendar of events, an interactive form for ordering Forum materials, and contact information.

Detroit Lions' Charities <http://www.detroitlions.com/charities.html>
Established by the NFL's Detroit Lions, the Detroit Lions Charities support education, civic affairs, and health and human services in the state of Michigan. Programs currently funded by the DLC include learning initiatives for youth, housing for less fortunate families, mentoring projects, domestic violence education, athletic programs for youth, substance abuse programs, and a visiting lecturer series at a creative studies center. Visitors to the Lions' Web site will find a description of the DLC and its activities, funding request deadlines, a press release on current grants and annual giving totals, and contact information.

Do Something, Inc. <http://www.dosomething.org/>

The Drug Policy Foundation <http://www.dosomething.org/>

**The Dystonia Medical Research Foundation
<http://www.dystonia-foundation.org/dmrf.html>**

The Enterprise Foundation <http://www.enterprisefoundation.org>
Launched by visionary developer Jim Rouse and his wife Patty in 1982, the Enterprise Foundation focuses its activities on providing "all low-income people in the United States the opportunity for fit and affordable housing." The Foundation's Web site offers extensive information about the plethora of loans, investments, training programs, and technical assistance supported by the foundation and its subsidiaries. Visitors to the site can also access information on the Foundation's annual Network Conference; read various Foundation publications, news releases, and newsletters; and search the "Best Practices Database," which shares experiences, strategies, and techniques for assisting low-income people.

Entrepreneurs' Foundation <http://www.the-ef.org/>

The Eurasia Foundation <http://www.eurasia.org/>
The Washington, D.C.-based Eurasia Foundation is a privately managed grantmaking organization dedicated to funding programs that build democratic and free market institutions in the Newly Independent States of the former Soviet Union—Armenia, Azerbaijan, Belarus, Georgia, Kazakstan, Kyrgyzstan, Moldova, Russia, Tajikistan, Turkmenistan, Ukraine, and Uzbekistan. The Foundation concentrates its support in eight priority areas: business development, business education and management training, economics education and research,

public administration and local government reform, NGO development, rule of law, media, and electronic communications. Visitors to the Foundation's Web site will find program descriptions and application guidelines; a searchable database of grants; a directory of Foundation offices, staff, and board members; links to Web sites of interest; job opportunities; news; and contact information.

First Nations Development Institute <http://www.firstnations.org/>
The First Nations Development Institute was formed in 1980 to help Native American tribes build sound, sustainable reservation communities by linking grassroots projects with national programs. Through its Eagle Staff Fund: A Collaborative For Native American Development, the Institute offers grants in support of "holistic" economic development projects that consider communities' economic, environmental, spiritual, cultural, political, social, and health needs. In addition, the Institute's Oweesta Program provides technical assistance to communities in creating and controlling capital assets for financing reservation and community development. Detailed information on these programs, a list of related links, and contact information are available at the First Nations Web site.

A.J. Fletcher Foundation <http://www.ajf.org/>
Originally formed to provide operating support for A.J. Fletcher's Grass Roots Opera, which later evolved into the National Opera Company, the A.J. Fletcher Foundation today supports a broad range of "nonprofit organizations in their endeavors to enrich the people of North Carolina." The Foundation makes grants in five areas: Arts and Humanities, Organizational and Administrative Development, Education, Programs Benefiting Children and Youth, and Community Initiatives and Human Services. The Foundation's Web site provides a description of the foundation, a biography of A.J. Fletcher, grants lists by giving area, grant guidelines and a downloadable application form. Visitors to the site can also read about the National Opera Company and another major beneficiary, the Fletcher School of Performing Arts.

Florida Humanities Council <http://www.flahum.org/>

First Nations Development Institute <http://www.firstnations.org/>

Foundation for Middle East Peace <http://www.fmep.org>

Frameline, Inc. <http://www.frameline.org/>

The Milton and Rose D. Friedman Foundation
<http://www.friedmanfoundation.org/>

Gay and Lesbian Medical Association <http://www.glma.org/>

General Health System Foundation
<http://www.generalhealth.org/foundation.html>
Based in Baton Rouge, Louisiana, the General Health System Foundation is committed to improving that community's access to health care services. GHS provides opportunities for education and assistance, as well as support for affiliates of

the General Health System, a network of health care providers. The Foundation is described briefly on a page of the GHS Web site.

Georgia Humanities Council <http://www.emory.edu/GHC/ghc.html>
The Georgia Humanities Council, the state affiliate of the National Endowment for the Humanities, was founded in 1970 to support and conduct local and state-wide educational programs in the humanities. In addition to descriptions of and guidelines for its four grant programs—Special Program Grants, Community Program Grants, Conference Program Grants, and Teacher Enrichment Grants—the site also provides information about a range of humanities resources (Web sites, book discussion groups, video resources, etc.) and contact information.

German-American Academic Council Foundation <http://www.gaac.org/>

Gifts In Kind International <http://www.GiftsInKind.org/>

Elizabeth Glaser Pediatric AIDS Foundation <http://www.pedaids.org/>

Glaucoma Research Foundation <http://www.glaucoma.org/>

Global Fund for Women <http://www.igc.apc.org/gfw/>
The Global Fund for Women strives to advance female human rights and improve women's economic autonomy and access to communications in countries around the world. It does not fund in the United States, however, nor does it fund individuals. As a non-endowed foundation, it relies on the annual support of individuals, foundations, corporations, and other nongovernmental and multilateral organizations. The Fund's Web site provides program descriptions, a FAQ section, grant application guidelines and criteria, a listing of the Fund's board of directors and advisory council, detailed accounts of many of its recent activities, dozens of links to nonprofit resources and sites concerned with women's issues, and an appeal for support (accompanied by an interactive donation pledge form).

Group Health/Kaiser Permanente Community Foundation
<http://www.ghc.org/foundatn/foundatn.html>

Hawai'i Committee for the Humanities <http://www.planet-hawaii.com/hch/>
The Hawai'i Committee for the Humanities was founded in 1972 to promote and support public awareness in Hawai'i of the humanities (defined on the HCH's Web site as studies examining philosophy, ethics, comparative religion, history, archaeology and anthropology, literature, languages, and art history). HCH offers grants primarily to nonprofit organizations that operate humanities programs, although a limited number of smaller grants are temporarily available for research by individuals and preservation and publications projects by nonprofits. The Web site provides detailed information about its grant programs and downloadable applications and instructions in .pdf format. The site also lists humanities resources and links to those with Web sites, information on Hawaii History Day and other programs, and contact information.

Headwaters Fund <http://www.fex.org/headwater/headwate.html>
Founded on the belief that the capacity for fundamental social change lies in the
hands of ordinary people, the Headwaters Fund provides financial and organizational resources to grassroots organizations in the Minneapolis/St. Paul metropolitan area. The Fund tends to support smaller organizations (i.e., with budgets under
$200,000) whose programs address the root causes of social, political, environ-
mental and economic injustice, and its grantmaking decisions are made by community activists, including people of color, women, poor and working class individuals, gays and lesbians, and people with disabilities. Visitors to the Fund's Web
site will find grant guidelines, information about donor opportunities, and contact
information.

Health Foundation of South Florida
<http://www.target.net/~wwdir/hlthfoun.html>

Health Trust of Santa Clara Valley <http://www.healthtrust.org/>

Idaho Humanities Council <http://www2.state.id.us/ihc/>
The Idaho Humanities Council partners with civic groups, citizens, and educators
to expand public humanities programs in the state. It accomplishes this mission by
supporting educational programs for the general public as well as various target
audiences. Although the Council's Web site offers comprehensive information on
its grants programs, applicants are "strongly advised to seek more detailed information through staff consultation before completing and submitting grant proposals," and an e-mail contact is provided for this purpose. The Council's Web site
also provides news, information on programs for teachers, humanities resources
and links of interest, and contact and donor information.

Jimi Hendrix Family Foundation <http://www.jimi-hendrix.com/foundation/>

Hogg Foundation for Mental Health <http://hogg1.lac.utexas.edu/>
Since 1940, the mandate of the Hogg Foundation has been "to develop and conduct a broad mental health program of great benefit to the people of Texas"
through education and grants supporting mental health service projects and
research efforts. The Foundation gives priority to projects in the areas of children
and their families, youth at risk, and minority health; it does not make grants for
projects located outside the state of Texas. Offerings at the Foundation's Web site
include a short history of the Hogg family, grant restrictions and application
guidelines for its mental health service and research programs, a 1996–97 grants
list, a staff listing with e-mail addresses, and information about its Regional Foundation Library, a longtime member of the Foundation Center's Cooperating Collections network.

Hospice Foundation of America <http://www.hospicefoundation.org/>
The mission of the Hospice Foundation of America is to "provide leadership in
the development and application of hospice and its philosophy of care for terminally ill people, with the goal of enhancing the American health care system and
the role of hospice within it." The Foundation designs and implements programs that assist hospices and the terminally ill, and makes grants that are sup-
portive of hospice concepts. Grants are not normally awarded for endowments,

debt reduction, religious efforts, or to individuals. Priority is given to those communities from which the Foundation collects donations. The Web site serves as an online resource for hospice care, providing excerpts from the Foundation's own publications in addition to numerous links to online hospice resources. The online version of the Foundation's 1996 annual report provides descriptions of grant programs, grant guidelines, a listing of 1996 grants, Foundation history, board and staff lists, and contact information. Visitors to the site will also find information on an array of Foundation projects, as well as interactive order and donation forms.

The Whitney Houston Foundation for Children, Inc.
<http://www.whfoundation.com/>

The Howard Hughes Medical Institute <http://www.hhmi.org/>
In addition to supporting more than 60 medical research laboratories worldwide, the Howard Hughes Medical Institute, the nation's largest philanthropy, awards both institutional and individual grants to strengthen education in medicine, biology, and the related sciences. HHMI's grants program also supports the research of biomedical scientists outside the United States. Although portions of this large site are under construction, visitors will find detailed program descriptions, application guidelines and requirements, a short history of the organization, press releases and the HHMI Bulletin, online versions of 1994, 1995, and 1996 annual reports, a map of HHMI locations, and an interactive form that allows for direct communication with HHMI staff.

Humanities Council of Washington, D.C.
<http://www.notegg.com/humanities/dchumanities.htm>

Idaho Humanities Council <http://www2.state.id.us/ihc/>

Independent Accountants International Education Foundation
<http://dev.expressweb.com/ia2/educationf.html>
The Independent Accountants International Educational Foundation administers the Robert Kaufman Memorial Scholarship Fund to assist young people pursuing education in the field of accountancy. The scholarship program is described on the Foundation's page of the IAI Web site; the page also provides links to the scholarship application form and a list of last year's award winners.

Indiana Humanities Council <http://www.ihc4u.org/>

The Initiative Fund <http://www.semif.org/>

International Center for Research on Women <http://www.icrw.org/>

International Youth Federation <http://www.iyfnet.org/>

Jewish Community Federation of Cleveland
<http://www.jewishcleveland.org/>

Elton John AIDS Foundation <http://www.ejaf.org/>

The London and Los Angeles-based Elton John AIDS Foundation was founded in 1992 by entertainer Elton John to fund programs that "provide services to people living with HIV/AIDS and educational programs targeted at AIDS prevention, and/or elimination of prejudice and discrimination against HIV affected individuals." Services supported by the Foundation include food banks and meal programs, legal aid, hospice and housing, counseling and support groups, education outreach programs, at-home care, and pediatric treatment centers. The Foundation's Web site provides a description of its programs, contact information for those seeking grants, and areas for purchasing merchandise or otherwise contributing to the Foundation.

Magic Johnson Foundation <http://www.magicjohnson.org/>

Kansas Humanities Council
<http://www.cc.ukans.edu/kansas/khc/mainpage.html>

Kentucky Humanities Council <http://www.uky.edu/~vgsmit00/khc/khc.htm>

The Kentucky Humanities Council, an independent, nonprofit affiliate of the National Endowment for the Humanities, provides grants and services to nonprofit organizations seeking to foster greater understanding of the humanities. The sort of programs traditionally funded by the Council include, but are not limited to, conferences, lectures, radio and video productions, exhibits, teacher training and development of curricular materials, interpretive programs for festivals, book discussions, and planning for future projects. Visitors to the Council's Web site will find grant guidelines as well as information about its speakers bureau, living history performances, book discussion programs, a listing of board and staff members, and contact information.

Susan G. Komen Breast Cancer Foundation <http://www.komen.org/>

Founded in 1982 and best known as the sponsor of the 5K "Race for the Cure" runs to raise funds for national and local breast cancer initiatives, the Susan G. Komen Breast Cancer Foundation is the largest private funder of research dedicated solely to breast cancer in the United States. The Foundation's National Grant Program awards grants and fellowships in basic and clinical research, as well as grants for breast cancer education, treatment, and screening projects for the medically underserved. Descriptions of the Foundation's programs and downloadable application forms are available on the Web site, as is a list of Komen affiliates who award grants locally. Visitors to the site will also find information about "Race for the Cure," an online version of the Foundation's annual report, and "breastcancerinfo.com," which provides general health and breast cancer news and information, an online forum, and a calendar of events.

The Kosciuszko Foundation <http://www.kosciuszkofoundation.org/grants/>

Leukemia Society of America <http://www.leukemia.org/>

In addition to sponsoring a broad range of public conferences about leukemia treatment and research, the Leukemia Society of America supports worldwide research efforts—both in the lab and clinical applications—toward controlling and finding a cure for leukemia, lymphoma, and myeloma. Grant information, guidelines, and application forms in a mix of Word 6.0 and .pdf formats are available in the "Research" area of the Society's Web site.

The Charles A. and Anne Morrow Lindbergh Foundation
<http://www.mtn.org/lindfdtn/>

The Lindbergh Foundation awards grants to individuals whose "initiative and work in a wide spectrum of disciplines furthers the Lindberghs' vision of a balance between the advance of technology and the preservation of the natural/human environment." The Foundation pursues its mission through three major programs: the presentation of Lindbergh Grants of up to $10,580 (a symbolic amount representing the cost of the "Spirit of St. Louis"); presentation of the Lindbergh Award to an individual for his or her lifelong contributions to the Lindberghs' shared vision; and the sponsoring of educational programs and publications which advance the Lindberghs' vision. In addition to a brief history of the Foundation, contact information, and application guidelines, the foundation's Web site offers visitors a 1999 grant application to view and print, or to download in Microsoft Word format; a list of Lindbergh Grants awarded from 1978–1996; an online version of the Foundation's 1995 annual report; a listing of the Foundation's officers, board, and staff; and links to other sites.

Louisiana Endowment for the Humanities
<http://home.communique.net/~leh/>

Lymphoma Research Foundation of America <http://www.lymphoma.org/>

James Madison Memorial Fellowship Foundation <http://jamesmadison.com/

The James Madison Memorial Fellowship Foundation seeks to "strengthen secondary school teaching of the principles, framing, and development of the U.S. Constitution," and works to foster the spirit of civic participation in teachers and students. The Foundation annually awards fellowships for graduate study of the principles, framing, and history of the U.S. Constitution to teachers of American history, American government, and social studies in grades 7–12, as well as to college seniors and college graduates who plan to become secondary school teachers of these subjects. At least one Junior or Senior Fellow is selected from each state every year. The Foundation's Web site provides a thorough description of the application process, and allows visitors to sign up to be notified electronically when new applications are posted to the site for downloading. The site also offers a password protected "Fellows Only" area; news announcements; a listing of staff, trustees, academic advisors, and faculty reps by state; and contact information.

March of Dimes <http://www.modimes.org/>

Mary's Pence <http://www.igc.apc.org/maryspence/>

Massachusetts Environmental Trust
<http://www.agmconnect.org/maenvtr1.html>

MAZON: A Jewish Response to Hunger
<http://www.shamash.org/soc-action/mazon/funding.html>

McKenzie River Gathering Foundation
<http://www.fex.org/mckenzie/front.html>

Meet the Composer <http://www.meetthecomposer.org/programs/>

The Michigan AIDS Fund <http://www.michaidsfund.org/>

Michigan Humanities Council <http://mihumanities.h-net.msu.edu/>

Mid Atlantic Arts Foundation <http://www.charm.net/~midarts/index.html>
One of six regional arts organizations in the continental United States, the Mid Atlantic Arts Foundation addresses the support of the arts in a multi-state region comprised of Delaware, the District of Columbia, Maryland, New Jersey, New York, Pennsylvania, the U.S. Virgin Islands, Virginia, and West Virginia. The Foundation, which is primarily concerned with providing increased access to quality arts programs, provides financial support, technical assistance, and information to artists and arts organizations through a variety of programs and services. Visitors to the Foundation's Web site will find general program descriptions for the visual arts, performing arts, jazz, and traditional and folk arts; some recent grant awards and descriptions; listings of the Foundation's board and staff; links to the nine Mid-Atlantic state arts agencies' Web sites; and an online version of ARTSINK, the Foundation's newsletter.

The Mississippi Humanities Council
<http://www.ihl.state.ms.us/mhc/index.html>

Missouri Humanities Council <http://www.umsl.edu/community/mohuman/>

Montana Committee for the Humanities <http://www.umt.edu/lastbest/>

Ms. Foundation for Women <http://www.ms.foundation.org/>

Muscular Dystrophy Association
<http://www.mdausa.org/research/index.html>

A.J. Muste Memorial Institute <http://www.nonviolence.org/ajmuste/>

NAFSA: Association of International Educators <http://www.nafsa.org>
NAFSA, a membership organization created in 1948, promotes the international exchange of students and scholars through training workshops and in-service training grants, grants for professionals to travel to NAFSA conferences, and a variety of overseas opportunities. The "Education and Training" area of the NAFSA Web site provides information on these programs. Visitors to the site can also find information on or about financial aid and re-entry job searching ("Students, Scholars, and . . ."); funding programs for study abroad ("Inside NAFSA"); and upcoming conferences and publications by NAFSA members.

National Blood Foundation of the American Association of Blood Banks
<http://www.aabb.org/docs/nbf.html>

National Council for the Social Studies <http://www.ncss.org/>

National Fish and Wildlife Foundation <http://www.nfwf.org/>

National Foundation for Advancement in the Arts <http://www.nfaa.org/>

The National Foundation for the Improvement of Education
<http://www.nfie.org/>

National Foundation for Infectious Diseases <http://www.nfid.org>

National Geographic Society Education Foundation
<http://www.nationalgeographic.com/society/ngo/foundation/>
The National Geographic Society Education Foundation currently awards more
than three million dollars in grants annually to programs nationwide in support of
their mission "to revitalize the teaching and learning of geography in the nation's
K–12 classrooms." Ninety percent of the Foundation's grants budget is "earmarked for a state-based network of geographic alliances, grassroots organizations of classroom teachers and university geographers dedicated to improving
geography education." In addition to funding the alliances, the Foundation awards
grants to individual teachers who work with the alliances to implement innovative
educational strategies relating to geography. The Foundation also funds an urban
initiative program, which awards grants to address the special needs of urban
schools, and offers discretionary grant endowments for geography education in
Colorado, Mississippi, and Oklahoma. Visitors to the Foundation's Web site will
find detailed descriptions of the Foundation's programs, application guidelines, a
list of sample teacher grants, a downloadable teacher grant application form, and a
contact list for each state alliance.

National Hemophilia Foundation <http://www.hemophilia.org/>

National Hispanic Scholarship Fund <http://www.nhsf.org/>

National Park Foundation <http://www.nationalparks.org/programs.htm>

National Press Foundation <http://www.natpress.org/>

National Society of Accountants <http://www.nsacct.org/>

National Trust for Historic Preservation <http://www.nthp.org/>

Nellie Mae Fund for Education <http://www.agmconnect.org/nellie1>

The New Jersey Council for the Humanities <http://www.njch.org/>

New England Foundation for the Arts <http://www.nefa.org/>
One of six regional arts organizations in the continental United States, the New
England Foundation for the Arts links the public and private sectors in a regional
partnership to support the arts in Connecticut, Maine, Massachusetts, New Hampshire, Rhode Island, and Vermont. Organized on a "community foundation"
model, the Foundation has three program areas: the Culture in Community Fund,
to strengthen the role the arts play in community development; the Connections
Fund, to expand knowledge concerning the roles, practices, and social impact of

the arts; and the Creation and Presentation Fund, to enable the development and presentation of high quality artistic work. Most grants are made through the Creation and Presentation Fund's New England Arts Access programs providing support to artists for art-making and to arts organizations for presenting activities in the New England area. NEFA's Web site provides descriptions of the Foundations programs; grant program descriptions, guidelines, and deadlines; a calendar of events; news; links to other Web sites related to the arts; and a staff list with e-mail addresses.

New Israel Fund <http://www.nif.org/>

The New Israel Fund supports activities and groups that defend civil and human rights, promote Jewish-Arab equality and coexistence, advance the status of women, nurture tolerance and pluralism, bridge social and economic gaps, seek environmental justice, and press for government accountability within Israel. "The NIF's primary strategy is building Israel's public interest sector: it nurtures the growing network of nonpartisan, nonprofit organizations that enable Israelis to advocate more effectively to improve their lives, the conditions in their communities, and the policies of their government." To further its objectives, NIF makes grants ($6 million, including NIF's own projects, in 1995); supports Shatil, its "capacity-building center," which provides technical assistance to some 170 Israeli public-interest groups and promotes action by coalitions of like-minded organizations; trains civil-rights and environmental lawyers; and conducts public education globally about the challenges to Israeli democracy. NIF's Web site offers detailed information about its programs; an online version of its 1995 annual report; links to NIF grantees; board members, and senior staff; NIF contact information worldwide; and information on volunteer and donor opportunities.

The New Mexico Women's Foundation <http://worldplaces.com/nmwf/>

New Visions for Public Schools <http://www.newvisions.org/>

New York Foundation for the Arts
<http://www.tmn.com/Artswire/www/nyfa.html>

Through its fellowships, residencies, sponsorships, loans, information and advocacy services, the New York Foundation for the Arts "works with artists and arts organizations throughout New York State and other parts of the country to bring the work of contemporary artists to the public." NYFA's charitable vehicles include the Artists' Programs and Services division, which provides cash grants, sponsors artists' projects, and provides financial and administrative services to individual artists and their organizations; and the Revolving Loans Program, which provides short-term loans to nonprofit cultural organizations. The Foundation also provides educational and informational services to benefit the arts. NYFA's Web site offers detailed program information and specific contact information for each program, as well as a number of links to other grantmakers in the arts.

Northland Foundation <http://www.northlandfdn.org/>

Northwest AIDS Foundation <http://www.nwaids.org/>

Orangewood Children's Foundation <http://www.InOrangeCounty.com/orangemedia/sites/orangewood/default.asp>

Pediatric Brain Tumor Foundation of the United States
<http://www.ride4kids.org/>
The Pediatric Brain Tumor Foundation of the United States seeks to find the cause of as well as a cure for childhood brain tumors; aid in the early detection and treatment of such tumors; and provide hope to the families of children afflicted with brain tumors. The Foundation also supports the development of a national database on all primary brain tumors and provides funding for research on new therapies designed to extend the lives of stricken children. Although the Foundation's Web site is geared toward attracting new donors and participants in Ride 4 Kids, a motorcycle fundraising event started in 1984 in Atlanta, Georgia, it does provide a list of recent grant recipients and contact information.

Pennsylvania Humanities Council <http://www.libertynet.org/phc/>

The Pet Care Trust <http://petsforum.com/petcaretrust/>

Pharmaceutical Research and Manufacturers of America Foundation
<http://www.phrmaf.org/>

Philanthrofund Foundation <http://www.scc.net/~philanth/>

The Ploughshares Fund <http://www.ploughshares.org/>
Founded at a time when global nuclear conflict seemed a real and immediate possibility, the Ploughshares Fund was designed to provide financial support to people and organizations working to eliminate the threat of nuclear war. Ploughshares now focuses its support on combatting the burgeoning trade in conventional weapons, the explosion of regional conflict in the aftermath of the Cold War, and the growing danger of nuclear weapons proliferation following the breakup of the Soviet Union. Ploughshares has made over 1,000 grants totaling more than $15 million. Visitors to the Foundation's Web site will find detailed information on its main areas of interest: banning land mines, preventing armed conflict, restraining the weapons trade, cutting Pentagon waste, cleaning up our radioactive environment, and fighting nuclear terrorism and proliferation. A 1997–1998 grants list—with links to grantee Web sites—is available, along with grant application guidelines, an interactive subscription form for the Foundation's free newsletter, board and staff lists, and contact information.

Princess Grace Foundation - USA <http://www.pgfusa.com/>
Established in 1982 in memory of Princess Grace of Monaco, the Princess Grace Foundation - USA supports emerging young artists nationwide in the the fields of theater, dance, and film. Students in their last year of schooling or training are eligible for tuition assistance through scholarships, while young artists working in the areas of theater and dance qualify for apprenticeships and fellowships. The Foundation, which has awarded over $1.6 million in grants since 1984, also recognizes exceptional and continuing professional achievement through the awarding of Princess Grace Statuettes, its highest honor, to two or three recipients annually. The Foundation's Web site provides a fact sheet and background information

about the Foundation, application guidelines, a list of 1997 grantees, and contact information.

Ayn Rand Institute/The Center for the Advancement of Objectivism
<http://www.aynrand.org/>
The Ayn Rand Institute was founded in 1985 by philosopher Leonard Peikoff to advance Objectivism, Ayn Rand's philosophy of reason, egoism, individualism, and laissez-faire capitalism. The Institute influences the public through opinion pieces and its own media projects; runs a "Campaign Against Servitude" opposing volunteerism; sponsors essay contests; supports college and university campus clubs; and produces materials and training on Objectivism. The Institute's Web site provides a fair amount of information on Objectivism and Ayn Rand, and describes the activities of the Institute.

The Donna Reed Foundation for the Performing Arts
<http://www.frii.com/donna_reed/>

Rex Foundation <http://grateful.dead.net/cavenWeb/rex/>
The Rex Foundation, a charitable foundation established by members and friends of the Grateful Dead, "aims to help secure a healthy environment, promote individuality in the arts, provide support to critical and necessary social services, assist others less fortunate than ourselves, protect the rights of indigenous people and ensure their cultural survival, build a stronger community, and to educate children and adults everywhere." Virtually all the Foundation's grant recipients are preselected; therefore, unsolicited requests are not considered. Visitors to the Foundation's Web site will find the 1997 annual report, a listing of all grant recipients from 1992–1995, profiles of selected Foundation beneficiaries, a listing of board bembers, and information about the 1997 Rex Awards: the Jerry Garcia Award, which honors and supports those working to encourage creativity in young people; the Bill Graham Award, which is designated for those working to assist children who are victims of political oppression and human rights violations; and the Ralph. J. Gleason Award, which recognizes individuals making outstanding contributions to culture.

Jackie Robinson Foundation

Rockefeller Family Fund <http://www.rffund.org/>
The New York City-based Rockefeller Family Fund made grants in five major program areas in 1996: citizen education and participation, economic justice for women, the environment, institutional responsiveness, and self-sufficiency. The Fund supports tax-exempt organizations engaged in educational and charitable activities of national significance. It does not usually fund projects pertaining only to a single community. In addition to general program descriptions, visitors to the Fund's Web site will find a list (by program and alphabetically) of 1996 grantees and links to those with Web sites, application procedures, a letter from the Fund's president, a listing of the Fund's trustees and staff, and information about the Rockefeller Technology Project, which helps grantees to learn about and effectively use new communication technology.

The Rotary Foundation of Rotary International
<http://www.rotary.org/foundation/>
As the philanthropic arm of Rotary International, the Rotary Foundation supports efforts to "achieve world understanding and peace through international humanitarian, educational, and cultural exchange programs." The Foundation sponsors activities in two main areas: the Humanitarian Programs, which fund projects designed to improve quality of life, primarily in the developing world; and the Educational Programs, through which the Foundation provides funding for students to study abroad each year, for university professors to teach in developing countries, and for exchanges of business and professional people. In addition to general program descriptions, visitors to the Foundation area of Rotary International's Web site will find information on the Foundation's history, support, and governance, including a list of trustees.

Albert B. Sabin Vaccine Institute at Georgetown University
<http://www.sabin.georgetown.edu/>
The Albert B. Sabin Vaccine Institute was established to promote "rapid scientific advances in vaccine development, delivery and distribution worldwide." (Albert B. Sabin developed the original polio vaccine.) In the field of vaccine development, the Institute supports the academic development of scientists and physicians; provides grants for research, development, and testing; advocates for the integration of scientific advances and public policy; and promotes public awareness of vaccine research and the development of educational materials. The Institute's Web site offers brief descriptions of its programs and activities and contact information.

Stanley J. Sarnoff Endowment for Cardiovascular Science, Inc.
<http://www.sarnoffendowment.org>

The Sierra Club Foundation
<http://www.sierraclub.org/affiliated/foundation.html>

Nicole Brown Simpson Charitable Foundation <http://www.nbscf.org>

Social Science Research Council <http://www.ssrc.org>

Society of Manufacturing Engineers Education Foundation
<http://www.sme.org/foundation>

Sonoma County AIDS Foundation <http://www.sonoma-aids.org/>

Sons of Italy Foundation <http://www.osia.org/sif.html>

South Dakota Humanities Council
<http://www.sdstate.edu/~whum/http/home.html>

Southern Education Foundation, Inc. <http://www.sefatl.org/>

Special Libraries Association <http://www.sla.org/research/index.html>

Spirits of the Land Foundation <http://greatspirit.earth.com/>

St. Luke's Charitable Health Trust <http://www.sltrust.com/>

TAPPI Foundation, Inc. <http://www.tappi.org/membact/found/main.htm>
Created in 1990 by the Technical Association of the Pulp and Paper Industry to
support research and education, the TAPPI Foundation awards research grants to
scientists and engineers for projects that will assist in securing the future of the
paper and pulp industries. Research needs of the industry are available for download in .pdf format on the Foundation's Web site, and the Foundation encourages
proposal submissions from newcomers to the industry. The site also provides
guidelines, the application in .pdf format, 1997 award recipients, grant executive
summaries, and a funding evaluation form.

A Territory Resource Foundation <http://www.atrfoundation.org/>

Texas Council for the Humanities <http://www.public-humanities.org/>

Theater Communications Group <http://www.tcg.org/>

Travel Industry Association of America Foundation
<http://www.tia.org/whatsTIA/found.stml>

Trinity Grants Program
<http://www.trinitywallstreet.org/Programs/grants.html>

Richard Tucker Music Foundation <http://www.rtucker.com/>

An Uncommon Legacy Foundation, Inc. <http://www.uncommonlegacy.org/>
The Uncommon Legacy Foundation, was founded in 1990 to enhance the visibility, strength and vitality of the lesbian community. The Foundation awards scholarships to openly lesbian students with leadership potential, and funds projects
and organizations that contribute to the health, education, and culture of the lesbian community. The Foundation's Web site provides grant guidelines and a
downloadable application form in .pdf format; scholarship guidelines, and a list of
1997 scholarship recipients; an online version of the Foundation's newsletter; and
information for prospective donors.

Union League (Chicago) Civic & Arts Foundation
<http://www.ulcc.org/c&a.htm>

United States Institute of Peace <http://www.usip.org/>

Utah Humanities Council <http://www.nonprofit.utah.org/uhc/>

V Foundation <http://www.jimmyv.org/
Founded by the late Jim Valvano and ESPN, the cable sports network, the V Foundation seeks to raise awareness of and support for cancer research. Although grant
information on the Foundation's Web site is limited to a list of recent grant recipients, visitors to the site can read about the life and times of Jimmy "V," learn more
about events staged in support of the Foundation, and sign up for e-mail updates
about the Foundation and its activities.

Virginia Health Care Foundation <http://www.vhcf.org/>

Washington Commission for the Humanities <http://www.humanities.org/>
The Washington Commission for the Humanities supports humanities projects—
which it defines as "the stories, ideas and writings that help us make sense of our
lives and enhance our ability to think creatively and critically about our world"—
in Washington State. Grants are awarded for a range of programs and activities,
including exhibits, public forums, school programs, reading and discussion series,
and cultural events. The WCH Web site provides grant guidelines—applicants are
encouraged to contact WCH before applying—along with information about past
recipients. WCH also gives two annual awards, the Washington Humanities
Award and the Governor's Writers Award, with eligibility requirements provided
on the site.

West Central Initiative <http://www.wcif.org/>

Western States Arts Federation <http://www.westaf.org/>

Wheat Ridge Ministries <http://www.wheatridge.org/>

**The Woodrow Wilson National Fellowship Foundation
<http://www.woodrow.org/>**

Wisconsin Humanities Council <http://www.danenet.wicip.org/whc/>

Women's Funding Alliance <http://www.wfalliance.org/>

**Women's Sports Foundation
<http://www.lifetimetv.com/WoSport/stage/GRANTS/>**

World Wildlife Fund <http://www.worldwildlife.org/>

Wyoming Council for the Humanities <http://www.uwyo.edu/special/wch/>

CHAPTER FOUR

Corporate Giving Information on the Web

Corporate Grantmaking: An Overview

Companies large and small in the United States traditionally have provided philanthropic support to the communities in which they operate as well as to worthy
charitable causes. The motivations behind individual corporations' giving vary
widely and can be complex. Before delving into corporate giving research using
the Web, a brief description of why and how corporations may give can offer
grantseekers a better understanding of what to look for in undertaking this
research.

Corporate giving usually entails a combination of altruism and self-interest.
Unlike foundations and other charitable agencies, corporations don't exist to give.
Their main responsibilities are to their employees, customers, shareholders, and
the bottom line. They give to support employee services, to guarantee a supply of
well-trained potential employees, to build community relations and community
life, both local and national, to enhance company image, to return favors, to get
tax deductions, and to influence policy makers and other opinion makers.

Companies understand the power of publicity and that charitable giving helps
build a strong community image. That makes giving essential for good corporate
business and citizenship. However, corporations expect concrete rewards for their
generosity.

Many companies have begun to use the Internet as a means to advertise their
philanthropic activities. By posting grantmaking activities on the Web, companies
make the public aware that they are involved in improving the quality of life,

133

particularly in areas of company operations. This exposure gives the company a positive image and improves public relations.

TRENDS IN CORPORATE GIVING

Corporations have reshaped and rethought their giving programs, narrowing their focus to specific objectives, examining how grants are used, and thinking in terms of possible benefits. They also have developed additional non-cash giving programs.

Companies often favor causes in the public eye like education, with a focus on math, science, minority education, and school reform. Environmental issues, low-income housing, and preventive health maintenance are also popular areas of giving.

In addition, companies want to maximize the impact of their giving. Direct involvement with students and teachers, in projects like the Adopt-A-School program and other tutoring and mentoring programs, is one approach. Across the board, companies want to plan and manage, foster collaborative donor and non-profit efforts, and take on long-term projects. They also look to volunteerism in the bid for community standing.

Company-Sponsored Foundations and Corporate Giving Programs

Companies provide support to nonprofits through private "company-sponsored" foundations, direct giving programs, or both.

Company-sponsored foundations usually maintain close ties with their sponsoring company, and their giving reflects that corporation's interests. Most maintain relatively small endowments and rely on contributions ("gifts received") from the company to support their programs. Corporations build their foundations' endowments in fat years and tap into them in lean ones.

Foundations must adhere to the appropriate regulations, including filing a yearly IRS Form 990-PF, which includes a report on contributions. These returns are publicly available from the IRS and at Foundation Center Cooprating Collections. They can be very helpful in researching individual corporate foundations.

Direct corporate giving—all charitable activities outside the company's foundation—is less regulated than foundation giving. Corporations are not required to publicize direct giving programs or sustain prescribed funding levels. They may also may give to nonprofits out of operating funds, and these expenditures won't show up in their giving statistics. Direct giving programs and foundations often share staff, adding to the confusion. For these reasons, funding information on direct company giving programs can be difficult.

"In-kind gifts" (such as donated products or loaned employee services) constitute an estimated 20 percent of corporate giving, although these numbers may be inflated due to the fact that many companies report their in-kind donations at market value rather than at their cost. Whatever the true percentage of corporate giving they represent, in-kind gifts are sometimes overlooked by organizations seeking company support.

For all the reasons noted above, most of the corporate giving information available on the Web concerns company-sponsored foundations. Foundations usually provide much more specific information concerning their grantmaking activities, including information on application addresses, contact persons, geographic limitations, fields of interest supported, types of support offered, and so on. One of the advantages to a company of using a direct giving program rather than a company-sponsored foundation is precisely that the company need not disclose how much or to whom they contribute. Therefore, finding out about direct corporate giving programs, grantseekers must use a little more strategy and a discerning selection process.

One of the basic handicaps is that companies often use their Web site primarily as a public relations tool. They may put up several pages concerning some of the grants they have given in the recent past and little else. Unfortunately, this kind of Web site can lead a grantseeker to believe that they are eligible for a grant when in fact they are not. Sites like these often generate hundreds, if not thousands, of applications to companies that do not accept unsolicited applications or who will not support the causes for which they are receiving applications.

THE COMMUNITY REINVESTMENT ACT

The passage of the Community Reinvestment Act (CRA) as a federal law in 1977, requires banks to help meet the credit needs of their entire community, including low- and moderate-income neighborhoods. Banks failing to do so may be denied permission by the government to expand their business locations, buy or merge with other banks, or engage in interstate banking. So, grantseekers looking for *loans* rather than cash or in-kind gifts should concentrate on banking firms in their communities.

It is debated within the philanthropic field whether these CRA loans represent a form of corporate giving at all. Some companies include their loans as part of their fiscal information for total giving, at the same time that they earn interest on these investments.

The Community Reinvestment Act does not require banks to make unsound business decisions. Banks are not obliged to make loans to organizations or individuals believed to be a great risk. CRA gives banks a general direction in order to serve the needs of the community in which they are located rather than direct them to make specific loans. CRA stimulates banks to make loans on low-income family housing, invest in community development, and support small businesses. Whether a true form of corporate giving or not, we mention CRA loans here as an avenue of potential assistance for some people.

How to Find Corporate Funders

Corporate giving is often in fields related to corporate activities and in company communities. The grantseeker's search should focus on local businesses as well as major corporations. Corporate directories and corporate giving studies are key resources.

A company foundation's tax return (Form 990-PF) is available through IRS district offices, at the foundation's office, through the attorney general for the state in which the foundation is chartered, and at Foundation Center libraries and cooperating collections.

In addition to the Web strategies outlined below, grantseekers should consult public libraries for regional and business indexes. The local Chamber of Commerce and Better Business Bureau may also have such guides. Do not overlook the yellow pages and staff community knowledge. In corporate grantseeking, personal contacts are invaluable. A grantseeker should consider their staff, board members, and volunteers as assets who may know corporate funders; they should be encouraged to investigate giving policies at these companies.

USING THE INTERNET

Many companies now maintain a presence on the World Wide Web, an important potential source for information about corporate community involvement and grantmaking activities.

Searching: Let Others Do the Searching for You

Several Web sites are good starting points for grantseekers on a quest for funding from corporate giving programs and company-sponsored foundations. Two are the Foundation Center's Corporate Grantmakers on the Internet <http://fdncenter.org/grantmaker/corp.html> and the U.K.-based Charities Aid Foundation's CCInet <http://www.charitynet.org/CCInet/frames/fpages.html>. These sites have extensive lists of hypertext links to corporate giving programs and company-sponsored foundations. (See Chapter 10 for more detail on the Foundation Center's Web site.)

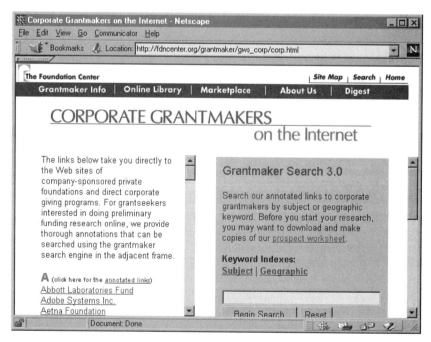

Another place to get started is the Council on Foundations' Web site <http://www.cof.org>. This site includes an FAQ page addressing corporate grantmaking and community involvement.

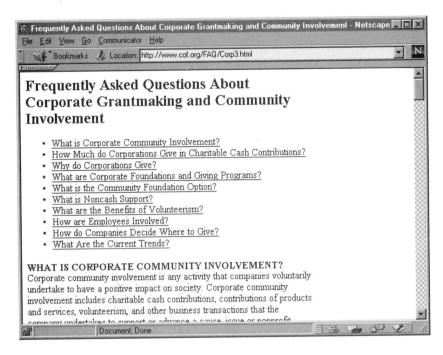

There is also a listing of member foundations and corporate giving programs with Web sites <http://www.cof.org/links/members.html> which, like the CCInet and the Foundation Center's pages, has links to corporate giving programs and company-sponsored foundations as well as independent foundations.

Other Web pages worthy of mention for corporate giving information include Internet Prospector's Corporate Giving Page <http://w3.uwyo.edu/~prospect/corp-giv.html>, which contains links and descriptions to several corporate giving programs and company-sponsored foundations, and *Philanthropy Journal*, whose Web site <http://philanthropy-journal.org/index.html> is full of interesting links to a corporate giving newsletter, a hypertext directory of company-sponsored foundations and corporate giving programs, and a hypertext list of other prospect research pages. The Northern California Community Foundation's homepage <http://www.foundations.org/index.html> is another good hypertext directory of foundations and corporate grantmakers. Access Point developed the Nonprofit Professionals Network <http://www.accesspt.com/npn/main.html> to help grantmakers and grantseekers. It includes free articles and a fee-based database.

Searching: Doing It Yourself Using a Search Engine

When searching for corporate giving information on the Internet, another way to find information you want is by using a search engine such as:

- AltaVista <htp://www.digital.altavista.com>
- Excite <http://www.excite.com>
- Infoseek <http://www.infoseek.com>
- Lycos <http://www.lycos.com>
- Hotbot <http://www.hotbot.com>
- Yahoo <http://www.yahoo.com>

There are myriad others. Try each one out to see which search engine is most to your liking. The key to retrieving a reasonable number of sites that contain useful information, rather than a list of thousands of irrelevant Web sites, is choosing the proper wording and knowing the rules pertaining to the specific search engine you may be using at the time. There are differences in how they work and what you can expect from them.

The words you select can greatly improve the search results you get. Try to search initially with phrases like "corporate giving," "community relations," and "corporate contributions." Once you have gotten an idea about what kind of information is available on the Web, you may be able to further narrow your searches by adding words more specific to your needs (e.g., "arts corporate giving"). You may also want to try the same search using various search engines; you will often get vastly different results. Other terms to try are "in-kind gift," if looking for product donations, or "community reinvestment act" for those seeking loans.

Searching: Looking Within a Corporate Web Site for Grantmaking Information
A different strategy is required to research the corporate giving policies regarding a specific company. Often there is no "search" option within the Web site. Therefore, you must search for the hypertext categories that may lead you to the information you need. Often these categories are within a menu list containing items such as "Products and Services," "Annual Report," etc. The categories most likely to contain the direct giving policies of the company are subjects like "About Us," "History," "Community," "Corporate Relations," and even "News Releases."

For more on searching within individual Web sites, see the section in this chapter called "Comparing Individual Corporate Web Sites."

Frequently, the corporate giving program information is contained on a "page within a page." In other words, you have to go through a lot to get to it. The best way to circumvent this is to find the Web site's site map, a listing of all of the pages contained within the Web site. These listings are usually the simplest way to cut to the heart of the subject you are looking for and are often more reliable than the hit-or-miss process of doing a search within a Web site.

RESEARCHING CORPORATE INFORMATION

In order to learn about a company's philanthropic efforts, it is often easier when basic information about the company itself is available, including: their areas of company operations, if the corporate giving program has geographic limitations; the products and services the company provides, when seeking in-kind gifts; a list of corporate officers, to help find a contact person when none is evident; and fiscal information, to give an idea about the possible size of the corporation's philanthropic efforts.

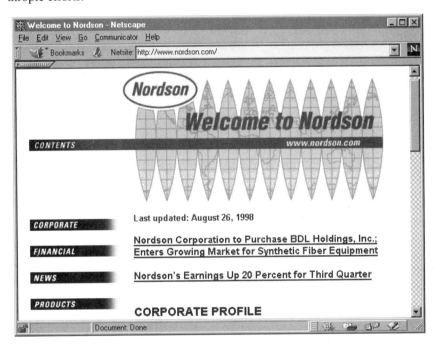

A good place to start when looking for any information about a public company, that is, a company whose stock is traded publicly, is the Security and Exchange Commission's (SEC's) EDGAR Database <http://www.sec.gov/edgarhp.htm>. This is a text-only database that contains an archive of all the financial documents filed with the SEC over the past three years

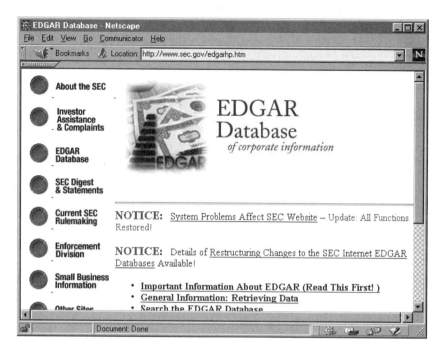

This site contains more information than you could ever want about a company and its operations. Thus, the main challenge is digging through a lot of irrelevant material to find the information you need.

One of the most comprehensive sites for links to corporate information on public and private companies, not only in the United States by abroad as well, is aptly named Corporate Information <http://corporateinformation.com>. This site lists separate links for corporate information in over 100 countries.

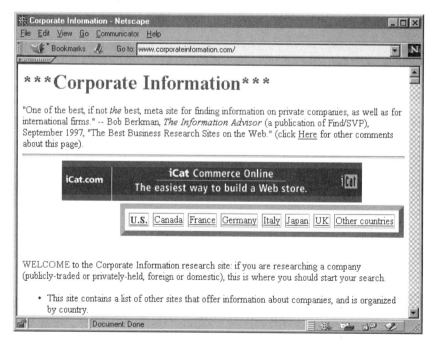

Other helpful pages for information about businesses include Internet Prospector's Corporations <http://plains.uwyo.edu/~prospect/company.html>, *Philanthropy Journal*'s Corporate/Business Links <http://www. philanthropy-journal.org/plhome/plcorp.htm>, and David Lamb's Prospect Research Page <http://weber.u.washington.edu/~dlamb/research.html#corp>. All of these sites have many hypertext links to corporate directories and other types of business information. Any one of these is a good starting point when looking for corporate information. Most of the corporate information available on these sites is for publicly traded companies. To find information on privately held corporations takes more research and may require using a search engine, looking for the company in question by name.

COMPARING INDIVIDUAL CORPORATE WEB SITES

Corporations present their giving information in widely varying formats. Some companies have Web pages dedicated to their philanthropic activities, while others may have information on their grantmaking programs hidden within other pages on their Web sites. Grantseekers must be diligent in order to find the information they need from a corporate Web site and must examine the information given very carefully before applying for a grant.

Buried Information

It is often the case that a company provides some basic philanthropic information within a Web page called, for example, "About Us" or "Corporate History." An example of an Internet site containing corporate giving information buried within its pages is Minolta USA's Web site <http://www.minoltausa.com/80s.html>.

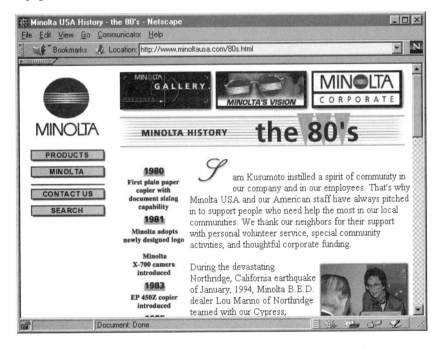

The data on the corporation's grantmaking activities is inside the documents referring to corporate history, listed by decade and beginning in the 1950s. The relevant information concerning corporate giving is in the page chronicling the company in the 1980's. There is no reference to this information on the company's homepage, and once found, it is not very specific, only listing past recipients, not the company's current philanthropic activities.

Like Minolta USA, the philanthropic information in Blockbuster Video's Web site <http://www.blockbuster.com/history/assets.html> is hard to uncover.

It is within the company's history and only accessible by following a link to a section called "Assets." There is no reference to the fact that this area contains information on the company's grantmaking program, nor is there much information once we get there, providing no information on giving criteria or how to apply for a grant.

More Transparent Sites

In comparison, ALZA Corporation's home page has a hypertext link to its Community Relations page <http://www.alza.com/cmnty.htm> which, like many other companies' Web sites, is the area containing information on its charitable contributions.

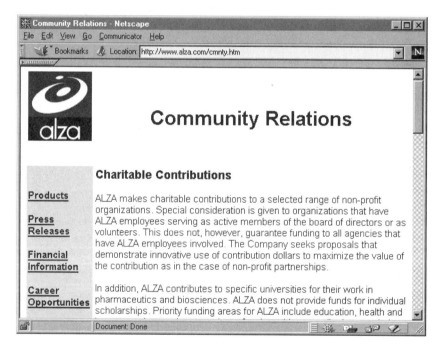

This page provides brief descriptions of the company's fields of interest, application procedures, and an application address. Grantseekers should never ignore the content of these guidelines and automatically send a proposal to the company's application address. Read the material carefully and use your judgment to decide whether you are a logical candidate for this program. An inappropriate application is a waste of time for both the candidate and the corporation.

One of the more well organized Web sites covering a company's grantmaking activities is Hewlett Packard's "Philanthropy" site <http://webcenter.hp.com/grants/index.html>.

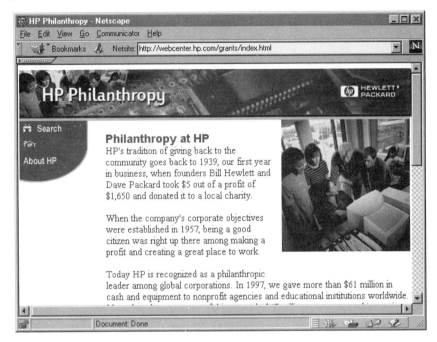

It contains links to succinct descriptions of each of Hewlett Packard's grantmaking programs and grant lists, including contacts, application addresses, telephone numbers, e-mail addresses, and other pertinent information. This is an exemplary corporate giving Web site in that its information leaves no doubt in the grantseeker's mind about how the company's philanthropic activities are organized.

Combination Sites

Nissan North America's site <http://www.nissan-na.com/1.0/1-1.html> contains information on both a company-sponsored foundation and a direct corporate giving program.

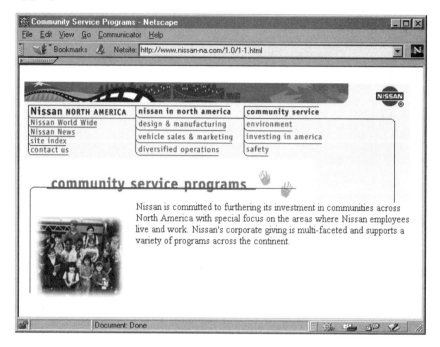

Grantseekers need to be a little careful when coming upon Web sites such as these. There is good information presented here about company giving, but it can be difficult to differentiate between the company's two grantmaking bodies. Sometimes they are operated out of the same office and by the same staff, while other times they act completely independently. In some cases they each require separate proposals. For a number of procedural or policy reasons, the foundation may not be able to support a worthy organization, and so the company will choose to supply support directly. You will need to do further research to choose the appropriate approach.

The pages describing Sumitomo Bank of California's Corporate Donation Program <http://www.sumitomobankcal.com/comm/donation.htm> primarily deal with the company's involvement with the Community Reinvestment Act (CRA). Since the company states up front that two-thirds of its giving is related to the CRA, the grantseeker should be wary of applying for support unless a loan is as desirable as other types of support.

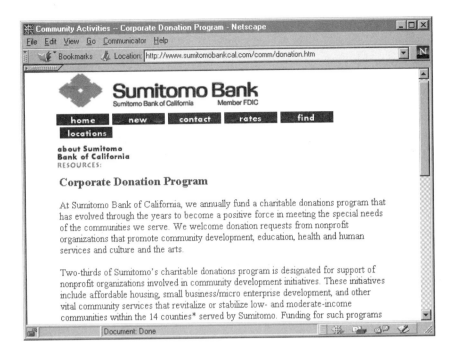

Utilizing the Material at Hand

THE SUBJECT, GEOGRAPHIC, AND TYPE OF SUPPORT APPROACHES

The subject approach leads grantseekers to corporations with an interest in funding programs in certain fields and businesses whose activities are related to nonprofit programs. Some nonprofit/corporate relationships will be obvious: a sporting goods manufacturer expresses interest in an athletic program for disadvantaged youth; a musical instruments manufacturer supports a music appreciation program; a pharmaceutical company or alcoholic beverage manufacturer funds a drug education program.

Most corporate giving programs are limited by giving to the communities in which the company operates. Therefore, a grantseeker's research should include a company's areas of operation, including corporate headquarters, subsidiaries, divisions, joint ventures, and community plants and offices. A company will often support programs that provide direct service to employees and other community residents, that promise public recognition, and that improve customer relations in specific geographic areas.

A type of support approach is usually equally productive. Corporations will often provide funds for capital improvements, operating budgets, and employee matching gifts. They may also make noncash contributions. For example, a clothing manufacturer may have "irregulars" or extra clothing to donate to a homeless shelter. Some connections, however, are more indirect. Charities such as *Gifts In Kind International* <http://www.giftsinkind.org>, *Share Our Strength* <http://www.strength.org>, *Volunteers of America* <http://www.voa.org>, and New York's *City Harvest* <http://www.cityharvest.org> act as pass-through organizations for corporations wishing to provide in-kind gifts, to see that the donations reach those who most need them in an efficient manner. In such cases, rather than applying to the company, giftseekers are encouraged to apply to the appropriate charity.

DO YOUR HOMEWORK

Learn about a corporation's funding before submitting a request. The funder may have an annual report or printed guidelines as well as information about the company and its giving on a Web page. These will help you target your appeal. Business reports present company philosophy and describe company plans for the community, providing vital background in linking a grant request to company interests. Economic conditions and business news should also be followed. A company laying off employees or running up a deficit may not be the one to ask for a donation.

Follow a corporate giver's guidelines to the letter, especially in regard to submission deadlines. Find out to whom the request should be addressed and the preferred format. At some companies, sponsorships and nonmonetary support may be handled by the marketing or public relations department; employee volunteerism may be coordinated in human resources. Different areas of company operations may have different contact persons. Some companies want a preliminary letter of inquiry, and a full proposal only after they have expressed an interest; others require full applications, and some ask for multiple copies of a proposal. Find this out in advance if you can.

PERSONAL CONTACTS

How important is it to know someone? In the electronic age, interpersonal contact is becoming less prevalent. With e-mail, fax machines, voice mail, and the World Wide Web all competing for attention, it is sometimes difficult to get in direct touch with someone you know, much less a stranger. Personal contacts can sometimes help, but their impact varies from organization to organization. Grantseeking from company foundations and direct corporate giving programs with specific philanthropy personnel and explicit guidelines for grantseekers is unlikely to require personal contacts. Personal contacts may be more important when seeking support from the companies with informal giving programs and no formal guidelines.

Nonprofit grantseekers with no personal contacts are not necessarily out of the running. They can begin to build relationships and establish contacts at a professional level. Write an introductory letter to the relevant contact describing your program and expressing interest in a meeting date. Send printed literature and articles that are relevent to your program; send nothing extraneous. Invite decision makers to see your organization in action and to attend special events. Ask if you should send a preliminary letter of inquiry or a full proposal. Establishing rapport with a wary grantmaker can be difficult, but it isn't impossible. Cultivation should be taken on as a long-term effort.

If you receive a grant, send a letter of thanks and submit all agreed-upon reports, following the established timetable. Corporate funders will expect you to follow through and will notice a missed deadline. Keep them informed regardless of the agreement. You may want to suggest forms of recognition, such as programs and posters, reception and dinner honors, certificates, plaques, and newspaper coverage. However, grantmaker recognition depends on nonprofit resources as well as the desires of the corporation, and given the small size of most corporate donations, such formal recognition is not often required.

Even if you are rejected, continue to nurture the relationship. Thank those in charge for considering your request. Ask why you were not funded if they have not made this clear. Determine whether you will reapply in the next cycle.

Getting corporate support demands creativity, ingenuity, and persistence. Competition will be stiff, but the possibility of support cannot be ignored.

PRESENTING YOUR IDEAS TO A CORPORATE GIVER

A proposal must be honest, clear, concise, and appropriate in tone. Draw up a realistic budget, and be prepared to divulge all sources of income and how that money was used, since corporate grantmakers emphasize the bottom line. Many ask for evidence of fiscally responsible, efficient management. Be explicit. State program or agency goals, a plan of action, a timetable, and a method of evaluation. Be brief but comprehensive.

Highlight an innovative program, a program that tackles a new issue, or that addresses an unfulfilled need—without undue self-promotion. Nonprofits should consider asking not only for money and in-kind support. They should target local businesses for board members and volunteers, likely paths to further contributions. Nonprofit leaders should remember that a good relationship with one company may point the way to others or provide an actual introduction to other funding prospects.

First and foremost, the grantseeker should always consider the funder's motivation for giving. Establishing the connection with the grantmaker's goals is the grantseeker's key to success. Focus on company self-interest more than benevolence. For example, a corporate giver may want to develop a trained pool of potential employees, support research, expand its markets, respond to related social issues, and increase sales. Consider what a business stands to gain from the program. Point out the potential benefits to the company in your proposal.

Links and Abstracts of Corporate Grantmaker Web Sites

The annotated list below includes company-sponsored private foundations and direct corporate giving programs.

Abbott Laboratories Fund <http://www.abbott.com/community/abtfund.htm>
The Abbott Laboratories Fund makes grants to nonprofit organizations operating in "Abbott Communities" in the areas of human health and welfare; elementary, secondary, and higher education; and culture, the arts, and civic activities. The Fund generally favors requests for one-time contributions and for programmatic and operating purposes; its guidelines preclude it from making grants for individuals, purely social organizations, political parties or candidates, religious organizations, advertising, symposia and conferences, ticket purchases, memberships, or business-related purposes. In addition to general facts about the Fund's 1997 giving, visitors to the "In the Community" section of the Abbott Laboratories Web site will find general program guidelines and Fund contact information.

Adobe Systems, Inc.
<http://www.adobe.com/aboutadobe/philanthropy/main.html>

Adobe's corporate giving is centered around its "Philanthropy Council," a representative group of Adobe employees committed to supporting programs that improve the quality of life for everyone. The company specifically supports nonprofit organizations that service "disadvantaged youth, the homeless, minorities, the elderly, and victims of abuse; provide disaster relief, medical and hospice care, and meal services; provide education and literacy programs; support human rights; support the arts; protect the environment; and support animal rights." Both cash grants and equipment donations are available. The single page devoted to the company's philanthropic activities provides visitors with a brief description of program and application guidelines, downloadable application forms (in .PDF format), information about Adobe's software donation program, and contact information.

Aetna Foundation <http://www.aetna.com/foundation/>

As the Hartford-based insurance giant's primary philanthropic vehicle, the Aetna Foundation focuses its activities in the areas of children's health, where it looks for initiatives that "focus on cardiac disease prevention and detection initiatives; and education where it favors college preparation, school-to-career initiatives, and entrepreneurial education for middle school students whose parents actively participate in the programs." The grant awards made by the Foundation reflect a geographic emphasis on organizations and initiatives in selected communities of strategic importance to Aetna, and is limited to proposals submitted by invitation. Grant proposals are accepted year-round and must be submitted in writing. In addition to detailed application guidelines, visitors to the Foundation section of the parent company's Web site will find general program information, profiles of successful Foundation-sponsored initiatives, and a section devoted to the company's Voice of Conscience Award, created as a tribute to the late Arthur Ashe. Additionally, the Foundation makes grants to participants in its Academic Medicine and Managed Care Forum for research that will directly improve practices impacting the quality of care and health outcomes for patients.

Alliant Utilities
<http://www.ies-energy.com/ies/company_information/corporate_giving.html>

ALZA Corporation <http://www.alza.com/cmnty.htm>

Aluminum Company of America <http://www.alcoa.com/grant.html>

American Express Company
<http://www.americanexpress.com/corp/philanthropy/>

The philanthropic program of the American Express Company includes the activities of the American Express Foundation and the company's corporate giving program, and encompasses both U.S. nonprofits as well as organizations outside the U.S. that can document non-for-profit status. The company makes grants in three program areas: community service, with funding primarily supporting the volunteer efforts of employees and advisors in their local communities; cultural heritage, with the twin themes of protecting "the built and natural environment" and supporting "art and culture unique to countries and regions"; and economic independence, with an emphasis on supporting initiatives that "encourage, support or develop economic self-reliance." In addition to general program information and application guidelines, visitors to the company's Web site will find a list of 1996 grant recipients and descriptions of major programs to which the company has recently made grants. An online version of the company's 1996 annual report is also available.

Ameritech Corporation <http://www.ameritech.com/community/index.html>

Ameritech, the Chicago-based communications company, provides local phone, data, and video services in Illinois, Indiana, Michigan, Ohio, and Wisconsin. The company gives priority "to grants that improve education, economic development, and quality of life." Ameritech also considers organizational support for "projects and special programs which make communities where it operates better places to live, learn and work. . . ." The company posts a good deal of information about its contributions program on its Web site, including program guidelines and limitations, application procedures, and links to grantee organizations that have their own Web sites. The contributions report is available to download as a .PDF file. Visitors to the Ameritech site can also access an online version of its 1997 annual report.

AMR/American Airlines Foundation <http://www.amrcorp.com/corp_fdn.htm>

Apple Computer <http://www.apple.com/education/>

The primary philanthropic activity of Apple Computer is the donation of new computer equipment to K–12 schools. In the area of higher education, Apple helps institutions to use technology more effectively "to deliver learning experiences that are rich in communication, collaboration and construction of knowledge." The Cupertino, California-based company does not fund religious groups, political groups, or individuals, and does not make donations in support of raffles, fundraising events, auctions, or door prizes. The Education section of the Apple Web site offers general information about Apple's support of K–12 and higher education; information about the Apple Education Grants program, the Apple Distinguished Schools initiative, the Apple Classroom of Tomorrow (ACOT) project, and other education-oriented initiatives; and a helpful FAQ section with, among other things, specific guidelines for contacting the company about its philanthropic programs.

ARCO Foundation
<http://www.arco.com/Corporate/reports/foundation/home.htm>

As the principal philanthropic vehicle of the Atlantic Richfield Company, the ARCO Foundation "has shaped its grantmaking around the belief that corporate philanthropy and individual participation in the nonprofit world go hand in hand." The Foundation relies heavily on the personal involvement of ARCO employees and retirees as volunteers and donors, and to reinforce employee and retiree support of community causes, the Foundation gives its Employee Programs—namely Matching Gifts and Volunteer Grants—precedence over direct grants in the allocation of available funds. The online version of the Foundation's annual reports from 1996 and 1997 which provide grantmaking objectives, priorities, and grants lists in five broad program areas (arts and humanities, community initiatives, education, the environment, and public policy); information about the

Foundation's employee programs; application procedures; and regional contact information.

Ashland Inc./Ashland <http://www.ashland.com/community/>

Aspect Telecommunications
<http://www.aspect.com/commcomm/cocous.htm>

AT&T Foundation <http://www.att.com/foundation/>
As the principal philanthropic arm of AT&T, the AT&T Foundation makes grants in the program areas of education, arts and culture, and civic and community service. While the scope of the Foundation's activities is global, the majority of its funds support U.S.-based institutions. The Foundation also maintains a local corporate contributions program to focus support on cities and regions with large concentrations of AT&T employees and business operations. The parent company's newly redesigned Web site includes a separate area for Foundation information where visitors will find detailed program descriptions; application guidelines and procedures; complete 1994–95, 1996, and 1997 grants listings for each program area; and an interactive form for requesting additional information.

Baltimore Gas and Electric Company
<http://www.bge.com/aboutbge/contrib/contrib.html>
Through "thoughtful social investments," BGE's corporate contributions program seeks to "enhance the health, welfare, financial strength, and quality of life" of those living in communities where BGE operates. The nation's first gas utility supports the following program areas: education, health and welfare, cultural enrichment, civic and environmental improvement, and economic development in communities where the company has a significant business interest. Visitors to the company's Web site will find program ad application guidelines, a graphic illustrating its 1997 giving by program area, and contact information.

BankAmerica Corporation
<http://www.bankamerica.com/community/community.html>
Through its Foundation, the San Francisco-based BankAmerica Corporation provides "opportunities for individual employees to contribute their talents for the good of the communities where they live" and "actively invests in nonprofit groups engaged in community development." Although the company supports programs in a number of funding areas, its Web site provides detailed information on only two of them: community development, with extensive information on the bank's Community Economic Development Initiative; and the environment, with helpful links and information on a variety of programs, including paper recycling and reduction and sustainable development.

Bankers Trust Corporation
<http://www.bankerstrust.com/corpcomm/communi/report/index.html>
Through its Foundation and corporate contributions program, New York City-based Bankers Trust concentrates its philanthropic activities in seven program areas: community development, education, arts and culture, health and hospitals, environment, international, and a general category (i.e., public policy research, and national and international emergencies). Bankers Trust also allocates funds to

special categories and through employee programs. Although the company's activities are focused on major institutions either operating in or committed to improving the quality of life in NewYork City, it also has a "coordinated strategy of overseas philanthropy" in communities where it has employees or conducts business. The parent company's Web site provides detailed program descriptions; grant policies and guidelines; a report of 1997 contributions; Community Focus, a periodic newsletter about Bankers Trust's philanthropic efforts; and contact information.

The Bayer Foundation <http://www.bayerus.com/about/index.html>

Baxter Allegiance Foundation
<http://www.baxter.com/investors/citizenship/index.html.>

BCI Corporation <http://www.bcicorp.com/CHARITY.HTM>

BDM International, Inc. <http://www.bdm.com/bdm/newscorp.htm>

Bectel Foundation <http://www.bechtel.com/buildingminds/bechfoun.html>

Bell Atlantic Foundation <http://www.bellatlanticfoundation.com>
The merger of Bell Atlantic and NYNEX, announced August 14, 1997, joined the two corporations' foundations to create a new Bell Atlantic Foundation. The Foundation provides "opportunities for non-profit organizations to apply new technology to the programs and services they offer," focusing its efforts on the communities from Maine to Virginia served by Bell Atlantic, particularly those communities' children and young people. Most of the Foundation's support aims to make technology more available to students, teachers, service organizations, and cultural institutions with youth programs. Priority is given to activities in education, health and human services, arts and humanities, and community service that facilitate collaborations through network solutions and enhanced communications systems. The Foundation's sophisticated Web site comes in Java and non-Java versions. Visitors to the Web site will find summaries of giving by state, grants lists by state going back to 1994, an overview of the Foundation, grant guidelines, detailed program descriptions, contact information (e-mail is the preferred form of communication), news, and a list of the Foundation's board of directors. Grantseekers can locate their community relations manager by entering their zip code in a form on the Web site, and the Foundation encourages online submission of grant applications, guaranteeing a response within 48 hours.

BellSouth Foundation <http://www.bellsouthcorp.com/bsf/>
The BellSouth Foundation seeks to improve outcomes and stimulate active learning for students in elementary and secondary education in nine southern states—Alabama, Florida, Georgia, Kentucky, Louisiana, Mississippi, North Carolina, South Carolina, and Tennessee. In its current grantmaking cycle (i.e., 1996–2000), the Foundation focuses its efforts in three areas: developing individual capacity to improve learning; creating environments to improve learning; and promoting partnerships through technology to improve learning. BellSouth's Web site offers visitors a broad range of information about the activities of its Foundation, including online versions of two reports on the Foundation's grantmaking

initiatives; detailed program descriptions; application guidelines, deadlines, and restrictions; and an interactive application form.

The Ben & Jerry's Foundation
<http://www.benjerry.com/foundation/index.html>
Ben & Jerry's gives away 7.5 percent of its pre-tax earnings through its foundation, through employee Community Action Teams (CATs) at five Vermont sites, and through a corporate giving program. The company supports projects that are "models for social change" in three focus areas: children and families, disadvantaged groups, and the environment. Ben and Jerry's does not support basic or direct-service programs. The company's Web site provides basic information on grant restrictions and size; application procedures; recent grants lists; a letter of interest to view and print; information on other funding sources; and tips on writing a successful proposal. Visitors to the site can also access the Foundation's 1994, 1995, and 1996 annual reports.

BHP Hawaii <http://www.energypeople.com/bhp/community/>
Through its charitable giving arm, the BHP Hawaii Foundation, and the individual efforts of its employees, BHP Hawaii contributes to a variety of organizations and causes, keeping a focus on education and the environment. Grant applications are reviewed once a year by the company's board, and awards generally are limited to organizations based in the State of Hawaii or other geographical areas in which BHP Hawaii has business interests. Application guidelines, general program descriptions, and contact information are available in the "Community" section of the parent company's Web site. The "1997 Community Investment Report" provides a listing of grantees for fiscal year 1997.

Boston Globe Foundation
<http://www.boston.com/extranet/foundation/index.html>

BP America, Inc. <http://www.bp.com/_nav/commun/index.htm>

Broderbund Foundation <http://www.broder.com/company/foundation.html>
The Broderbund Foundation, the philanthropic arm of California-based Broderbund Software, Inc., awards grants to health, social service, and environmental organizations primarily serving the San Francisco Bay Area. Grant applications must be sponsored by a Broderbund employee, and "involvement by a Broderbund employee or a member of the extended Broderbund family continues to be an important factor in the choice of recipients." The "Foundation" page of the parent company's Web site provides a general statement of purpose, initial application procedures, and contact information.

Bristol-Myers Squibb company <http://www.bms.com/profile/index.htm>

Ceridian Corporation <http://www.ceridian.com/who_we_are.htm>
In the Who We Are section of Ceridian's Web site, visitors should select "In the Community" to learn about the company's corporate giving program. The primary emphasis of Ceridian's corporate giving is on innovative policy initiatives and programs that help people balance the growing demands of work and home life. The Minneapolis-based information services and defense electronics

company also emphasizes giving in the areas of health, education, and the arts. The In the Community section of the company's Web site provides general program information as well as application guidelines and an interactive application form. Visitors to the site can also access an online version of the company's 1996 and 1997 annual reports.

Chevron Corporation <http://www.chevron.com/community/index.html>
Chevron, the San Francisco-based petroleum and chemicals concern, has a long history of supporting communities where it does business and where its employees live and work. Those communities are scattered around the globe—from the Americas (Bolivia, Canada, Mexico, the U.S.), to Europe and Africa (Angola, Scotland, Wales, Zaire), to Asia and the Pacific (Australia, China, Indonesia, Kazakhstan, Papua New Guinea). Currently, the company focuses its giving in the areas of math and science education, with an emphasis on kindergarten through 12th grade (K–12); environmental conservation, with an emphasis on habitat preservation, wildlife protection, and environmental education programs; crime; and substance abuse. The "Community" section of the Chevron Web site offers a good deal of general program information, grant guidelines, a 1997 grants list organized by program area, answers to frequently asked questions, and a simple interactive application form.

CIGNA Corporation <http://www.cigna.com/corp/contributions/>

Cinergy Foundation <http://www.cinergy.com/foundation/default.htm>

Citibank/Citicorp Foundation
<http://www.citicorp.com/corporate_affairs/pfoco.htm>
Citibank and the Citicorp Foundation contributed more than $31 million in 1996 to community development and education programs, both nationally and internationally. Funding is provided to nonprofit institutions through initiatives such as the Foundation's Banking on Enterprise, which supports microenterprise lending in inner-city neighborhoods in the U.S. and emerging markets worldwide, and Banking on Education, a program that supports the use of technology in inner-city schools and provides scholarships for higher education. Citibank also sponsors art programs worldwide through its contributions to museums, symphony orchestras, theater and dance companies, performing arts centers, and libraries. Among a wide variety of features, the Citibank/Citicorp Web site includes descriptions of the company's international community activities and programs, performance strategies, financial statements, and listings of corporate officers.

The Clorox Company Foundation <http://www.clorox.com/community.html>
The Clorox Company Foundation is dedicated to improving the quality of life in communities where Clorox employees live and work—primarily in 23 "Clorox cities" in the U.S., Canada, and Puerto Rico. The Foundation focuses its grants on programs that serve youth, core cultural and civic organizations, plant programs, and organizations in which Clorox employees are involved. Grants typically support innovative programs in their developmental stages. The Community Affairs section of the parent company's Web site offers a brief description of the Foundation's philanthropic interests and activities, contact information, and links to the Web sites of organizations receiving support from Clorox.

Coca-Cola Company <http://www.cocacola.com/co/scholars/index.html>

Columbia Gas <http://www.columbiaenergy.com/>
The principle goal of the Corporate Contributions Program of Columbia Gas of Pennsylvania and Columbia Gas of Maryland is to address community priorities, primarily where Columbia has a presence. To learn about it, first select "About the Company" and then "community relations." The company focuses its charitable activities on education, community development, community safety, and civic leadership. Within each of these areas, Columbia actively encourages programs that meet the needs of young people, the elderly, persons with disabilities, minorities, and women. Visitors to the Community section of the parent company's Web site will find general information on Columbia's outreach and grantmaking activities.

Compaq Computer Corporation
<http://www.compaq.com/corporate/contrib/index.html>

The ConAgra Foundation <http://www.conagra.com/commun.html>
Through its company-sponsored foundation, ConAgra, a diversified international food company based in Omaha, Nebraska, seeks to improve the quality of life in communities where the company's employees work and live. To that end, the ConAgra Foundation focuses its resources in the areas of education, health and human services, arts and culture, sustainable development, and civic and community betterment. The ConAgra Web site provides very general information about the Foundation's guidelines, restrictions, deadlines, as well as contact information for written requests only.

Cooper Industries <http://www.cooperindustries.com/about/giving/toc.html>
Houston-based Cooper Industries, Inc., a diversified manufacturing company with 40,000-plus employees in 24 countries, makes contributions through its foundation and corporate giving programs in the areas of community development, the environment, education, health and human services, arts and culture, and workplace safety in communities where it has a strong presence. The Cooper Industries Web site provides a good deal of information about the company's charitable activities, including guidelines and application procedures, 1997 grants of $1,000 or more arranged by program area, a listing of the communities in which Cooper has operations, and online versions of the company's 1997 and 1996 annual reports.

Corning Foundation <http://www.corning.com/news/index.html>

Datatel Scholars Foundation <http://www.datatel.com/scholars.htm>

John Deere & Company
<http://www.deere.com/aboutus/general/support.htm>
The John Deere Foundation and Contributions Committe award grants and give support to a variety of nonprofit organizations nationwide, with an emphasis on human services, community development, educational issues, and cultural opportunities. The Corporate Contributions page of the Deere & Company Web site provides general infomation about the company's contributions program, Deere

Foundation policies and procedures, and contact information for both. A link to the November '95 issue of the JD Journal provides a somewhat more detailed look at the scope and impact of various Foundation-sponsored initiatives. HTML and/or .PDF versions of recent Deere & Company annual reports are also available at the site.

Detroit Edison Foundation
<http://www.detroitedison.com/aboutus/whoweare/96ar/96found.html>

Digital Equipment Corporation <http://www.digital.com/community/>
DIGITAL's corporate contributions program provides cash grants for programs that benefit children and youth, particularly in the areas of education, health and leadership. The company also provides computer and technology grants to "organizations and programs outside the children and youth theme, specifically in the areas of education, healthcare and community programs." Favorable projects will demonstrate employee involvement or interest and a direct impact on DIGITAL communities. In addition to a statement of the company's giving philosophy, visitors to the site will find application guidelines, support limitations, and general information about the company's programs, partnerships, and community activities.

R.R. Donnelley & Sons Co. <http://www.rrdonnelley.com/public/community/>

Dow Chemical Company <http://www.dow.com/about/charitable/charity.html>

Dreyer's Charitable Foundation
<http://www.dreyers.com/corporate/charity.html>
The mission of the Dreyer's Grand Ice Cream Charitable Foundation is "to promote a family, school and community environment which enables young people to develop their individual initiative and talents to the maximum extent in order for them to become contributing members of their community and caretakers of the community's values and ideals for the next generation." Through its direct grant program, the Foundation supports projects that benefit young people in the Oakland, California/East Bay Area, with particular priority given to support low and middle income youth and minority youth. Visitors to the philanthropy section of the parent company's Web site will find program guidelines and application procedures for the direct grants program, as well as a number of other Foundation-sponsored programs, including the Employee Community Involvement Fund, the "Dream the Dream" Competition, small grant and product donation opportunities. Visitors will also find 1996 support highlights and Dreyer's 1996 annual report.

Eastman Kodak Company
<http://www.kodak.com/US/en/corp/community.shtml>

Eaton Corporation <http://www.eaton.com/corp/contribute/index.html>

Electronic Data Corporation <http://www.eds.com/community_affairs/>

Exxon Corporation & Exxon Education Foundation
<http://www.exxon.com/exxoncorp/main_frame_3_ie4.html>

Exxon makes direct contributions to charitable organizations in the U.S. and funds the Exxon Education Foundation. Exxon's direct contributions program concentrates on the following program areas: the environment; public policy and public research; united appeals and civic and community-service organizations; arts, museums, and historical associations; and education. The Exxon Education Foundation provides funds to launch new activities or to expand existing programs in mathematics education; elementary and secondary education; and undergraduate science, technology, engineering, and mathematics. Three other Foundation programs, which are currently closed, are not described on the Web site. The "Working With Others" area of Exxon's Web site offers thorough program descriptions and grant application guidelines; Dimensions 97, a report on Exxon's 1997 contributions, including the Exxon Education Foundation report, which provides a grant summary and 1997 grants list; reports on special funding areas; and an online version of Intersections, the Foundation's newsletter.

The Fannie Mae Foundation **<http://www.fanniemaefoundation.org/>**

The mission of the Fannie Mae Foundation is "to expand decent and affordable housing opportunities and improve the quality of life in communities throughout the United States." The Foundation supports national and local nonprofit organizations dedicated to helping more families afford homes, provides prospective buyers and immigrants with information on the home-buying process, conducts local home-buying fairs as well as research on a broad range of housing and urban issues, and supports organizations addressing housing and community development issues across the country. In addition to detailed information on the Foundation's initiatives, the Web site provides complete grant program guidelines, current RFPs, and information about the Maxwell Awards for Excellence. Grant applications can be downloaded as .PDF files or requested through an interactive form. An online version of the Foundation's 1996 annual report provides lists of program-related investments; national and local grants; Washington, D.C., grants; and officers and board members.

The Fieldstone Foundation **<http://members.aol.com/mmfieldsto/index.htm>**

As the philanthropic vehicle of the Fieldstone Group, a home builder based in Southern California, the Fieldstone Foundation is primarily interested in programs serving children and families. The Foundation funds capacity building of nonprofits through leadership programs; school retention programs; prevention of drug and alcohol abuse, child abuse, and community violence. It also supports organizations that provide child care services, emergency assistance for youth and families, positive alternatives for youth, and positive responses to diversity. Contributions are made primarily within Southern California, and to national organizations that earmark Foundation funds for use in these communities. Visitors to the Foundation's Web site will find a listing of the Foundation's 1996 and 1997 grants; grant guidelines and criteria; information on the Fieldstone Leadership Network, which provides technical and management training to nonprofits in Fieldstone communities; a listing of the Foundation's staff and board members; and contact information.

FirstEnergy Corp. <www.FirstEnergyCorp.com/community/>
FirstEnergy Corp is a newly formed holding company that resulted from the merger between Ohio Edison and Centerior. While no information related to their corporate giving program can currently be found on the site, the company is expected to develop a giving program similar to the Centerior Energy Foundation, previously run by Centerior Energy. The Centerior Energy Foundation povided funding to support "health, welfare, civic, cultural, and educational endeavors" to improve the quality of life for its customers, employees, and other stakeholders. Funding was limited to organizations located within Centerior's service territories. The Foundation generally provided support for building funds, equipment, and operating budgets. Visitors to the site will find information on their education grants and the required application.

FMC Foundation
<http://www.fmc.com/Corp/Community/Foundation/foundation.html>
Chicago-based FMC is one of the world's leading producers of chemicals and machinery for industry, government, and agriculture. The company's charitable-giving arm, the FMC Foundation, contributes more than $1.5 million annually in five major areas—health and human services, education, community improvement, urban affairs, and public issues—to nonprofit organizations in FMC communities, as well as to national organizations working on issues relevant to FMC's businesses. Visitors to the parent company's Web site will find brief descriptions of the Foundation's philosophy and purpose; program descriptions and guidelines; detailed submission requirements; and basic contact information.

Freddie Mac Foundation <http://www.freddiemacfoundation.org/>

Gap, Inc. <http://www.gap.com/company/community.asp>
Through its Community Relations program, Gap, Inc. gives cash grants and contributions of merchandise to nonprofit organizations in program areas of particular concern to Gap employees. While the Gap makes grants in a variety of areas of importance to its communities, including health and human services, education, and arts and culture, it has a special interest in supporting environmental projects. The Gap also makes contributions of t-shirts, sweatshirts, and gift certificates. Visitors to the "Our Community" section of the company's Web site will find general program descriptions, funding limitations, application instructions, and contact information.

Gannet Foundation <http://www.gannett.com/map/foundation.htm>

GE Fund <http://www.ge.com/fund/>
The GE Fund places education at the crux of its international grantmaking efforts, with support to programs in the areas of science and engineering, pre-college education, public policy, international programs, management, and arts and culture. Online versions of the Fund's 1994, 1995, 1996 and 1997 annual reports, featured within parent company General Electric's well-organized Web site, each include a letter from the Fund's president, profiles of the Fund's major initiatives, program descriptions, grants lists, and application guidelines.

General Mills, Inc. <http://www.genmills.com/explore/community/>

Genentech, Inc. <http://www.gene.com/Company/Responsibility/>

GTE Foundation <http://www.gte.com/g/ghcomm.html>
The GTE Foundation, one of the country's 20 largest corporate philanthropies, gives nearly $25 million annually to educational, scientific, and charitable organizations on behalf of GTE and its business units. As a corporation, the telecommunications giant is concerned about America's ability to produce a well-educated, highly productive workforce and has committed significant resources to improving education, with special emphasis on mathematics and science. The GTE Web site offers information about GTE's philanthropic efforts in education, health and human services, the arts, and community involvement; and a brief description of the Foundation itself, including contact information. Visitors can also access the company's 1997 annual report.

Halsey Street Interactive Design <http://www.halseystreet.com/105.html>

John Hancock Company
<http://www.jhancock.com/company/community/index.html>

Hannaford Bros. Company
<http://www.hannaford.com/community/charitbl.htm>

HEI Charitable Foundation <http://www.hei.com/heicf/heicf.html>
The Hawaiian Electric Industries Charitable Foundation awards grants to 501(c)(3) organizations in the State of Hawaii in the categories of community development, education, environment, and family services. The company's Web site provides financial highlights from its 1997 annual report, a message from HEI's president, summaries of giving for each program area, and general guidelines and application information.

Hewlett-Packard Company <http://www.corp.hp.com/Publish/UG/>
Hewlett-Packard's Web site offers application guidelines and selection criteria for the primary components of its corporate giving program: The University Grants Program, which emphasizes the donation of equipment over cash; the National Grants Program, primarily supporting K–12 education; U.S. Education Matching, which provides cash matching to universities and equipment matching to educational institutions of all levels; U.S. Local Grants, which support local organizations and K–12 education; and European Grants Programs to help fulfill HP's European citizenship objective. Visitors to the site will also find a corporate philanthropy overview and 1997 annual report, program and application guidelines, grant and product request forms to download as .PDF or text files, and philanthropy contacts at HP.

The Home Depot <http://www.homedepot.com/>

IBM Corporation <http://www.ibm.com/IBM/IBMGives/index.html>
IBM is guided by a new corporate strategy that aims to combine the company's "technology and people in effective partnerships to bring solutions to the systemic problems that impact society, business, and our quality of life." The four key elements in all new IBM contributions are IBM technology and service, IBM

expertise, IBM partnerships, and rigorous measurement. The "philanthropy" section of Big Blue's Web site offers a listing of "Recent Events" (i.e., press release-style narratives about the company's recent charitable endeavors); a statement of the company's new corporate giving strategy and a summary of its current philanthropic initiatives, including K–12 education, reinventing education, workforce development, adult education and job training, and the environment; examples of funding to IBM communities worldwide; and a link to the IBM-sponsored 1996 National Education Summit Web site. A snazzy online version of the company's 1997 annual report is also available.

Inland Paperboard and Packaging, Inc.
<http://www.iccnet.com/content/social/default.htm>
Indianapolis-based Inland Paperboard and Packaging, a wholly-owned subsidiary of Temple-Inland, Inc., places a substantial emphasis on action-oriented social responsibility. The company embraces the values of its founder, entrepreneur and philanthropist Herman Krannert, and his wife, Ellnora, who were committed to improving educational and cultural opportunities for all people. The Inland Foundation, established in 1951, makes grants in the areas of health and welfare, education, art and culture, and civic issues. Inland's Web site provides visitors with a strong sense of the company's mission, its activities vis-a-vis its stewardship of the environment, and initiatives that comprise its Partners in Education program.

Intel Corporation & Foundation <http://www.intel.com/intel/community/>
The focus of Intel's giving and outreach programs is on bettering education, supporting Intel communities, improving life with technology, and protecting the environment. The company's Foundation funds programs which "advance math, science and engineering education, promote women and under-represented minorities entering science and engineering careers, and increase public understanding of technology and its impact on contemporary life." All information on the company's philanthropic activities is provided at its Web site under the heading "Intel's Community Involvement." The "Grant Information" section in this area offers grant guidelines, downloadable application materials (as MS Word executable files—you don't need MS Word to view them), additional information on local community grant programs, and links to information on research grants, scholarships, and fellowship programs. An online version of Intel's 1997 annual report is located in the "Investor Relations" area of the Web site.

Ipalco Enterprises <http://www.ipalco.com/>

SC Johnson Wax Fund, Inc. <http://www.scjohnsonwax.com/whocmovw.html>

KN Energy Foundation
<http://www.kne.com/pages/community/foundation.htm>

Lincoln National Foundation
<http://www.lnc.com/public_involvement/>

MCI Communications Corporation
<http://www.mci.com/aboutus/company/corporate/community/>

MCI, which operates the world's largest and fastest Internet network, "is dedicated to educating America's children through cutting-edge technology to provide [them] with the knowledge and skills they need to succeed in the 21st century." Recently, the telecommunications giant has refocused its philanthropic activities on its Corporate Community Partnership Programs, which comprise five distinct entities: the MCI Foundation, Corporate and Field Community Relations, In-Kind Donations, Employee Voluntarism, and Academic and Community Support. In addition to a general overview, the "Community Partnerships" area of the MCI Web site provides information about a number of its Partnership programs, including MCI Smart Surfing, educationMCI, Disaster Response, and the MCI International Scholar Awards; and a selection of press releases.

Lucent Technologies <http://www.lucent.com/what/community/>

Matsushita Electric Corporation of America
<http://www.panasonic.com/host/company/index.html>

McDonald's Corporation
<http://www.mcdonalds.com/community/index.html>

McKesson Corporation <http://www.mckesson.com/>

The Medtronic Foundation
<http://www.medtronic.com/foundation/index.html>

The Medtronic Foundation directs the worldwide philanthropy and community affairs of Minneapolis-based Medtronic, Inc., a manufacturer of medical equipment and devices. Most of the Foundation's grant dollars are spent in three areas: education, with an emphasis on K–12 science education through its STAR (Science and Technology Are Rewarding) program; health; and community affairs, which includes human services, civic, and arts grants. In all three areas, priority is given "to programs that benefit people of color and those who are socioeconomically disadvantaged." The Foundation's Web site offers program descriptions, grant guidelines and application procedures, an application form to print out, a list of Foundation grants made between May 1, 1996, and April 30, 1997, a listing of Medtronic communities, a selection of press releases, and a handy interactive correspondence page. Visitors can also browse an online versions of Medtronic's 1997 annual report.

Merrill Lynch & Co., Inc. <http://www.ml.com/woml/phil_prog/index.htm/>

Metropolitan Life Insurance Company
<http://www.metlife.com/Companyinfo/Community/>

MetLife's Web site provides visitors with detailed program guidelines and limitations, application procedures, and contact information for the insurance giant's three distinct giving programs: the Metropolitan Life Foundation, which awards grants in the areas of health, education, culture, civic affairs, and anti-violence; MetLife's Social Investment Program, which provides aid primarily in the form of loans to help "local and national groups build stronger communities across the country"; and the Targeted Suppliers program, which is "designed to increase MetLife's purchasing of goods and services from minority and women-owned firms."

Micron Technology, Inc. <http://www.micron.com/html/community.html>

Microsoft Corporation <http://www.microsoft.com/giving/>
The Microsoft Corporation supports organizations in its communities of operation, primarily the Puget Sound region of Washington State where its headquarters are located and where most of its employees reside. Community grants are made in the areas of human services, education, arts and culture, the environment, access to technology, and civic activities. The world's largest software manufacturer also makes cash and in-kind contributions nationally to K–12 and higher education institutions. The Community Affairs section of Microsoft's Web site offers brief program descriptions, application guidelines, 1997 giving highlights, and information on its employee giving and Libraries On-Line programs.

The Millipore Foundation <http://www.millipore.com/corporate/foundation/>
The Millipore Foundation's objectives are to foster advances in science and technology related to Millipore's business objectives, which include developing purification products for the microelectronic, biopharmaceutical, and analytical laboratory markets; to improve the quality of life in those communities in which Millipore employees live and work, particularly in its headquarters city of Bedford, Massachusetts; and to stimulate voluntarism and active community involvement by Millipore employees. Through its Grants Program, the Foundation supports projects in the areas of education and research, social services, health care, and the arts. Visitors to the parent company's Web site will find a brief overview of the Foundation, program guidelines, application instructions, and contact information. There is an online version of the parent company's 1997 annual report, and the Foundation's 1997 annual report is available for downloading as a .PDF file.

Minnesota Mining & Manufacturing Company
<http://www.mmm.com/profile/community/index.html/>

Mitsubishi Electric America Foundation
<http://www.meaf.org/meafhome.html>
The MEA Foundation is dedicated to the "improvement of quality of life and the empowerment of disabled youth." Its Web site details the Foundation's history and mission, and includes extensive program descriptions, application guidelines, and recipient information on grants awarded by the Foundation. Visitors to the site will also find a list of Foundation staff and officers, and Foundation contact information.

Mitsubishi Motors of America <http://www.mitsucars.com/>

Monsanto Fund
<http://www.monsanto.com/Monsanto/Media/archive/docs/monsantofund/>
The mission of the Monsanto Fund, the philanthropic arm of the Monsanto Company, is "to enhance the value of Monsanto by improving the quality of life in

communities of particular importance." The Fund's annual budget of approximately $11 million is distributed for science education, the United Way, arts and culture, and other charitable purposes. Approximately 25 percent of the Fund's annual contributions support programs to improve the quality of life in Monsanto's plant communities. Visitors to the one-page Fund section of the parent company's Web site will find general program goals, descriptions of recent grants, and a handful of links to recent grant recipients. The site also offers an online version of the company's 1997 annual report.

J.P. Morgan & Co., Inc. <http://www.jpmorgan.com/>

J.P. Morgan & Co., the global financial services firm established more than 150 years ago, makes charitable contributions to a wide range of organizations involved in the arts, education, the environment, health and human services, international affairs, and urban affairs through both the J.P. Morgan Charitable Trust and the firm's offices and subsidiaries around the world. Morgan's Community Relations and Public Affairs department, which is responsible for the firm's relationships with nonprofit organizations, supports "recognized and competent groups" with financial grants, donations of equipment, volunteer services, technical advice, and other services. The department also supports Morgan's efforts to comply with the Community Reinvestment Act. Visitors should select "Community Relations" under "Corporate Information" to find general information about the firm's charitable activities, back issues of Capital Ideas, a biennial newsletter, and contact information.

Morton International, Inc. <http://www.morton.com/comm/overcomm.html>

Nalco Foundation <http://www.nalco.com/1_about.html#foundation/>

NEC Foundation of America
<http://www.nec.com/company/foundation/index.html>

The NEC Foundation was established in 1991 by NEC and its United States subsidiaries to promote NEC's corporate philosophy: the integration of computers and communications to help societies worldwide move toward deepened mutual understanding and fulfillment of human potential. The particular focus of the Foundation is on organizations and programs with national reach and impact in one or both of the following areas: science and technology education, principally at the secondary level; and/or the application of technology to assist people with disabilities. Visitors to the parent company's Web site will find extensive information about the Foundation's activities, including funding guidelines, application procedures, deadlines, and restrictions; a list of recent grant recipients indexed by organization type, geographic location, and grant purpose; and a financial statement.

New England Financial <http://www.tne.com/aboutus/comminv.htm>

Newport News Shipbuilding
<http://www.nns.com/overview/97_community_affairs/community.htm/>

Oxford Health Plans Foundation <http://www.oxhpfoundation.org>

Pacific Bell Foundation
<http://www.pactel.com/community/foundation/index.html>
As the principal philanthropic vehicle of the Pacific Telesis Group, the Pacific Bell Foundation is dedicated to "preparing people from all cultures to participate in the economic, social and civil life of their communities by improving the quality of public education, providing access to technology, and building the capacity of community-based organizations" in California and Nevada. The online version of the Foundation's 1997 annual report includes a letter from the Foundation's president, a grant summary and searchable grants database, a description of the organization with grant guidelines, application procedures, a list of public affairs offices, and a contact information page where visitors can request a copy of the Foundation's annual report.

Pacific Gas & Electric
<http://www.pge.com/about_us/communities/contributions.html>
Through its corporate contributions program, Pacific Gas & Electric makes grants exclusively to nonprofit organizations in northern and central California, primarily in two areas: 1) job training and economic development and 2) education. It also makes a limited number of grants for emergency preparedness and response, environmental stewardship, and civic and cultural activities. Although the company prefers to fund special projects and new or existing programs, it does makes grants for general operating support and, on a limited basis, for capital campaigns. Grants typically range from $1,000 to $15,000. In addition to a general description of PG&E's philanthropic programs, visitors to the company's Web site will find a rundown of its grant application procedures and contact information.

J. C. Penney Company <http://www.jcpenney.com/commrel/content/>
J.C. Penney makes grants to national organizations in the areas of health and welfare, education, civic betterment, and arts and culture. Special attention is given to the support and promotion of voluntarism and the improvement of pre-college education, with a focus on the areas of K–12 reform, restructuring, and dropout prevention. Funding emphasis is given to projects that serve abroad sector of a particular community, national projects that benefit local organizations across the country, organizations that provide direct services, and organizations with a proven record of success. Grants for projects with a local scope, hospitals, museums, and individual colleges and universities are made by local units of the company. Visitors to the "Community Involvement" area of the parent company's Web site will find general funding guidelines, application procedures and limitations, and the company's Community Relations Annual Report.

Pfizer Inc. <http://www.pfizer.com/pfizerinc/philanthropy/home.html>
Through its "Venture Philanthropy" program, pharmaceutical giant Pfizer Inc. makes grants to nonprofit organizations within the broad categories of health, education, and community and cultural affairs. Through both product donations and cash grants, Pfizer's health program seeks to "expand access to compassionate, high-quality health care, especially for those most at risk of poor health outcomes." The goal of its education programs is to "excite students, primarily K–12, about science and to increase their understanding of scientific principles and the importance of scientific progress." And the company's community and cultural affairs program "is committed to strengthening and enhancing the quality of life

in communities" where Pfizer operates, particularly New York City. Visitors to the philanthropy section of the Pfizer Web site will find extensive descriptions of the company's philanthropic philosophy, general program descriptions, listings of selected grant recipients in each program area, and application instructions.

Pillsbury Company Foundation <http://www.pillsbury.com/community/foundation.html>

Piper Jaffray Companies
<http://www.piperjaffray.com/pj/pj_ci.asp>

The Playboy Foundation
<http://www.playboy.com/pb-foundation/foundation.html>
Established in 1965, the Playboy Foundation's mission is "to pursue, perpetuate and protect the principles of freedom and democracy." Today, the Foundation "seeks to foster social change by confining its grants and other support to projects of national impact and scope involved in fostering open communication about, and research into, human sexuality, reproductive health and rights; protecting and fostering civil rights and civil liberties in the United States for all people, including women, people affected and impacted by HIV/AIDS, gays and lesbians, racial minorities, the poor and the disadvantaged; and eliminating censorship and protecting freedom of expression." The Foundation also awards grants for postproduction and distribution of documentary films and videos that address issues of social change. It has established the Freedom of Expression Award given at the Sundance Film Festival each year to honor the documentary film that best educates the public on an issue of social concern. The Foundation component of Playboy's Web site provides visitors with general program guidelines, grant application and award nomination guidelines and limitations, a selected 1997 grants listing, and contact information.

Polaroid Foundation
<http://www.polaroid.com/polinfo/foundation/index.html>

Procter & Gamble <http://www.pg.com/docCommunity/activity/>
Procter & Gamble makes charitable contributions worldwide in excess of $50 million annually. Roughly 60 percent of the company's annual contributions support education, through grants to colleges and universities, public policy research programs, economic education organizations, and P&G's scholarship program for employee children. P&G also makes grants to health, social service, civic, cultural, and environmental organizations. Visitors to the "Community Activity" section of the P&G Web site will find a brief description of the company's philanthropic interests and a brief accounting of its contributions by interest area.

The Prudential Foundation
<http://www.prudential.com/community/cmzzz1000.html>
Founded in 1977, the Prudential Foundation "works to improve the quality of individual and community life by focusing on critical children's issues and community, education, and health needs." The Foundation's grantmaking efforts fall into six categories: health and human services; education; urban and community development; children; business and civic affairs; and culture and the arts. The

Foundation makes grants in all regions of the U.S., and the Web site's community locator identifies specific communities where Prudential has a presence. Visitors to the Foundation's Web site will find program area guidelines and contact information for obtaining application forms or the Foundation's 1997 annual report. The site also contains information on Prudential direct corporate giving initiatives, including the "Spirit of Community Awards," granted to middle and high school students in recognition of community service; the "Helping Heart Program," which helps voluntary emergency medical service squads purchase semi-automatic cardiac defibrillators; and the "Social Investment Program," which finances projects designed to provide affordable housing, economic revitalization, and healthcare cost containment to communities where Prudential has a significant presence.

Rite Aid Corporation <http://www.riteaid.com/commun.htm>

Sara Lee Foundation <http://www.saraleefoundation.org/>

SBC Foundation <http://www.sbc.com/About/Foundation/Home.html>
The SBC Foundation, the philanthropic unit of SBC Communications, Inc., and two of its subsidiaries—Southwestern Bell and Cellular One—seeks to help "communities search for lasting solutions to critical and complex problems." To that end, the Foundation focuses on education, community economic development, health and human services, and culture and the arts. Most grants are directed toward Southwestern Bell's five-state region—Texas, Missouri, Kansas, Oklahoma, and Arkansas—but the Foundation does support a number of relevant initiatives that are national in scope. The SBC Web site provides visitors with a thorough, user-friendly overview of the grantseeking process, including grantmaking guidelines, a grant application form, and contact information.

The Sega Foundation <http://www.sega.com/central/foundation/index.html>
The Sega Foundation is committed to improving the lives of young people, and has a particular interest in children's education and health. While not readily accessible from the parent company's home page, the Foundation area of the Sega Web site offers a good deal of information about Sega-funded projects and initiatives, past, present, and future. The Foundation initiates most of its funding discussions with nonprofit organizations, but it accepts unsolicited proposals for small grants, typically ranging from $500 to $2,500. The Web site provides thorough funding information, grant application and eligibility guidelines, and lists of grants.

SmithKline Beecham <http://www.sb.com/company/c_commun.htm>

Sonoco Products Company <http://www.sonoco.com/grant/grant.htm>
The Sonoco Foundation, the principal philanthropic conduit for the South Carolina-based Sonoco Products Company, focuses its giving on education, health and welfare, arts and culture, and the environment in locations where the company has operations. The majority of its grants are awarded to United States institutions with a local, rather than a national, perspective. The Foundation does not support projects in areas where the company has minimal or no operations; grants to individuals or sponsorship of individuals in fund-raising projects; private

foundations; sectarian or denominational religious organizations, missionary groups, or projects serving religious purposes; courtesy advertising or testimonial dinners; loans or investments; or pledges longer than five years. Visitors to the Foundation's Web site will find general policy, program, and application guidelines, grant application format, and contact information.

Southwire Company <http://www.southwire.com/sw/comm/resume.htm>

Sprint Corporation <http://www.sprint.com/sprint/overview/commun.html>
Commitment to community, with an emphasis on "support of local and regional organizations in which the corporation has a major presence," is the basis for Sprint's corporate philanthropy. Through its Foundation and its corporate giving programs, Sprint supports education, arts and culture, community improvement, and youth development. The "Community Service" area of the Sprint Web site includes information on the company's employee giving programs, a brief overview of the Sprint Foundation's activities, application guidelines, and contact information. Online versions of the company's annual reports from 1993 through 1997 are also available at the site. The 1994–1997 reports can be downloaded as .PDF files.

State Farm Companies <http://www2.statefarm.com/commun/commun.htm/>

Sun Microsystems Foundation
<http://www.sun.com/corporateoverview/corpaffairs/giving.html>
Through its Community Development Grants Program, the Sun Microsystems Foundation "invests in communities that are often characterized by low income, high unemployment, and disturbing school drop-out rates." Grants are awarded in the areas of education (grades 7–12 in the U.S., and secondary schools S1-S6 in Scotland) and employment and job development in the southern San Francisco Bay Area, the Merrimack Valley of Massachusetts, and the West Lothian District of Scotland. Visitors to the Sun Web site will find information on the Program's funding criteria (and what it doesn't fund), application guidelines, and online versions of the company's 1995–1997 annual reports.

Texaco Foundation
<http://www.texaco.com/corporate/foundation/foundation.htm/>

Texas Instruments Foundation
<http://www.ti.com/corp/docs/foundation/home.htm>

360 Degrees Communications <http://www.360.com/cc/>

Toshiba America Foundation <http://www.toshiba.com/new/taf.shtml>
As the charitable arm of Toshiba America, Inc., a leading consumer electronics company, the Toshiba America Foundation focuses on the improvement of classroom teaching in grades 7–12, especially in the areas of science, mathematics, and technology. Although the Foundation welcomes proposals from communities across the United States, it "feels a special responsibility toward . . . communities where the Toshiba America group companies have a corporate presence." In addition to information about the Foundation's current program interests, Toshiba

America's attractive, well-organized Web site provides a summary of projects funded by the Foundation in the last twelve months, detailed instructions on preparing a grant application, a proposal format outline and sample proposal cover page, and contact information.

Toyota USA Foundation <http://www.toyota.com>

With a primary emphasis on improving the teaching and learning of mathematics and science, the Toyota USA Foundation is committed to improving the quality of K–12 education in the U.S. Grants are made to accredited colleges, universities, community colleges, vocational or trade schools, and to nonprofit organizations engaged in pre-collegiate math and/or science education; K–12 public and private schools may not apply directly to the Foundation, though they may be the recipient of an independent nonprofit agency's funding request. In addition to contact information and a general overview of its activities, visitors to the Foundation's Web site will find detailed application guidelines and restrictions, highlights of recent grants and a list of Foundation grantees since 1989, and a grant application form.

Union Electric Company <http://www.ue.com/community/>

United Airlines Foundation <http://www.ual.com/airline/>

United Technologies <http://www.utc.com/commun2.htm>

United Technologies, a diversified $23 billion Fortune 500 conglomerate, makes grants to tax-exempt 501(c)(3) organizations in the areas of education, health and human services, cultural arts, and civic involvement. UTC focuses its grantmaking in communities where it has a substantial corporate presence, including Hartford, East Hartford, Stratford, Windsor Locks, and Middletown, Connecticut; Syracuse, New York; Dearborn, Michigan; Bloomington, Indiana; West Palm Beach, Florida; and Washington, D.C. The application form available on the Web site must be filled out and submitted by July 15 of the current year for projects to be considered for the next year's budget. The "Community Involvement" area of the United Technologies Web site provides visitors with general descriptions of each area of support, guidelines and limitations for grant and matching gift programs, summaries of funded projects in UTC's program areas, and appropriate contact information.

U S WEST Foundation
<http://www.uswest.com/com/communities/foundation/>

The US West Foundation seeks to "strengthen the link between developments in the communications world and the kinds of projects it funds" through its Major Initiative and Community Outreach programs. The Foundation's major initiatives include "Widening Our World," a mobile interactive school teaching people how to interact through computer and telecommunication technologies; "Connecting People Through Communications Technologies for Education," an information technology training program for teachers; "Connecting People to Economic Growth," supporting programs designed to nurture small businesses and other economic development efforts; and "Creating Content for the Future," improving lives of individuals with multimedia technologies. Through its Community Outreach program, the Foundation supports nonprofit organizations in the areas of

arts and culture, civic and community improvement, education, and human services. The Foundation's previous General Grant application process has been
replaced with a Request for Proposal (RFP) process, therefore unsolicited proposals will not be reviewed. The Web site provides general guidelines for RFPs,
deadlines for each program area, and contact information for regional program
officers.

USX Foundation <http://www.usx.com/grant.htm/>

Wells Fargo & Company <http://wellsfargo.com/cra/contrib/>

Wells Fargo, the San Francisco-based banking and financial services concern,
directs the bulk of its corporate giving to three areas: community development,
especially programs that provide affordable housing, provide job training, revitalize or stabilize low and moderate income communities, or promote economic
development; pre-K through grade 12 education, with a focus on math, literacy,
and the history of the American West; and human services, especially organizations whose work in child care, health services and education, and basic needs
assistance benefits low and moderate income individuals. Geographically, the
company's grantmaking is concentrated west of the Mississippi in the states of
Arizona, California, Colorado, Idaho, Nevada, New Mexico, Oregon, Texas,
Utah, and Washington. Visitors to the Community Reinvestment section of the
Wells Fargo Web site will find general program information, application guidelines and procedures, and contact information. The site also offers information
about the company's $45 billion/10-year Community Reinvestment Lending and
Investment Leadership Pledge.

Westinghouse Foundation
<http://www.westinghouse.com/corp/wesfound.htm>

Through its Foundation, the Westinghouse Electric Corporation focuses its philanthropic efforts on education and a qualified, well-educated workforce, placing a
special emphasis on science, math, and engineering programs that reach students,
teachers, and education institutions and associations at all levels. The Foundation
is currently not accepting requests for funding, but will update the site when it is.
Visitors to the "Foundation & Community Affairs" section of the Westinghouse
Web site will find an historical overview of the Foundation's activities; detailed
information about the Westinghouse Science Talent Search and the Service
Uniting Retired Employees; and an online version of the Foundation's annual
report, with application guidelines and procedures, a list of grant recipients, and
descriptions of some recent Foundation grants, among other items.

Weyerhaeuser Company Foundation
<http://www.weyerhaeuser.com/who/foundation/>

The Whirlpool Foundation
<http://www.whirlpoolcorp.com/ics/foundation/index.html>

Through the Whirlpool Foundation, the appliance manufacturer seeks to
"improve the quality of family life primarily in [Whirlpool] communities, worldwide." The Foundation particularly likes to partner with "organizations that target
women and family life issues." In 1996, the Foundation awarded $4.5 million in
grants, scholarships, and gifts to a variety of nonprofits through four programs:

the Strategic Grants Program, the Citizenship Grants Program, the Employee-Directed Programs, and the Sons and Daughters Scholarship Program. Visitors to the Whirlpool Corporation Web site will find general descriptions of the Foundation's areas of interest, information on Whirlpool's research in women's studies, a sampling of recent grants, and contact information. An online version of the company's 1997 Corporate Citizenship report is also available.

Wisconsin Power and Light Foundation
<http://www.wpl.com/ewpl/who/founda.html>
The Wisconsin Power & Light Foundation supports programs in the areas of health and welfare, education, arts and culture, and community development that primarily benefit communities in a 16,000-square-mile section of south-central Wisconsin. The Foundation does not support direct grants or scholarships to individuals; advertisements, door prizes, raffle tickets, or organized sports teams; religious, fraternal, or social clubs; endowments; registration or participation fees for individuals or teams for fundraising events; travel funds for tours or tournaments; political activities; or organizations that don't have tax-exempt status. Visitors to the WP&L Web site will find general program descriptions, downloadable versions of the Foundation's Request Profile and Request for Financial Support forms, and contact information.

CHAPTER FIVE

Government Resources on the Web

In an environment of government cutbacks and the call for balanced budgets, the abundance of government grants for nonprofits and individuals may come as a surprise to some. Also surprising may be the U.S. government's notable presence on the Internet, which attests to the wealth of resources for grantseekers at all levels as well as to the government's interest in keeping pace with technological change.

Because printed government documents and information tend to be dense and laborious to search through (not to mention difficult or inconvenient to find), the Internet is an ideal place to conduct such research. Online government resources of interest to grantseekers include general information about the government, databases and statistics about philanthropy, legal and financial information, funding availability announcements, and guides to proposal writing. Although government resources on the Internet are plentiful and therefore potentially overwhelming, a number of Web sites exist whose creators—often at universities or nonprofit organizations—have culled, categorized, organized, and annotated government and government-related sites. These sites vary greatly in design, amount and type of information, and usefulness to grantseekers. This chapter is intended to suggest starting points and, especially, to help identify those sites most useful for grantseekers.

Start at the Top

The top is a logical place to start to get the broadest possible view of resources. Each branch of the federal government has its own Web site, as do many departments, agencies and state and local governments. The executive branch, for instance, provides access to information from the White House, the President's cabinet, and independent federal agencies and commissions <http://www.whitehouse.gov/WH/EOP/html/3_parts.htm/>.

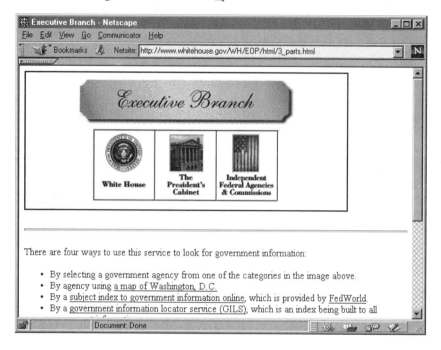

The executive branch site is also a place to start your search for general government resources. Follow the links to FedWorld <http://www.fedworld.gov/>, a subject index to government information online, and the Government Information Locator Service (GILS) <http://www.gils.net/index.html>, an index to all government information.

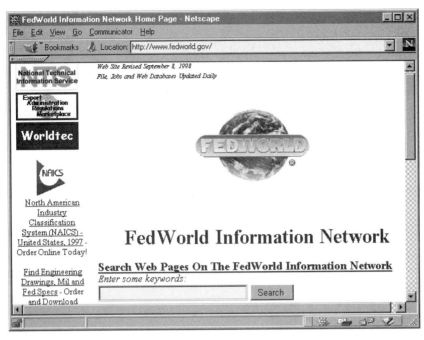

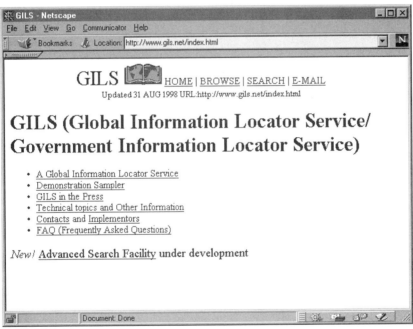

The House of Representatives site <http://www.house.gov/> and the Senate site <http://www.senate.gov/> include access to information about legislation recently passed and being considered.

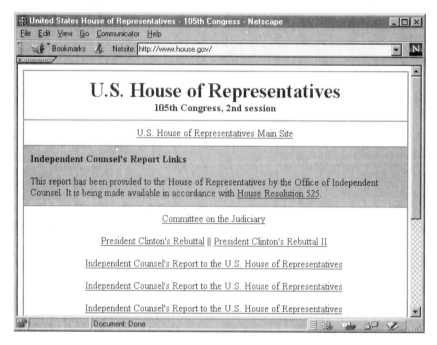

The frequently updated databases of THOMAS, the official site of the U.S. Congress <http://thomas.loc.gov/>, include information on congressional activity, committee reports, and the legislative process.

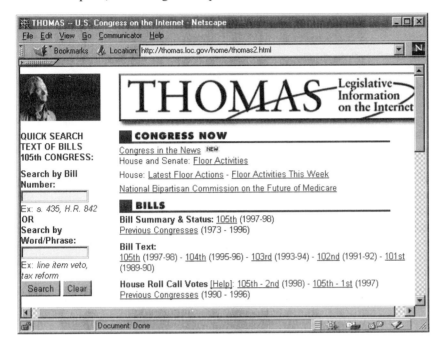

GENERAL GOVERNMENT INFORMATION SITES

In addition to the official government branch home pages, many government departments and nongovernmental organizations compile and list links, providing entrance to government and related sites. The Library of Congress's Internet Resource Page series <http://lcweb.loc.gov/global/executive/fed.html>, for example, has a comprehensive set of links organized by departments and agencies. Here are some other places to start:

Federal Web Locator <http://www.law.vill.edu/Fed-Agency/fedwebloc.html>
A service provided by the Villanova Center for Information Law and Policy, this site offers a comprehensive search engine using keywords or "federal quick jumps" to find an agency or organization.

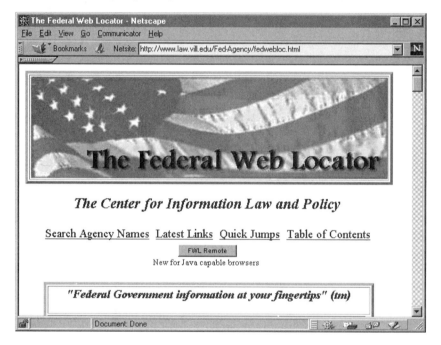

   This site is "intended to be the one-stop-shopping point for federal government information on the World Wide Web. This list is maintained to bring the cyber citizen to the federal government's doorstep."

GovBot <http://ciir2.cs.umass.edu/Govbot/>

Developed by the Center for Intelligent Information Retrieval, the GovBot data-base consists of over 500,000 Web pages from U.S. government and military sites and can be searched by means of a simple form with keywords.

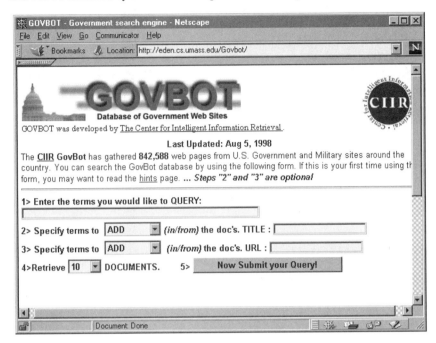

World Wide Web Virtual Library: US Government Information Sources
<http://iridium.nttc.edu/gov_res.html>

This site, maintained by the National Technology Transfer Center, is similar to the Federal Web Locator but on a smaller scale (about 1,000 government links). It is notable for highlighting all new links in a separate category.

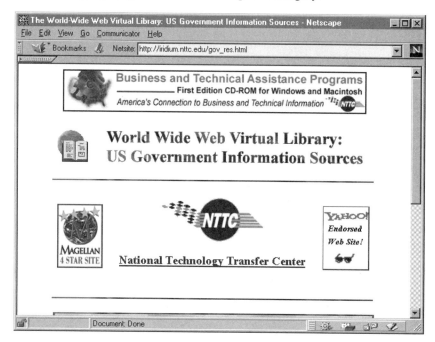

Louisiana State University's Libraries List of U.S. Federal Government Agencies <http://www.lib.lsu.edu/gov/fedgov.html>

This site provides a comprehensive list of links to government departments, agencies, and related organizations right on the first page so that you can simply search or scan for relevant words or appropriate departments.

University of Texas Health Center United States Government and Grant Resources <http://pegasus.uthct.edu/OtherUsefulSites/Govt.html>

This site provides useful links organized in categories such as Foundations and Grant Information, Minority Funding Opportunities, U.S. Federal, State, and Local Grant Funding Opportunities, and specific grantmaking foundations, government departments, and institutes.

The Foundation Center's Links to Nonprofit Resources
<http://fdncenter.org/2onlib/2govt.html>
The Government Resources section of "Links to Nonprofit Resources" in the Foundation Center's Online Library provides easy access to sites highlighted in this chapter in addition to several specific federal and state agencies of interest to grantseekers and nonprofit organizations. (See Chapter 7 for more on the Center's "Links to Nonprofit Resources.")

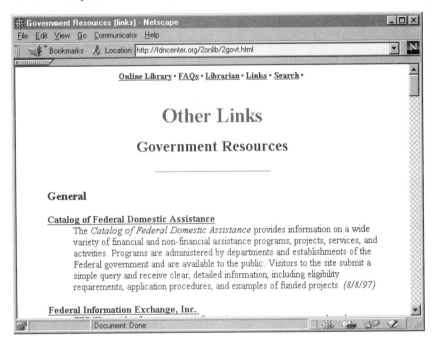

Federal Acquisition Jumpstation (part of NASA Acquisition Internet Service)
<http://procure.msfc.nasa.gov/fedproc/home.html>
This site, which links to Internet sites of federal procurement information, is designed for the business community but is also relevant to grantseekers because it delineates how the government spends its money. Simply searching for the word "grant" on the front page takes you to specific grantmaking bodies.

STATE AND LOCAL GOVERNMENT INFORMATION SITES

The government Internet presence extends deep into all levels and, therefore, so can your grantseeking. To find state and local government resources, try these sites:

State and Local Government on the Net
<http://www.piperinfo.com/state/states.html>
This site consists of links to each state (plus tribal governments), and in turn each state page provides links to the branches, departments, boards, and commissions that have Web sites. This site can be helpful in searching for local grantmaking bodies such as arts councils.

StateSearch <http://www.nasire.org/ss/index.html>

This site is "designed to serve as a topical clearinghouse to state government information on the Internet." Linking to a subject area results in a list of all departments, listed by state, that are involved in that subject and have a Web presence.

Library of Congress: State and Local Governments
<http://lcweb.loc.gov/global/state/stategov.html>

This site offers a combination of the previous two sites—a meta-list of links to state and local government information. (e.g., City Net, a searchable site providing access to cities' government information) and links to each state's Web pages.

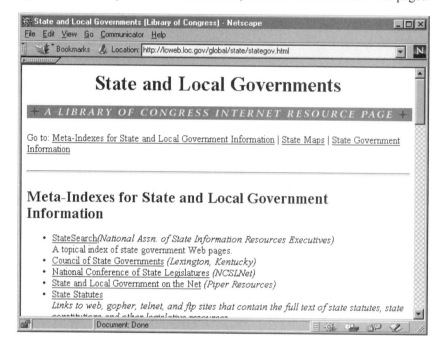

Focusing Your Research on Government Funding

Government-related sites can contain an enormous amount of information, much of it not very useful to the focused grantseeker. As with corporate Web sites (see Chapter 4), grants and funding information is often buried within a site and can easily be missed. In addition, funding information may not be situated in one area of the site but rather by department or subject matter. Because most of these sites are so information-rich, many of them have internal search engines and grantseekers should make a habit of using them. By using the search terms "grants," "funding," "opportunities," or even "research and development," in addition to key words describing the particular subject matter of interest, you are less likely to miss relevant information.

The majority of grants offered by the government—especially at the federal level—are in the fields of education, health and scientific research, human services, environment, agriculture, and industry, though they are not limited to these subject categories. The government also funds historical research, arts and humanities. Looking at the more specialized departments, grants are awarded in a wide range of disciplines. Federal funders generally prefer projects that serve as prototypes or models for others to replicate, whereas local government funders look for strong evidence of community support for the project.

Though a fair number of individual awards exist, the majority of government grants (as is true for private grants as well) are awarded to eligible nonprofit organizations, not to individuals.

GENERAL GOVERNMENT GRANT INFORMATION SITES

There are a number of general sites that focus specifically on government funding, which can be very useful to grantseekers.

NonProfit Gateway <http://www.nonprofit.gov>

This is the starting point for nearly one-stop federal grant shopping. Created by the White House Office of Public Liaison, the site provides extremely valuable and easy-to-use information and services from federal agencies.

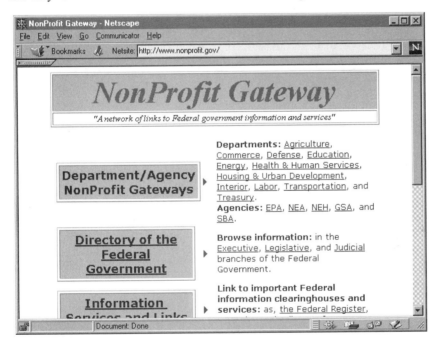

You can link to related Web sites hosted by federal departments and agencies, search for grant programs, and get information about federal laws that apply to nonprofits. The most useful feature of the site is the set of charts that list government cabinet departments and agencies and note whether or not they offer grants. Bullets in the charts link to the department or agency's Web site and directly to the grantmaking section of each site.

Federal Register <http://www.access.gpo.gov/su_docs/aces/aces140.html>
This is the official daily record of the federal government. It has the most current and comprehensive information regarding governmentally funded projects and funding availability.

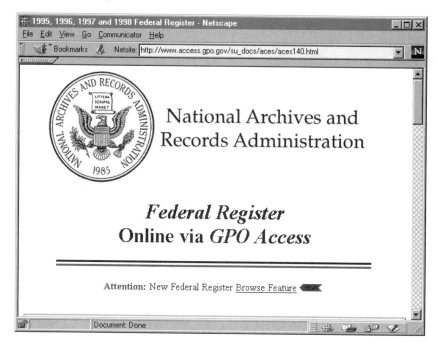

You can search the database in a variety of ways, guided by detailed instructions and sample searches. Alhough there is no section devoted entirely to grants or requests for proposals (RFPs), grantseekers can enter key words to generate a list of potential funding notices. The Federal Register is an essential stopping point in the grantseeker's journey because it provides information on all government grants. Other departments often link to this site in their grants information, and their own compilations may not be as current.

EZ/EC Notices of Funding Availability <http://ocd.usda.gov/nofa.htm>

As noted above, although comprehensive, the Federal Register is not solely dedicated to serving the grantseeker. So a visit to this site, developed by the Empowerment Zone and Enterprise Community Program Offices of the U.S. Department of Agriculture and the U.S. Department of Housing and Urban Development, allows grantseekers to customize a search for Notice of Funding Availability announcements (NOFA), thereby making the Federal Register database more relevant and manageable.

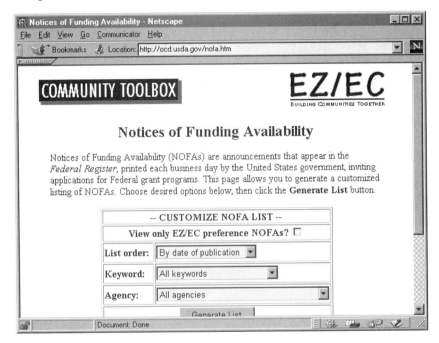

**Catalog of Federal Domestic Assistance
(CFDA) <http://www.gsa.gov/fdac/default.htm>**

This site is part of the General Services Administration and provides information on a wide variety of financial and non-financial assistance programs, projects, services, and activities. This is probably the government resource most familiar to grantseekers, with good reason. You can submit a simple query and receive clear, detailed information, including eligibility requirements, application procedures, and examples of funded projects. Suggested keywords to use are "grants," "money," "assistance."

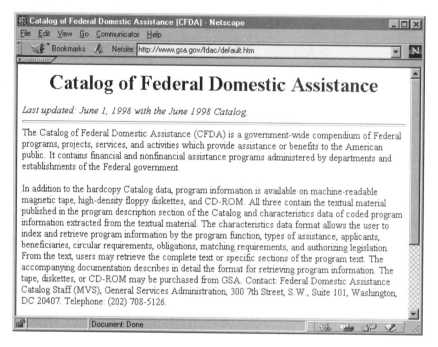

Federal Information Exchange (FEDIX) <http://web.fie.com/fedix/index.html>
This page is run by several federal agencies and provides access to information on
government research and education grants, programs, contracts, and more. The
site is comprehensive and easy to use.

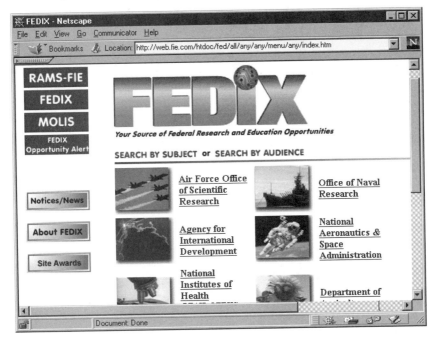

You can search by audience (e.g., Higher Education and Research Organizations, Public Outreach, Elementary/Secondary Schools, Minority Federal Opportunities) or subject and you can also receive targeted funding opportunities via e-
mail.

GrantsNet (Department of Health and Human Services)
<http://www.hhs.gov/progorg/grantsnet/>

The Department of Health and Human Services has an exemplary Web site for grantseekers. Visitors to the GrantsNet portion of the site will find relevant headings, including "How to Find Grant Information," "Search for Funding," "How to Apply," "Useful Grants Management Information," as well as links to other federal grant programs.

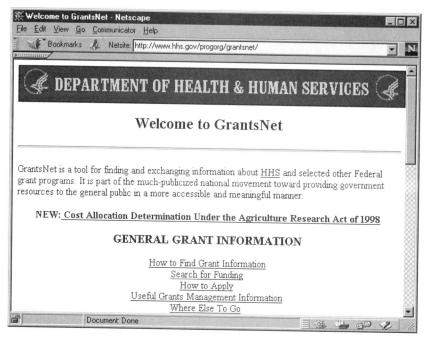

GrantsNet has a search tool to use as a guide to find specific funding opportunities. The HHS Partner Gateway <http://www.odphp.osophs.dhhs.gov/partner/funding.htm>, also a service of the Department of Health and Human Services, is "an easily navigable roadmap to HHS resources" that highlights Web pages with grant information if you are seeking funding for projects in this area.

NARROWING YOUR FOCUS ON FUNDING INFORMATION

Like FEDIX, the following sites list resources specifically geared towards government grant information and therefore help reduce searching time.

Grants Web <http://web.fie.com/cws/sra/resource.htm>

This is a comprehensive, well-organized site, created by the Research Administrator's Resource Center, that highlights government grantmaking areas with links to federal agencies and the NonProfit Gateway.

Grants Information Service (Penn State)
<http://infoserv.rttonet.psu.edu/gis/>

This site provides links to several searchable government databases, most of which have been previously mentioned here, in addition to several university gateways and new, featured databases.

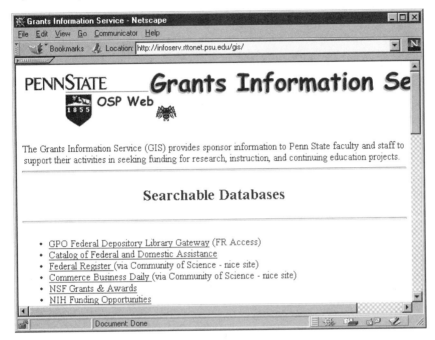

University of Michigan Documents Center
<http://www.lib.umich.edu/libhome/Documents.center/fedgt.html>

Annotated links provide access to some of the major government databases and grantmaking sites, such as the Federal Register, a few searchable university databases, Education Department Grants, etc. Again, this site provides access to most of the previously mentioned sites but is well-organized and worth visiting.

The National Adjunct Faculty Guild At-a-Glance Guide to Grants
<http://www.sai.com/adjunct/nafggrant.html>

This site has a section called "Databases of Funding Opportunities" that includes links to federal and state grant catalogs, several of which require subscription or university affiliation, but again, worth a visit.

SPECIFIC SUBJECT AREAS

Grantseekers who have a very clearly defined project in a specific discipline or subject area may choose to go directly to the government department that would be most likely to offer such funding. A project may even be developed with a particular funder in mind. Some of the federal government agencies or departments commonly known to provide funding assistance are (these URLs indicate grants/ funding information pages, not the departmental home page):

Department of Education <http://www.ed.gov/money.html>
The "Money Matters" section of the Department of Education contains information about student financial assistance and links to a host of grants and contracts information.

Department of Housing and Urban Development
<http://www.hud.gov/fundopp.html>
This site provides information about various types of grants, including community development, affordable housing, and research.

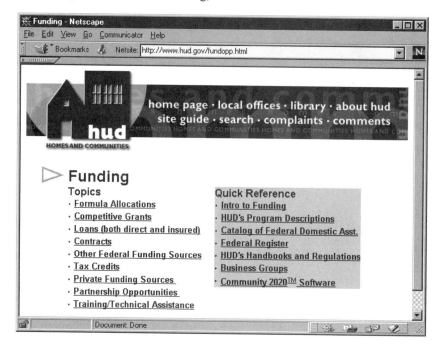

Department of Transportation <http://www.dot.gov/ost/m60/grant/>
Grants for planning, design, and construction of transportation improvements are generally made to state and local governments (with some to Indian tribes, universities, and nonprofit organizations). There is also a limited amount of funding available for research and development projects.

National Science Foundation <http://www.nsf.gov/home/grants.htm>
This is an attractive, user-friendly, grantseeker-friendly site. The Foundation is an independent U.S. government agency responsible for promoting science and engineering through research and education projects in science and engineering.

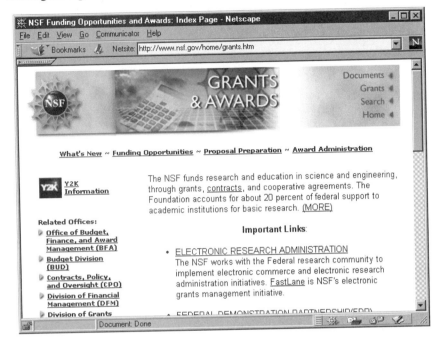

National Endowment for the Arts <http://arts.endow.gov/>
National Endowment for the Humanities <http://www.neh.fed.us/>

These are two very well known and thus highly competitive grantmaking programs. Their main purpose is to fund projects, so both sites are worth browsing.

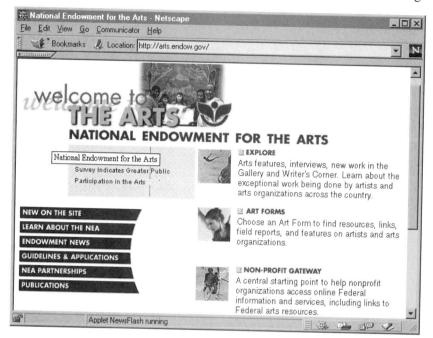

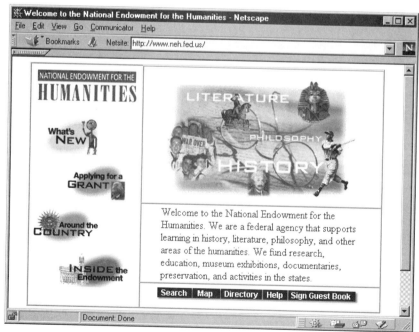

National Institutes of Health <http://www.nih.gov/grants/>
This is an easy-to-use site with clear information about funding for health and research projects.

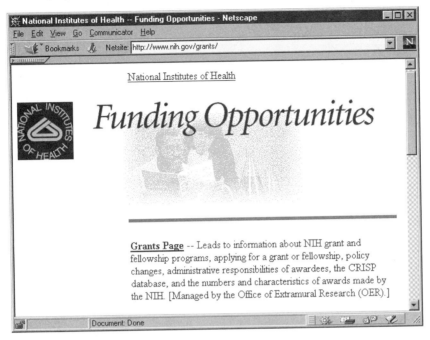

Smithsonian Institution <http://www.si.edu/organiza/offices/fellow/start.htm>
The Smithsonian offers predoctoral, postdoctoral, and graduate student fellow-ship programs, the Minority Internship Program, and the Native American Intern-ship Program.

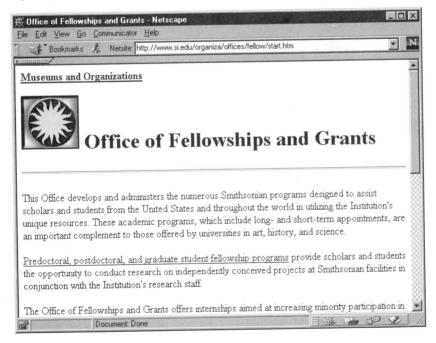

Office of Minority Health Resource Center <http://www.omhrc.gov/>
We show the main Web page here, but this site includes a database of funding and
grant resources for minority health projects, providing information on private and
public foundations; pharmaceutical and insurance organizations; and federal,
state, and community resources.

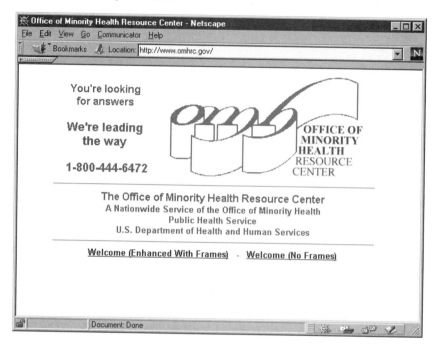

Environmental Protection Agency <http://www.epa.gov/ogd/grants.htm>
This site offers clear and plentiful information on research grants and graduate fellowships.

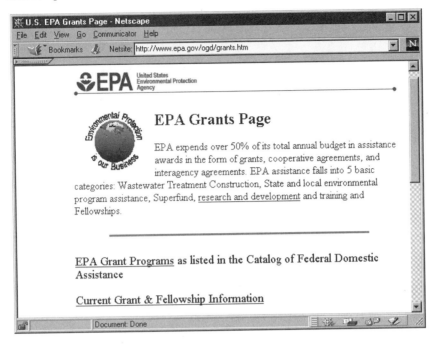

National Archives <http://www.nara.gov/nara/nhprc/>
The National Historical Publications and Records Commission (NHPRC) makes grants to preserve and provide public access to records, photographs, and other materials that document American history.

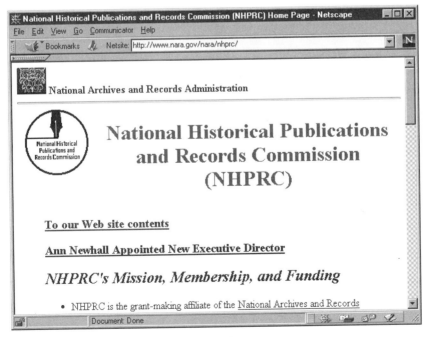

Small Business Administration
<http://www.sbaonline.sba.gov/specialinterests/ingrant.html/>

This is a well known independent governmental agency that assists small businesses through a variety of financial assistance programs. The Web site is easy to navigate, with concise descriptions explaining the variety of routes available to financing a small business.

National Telecommunications and Information Administration
<http://www.ntia.doc.gov/>

This site offers grants, training, information, and research services in the telecommunications arena.

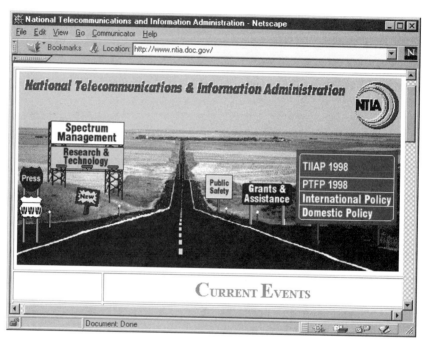

Department of Agriculture <http://www.reeusda.gov/new/funding.htm>

The Cooperative State Research, Education, and Extension Service of the USDA administers a variety of grant programs available to researchers, educators, and small businesses.

Department of Justice <http://www.usdoj.gov/grants.html>

This site offers grant information, including the ADA Technical Assistance Grant Program, Bureau of Justice Assistance, COPS Grant Information, and Violence Against Women Grant Information.

OTHER GOVERNMENT RESOURCES

In addition to online grant announcements, you may find the following government-related sites useful both in your grants search and in gaining a better understanding of the nonprofit sector and its relationship to the government.

FedWorld <http://www.fedworld.gov/about.htm>

This is a comprehensive, easy-to-use resource for government databases and general government information.

FedStats <http://www.fedstats.gov/>

This site provides a variety of statistics produced by more than 70 agencies in the federal government, such as the National Center for Education Statistics and the Federal Assistance Awards Data System.

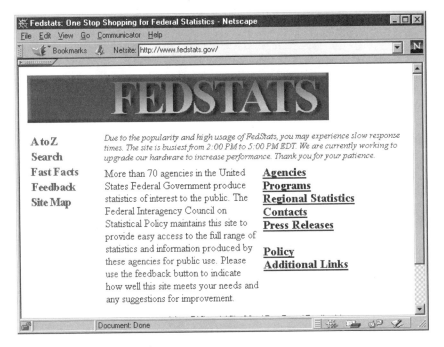

IRS Exempt Organization Search <http://www.irs.ustreas.gov/prod/search/ eosearch.html>

This is a very useful site for tax information. The Exempt Organization Search allows visitors to learn about the exemption process and conduct a search for any exempt organization. There are a number of links to explore on this page.

This list of resources is by no means exhaustive, but rather a guide to some user-friendly points along the grantseeking journey. As with any grant search, it is essential to start out with a clear idea of what is needed. This proves especially true when combing through the profusion of government resources. As a rule, it is a good idea to contact the agency you are considering applying to in order to obtain the most up-to-date information on its programs and procedures.

CHAPTER SIX

Databases on the Web, Free and Fee

A database is a collection of data organized for rapid search and retrieval. This chapter focuses on World-Wide-Web-accessible resources that offer this search and retrieval capability and which may be of special interest to grantseekers.

Many grantseekers use Web-spanning search engines as an integral component of their investigations. Because the Internet itself is indexed by search engine services, you could say that it is a sort of database, albeit sprawling and without the important data consistency provided by a single-source database. However, a variety of specific government, nonprofit, and corporate databases, some of them completely free, have become available on the Web. Such publicly accessible databases generally offer keyword searching in one or more searchable fields and can be effectively utilized by even the most inexperienced researcher. Additionally, veteran information service providers, some of whom have utilized database technology for decades, have begun making their databases available online via the Internet, often modifying their search technology in the process—introducing natural language searching and combining data sources, for example—to ease access by novice researchers. As a result of these Web-based modifications, database searching, once the sole province of research professionals, has become an option for a wide and varied audience of grantseekers. The Web has brought the search and retrieval of organized data sets within reach of a much wider audience.

Web-available databases cover a wide spectrum—from the funding-specific that let you search on consistently fielded data as a way to identify potential donors, to the more general and news-oriented types which may help you find potential donors but which certainly will help you conduct further research on the prospects you have identified from other resources. In this chapter, we describe various types of databases that are available for free and then list and describe

197

some of the more comprehensive databases available for a fee. While there is some overlap with other chapters (in particular, Chapter 4 about corporate funding research and Chapter 5 concerning government Web sites), this chapter focuses specifically on searchable databases.

Free Nonprofit Database Services

There are several large free databases containing information on nonprofits that can be very useful to the grantseeker in providing names, addresses, and financial information for foundations and other nonprofit grantmakers. The source for some of these services is publicly available IRS information. (See Chapter 5 to learn more about the wealth of government information available via the World Wide Web.)

Foundation Center—Foundation Finder <http:/fdncenter.org/>

If you know the name or partial name of any of the approximately 46,000 active grantmaking foundations in the U.S., Foundation Finder will provide you with that foundation's address, contact person, and basic financial information, as well as link you to its Web site if a URL exists.

Internet Nonprofit Center—Nonprofit Locator <http://www.nonprofits.org/library/gov/irs/search_irs.shtml>

The Internet Nonprofit Center's Nonprofit Locator allows you to find any nonprofit organization in the U.S. by searching a database of over one million tax-exempt entities.

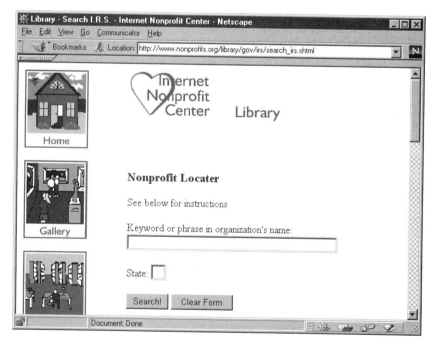

Using keywords from the organization's name, you can find the address of a particular organization, find organizations in your area, or check the exempt status of an organization. (Data is from the IRS, and explanatory information on the IRS fields and codes is accessible from the Nonprofit Locator site.) You may want to find organizations concerned with a certain issue by typing a short word or phrase that is likely to occur in the organization's name. The Locator also permits zip code searches to find nonprofits in a particular geographic area. It includes access to map location and a search engine for organization Web sites.

Action Without Borders <http://www.idealist.org>

Action Without Borders, formerly called the Contact Center Network, is a nonprofit organization that promotes the sharing of ideas, information, and resources to "help build a world where all people can live free, dignified and productive lives." Through the site's searchable indexes, visitors can access a global directory of 10,000 nonprofit Web sites, nonprofit news sites, jobs and volunteer opportunities, and resources for nonprofit managers. Search by organization name, region, or mission keyword.

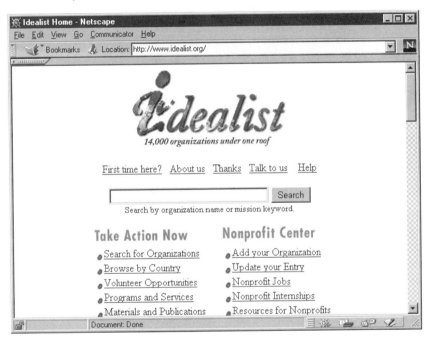

Guidestar <http://www.guidestar.org/>

Guidestar's database contains information on more than half a million American nonprofit organizations. All of these organizations are classified by the IRS as 501(c)(3) nonprofit organizations. This group includes public charities, private nonoperating foundations, and private operating foundations (operating foundations generally focus on specific foundation-administered programs). A Guidestar Report with a gray icon includes asset and income information from the IRS Form 990. A Guidestar Report with a blue icon includes financial and basic program information from the IRS Form 990, direct input from the individual organization about its goals, accomplishments, and program monitoring systems, and comments from its executive director. Financial data are taken from the IRS Business

Master File and/or the Form 990, a public report filed with the IRS by all 501(c)(3) public charities with revenues exceeding $25,000.

State Home Pages and Secretaries of State WWW Sites
<http://w3.uwyo.edu/~prospect/secstate.html#United>

The Internet Prospector has created a page of links to corporate and nonprofit corporation databases contained on state Web pages. These database listings frequently contain lists of donors, officers, and trustees and are sometimes searchable by keyword as well as by foundation name.

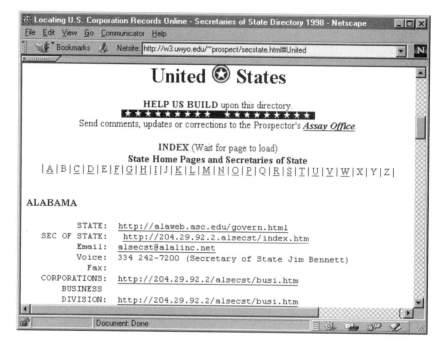

FOUNDATION GRANTS DATABASES

A number of foundations offer fully searchable Web sites. The W.K Kellogg Foundation, Charles Stewart Mott Foundation, and Pew Charitable Trusts have gone one step further and provided grantseekers with specialized databases of their grant awards.

Kellogg Foundation Online Database of Current Grants—W.K. Kellogg Foundation <http://www.wkkf.org/>

To access the database, visitors to the site should select "grants" and then "search database." The grants database is organized around the W.K. Kellogg Foundation's program interests—Health; Food Systems and Rural Development; Youth and Education; Higher Education; and Philanthropy and Volunteerism. Funding for the specific initiatives of Leadership; Information Systems/Technology; Capitalizing on Diversity; and Family, Neighborhood, and Community Development is represented throughout these programming interests. You can direct a search of the database (by grantee name, location, program information, timeframe, and purpose) or you can browse by thematic coding, country, or grantee name. (See Chapter 2 for more about this Web site in general.)

The Mott Grants Database—The Charles Stewart Mott Foundation
<http://www.mott.org/grants/search.html>
The Mott Grants Database contains detailed fact sheets on each grant made by the Foundation in recent years. Two ways to search for specific grant information are provided. The first allows users to search by keyword. The second method of searching allows users to search on specific fields, such as the project description or state location of the grantee. (See Chapter 2 for more about this Web site in general.)

Pew Charitable Trusts "Search Grants" Database—The Pew Charitable Trusts
<http://www.pewtrusts.com/>
The Pew Charitable Trusts Web site allows visitors to search all of its grants from the previous three years. A synopsis of the purposes, the amount, and the recipient of each grant is provided. A more expanded table containing the recipient contact's name, the relevant dates, and a longer grant description is available. The database search can be made extremely specific by narrowing it through the given categories.

Donors Forum of Chicago <http://www.donorsforum.org/>
The Donors Forum, an association of Chicago-area grantmaking institutions, promotes effective philanthropy through its educational, collaborative, and networking efforts. The main offering at the Forum's no-frills Web site is an updated 1994 version of its foundation grants database, searchable by foundation name, recipient, beneficiary type, support type, and grant purpose. Search results are displayed in plain-vanilla ASCII, but with approximately 7,500 grants made by some 50 Chicago-area funders, the Forum's database is worth exploring.

Corporate Funding Information (Fee-Based and Free— many services offer a combination.)

Corporate information on the Web is vast and varied. Many corporate information database services offer a variety of free and fee-based content. Some information available for free at certain sites will require fees at other sites, particularly those of database vendors.

Going directly to a company's Web site is the best way to locate corporate giving information. (See Chapter 4 for more information about corporate grantseeking on the World Wide Web.) There are many free search services for locating company Web pages, including:

- Company Name <www.companyname.com>
- Domain Name Search <http://www.internet.org>
- Companies Online <http://www.companiesonline.com>

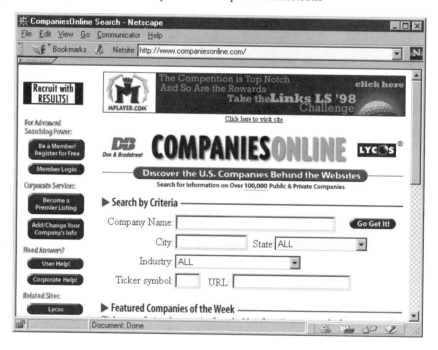

CORPORATE FINANCIAL INFORMATION

Hoovers Online <http://www.hoovers.com>

An easy-to-use site with links to over 4,000 corporate Web sites, over 10,000 Company Capsules, and 1,100 sites with job listings. Free Company Capsules provide news and information—company profile, key personnel, full stock quote, selected press coverage—on more than 11,000 public and private enterprises. Subscribers (two options: personal or multi-user) get the same information but in much greater depth and detail. And coming soon will be coverage of large non-publicly traded U.S. enterprises, including not-for-profits, foundations, health care companies, cooperatives, and universities.

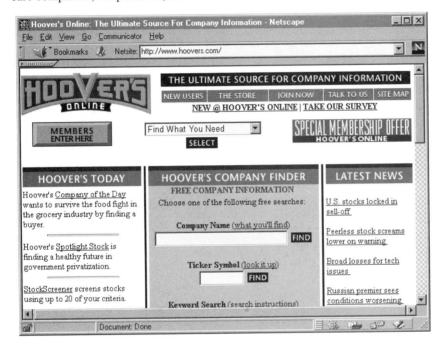

EDGAR Database of Corporate Information
<http://www.sec.gov/edgarhp.htm>

The Securities and Exchange Commission's EDGAR (Electronic Data Gathering, Analysis, and Retrieval) system contains basic but often hard-to-find corporate information (e.g., fiscal data, officers, subsidiaries, recent merger and acquisition activity, etc.). EDGAR on the Web allows visitors to retrieve publicly available filings submitted to the SEC from January 1994 to the present.

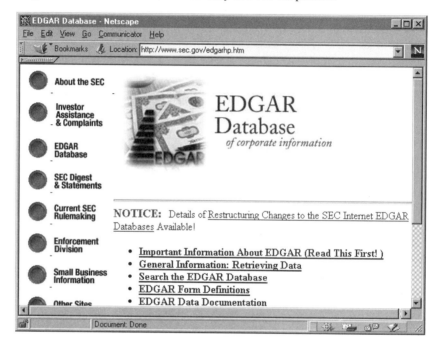

Edgar (NYU) <http://edgar.stern.nyu.edu/EDGAR.html>

This NYU site provides easier access to EDGAR filings. For example: reports are in reverse chronological order, the site includes descriptions for the more common filings, the ability to limit the number of answers, and a company-ticker resolver.

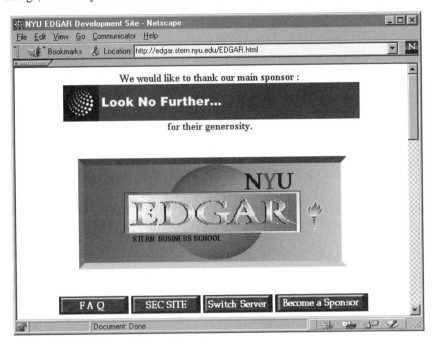

Inc. Online <http://inc.com/>

Inc. Online is an information resource for entrepreneurs and small business owners who are serious about growing their businesses. In addition to the most recent edition of *Inc.* and an archive of 5,000-plus articles on a wide variety of topics, the site offers a searchable database of America's 500 fastest-growing companies.

CORPORATE NEWS ONLINE

BusinessWire <http://www.businesswire.com>

This site includes searchable company press releases. It also includes selected corporate profiles and related URLs.

PR NewsWire <http://www.prnewswire.com>

This site includes searchable company press releases, with a one-year archive and company news on call.

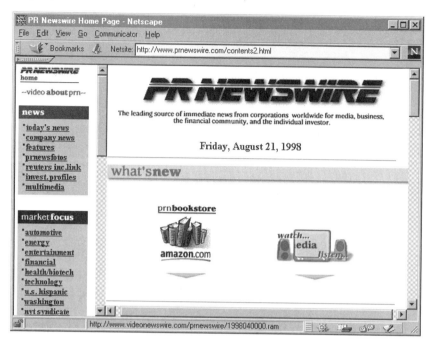

Forbes Toolbox <http://www.forbes.com/tool/html/toolbox.htm>

Forbes magazine has made available in database format a variety of its lists of wealthy individuals and of companies. (The 500 Largest Private Companies in the U.S., 400 Richest People in America, Technology's Richest 100, etc.)

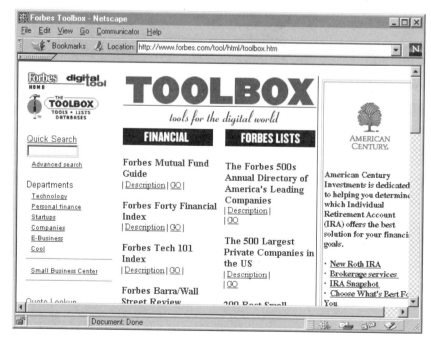

Newspaper Searching

Newspaper search sites are generally searchable by keyword. Articles are available until the source site deletes them (typically one day). Archived information is generally available only for a fee from the source publication or online vendor. Many regional business newspapers are now available online (indexed at most of the major news sites) and provide excellent information on local philanthropists, corporate giving, foundations, etc.

American Journalism Review <http://www.ajr.org>
This site includes worldwide links to some 3,500 news organizations online. You can also search other news sites from here (Total News, Newsindex.com, newsbots.com, etc.).

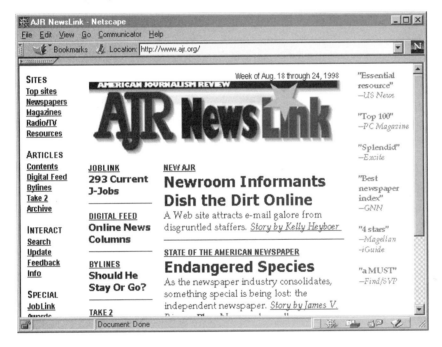

Biographical Information

Although not the primary focus of this book, below we list some of the sites from which to locate information about individuals.

American Medical Association's Physician Select
<http://www.ama-assn.org/aps/amahg.htm>

Congressional Directory
<http://www.access.gpo.gov/congress/ cong001.html>

Martindale Hubbell <http://www.martindale.com/locator/home.html>
900,000 attorney and firm profiles

Philanthropy News Digest-Foundation Center
<http://fdncenter.org/pnd/current/>

This service includes a searchable donor/trustee/officer index to Philanthropy News Digest stories on donations and donors. (See Chapter 10 for more detail on the contents and services of the Foundation Center's Web site.)

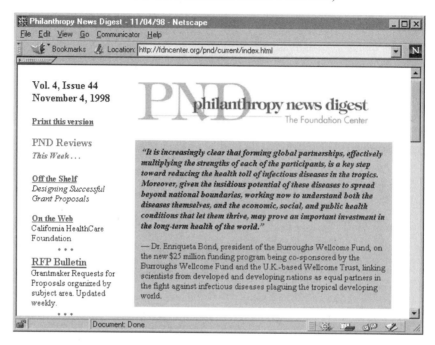

Fee-Based Databases Available from Database Vendors

Database vendors offer for-fee access to an enormous variety of databases. Most for-fee information vendors, including those that specialize in funding information, offer their database information in a variety of electronic formats, including CD-ROM and direct modem access (requiring software installation). Indexed print versions are also available for many directories. The choice of format depends largely on cost effectiveness (frequency of use, expense of support systems, etc.)

Web access offers users a great deal of flexibility. Fee-based services typically require only a user name and password for access from any online location. Internet database vendors offer pricing options which can be tailored to a user's particular needs, such as short-term, narrowly focused searches. Additionally, databases are updated on a regular basis, some daily. For-fee database searches can, however, be quite expensive. The World Wide Web has expanded rapidly, and the cost of data now varies greatly. While fee-based services are often very comprehensive and therefore efficient, the same information can sometimes be found through other sources for less cost (or even for free.) The major database vendors tend to simplify their search structures for Web presentation, gearing them toward a broad end-user audience. Experienced researchers may therefore prefer the wider range of search options available in direct dial-up services.

Other major database vendors offer legal and government documents, newspaper and periodical articles, and a wide variety of corporate information, including company profiles. These services are generally updated daily and offer easy-to-use search interfaces and a wide variety of search parameters. Newspaper searches, for example, can be restricted by date, source, geography, etc. You can search a single newspaper or thousands of sources at once. (Although many major and mid-sized newspapers now offer Web editions, they do not generally make archived information available. Those that do, such as the *Los Angeles Times*, frequently charge a single-use or subscription fee.)

The DIALOG Corporation <http://www.dialog.com/info/home/>

Knight-Ridder Information, Inc., formerly known as DIALOG Information Services, had been a source for online information for over 25 years with over 200,000 corporate users in 100 countries. Knight-Ridder Information, Inc. recently merged with M.A.I.D to form the Dialog Corporation, which offers hundreds of databases representing a broad range of disciplines: company directories, news sources, general reference, biographical information, etc.

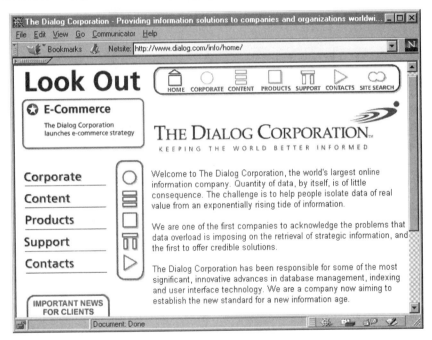

A complete list of online databases is available at DIALOG Web (see below). The online access rates vary by database (prices include output and search time costs, as well as telecommunications charges). There are annual service fees and start-up fees. Training is provided as online tutorials and/or guided tours.

DIALOG Web

This is a tool for intermediate and advanced online searchers. It offers a browser-enabled interface to the full DIALOG command language, an index to most of the DIALOG databases, plus a guided search component for search assistance. Other than an enhanced graphical Web interface, there are some features unique to DIALOG Web, which include a free database directory that lets you browse DIALOG databases by subject with a "Search DIALINDEX" feature that helps you find the exact databases for your topic.

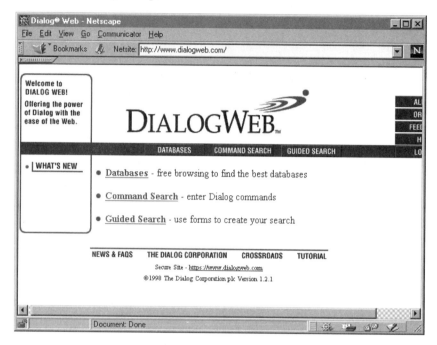

DIALOG Select

This service is designed for novice end-users, utilizing pre-defined search forms where users enter keywords and use pull-down menus to set up their searches. No prior search expertise is required.

Grantmaker/Grant Information on DIALOG

There are two Foundation Center databases provided via the DIALOG service. The "Foundation Directory" database is known as "File 26" and the "Foundation Grants Index" is known as "File 27." The two files can be used in conjunction through software functionality provided through the DIALOG service.

Foundation Directory—File 26 (available on DIALOG Web and DIALOG Select) is a comprehensive database providing descriptions of more than 47,000 grantmakers, including private grantmaking foundations, community foundations, operating foundations, and corporate grantmakers. Records include entries from the following Foundation Center print publications: *The Foundation Directory*; *The Foundation Directory, Part 2*; *Guide to U.S. Foundations: Their Trustees, Officers, and Donors*; and *National Directory of Corporate Giving*.

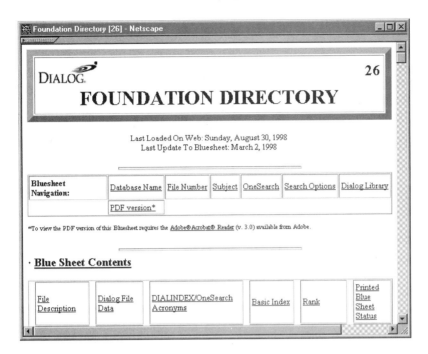

Use File 26 to identify foundations that provide funding for a specific subject area; identify foundations that provide certain types of support; identify grantmakers in a specific city, state, or zip code; determine on which foundation boards, if any, a certain individual serves; identify company-sponsored foundations and corporate giving programs; find additional information about foundations whose grants appear in File 27; find detailed information about a specific foundation or corporate giving program; create a list of the largest foundations that support a specific subject area or give in a specific geographic area. Full records (available for approximately 27,000 of the nation's largest foundations) include foundation name and address, parent company (for company-sponsored foundations); lists of donors, officers, and trustees; purpose and activities statements; grantmaking program descriptions; financial information, including assets and total giving; giving limitations statements; application information; a list of publications available from the foundation; fields of interest (descriptors); indication of whether grant records for a particular foundation exist in File 27. File 26 contains brief records for about 13,000 smaller foundations which include foundation name and address; donor, officers, and trustees; financial information, including assets and total giving; geographic focus; indication of whether or not the foundation accepts applications.

The file covers one year's data, based on the most currently available fiscal year. The file is reloaded annually, with a semi-annual update. Search and retrieval time is $0.50 per minute. Costs for displayed records are shown in the title list.

The Foundation Grants Index—File 27 (available only on DIALOG Web) is an index of grants of $10,000 or more awarded to nonprofit organizations by over 1,000 of the largest foundations in the U.S. (While these comprise a small subset of the foundations included in File 26, their grants represent over 50 percent of the total dollars awarded by all U.S. private, corporate, and community foundations during the latest year of record.) Information in File 27 includes grants found in the print *Foundation Grants Index* beginning with those included in the 1989 Edition. Each record in File 27 represents one grant. Grant records include the following elements: name/state of the foundation awarding the grant; geographic focus of the grantmaker; recipient organization (name, city, state); recipient type (hospital, museum, university); recipient auspices (religious, government, private non-sectarian); purpose of the grant and year authorized; amount (and duration) of the grant; intended beneficiaries (if specified); type of support represented (capital, research, etc.); fields of interest (descriptors).

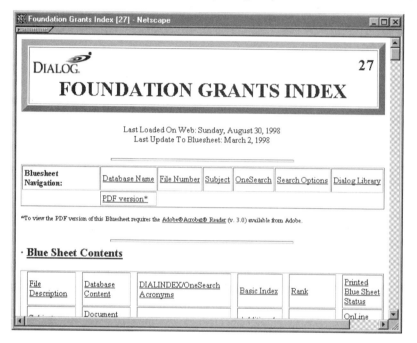

Use File 27 to find grants awarded in specific subject areas; locate grants that serve certain populations; examine a foundation's grants in one subject area; find grants awarded to organizations similar to your own; locate grants awarded to organizations in your city or state; identify the largest grants in a subject area. After locating appropriate grants in File 27, search for the grantmaking organizations in File 26. New grant records are added five times each year. No grants to individuals are included in the Grants Index. Search and retrieval time is $0.50 per minute. Costs for displayed records are shown in the title list.

The Center classifies grants according to its Grants Classification System, derived from the National Taxonomy of Exempt Entities (NTEE). The NTEE standardizes language used to describe the activities of the nonprofit sector. (See the Foundation Center's Grants Classification Manual and Thesaurus, Internet Edition at <http://fdncenter.org/trends/tax/txcont.html> for more information on the Grants Classification System.)

Use the *DIALOG User Manual and Thesaurus* (available from the Foundation Center <fdncenter.org>) as an aid to the most cost-effective searching of Files 26 and 27. The *User Manual* contains a fully revised and expanded list of subject terms and shows you how to retrieve facts from the Center's databases quickly, easily, and efficiently.

GRANTS Database—File 85 (available on DIALOG Web) is provided from Oryx Press and is also available on KEDSnet on the World Wide Web <http://www.knowledgeexpress.com/>.

The GRANTS Database offers access to information on more than 8,500 funding programs available through over 3,000 nonprofit organizations, foundations, private sources, and federal, state, and local agencies in the United States and Canada.

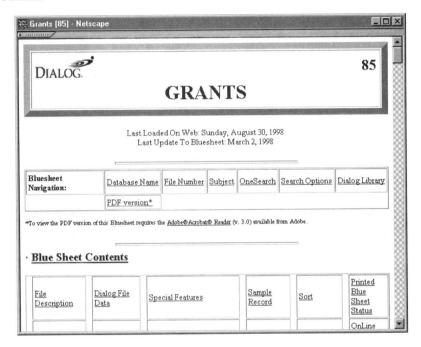

The GRANTS Database is searchable by title, sponsoring organizations, keyword, program type, or any combination of 20 searchable fields. It is updated monthly. Use the Grants Subject Authority Guide to become familiar with the 2,422 subject terms used to index the database. The database also features "see" and "see also" references to help users target the most appropriate files.

Other DIALOG Databases

Files on grants and grantmakers comprise a small percentage of the information available on DIALOG (as elsewhere on the Web). The DIALOG corporate and biographical databases are extensive and varied and can be extremely useful to grantseekers. Because information on corporate funding is subject to somewhat less stringent reporting standards than information on company-sponsored foundations, it can be more difficult to locate. Corporate information on DIALOG (DIALOG Corporate Information, Standard & Poor's American Business Directory, Corporate Descriptions, etc.) can be searched geographically, providing you with a potentially enormous list of companies to research to find prospective sponsors for your project or organization. Archived business newspapers and journals as well as press releases can be used to narrow the search, giving indications of past corporate giving and likely company giving interests. Stock prices and other indicators of corporate wealth also can be used in the formulation of a realistic charitable solicitation. (See Chapter 4 for more on corporate grantseeking on the Web.)

The lists of top executives included in many corporate profiles also provide you with lists of potentially wealthy individuals in your geographic area. Because individual giving accounts for almost 80 percent of all charitable funding, the biographical resources available on DIALOG provide a huge pool of possible funders. Biographical information, such as alumni affiliations, foundation or charity board membership, and volunteer involvement can be used in conjunction with corporate indicators of wealth, such as stock proxy listings and professional affiliations, to develop a fairly comprehensive potential donor profile. (You can cross-reference names with the officer, trustee, and donor search capacity of File 26.) Running an archived newspaper search on an individual's name in conjunction with search words such as "donate," "give," etc. can return information on past charitable donations.

DIALOG offers many comprehensive corporate and biographical databases, including:

Corporate
- DIALOG Corporate Information (Directories, News Sources)
- American Business Directory (531, 532)
- Standard & Poor's Corporate Descriptions plus News (133)
- Business Dateline (635)
- Commerce Business Daily (194, 195)
- Corporate Affiliations (513)
- DIALOG Company Name Finder (416)
- Trade & Industry Database (148)
- Moody's Corporate Profiles (555)
- Dunn & Bradstreet Dunn's (515, 519, 516)
- Financial Times Full Text (622)
- Harvard Business Review (122)

Biographical
- Biography Master Index (287)
- Bowker Biographical Directory (236)
- Standard & Poor's Register—Biographical (526)
- Marquis Who's Who Database

Check the full list of DIALOG databases by name accessible from the Databases page of DIALOG Web.

LEXIS-NEXIS on the World Wide Web (Mead Data Central)
<http://www.lexis-nexis.com/>
LEXIS-NEXIS provides online access to legal, news, and business information services. There are 7,300 databases between the two services. More than 9.5 million documents are added each week to the more than one billion documents online. Information on LEXIS-NEXIS is organized into "libraries." LEXIS-NEXIS information is accessible with a user name and password.

The LEXIS-NEXIS service offers three options of searching: FREESTYLE, Boolean, and Easy Search. The FREESTYLE feature is a plain English search feature that allows the user to search both legal and non-legal materials all in one commercial database. Experienced searchers most often select the traditional Boolean search option for precision searching of specific data sets. The Easy Search feature, on the other hand, uses online menus and screen prompts to assist novice users in formulating precise search requests and then to select the best parts of the database to search for the user.

The LEXIS service

The LEXIS service contains major archives of federal and state case law, continuously updated statutes of all 50 states, state and federal regulations, and an extensive collection of public records from major U.S. states and counties. The LEXIS service has 40 specialized libraries covering all major fields of practice, including tax, securities, banking, environmental, energy and international. Although the LEXIS service is not directly related to grantseeking research needs, a subscriber to the LEXIS service also has access to the NEXIS service and its related services.

The NEXIS service

The NEXIS service is a news and business information service which contains more than 13,500 sources. These include regional, national, and international newspapers, news wires, magazines, trade journals, and business publications. The NEXIS service also offers: brokerage house and industry analyst reports; business information from Dunn & Bradstreet; public records such as corporate filings, company records, and property records; and tax information.

Useful NEXIS Libraries for Grantseekers

The People Library (PEOPLE) brings together information sources concentrating on biographical or people-related news, issues, and events. This library allows you to use custom file selection. Within the PEOPLE library you will find a combined news and biographical information set called ALLBIO. This includes Gale biographies from January 1990 (Newsmakers from January 1985), Marquis Who's Who biographies, and the most recent edition and selected full-text articles from major newspapers and periodicals, including the *Washington Post*, the *Los Angeles Times*, and the *New York Times*.

The Assets Library (ASSETS) provides access to real estate assessment records and current deed transfer information gathered from county assessors' and recorders' offices in selected counties (metropolitan areas) nationwide, U.S. Federal Aviation Administration Aircraft Registrations, Florida Boat registrations from Florida Department of High Safety and Motor Vehicles, U.S. Coast Guard Merchant and Recreational Vessel Registrations, and Texas Motor Vehicle Registrations. The information available in this library can be useful in providing indicators of the wealth of a potential funder.

The Entertainment Library (ENTERT) combines facts pertaining to the entertainment industry such as: litigation, credits, grosses, contacts, company profiles, biographies and industry profiles, along with a variety of daily and weekly news sources. This library allows you to use custom file selection. It contains some biographical information sources.

There are a number of corporate libraries. (See Chapter 4 for suggestions on how to plumb other resources in your corporate grantseeking efforts.) Several are described below.

The Company Information Library (COMPNY) contains business and financial information, including thousands of in-depth company and industry research reports from leading national and international investment banks and brokerage houses. The materials may be searched in individual files, such as brokerage house reports, or in group files organized by subject, such as SEC filings.

The Dunn & Bradstreet Library (D&B) provides a vast base from which information can be obtained on more than 50 million domestic and international businesses. This library allows you to use custom file selection.

The Corporation Library (INCORP) provides access to records on active and inactive limited partnerships and limited liability companies, and corporations registered with the office of the Secretary of State or other appropriate agency. These records include information extracted by the State's staff from articles of incorporation, annual reports, amendments, and other public filings. "Doing Business As" records titled in over 1,000 counties nationwide are also provided.

The Business/Finance Library (BUSFIN) contains a wide variety of sources that provide business and finance news, including business journals as well as investment and merger and acquisition news sources. This library allows you to use custom file selection.

Other LEXIS-NEXIS Features and Products

EdgarPlus, offered on the LEXIS-NEXIS services through an agreement with Disclosure Incorporated, allows access to SEC filings and a series of SEC products developed from EDGAR (Electronic Data Gathering, Analysis and Retrieval system) data.

Martindale-Hubbell is a professional directory database of over 900,000 lawyers and law firms in 150 countries. Listings are updated monthly and include such details as contact data, areas of practice, education, clients, languages, and representative cases.

Dow Jones Interactive (Formerly Dow Jones News/Retrieval) (Dow Jones) <http://ip.dowjones.com/>

Dow Jones Interactive, based on the Dow Jones News/Retrieval service, is an online business news and research tool that provides access to breaking news from 3,800 sources, a custom news-tracking tool that automatically filters news and information based on an individual's needs, and a financial center that covers more than 10 million public and private companies around the world. Dow Jones provides access to the local newspapers formerly available through UMI's DataTimes. In addition to UMI content, Dow Jones is the exclusive online source of the combined same-day, full-text editions of the *Wall Street Journal*, *New York Times*, *Washington Post*, *Financial Times*, and *Los Angeles Times*. Dow Jones offers a wide variety of flexible pricing plans (based on per article usage), including monthly flat-free pricing.

ProQuest Direct (UMI) <http://www.umi.com/proquest>

ProQuest Direct provides "one of the world's largest collections of information," including summaries of articles from over 5,000 publications, with many in full-text, full-image format. ProQuest Direct offers a free trial period.

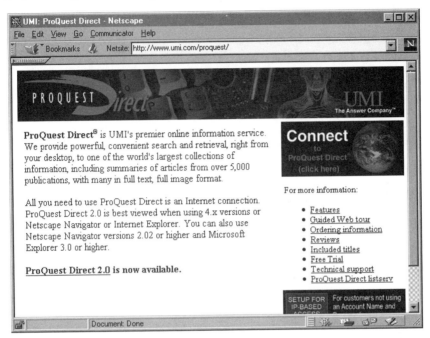

Useful ProQuest Database Files for Grantseekers:

The list of databases is accessible from the Guided Tour page.

ABI/INFORM provides in-depth coverage of business conditions, trends, corporate strategies and tactics, management techniques, competitive and product information, and a wide variety of other topics.

Business Dateline contains fully searchable full-text articles, in ASCII format, from more than 450 North American business tabloids, magazines, daily newspapers, and news wire services. Each record includes complete bibliographic, geographic, and indexing information as well. Current material is from 1994 forward, with retrospective coverage on tape available from 1985. The database covers a variety of subject areas, including employment opportunities; benefit packages and compensation plans; businesses and industries in particular locations; corporate strategies, mergers, acquisitions, and expansions; marketing trends and new products; local effects of regulation and legislation; and more.

Business Periodicals provides coverage of business and management publications available, with three different editions to choose from. The database links full images of articles from the most important and popular ABI/INFORM sources. Each edition contains abstracts and indexing to articles from top publications, plus cover-to-cover page images from about half of the cited journals. Coverage for current subscriptions begins in 1992, with backfile availability to 1971. Full-image coverage begins in 1988.

Wilsonline (H.W. Wilson Company) (Readers Guide to Periodical Literature) <http://www.hwwilson.com/>

H.W. Wilson's Information Retrieval System for the World Wide Web, WilsonWeb, provides several search tools for accessing information in Wilson databases. You can search for records pertaining to a topic of interest, then show, print, and download those records. WilsonWeb's interface is customizable. WilsonWeb offers a free trial.

Useful Wilson Databases for Grantseekers

The Wilson offerings include lists of Index and Abstract Databases and Full-Text Databases.

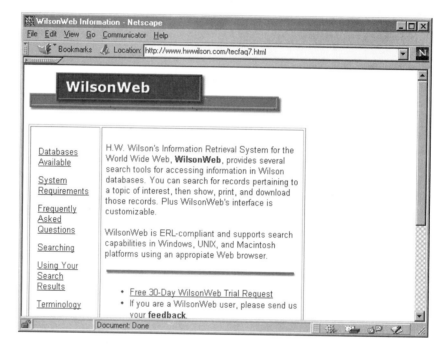

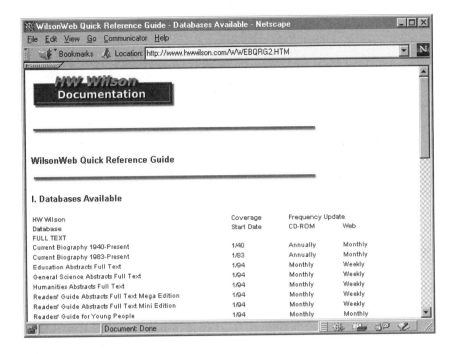

H.W. Wilson's Biography Index Database cites biographical material appearing in more than 2,800 periodicals indexed in other H.W. Wilson databases and additional selected periodicals; some 2,100 books annually of individual and collective biography; and incidental biographical material in otherwise non-biographical books. Periodicals indexed are selected from all subject areas represented by other H.W. Wilson databases. Biographical subjects indexed range from antiquity to the present and represent all fields and nationalities.

H.W. Wilson's Business Periodicals Databases cover 400 English-language general business periodicals and trade journals, plus the *Wall Street Journal* and the business section of the *New York Times*. Topics include management, accounting, advertising and marketing, construction, entertainment and media, information technology, mergers and acquisitions, occupational health and safety, public relations, and small business. Users can access citations via SIC codes.

Wilson Business Abstracts includes abstracts of periodicals from June 1990 and indexing from July 1982. Wilson Business Abstracts Full-Text includes full-text coverage of 158 periodicals back to January 1995.

GaleNet (Gales Research, Inc.) <http://galenet.gale.com>
This subscription service requires a user name and password in order to access any Web pages.

Useful Gale Databases for Grantseekers
Associations Unlimited contains information for approximately 440,000 U.S. national, regional, state, local, and international nonprofit membership organizations in all fields, and U.S. 501(c)(3) nonprofit organizations. Subsets of Associations Unlimited are also available.

U.S. National Associations contains information for approximately 23,000 U.S. national nonprofit membership associations in all fields. Features include full contact information, description, SIC descriptors, convention dates, and more.

U.S. 501(3) Nonprofit Organizations contains information for approximately 300,000 U.S. 501(c)(3) nonprofit organizations, agencies, and service programs as registered with the U.S. Internal Revenue Service.

The Biography and Genealogy Master Index is an index to more than 10 million biographical sketches in over 1,000 current and retrospective biographical dictionaries, covering both contemporary and historical figures throughout the world.

Gale Business Resources integrates some 30 print volumes of Gale's business reference works. It contains listings for some 200,000 U.S. companies, extensive essays for 54 industrial categories, industry statistics, market share reports, and company rankings. In addition, company histories are available for 1,500 of the most prominent businesses in the United States. Gale Business Resources also provides access to the complete text of U.S. Securities and Exchange Commission Reports for 1,100 top U.S. companies and the U.S. Industrial Outlook.

For-Fee Database Services Specific to Grantmakers/Grants

In addition to specific DIALOG databases, there are a small number of database services specializing in information for grantseekers. These services are offered by people with a particular focus on nonprofits and who also often offer database management software and other electronic services geared to the needs of charitable organizations.

Prospect Research Online (PRO) Rainforest Publications Books
<http://www.rpbooks.com/>

The Prospect Research Database offers access to a full range of corporate data geared to the needs of grantseekers, such as company history, proxy statement information, lists of officers and directors, and links to various stock markets, EDGAR and SIC codes, and links to corporate Web sites. Each PROfile includes recent financial reports, announcements regarding senior officers, mergers, acquisitions and buy-outs, as well as information about corporate giving programs. There is an annual subscription fee. A free guided tour is available.

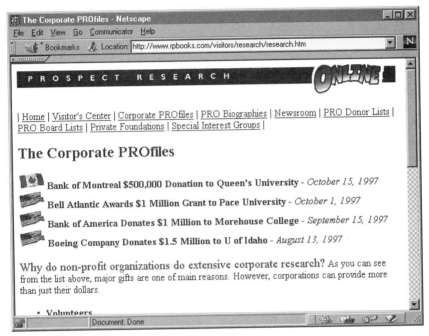

Access.Point Fundraising System
<http://www.accesspt.com/Fundraising/index.html>

The Access.Point Fundraising System includes the Foundation Database, containing information on more than 12,000 private and corporate foundations, and the Corporate Giving Database, which contains information on more than 4,000 corporate giving programs. Search by keyword or phrase.

Community Information Exchange **<www.comminfoexch.org/database.htm>**

The Community Information Exchange is a national, nonprofit information service founded in 1983 that provides community-based organizations and their partners with the information they need to successfully revitalize their communities. The Exchange provides comprehensive information about strategies and resources for affordable housing, and economic and community development. The Exchange provides information in easy-to-search databases containing case studies about innovative and replicable strategies, describes funding and financing sources, identifies technical assistance providers, and abstracts printed resources such as how-to guides and sample legal documents. Bulletin boards feature the latest funding announcements, including those from the Federal Register, and timely news items. The databases are available on a subscription basis for PCs,

CD-ROMs, and local area networks (LANs). In the future they will be available on the Web, and so we include them here.

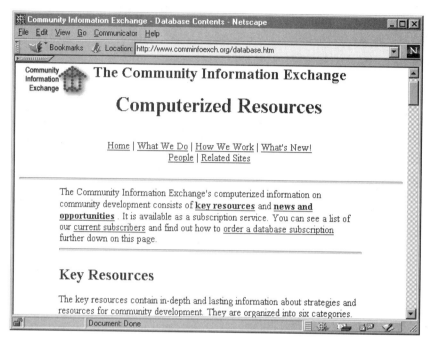

Target America <http://www.tgtam.com/>
The Target America Database offers comprehensive information (financial, employment, address, etc.) on the wealthiest 5 percent of the U.S. population.

FEE-BASED SERVICES FOR ACADEMIC PROFESSIONALS

There are also a number of grants databases, primarily intended for academic professionals, that offer access to a variety of government and private funding sources. These services are fee-based, but some also offer free information.

IRIS—Illinois Researcher Information Service
<http://carousel.lis.uiuc.edu/~iris/about_iris.html>
A unit of the University of Illinois Library at Urbana-Champaign, IRIS contains records on over 7,000 federal and non-federal funding opportunities in the sciences, social sciences, arts, and humanities. The file is updated daily. The Online Periodical Service (OPS) is a full-text database of selected items from the Commerce Business Daily and abstracts of research-related items from the Federal Register. The service is available free of charge to the University of Illinois at Urbana-Champaign community. It is available to other colleges and universities for an annual subscription fee.

Community of Science <http://www.cos.com> (some free information)
This site is maintained by a consortium of research institutions as a repository of scientific information searchable through the Internet. It offers several searchable grant databases for both private and federal funding. The Funding Opportunities Database is a good place to start. It includes grants in non-science areas.

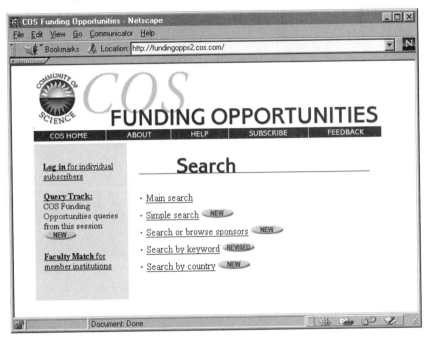

For federal grant database searching, this Web site provides access to the Federal Register and the Commerce Business Daily. Also note that searching federally funded research in the U.S. will provide summaries of research grants and projects from five agencies: the National Institutes of Health, the National Science Foundation, the U.S. Department of Agriculture, the Small Business Innovation Research awards, and the Advanced Technology Program of the National Institute of Standards & Technology. (See Chapter 5 for more on the wealth of government information on the Internet.)

AWARDS Database <http://cos.gdb.org/repos/fund/stanford>
Concerned with academic funding, this database is maintained by the Undergraduate Advising Center at Stanford University. It offers a 48-hour free trial search period.

SPIN (Sponsored Programs Information Network)
<http://www.infoed.org/Products.stm#spin>

This service includes funding for research, fellowships, exchange programs, travel, equipment, collaborative projects, and more. SPIN is the Sponsored Programs Information Network provided by InfoEd, Inc. The Web version requires a subscription. This service includes searching by deadline, academic discipline, and more. Federal and non-federal grants are listed with free access to key federal databases.

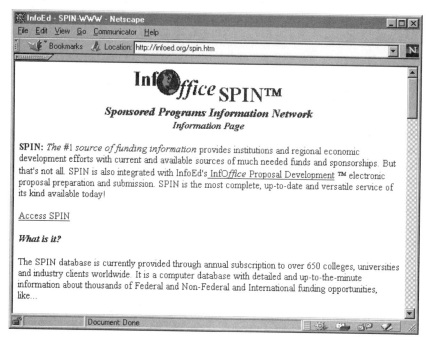

REGIONAL FEE-BASED SERVICES

Nonprofit Resource Center of Texas <http://www.fic.org>

This is a membership organization that offers technical assistance, consultation, and training opportunities for board members, staff, and volunteers of nonprofit and philanthropic organizations. This site includes access (for a fee) to the Database of Texas Foundations which contains profiles of over 1,700 foundations. Search by areas of interest and types of support. The database is updated throughout year.

The Greater Kansas City Council on Philanthropy <http://www.kcphilnet.org>

This is a professional organization that has provided a local forum for the exchange of information on philanthropy and fundraising since 1975. This site offers (for a fee) the Directory of Greater Kansas City Foundations, a quarterly updated directory of nearly 500 area funders, including who is on their boards, the types of programs they fund, grant recipients, grants awarded, and procedures for submitting a funding request.

CHAPTER SEVEN

Other Useful Sites for Grantseekers

How do you find out whether the foundation prospect you're interested in is on the Web? Although you can certainly start by searching on its name with a search engine like HotBot or AltaVista, remember that other people have done the job for you. Many Web sites now function as "portals" to the Web at large, sites that attempt to organize Web information and make it accessible in one location. The Yahoo Web page is pointed to as the primary example.

The Foundation Center continues to design and organize its own Web site to function as such a "specialty portal," providing access to the world of philanthropy, as well as providing information resources and guidance on how to do funding research and then to approach potential funders.

(See Chapter 10 for a description of the many resources and links available at the Center's Web site <http://fdncenter.org>, Your Gateway to Philanthropy on the Web.)

There are hundreds of annotated links to various types of grantmakers in the Grantmaker Information section of the Foundation Center's Web site. There is also a fairly large section of foundation links available through Yahoo, at http://www.yahoo.com/Society_and_Culture/Organizations/ Grant_Making_Foundations. If you need to locate information about a particular organization, or if you'd just like to browse for prospects, the resources that follow point the way to extensive online information about potential funders.

This chapter introduces some useful Web resources for grantseekers, many of which you'll find listed in the Links to Nonprofit Resources section of the Online Library found at the Foundation Center's Web site <http://fdncenter.org/onlib/linxtoc.html>.

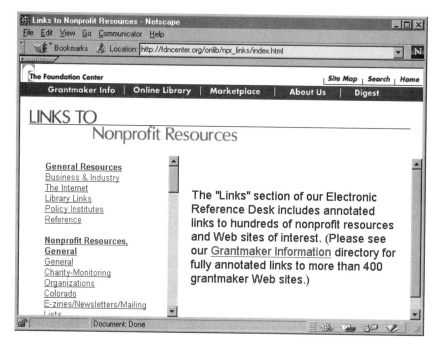

We continue to add to these categorized lists of sites and prepare annotations for them to aid in your exploration of funding opportunities and helpful resources. A comprehensive list of nonprofit resource links taken from the Center's Web site is included at the end of this chapter, organized into categories. We have condensed and revised this list because some of these sites are discussed in greater detail in other chapters (e.g., in those on corporate and government resources). However, some overlap remains, reflecting the hyperlinked nature of the Web environment.

A Selection of Useful Sites

Here are our recommendations for the best Web sites available for grantseekers. The categories we have used to organize the sites we describe in some detail are to a certain extent arbitrary; that is, many of the resources could fit into two or more categories, based on their features and content. What these sites have in common is that they reward deeper investigation. They are resources that you'll want to return to time and again in searching for online information about foundations, grants, fundraising, and nonprofit management. Our goal is not to be comprehensive—that often isn't practical when dealing with the Web—but to point the way to a manageable number of useful sites. Please refer to the more complete listing at the end of the chapter to make additional selections of sites of particular interest to you.

Council on Foundations <http://www.cof.org>

The Council, a nonprofit membership organization of foundations and corporations, offers a wealth of information at its Web site, which is organized into broad categories.

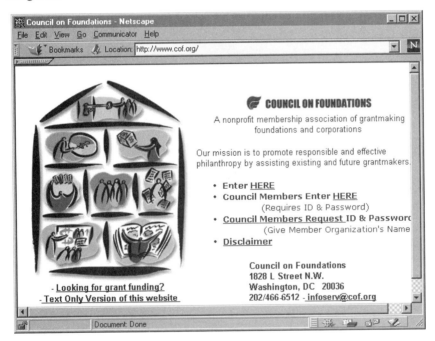

FundsNet <http://www.fundsnetservices.com>

This site, compiled and maintained by A. Gil de Lamadrid, includes links to over 500 foundations, corporations, and grantmaking public charities online. The Funders area offers links alphabetically, by grantmaker type and by area of grantmaking emphasis, within broad categories like arts, communities, education, health, and religion. This part of the site is especially helpful for grantseekers browsing for new prospects, and some of the links include a short note about the funder's mission or guidelines. The goal is comprehensive coverage of what's currently available on the Web from grantmakers, but the site also includes links to information on fundraising, proposal writing, government agency resources, and more. Best of all, the site is updated daily, and there's almost always something new.

Michigan State University Grants and Related Resources
<http://www.lib.msu.edu/harris23/grants/grants.htm>
The amount of information available on these pages is nearly overwhelming, but
Jon Harrison of the University of Michigan Libraries has created a site that is well
organized and cleanly designed. You won't get lost.

Most valuable here are the annotated lists of resources (print, electronic, and
online) for grant information in particular subject areas, from Arts and Cultural
Activities to Religion and Social Change. For each subject area, Harrison gives
abstracts of useful print resources, descriptions of databases, and hyperlinks to
online information. There is a substantial section of information on grants to individuals, including financial aid. Harrison also has assembled an impressive bibliography, with links, on techniques of grantsmanship, including lots of information
on fundraising research and proposal writing.

National Assembly of State Arts Agencies <http://www.nasaa-arts.org>
Sponsored by the National Endowment for the Arts, this site is a clearinghouse of
Internet information for arts organizations.

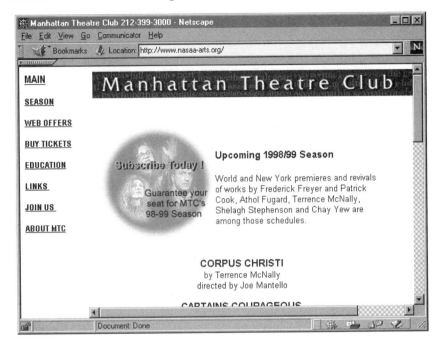

The Tangents section includes Major Grantmakers to the Arts and Culture, a
selected group of links to the Web sites of private foundations and corporations
with a track record in funding arts and culture programs. State arts agencies are
important funding sources for both arts nonprofits and individual artists (usually
through sponsorship programs), and visitors will find a comprehensive collection
of links to state arts agency Web sites as well as notices of arts events and conferences nationwide.

National Directory of Computer Recycling Programs
<http://www.microweb.com/pepsite/Recycle/recycle_index.html>

Of course, nonprofits don't live by foundation grants alone. If your organization is looking for a free or low-cost technology upgrade and you don't mind working with equipment that isn't brand new, you might want to stop by the Parents Educators and Publishers (PEP) site.

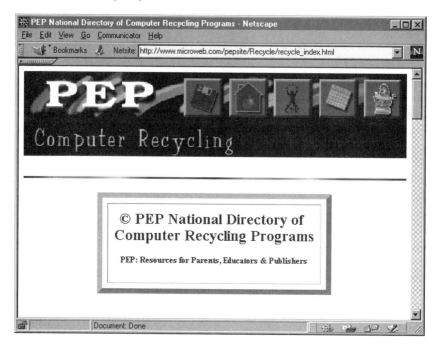

This site includes a directory of organizations that facilitate donations of computer hardware and software to schools and community-based nonprofits. Annotated entries describe each program's eligibility requirements, with complete contact information, including links to Web sites and e-mail addresses, when available. A wide variety of organizations are represented, and resources are classified by geographic scope, from international to state level.

Nonprofit News and Current Awareness

One of the most valuable features of the Web is the fast access it provides to current information about new developments affecting philanthropy, nonprofits, and fundraising. Stopping by some of the following sites on a weekly basis can help to keep your organization apprised of grant proposal deadlines, training opportunities, and pending legislation that could impact your operations.

The Web also offers you a way to learn about what organizations like yours are doing with programs and services, special events, fundraising, and public relations, making it possible to network with people who are working on similar issues the world over. Visiting the Web sites of other organizations active in your field of interest is a great way to see what seems to work (and what doesn't) in using the Web to promote services, recruit volunteers, and even raise money. Some of the sites that follow will lead you to nonprofits like yours, others will give you the opportunity to make information about your organization available on the Web.

Chronicle of Philanthropy <http://philanthropy.com>
Like its biweekly print analog, The *Chronicle of Philanthropy*'s Web site is full of useful information for grantseekers.

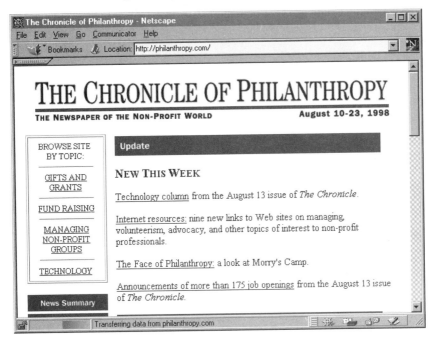

The site is organized into broad topic areas—Gifts and Grants, Fund Raising, Managing Non-Profit Groups, and Technology—and offers, among other items, a summary of the contents of the *Chronicle*'s current and previous issues, the full text of selected stories, award and RFP deadlines, job opportunities in the non-profit sector, and information about forthcoming conferences and workshops. The annotated links section is one of the best for finding nonprofit resources on the Internet. Visitors can also sign up for free updates via e-mail about changes at the site as well as breaking news stories.

Nonprofit Online News <http://www.gilbert.org/news>
Michael Gilbert of the Gilbert Center maintains this site, where he posts one to three news items per day, Monday through Friday. Visitors will find notices of meetings and conferences, links to new online resources for nonprofits, full-text articles about the sector, and especially, information about how nonprofits can use the Web as a resource for sharing information and making themselves more visible. The focus is on timely issues, and the news items tend toward the Web-centric.

Guidestar <http://www.guidestar.org>
In a partnership with Lexis/Nexis, the Guidestar News Service posts the full text of current news stories from newspapers around the country on charitable giving,

tax regulations, prominent philanthropists, and nonprofit organizations. The stories are searchable by topic, location, or revenue.

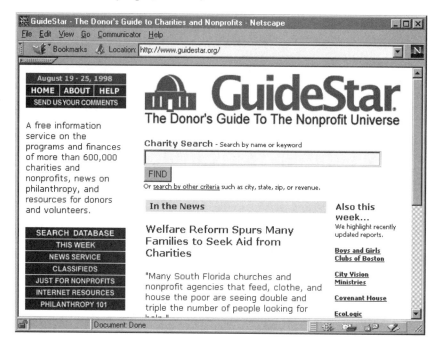

As noted in Chapter 6, Guidestar also provides a free, searchable database of information on the programs and finances of U.S. nonprofit organizations. Guidestar information is drawn from IRS Form 990 and includes a description of the organization and a summary of revenues and expenses. The goals of this service are to inform donors and promote nonprofit accountability. Thus, organizations are given the opportunity to supply Guidestar with additional information about their programs, services, and financial status. Simply click on Just for Nonprofits on the home page to get started.

Action Without Borders <http://www.idealist.org>

Action Without Borders (formerly the Contact Center Network) is a searchable directory of over 11,000 nonprofit organizations in 125 countries. You can search for nonprofits by subject or geographic area.

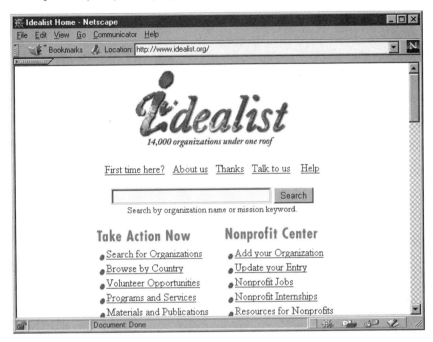

There are plenty of links here, but what's really nice about Action Without Borders is that nonprofits without Web sites of their own can submit information about their mission, programs, and services for posting. Raising your organization's profile in cyberspace is just a few mouse clicks away. Action Without Borders also includes links to nonprofit news, jobs and volunteer opportunities, and resources for nonprofit managers.

Internet NonProfit Center <http://www.nonprofits.org/>
The Center aims to provide, fast, free, and easy access to information on nonprofit organizations, wise giving practices, and issues of concern to donors and volunteers.

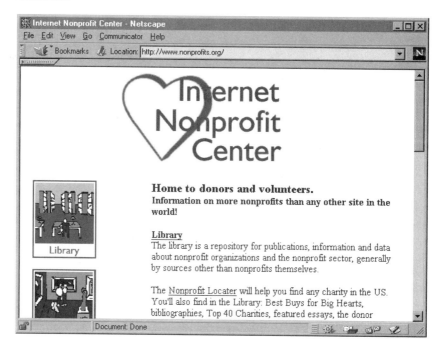

Major components of the site include a "library," which offers essays and data about the nonprofit sector, and a Nonprofit Locator that provides financial information from IRS filings on more than a million charities. It is searchable by keyword and state. Nonprofits can use the "gallery" to post online brochures, annual reports and home pages—like Action Without Borders and Guidestar, this site offers the chance to boost your online visibility. The "parlor" has volunteer opportunities and chat rooms, dozens of links, and information about setting up your own home page on the Web.

Impact Online <http://www.impactonline.org>

"Turning good intentions into action" is the motto of this organization, based in Palo Alto, California. Impact Online aims to use the Internet to promote community involvement by means of a searchable database of volunteer opportunities in major cities.

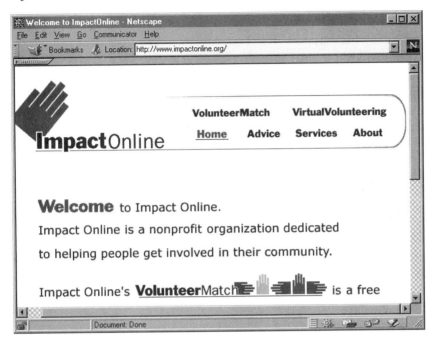

The site also allows nonprofits to post information about themselves in order to recruit volunteers. Through its "Virtual Volunteering" program, Impact Online seeks to expand the reach of voluntarism by matching nonprofits with individuals who can help out via a computer at home or at work.

Fundraising Tips and Training

Another advantage of the Internet is the opportunity it provides for consulting professionals in the nonprofit field. The Internet has been about sharing information since its very beginnings, and a great deal of expertise in areas like fundraising, taxation, legal issues, and nonprofit management is readily available. This is also true, of course, of the wide variety of mailing lists, bulletin boards, and discussion groups available online, which are discussed in detail in Chapter 9. Think of the Web as a constantly growing storehouse of knowledge that your organization can explore at some of the sites that follow.

The Grantsmanship Center <http://www.tgci.com>

The Grantsmanship Center specializes in training nonprofit managers and fundraisers, and its site offers the full text of stories from the Center's magazine, along with grant announcements and funding news from federal government agencies. An online subscription service featuring current grant opportunities on the Internet is under development, and a bulletin board area for fundraising tips has been added.

Support Centers of America <http://www.supportcenter.org/sca>

Support Centers of America provides management consulting, training, and information to the nonprofit sector at each of its 12 regional centers. Visitors to its Web site can find out about local training opportunities and access the "Nonprofit Genie" (Global Electronic Nonprofit Information Express), and a list of answers to frequently asked questions developed by its San Francisco office. Categories include strategic planning, financial management, board development, and fundraising, which addresses topics like "Why are people afraid to ask for money?" and "How do I figure out how much someone can give my organization? " The site also offers information on purchasing fundraising software and book reviews of notable titles in the field.

National Center for Nonprofit Boards <http://www.ncnb.org>
If you've wondered how to get the members of your board to take a more active role in your organization's fundraising efforts, you will find useful resources and publications at the NCNB's Web site.

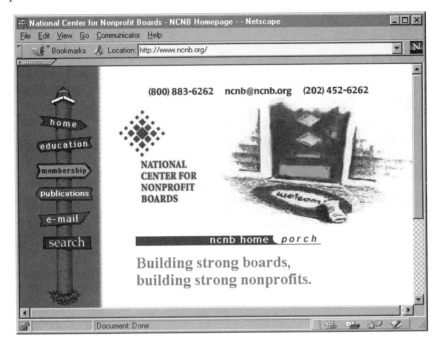

The NCNB FAQ section includes information about recruiting and communicating with board members, forming nonprofits, resolving board conflicts, and developing board job descriptions. For visitors who need further information, there is an electronic query form for submitting questions to NCNB staff.

Association of Professional Researchers for Advancement
<http://weber.u.washington.edu/~dlamb/apra/APRA.html>

APRA is a membership organization for professional fundraising researchers, and its Web site features "prospecting resources" links (including the PROSPECT-L discussion list and its archives; see Chapter 9) and several FAQs on topics ranging from determining an individual's net worth to finding biographical information on foundation executives.

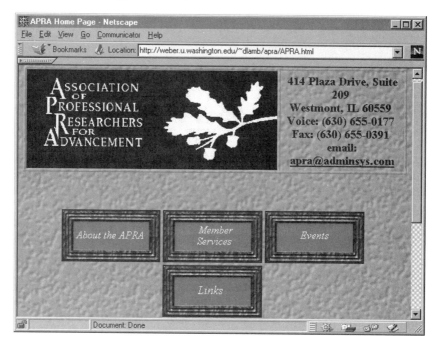

National Society of Fund-Raising Executives <http://www.nsfre.org>

The National Society of Fund Raising Executives is the premiere professional organization for nonprofit fundraisers, and its site is primarily for the use of NSFRE members. In addition to the full text of its Code of Ethical Principles and Standards of Professional Practice, visitors will find NSFRE's directory of fund-raising consultants, with contact information and areas of specialization.

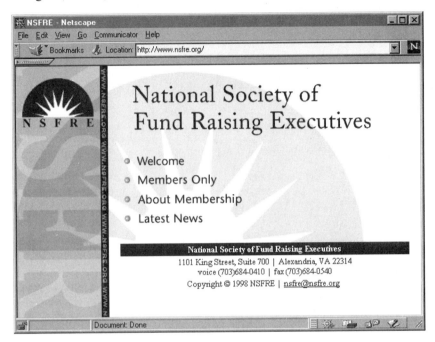

David Lamb's Prospect Research Page
<http://weber.u.washington.edu/~dlamb/research.html>

Lamb, a development officer at the University of Washington, has attempted to "separate the wheat from the chaff" in describing truly useful Internet sites for researching corporations, foundations, and individual donors. His page includes links to directories of doctors, dentists, lawyers, and airplane owners, as well as to online news sources and fee-based information providers like Dialog. What's nice about the Prospect Research Page is that Lamb has distilled the overwhelming number of potential sources of information on the Internet into a relatively small selection of sites, which he has thoughtfully annotated. The casual visitor can tell that he or she is in capable hands.

The Nonprofit FAQ <http://www.nonprofit-info.org/npofaq/index.html>
This page may be a good illustration of the adage that good things come to those who wait. The Nonprofit FAQ is a large file that takes a while to load even with a fast computer, but once you get to the section you need, you'll be rewarded with a wealth of information.

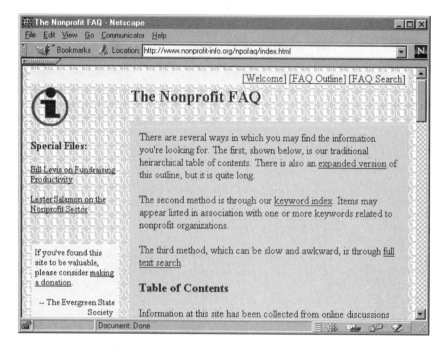

Based on online discussions at the UseNet newsgroup soc.org.nonprofit (see Chapter 9), this set of frequently asked questions is divided into 15 broad categories, including starting and marketing nonprofit organizations, volunteers, board governance, small and large donor fundraising, computer technology, and ethics. You get to see what professionals in the field have to say on topics like special events, direct mail, corporate sponsorship, and enlisting celebrity support for your organization.

Grantscape <http://www.grantscape.com>
The Web site of Capitol Publications, a publisher of many directories and newsletters for fundraisers, Grantscape offers a "Funder of the Day," a discussion forum for nonprofits, information about upcoming meetings and conferences, and Grantseeking 101, an overview of the process of fundraising research, proposal development, and good grantsmanship practices.

"How do we select fundraising software?"
<http://www.supportcenter.org/sf/frfaq7.html>
If your organization is thinking about purchasing specialized fundraising software to enhance its development efforts, this Support Center FAQ deals with hardware platforms, pricing options, staff training, and what sorts of questions you should be asking a software sales representative. Enter the Nonprofit Genie and choose "fundraising" under "Answers." This FAQ is the seventh question.

Grants for Individuals

Most foundations and corporations make grants to nonprofit organizations rather than to individuals. It shouldn't be surprising that most of the available online information for grantseekers focuses on funding for charities rather than for artists, writers, and researchers. One of the best starting places for the individual grantseeker is the Michigan State University Grants and Related Resources pages, previously introduced in the Funding Information section of this chapter. The MSU site includes a separate section for individuals that covers print resources as well as many federal, state, and university-based funding sources online. It is a very good place to browse for new Web-based resources. Some additional places to visit follow.

ArtsWire <http://www.artswire.org>

ArtsWire, a membership organization devoted to arts advocacy that is sponsored by the New York Foundation for the Arts, offers funding information for individual artists each week in the Current section of its Web site. Current includes late-breaking details on fellowships, residencies, exhibition spaces, arts events, and job listings. The site also includes an archive of Current postings going back to 1995.

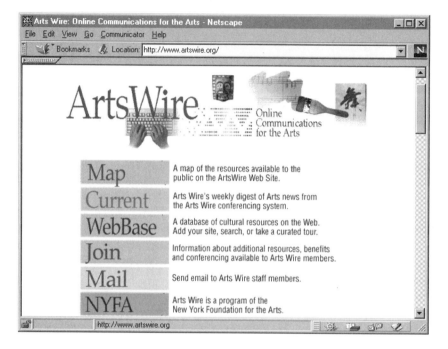

Art Deadlines List <http://custwww.xensei.com/adl/>

Richard Garner's Art Deadlines List is a monthly compilation of information about juried competitions, contests, jobs, internships, scholarships, residencies, fellowships, casting calls, auditions, tryouts, festivals, and grants for artists in the visual, literary and performing arts. Posted to the site is a free version of the list, which is also available via e-mail as a paid subscription service.

FinAid: The Financial Aid Information Page <http://www.finaid.org>
Sponsored by the National Association of Student Financial Aid Administrators and created by Mark Kantrowitz, FinAid is the most comprehensive Internet resource available on funding for education in the United States.

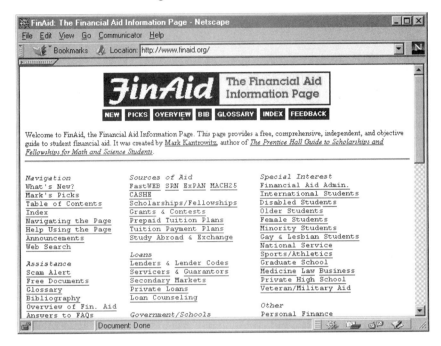

The site runs the gamut from general information about public and private sources of scholarships and loans to scam alerts to FASTWEB, a searchable database of funding. It would be difficult to pose a question about financial aid and not find a detailed response here.

International Resources

At this point, the Web's promise for creating a global network that links international nonprofits with prospective sponsors has yet to be realized. Online information for organizations is heavily concentrated in Europe and North America, areas of the world with well-developed philanthropic and telecommunications infrastructures. FundsNet, previously cited in the Funding Information section of this chapter, offers a collection of links to online information about grantmakers active outside the United States at <http://www.fundsnetservices.com/internat.htm.>

The sites that follow may be useful as well.

European Foundation Centre <http://www.efc.be/>

Visitors to this simply designed page will find information about the Foundation Center's European counterpart, including links to foundations and corporations active on the Continent, and advice about research and cultivation of potential funders.

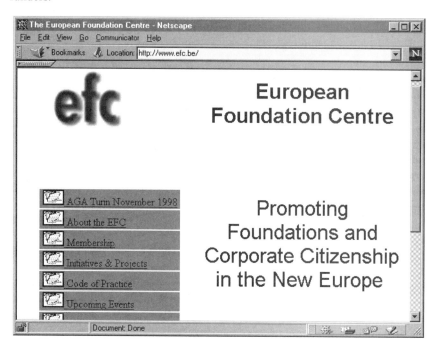

UK Fundraising <http://www.fundraising.co.uk/>

A wide variety of information for charities and fundraisers in the United Kingdom is made available here by the Charities Aid Foundation. The information offerings range from monthly news features to book reviews and statistical information about the nonprofit sector. Check the "Grants and Funding" section for useful links. "Fundraising Online" features examples of how to use the Web to publicize your organization, attract donations and in-kind gifts, and recruit members and volunteers.

Charity Village <http://www.charityvillage.com>

The online resource for all things nonprofit in Canada, this site combines news headlines, conference listings, job opportunities, a directory of Canadian organizations by subject area, and links to online publications and mailing lists. The Sources of Funding section has links to Canadian foundations, databases of funding for research, and grants opportunities from Canadian government agencies.

German Charities Institute <http://www.dsk.de>

This site is a clearinghouse of information on German and international charities which features a searchable directory of over 5,000 organizations, an immense collection of links, and information about everything from volunteer opportunities to e-mail discussion groups on philanthropy and social issues. Much of the information is available in English.

CONCLUSION

The Internet is growing so rapidly that it could be a full time job keeping current with what's available. Surfing for new Web sites, while time consuming, is an essential part of that process. Many of the sites we've reviewed will help keep you posted about new online resources, but it's important not to understate the value of simply spending time on the Web yourself. The Links to Nonprofit Resources section of the Foundation Center's Web site is a great jumping off point for further exploration. We'll continue to use that space to inform you about new sites of interest as well as changes to some of your old favorites. Below we reproduce those listings of links from the Center's Web site, condensed and revised for a print presentation.

Links and Abstracts of Nonprofit Resources on the Foundation Center Web Site

BUSINESS & INDUSTRY (See Chapter 4 for more about corporate information available on the Web)

Council of Better Business Bureaus <http://www.bbb.org/index.html>

Besides serving as a gateway to more than 150 local Better Business Bureaus throughout the U.S. and Canada, the CBBB Web site provides instant access to business and consumer alerts, charity reports and standards (through its Philanthropic Advisory Service), and other helpful resources. It also has begun to accept consumer complaints, which it forwards to the appropriate local BBB. An important service, and a nice site.

EDGAR Database of Corporate Information <http://www.sec.gov/edgarhp.htm>

The Securities and Exchange Commission's EDGAR (Electronic Data Gathering, Analysis, and Retrieval) system is a goldmine of basic but often-hard-to-find corporate information (e.g., fiscal data, officers, subsidiaries, recent M&A activity, et cetera). EDGAR on the Web allows visitors to retrieve publicly available filings submitted to the SEC from January 1994 to the present.

Hoover's Online <http://www.hoovers.com/>

Hoover's, the Austin, Texas-based publisher of corporate information, may not be the "Ultimate Source for Company Information," as it bills itself, but it sure is a good one. The site's offerings come in two flavors, free and fee-based. The former center around Hoover's Company Capsules, which provide news and information—company profile, key personnel, full stock quote, selected press coverage—on more than 11,000 public and private enterprises. Subscribers (two options: personal or multi-user) get the same—in much greater depth and detail. This site offers coverage of more than 1,500 nonpublic companies including not for profits and foundations.

Inc. Online <http://www.inc.com/>

Brought to you by the folks at Inc. magazine, the award-winning Inc. Online is a great resource for entrepreneurs and small business owners who are serious about growing their businesses. In addition to the most recent edition of Inc. and an archive of 5,000-plus articles on a wide variety of topics, the site offers interactive worksheets, case studies, online tutorials, a searchable database of America's 500 fastest-growing companies, and great links to other small business-related resources on the Net.

Project Involve! <http://www.alfsv.org/involve/>

The mission of the American Leadership Forum's Project Involve! is to build philanthropy, public service, and community in Silicon Valley. Among other features, the Involve! Web site offers a "Resource Guide," an online guide to organizations and resources for companies exploring or expanding their corporate contributions programs, and "Winning Strategies for Corporate Community Involvement," which contains the basics of how to plan, select, and initiate community-oriented programs. Although the site focuses on Northern California, many of the organizations listed are national in scope.

U.S. Small Business Administration <http://www.sbaonline.sba.gov/>

As an independent agency of the U.S. government, the SBA assists small businesses in order to encourage free enterprise and improve the nation's overall economy. Visitors to the site can retrieve exhaustive information about what the agency offers, including a variety of financial assistance programs. The SBA site also includes a section devoted to laws and regulations affecting small businesses, a "business card" registration center and links to other government resources. Easy to navigate, concise descriptions explain the variety of routes available to financing a small business.

THE INTERNET

Electronic Frontier Foundation <http://www.eff.org/>

The not-for-profit EFF is a high-profile clearinghouse for news and information about Internet-related issues such as free speech, encryption, privacy, and intellectual property rights. One of the four most-linked-to sites on the Web. This site also contains daily news updates and opportunities to participate in internet advocacy.

Internet Law & Policy Forum <http://www.ilpf.org/>

The ILPF was conceived as "a neutral venue in which to develop solutions to the challenging legal and policy questions of the Internet." Issues currently being addressed by the Forum include online certification of commercial transactions, digital signatures, and content blocking and regulation. This site also offers listings of internet law resources, conferences and an archive of press releases.

The 'Open Source' Page[New!] <http://www.opensource.org/index.html>

The "open source" movement is dedicated to the proposition that computer source code developed in an open, non-proprietary environment is chiefly responsible for the global popularity of the Internet. Examples of open-source software in commercial use include Apache, which runs 50 percent of the world's Web servers; the Perl programming language, in which most CGI applications are written; BIND, the software that provides the domain name service (DNS) for the Internet; and sendmail, the most widely used email transport software on the Net. The 'Open Source' Page explains the roots of the movement and where it's headed.

Technology Tip Sheets for Nonprofits <http://www.coyotecom.com/tips.html>

Tip sheets to help organizations and individuals reap money-saving, program-enhancing benefits from technology. Most of the material is geared to not-for-profit and public sector organizations.

Technology Resource Institute <http://www.techresource.org/>

TRI works with public libraries to ensure that communities have access to the Internet, and helps to train local library personnel in the use of emerging communications technologies. This site also provides listings of training opportunities, other web-based resources and a description of TRI's partnership with the Gates Library Foundation.

World Wide Web Consortium <http://www.w3.org/>

Under the direction of Tim Berners-Lee, the creator of the World Wide Web, the WC3 has played a leading role since 1994 in developing and articulating the specifications and protocols at the heart of the Web. A touchstone in the evolution of the Web, and a vitally important resource for Web developers.

LIBRARY LINKS

American Library Association <http://www.ala.org/>

The 57,000-member ALA, the oldest library association in the world, has been a leader in defending intellectual freedom and promoting quality library and information services for more than a century. Today, the association's interests and activities range from copyright and intellectual property issues, to library education and professional development. A great resource for library professionals as well as anyone interested in the critical role libraries and librarians will play in the emerging information-based economy.

Association of Research Libraries <http://www.arl.org/>

The programs and services of the ARL promote equitable access to, and effective use of, recorded knowledge in support of teaching, research, scholarship, and community service.

CAUSE <http://www.educause.edu/>

This membership organization, which recently consolidated with Educom, is dedicated to managing and using information resources in higher education.

IUPUI University Special Collections <http://foyt.iupui.edu/special/>

The Special Collections department at the University Library of Indiana University-Purdue University Indianapolis (IUPUI) encompasses the Manuscript Collections, University Archives, and Rare Books—located in the Ruth Lilly Special Collections and Archives—and the Joseph and Matthew Payton Philanthropic Studies Library (PPSL). (The Manuscript Collections' "Philanthropy" section houses the Foundation Center Historical Foundation Collection, 1896–1994.) Special Collections also compiles and maintains the Philanthropic Studies Index, a reference to literature, primarily periodicals and research reports, on voluntarism, nonprofit organizations, fund raising, and charitable giving.

Libri Foundation <http://www.teleport.com/~librifdn/index.html>

The Libri Foundation is a national nonprofit organization that donates new hardcover children's books to small rural public libraries in the U.S. through its "Books for Children" program.

Library of Congress <http://lcweb.loc.gov/>

The entire Library of Congress catalogue searchable online, as well as information on the LC's programs and services.

Technology Resource Institute <http://www.techresource.org/>

TRI works with public libraries to ensure that communities have access to the Internet, and helps to train local library personnel in the use of emerging communications technologies. This site also provides listings of training opportunities, other web-based resources and a description of TRI's partnership with the Gates Library Foundation.

POLICY INSTITUTES

Hoover Institution on War, Revolution and Peace
<http://www-hoover.stanford.edu/>
Before he became 31st president of the United States, Herbert Hoover founded the Hoover Institution, a public policy research center at Stanford University devoted to the advanced study of domestic and international affairs. Recognized as one of the first "think tanks" in the U.S., the Institution boasts one of the world's most complete libraries on political, economic, and social change in the 20th century. The Hoover Institution Web site offers information on the organization's research program, publications, and library collections, as well as subscription information for its electronic mailing lists.

NIRA's World Directory of Think Tanks
<http://www.nira.go.jp/ice/tt-info/nwdtt96/>
The Japan-based National Institute for Research Advancement provides a no-frills site with basic information on more than 250 policy organizations in 65 countries. Information available for each organization can include executive personnel, organizational history, areas of research, geographic focus, availability of research findings, and funding sources. Contact information is also available, as are individual Web site links (when available). Although the site lacks a master index, this is an excellent place to start for those interested in policy institutes and their work.

RAND <http://www.rand.org/>
RAND (an acronym for Research and Development) researchers assist public policymakers at all levels, private sector leaders in many industries, and the public at large in efforts to strengthen the nation's economy, maintain its security, and improve its quality of life. RAND's Web site offers information about the organization's research activities, technical capabilities, publications, educational opportunities, and board of trustees, along with a "Hot Topics in RAND Research" area.

REFERENCE

Fast Area Code Look-Up <http://www.555-1212.com/aclookup.html>
Brought to you by the folks at 555-1212.COM, Fast Area Code Look-Up does exactly that: Plug in the name of a city, add the name of a state or (Canadian) province, and voila!—it supplies that pesky area code you can never remember. Also works in reverse (though less well): Enter an area code and Fast Look-Up gives you a broad geographical location and the names of major cities in that location. Neat.

U.S. Census Bureau <http://www.census.gov/>
The Census Bureau's sprawling site is the source of social, demographic, and economic information about the U.S. on the Web. Offerings include all Census Bureau publications (in .PDF format) released since January 1996; statistical profiles for states, congressional districts, and counties; current economic indicators; state and county maps created on the fly; and much, much more. Who would have guessed that statistics could be this much fun?

GENERAL

Catalog of Federal Domestic Assistance
<http://www.gsa.gov/fdac/default.htm>
The Catalog of Federal Domestic Assistance provides information on a wide variety of financial and non-financial assistance programs, projects, services, and activities. Programs are administered by departments and establishments of the federal government and are available to the public. Visitors to the site submit a simple query and receive clear, detailed information, including eligibility requirements, application procedures, and examples of funded projects.

Federal Information Exchange, Inc. <http://web.fie.com/fedix/index.html>
FEDIX provides free access to information on government research and education grants, programs, contracts, and more. Supported by selected federal agencies under a cooperative agreement forged by the Department of Energy and the Office of Science Education and Technical Information, the FEDIX Web site is comprehensive and easy to use. Visitors can search by audience or subject and can also receive targeted funding opportunities via E-mail. Other features include news updates and a Grants Keyword Thesaurus, which can be downloaded by eligible nonprofit institutions.

Federal Register <http://www.access.gpo.gov/su_docs/aces/aces140.html>
The no-frills Federal Register site provides access to presidential documents, executive orders, rules, and proposed rules from federal agencies and organizations. Visitors to the site can search the database in a variety of ways, and detailed instructions and sample searches are provided to facilitate the process. The exhaustive information on governmentally funded projects and funding availability is especially helpful.

Grants Information Service <http://infoserv.rttonet.psu.edu/gis/>
A collection of links to (mostly) government sources of funding for research, instruction, and continuing education projects from the folks at Penn State's Office of Sponsored Programs.

OMB's Nonprofits and Technology Project
<http://www.ombwatch.org/ombwatch/npt/>
The goal of the Nonprofits and Technology Project is to improve communications linkages within the nonprofit sector to strengthen public policy participation. Through the project, OMB Watch will offer grants to nonprofits in the range of $5,000 to $25,000 to help fund innovative and creative applications of technology to the field of public policy participation.

THOMAS: Legislative Information on the Internet
<http://thomas.loc.gov/home/thomas2.html>
The online arm of the U.S. Congress Library, offering up-to-date information on the legislative activities of both Houses, and searchable databases of current and historical legislative documents of the U.S. Congress.

WWW Virtual Library: U.S. Federal Government Agencies
<http://www.lib.lsu.edu/gov/fedgov.html>
A meta-index of federal agencies on the Internet.

WWW Virtual Library: U.S. Government Resources
<http://iridium.nttc.edu/gov_res.html>
A searchable meta-index of federal agencies on the Internet.

FEDERAL AGENCIES (See Chapter 5 for more detail on government Web sites)

Administration on Aging <http://www.aoa.dhhs.gov/>
An exhaustive online resource for senior citizens and issues concerning aging and senior health.

Administration for Children and Families <http://www.acf.dhhs.gov/>
Information on the vast array of programs and services offered by this division of DHHS, dedicated to promoting the economic and social well-being of families, children, individuals and communities.

Agency for Health Care Policy and Research <http://www.ahcpr.gov/>
Grantmaking DHHS agency, dedicated to generating and disseminating information that improves the health care system.

Centers for Disease Control and Prevention <http://www.cdc.gov/>
Includes comprehensive program and application information for the CDC's many health-related funding opportunities.

Department of Health and Human Services <http://www.os.dhhs.gov/>
The DHHS Web site provides consumer and policy information, searchable databases, employment opportunities, and links to related government agencies.

Health Resources and Services Administration <http://www.hrsa.dhhs.gov/>
An overview of programs, services and grant opportunities from this DHHS agency.

Indian Health Service <http://www.tucson.ihs.gov/>
Dedicated to raising the health status of American Indians and Alaska Natives, the Web site of this DHHS agency provides information on the agency's activities, and serves as an online resource for Native American communities.

Internal Revenue Service <http://www.irs.ustreas.gov/prod/>
This highly regarded site provides comprehensive tax information and has a site-wide search engine.

National Endowment for the Arts <http://arts.endow.gov/>
The NEA's elegant Web site provides information on the endowment's programs and funding guidelines and serves as a comprehensive resource for the arts community and its supporters.

National Endowment for the Humanities <http://www.neh.fed.us/>
Program information and application guidelines for the NEH's grantmaking programs in the humanities.

National Institute on Alcohol Abuse and Alcoholism
<http://www.niaaa.nih.gov/>
One of 18 agencies that comprise the National Institutes of Health, NIAAA supports and conducts biomedical and behavioral research on the causes, consequences, treatment, and prevention of alcoholism and alcohol-related problems.

National Institutes of Health <http://www.nih.gov/>
Comprehensive information on the NIH's activities and programs, including grants and funding opportunities.

National Science Foundation <http://www.nsf.gov/>
The NSF is dedicated to fostering science and engineering research and education nationwide. As you'd expect from the agency that step-fathered the Internet into adolescence, the NSF Web site is comprehensive, well-organized, and fast. Site includes program and grants and awards info in biology, education, engineering, the geosciences, math and physical sciences, polar research, social and behavioral sciences and much more.

National Telecommunications & Information Administration
<http://www.ntia.doc.gov/>
Includes application guidelines and a listing of recent grants awarded through its Telecommunications and Information Infrastructure Assistance Program.

Oak Ridge Institute for Science and Education
<http://www.orau.gov/orise.htm>
The Institute supports national and international programs in education, training, health, and the environment.

Substance Abuse and Mental Health Services Administration
<http://www.samhsa.gov/>
The Web site of this DHHS agency provides information on its programs, events and funding opportunities, and serves as an online resource for substance abuse prevention.

U.S. Census Bureau <http://www.census.gov/>
The Census Bureau's sprawling site is the source of social, demographic, and economic information about the U.S. on the Web. Offerings include all Census Bureau publications (in .PDF format) released since January 1996; statistical profiles for states, congressional districts, and counties; current economic indicators; state and county maps created on the fly; and much, much more. Who would have guessed that statistics could be this much fun?

STATE AGENCIES

Nebraska Arts Council <http://www.gps.k12.ne.us/nac_web_site/nac.htm>
The NAC promotes the arts, cultivates resources, and supports excellence in artistic endeavors for all Nebraskans. Still under construction, the NAC Web site provides general information about its grant programs and application requirements; an artists directory; links to other art councils (community and state), state organizations, and art museums on the Web; and contact information.

North Carolina Arts Council <http://www.ncarts.org/>
The mission of the NCAC is to enrich North Carolina's cultural life by supporting the arts. The Council is a catalyst for the development of arts organizations, and awards grants and offers technical guidance statewide. The Council's colorful Web site provides, among other items, program and grant information; links to various arts organizations, government agencies, and regional and national arts partners; and contact information for 285 North Carolina arts organizations organized by county and by type of art group.

North Dakota Council on the Arts <http://www.state.nd.us/arts/>
Established in 1967 by the state legislature, the NDCA is responsible for the support and development of the arts and artists in North Dakota. In addition to making grants based on recommendations from artists and arts administrators, the Council administers the Cultural Endowment Fund, through which it secures private and public funds to enhance existing programs. The Council's Web site provides program information, application instructions, grant-writing tips, related arts resource links, and contact information.

Ohio Arts Council <http://www.oac.ohio.gov/>
Established in 1965 to "foster and encourage the development of the arts and assist the preservation of Ohio's cultural heritage," the OAC funds programs to make arts activities available to the public and also supports Ohio artists through 25 different grant programs. The Council's Web site provides information about all OAC programs, complete grant guidelines, an impressive search engine, links to both state and national arts resources, and e-mail links to staff members.

South Dakota Arts Council <http://www.sd.us/deca/sdarts/sdarts.htm>
The SDAC encourages and supports artists, strengthens arts organizations and arts education programs, and increases South Dakotans awareness of the arts. As a state agency of the Department of Education & Cultural Affairs, the Council makes grants to schools, individuals, and arts organizations. Grantseekers will especially appreciate the Council's online program guide, which includes detailed grant application guidelines and a handy glossary of terms.

INTERNATIONAL

Charities Aid Foundation <http://www.charitynet.org/index.html>
CAF, a British nonprofit whose aim is to encourage charitable giving in the United Kingdom as well as internationally, sponsors the Charitynet Web site, "a resource centre for the non-profit sector and its contributors." The site includes contact

information for thousands of charities and serves as a technical assistance provider to both funders and nonprofits. Of special interest is the site's Corporate Community Involvement Resource Center, an alpha list of links to more than 100 corporate (U.S.-based and multinational) Web sites with charitable giving information.

CIVICUS <http://www.civicus.org/>
An international alliance dedicated "to strengthening citizen action and civil society throughout the world."

Disaster Relief.Org <http://www.disasterrelief.org/>
An easy-to-navigate clearinghouse for worldwide disaster aid and information.

International Donors' Dialogue <http://www.internationaldonors.org/>
Almost everything you wanted to know about international philanthropy, from the clever, passionate folks who started the San Francisco-based IDD in 1996. The IDD Web site offers a list of international projects that need urgent, immediate action; a selection of worthwhile projects in need of funding arranged by region, organization, or issue; a calendar of conferences, films, workshops, and site visits; helpful answers to frequently asked questions about international philanthropy; and more. Check it out. You'll be inspired.

Internet Law & Policy Forum <http://www.ilpf.org/>
The ILPF was conceived as "a neutral venue in which to develop solutions to the challenging legal and policy questions of the Internet." Issues currently being addressed by the Forum include online certification of commercial transactions, digital signatures, and content blocking and regulation.

Internet Prospector <http://w3.uwyo.edu/~prospect/inter.html>
Check out IP's resources for international prospect research.

Novartis Foundation for Sustainable Development
<http://www.foundation.novartis.com/>
Established in December 1996, and formerly known as the Ciba-Geigy Foundation for Cooperation with Developing Countries, the Novartis Foundation supports a variety of projects in developing countries—among them Bangladesh, Bolivia, Brazil, China, Laos, Mali, Senegal, and Tanzania—in the areas of agricultural, health care, and social development.

The World Bank <http://www.worldbank.org/>
The sometimes-controversial World Bank strives to reduce poverty and improve living standards by promoting sustainable growth and investment in developing countries. The World Bank Group includes the International Bank for Reconstruction and Development, the International Development Association, the International Finance Corporation, the Multilateral Investment Guarantee Agency, and the International Centre for the Settlement of Investment Disputes. The Bank's Web site offers an imposing smorgasbord of economic facts and general information about the dozens of countries in which the Bank and its sister institutions do business.

USAID <http://www.info.usaid.gov/>
The United States Agency for International Development is an independent government agency that provides economic development and humanitarian assistance to advance U.S. economic and political interests overseas. The USAID Web site offers numerous links to governmental and non-governmental organizations concerned with international development.

AFRICA

Africa News Online <http://www.africanews.org/>
A one-stop source for up-to-date information on all of Africa, with reports from Africa's leading newspapers, magazines, and news agencies. An invaluable resource.

**Novartis Foundation for Sustainable Development
<http://www.foundation.novartis.com/>**
Established in December 1996, and formerly known as the Ciba-Geigy Foundation for Cooperation with Developing Countries, the Novartis Foundation supports a variety of projects in developing countries—among them Bangladesh, Bolivia, Brazil, China, Laos, Mali, Senegal, and Tanzania—in the areas of agricultural, health care, and social development.

EUROPE/EURASIA

European Foundation Centre <http://www.efc.be/>
Information about the Foundation Center's European counterpart, including a list of links to foundations and corporate funders active on the Continent.

**International Research & Exchanges Board
<http://www.irex.org/grant-opps/index.htm>**
Washington, D.C.-based IREX was founded in 1968 to administer academic exchanges between the U.S. and Soviet Union. Since then, its efforts have expanded to encompass professional training, institution building, technical assistance, and policy programs with the Newly Independent States, Central and Eastern Europe, and Mongolia and China. The "Grants & Fellowships" section of this information-rich site includes opportunities for international and U.S. scholars, and reports on library and archive access in a host of far-flung locales. The site also offers a database-driven links section showcasing the best of the World Wide Web.

National Forum Foundation <http://www.nff.org/>
Information on NFF's internship and volunteer programs and the NGO Regional Networking Project. Visitors to this site can also access the Freedom Forum's NGONet , an online database on Central and Eastern European NGOs.

**Regional Environmental Center for Central and Eastern Europe
<http://www.rec.org/Default.shtml>**
Comprehensive Web site offering information on REC's programs and grantmaking activities, as well as several searchable databases.

NGONet <http://www.ngonet.org/>

NGONet provides information to, for, and about non-governmental organizations (NGOs) active in Central and Eastern Europe. Visitors to the NGONet site will find resources for funders, grantseekers, organizations looking for project partners, and job seekers.

CANADA

Council of Better Business Bureaus <http://www.bbb.org/index.html>

Besides serving as a gateway to more than 150 local Better Business Bureaus throughout the U.S. and Canada, the CBBB Web site provides instant access to business and consumer alerts, charity reports and standards (through its Philanthropic Advisory Service), and other helpful resources. It also has begun to accept consumer complaints, which it forwards to the appropriate local BBB. An important service, and a nice site.

Charity Village <http://www.charityvillage.com/>

An excellent source of news, information, nonprofit resources, and discussions for the Canadian nonprofit community. Updated daily.

fastWeb Canada <http://www.fastweb.com/canada/>

A comprehensive, searchable database of scholarships, fellowships, grants, loans, and bursaries for Canadian students.

In Kind Canada/In Kind Exchange <http://www.inkindcanada.ca>

A collaborative effort between In Kind Canada, which distributes donated goods and services to other Canadian charities, and Charity Village, the award-winning Canadian Web site.

Ontario Arts Council <http://www.arts.on.ca/>

The OAC supports artists and arts organizations throughout the province of Ontario, and awards grants based upon a unique peer assessment process that "gives artists and arts organizations a voice in how funds are distributed." Visitors to the OAC Web site will find a thorough description of its grant programs, application procedures, eligibility requirements, and deadlines. Excerpts from past Council newsletters are also available, providing a clear picture of the OAC community and how it is affected by government policy.

Science's Next Wave <http://www.nextwave.org/>

Billed as "an electronic network for the next generation of scientists," the Next Wave site features profiles of and practical career advice for young scientists, as well as links to numerous scientific organizations and funding sources. Lots of material written by and of interest to Canadian scientists.

The Trillium Foundation <http://www.trilliumfoundation.org/>

The Trillium Foundation was established in 1982 "to ensure that a portion of the proceeds of the Ontario Lottery Corporation is directed toward social issues" in Ontario. The focus of the Foundation is on "the development of a new social vision which provides opportunity, and promotes both individual and collective responsibility." Through its grants program, the foundation encourages innovation and experimentation, cross-sectoral collaboration, citizen participation, and systemic change." English- and French-language versions.

GERMANY

German Charities Institute <http://www.dsk.de/>
More than 25,000 pages on German charity, philanthropy, and volunteering, including extensive listings of German and international nonprofit resources. German and English versions.

Lycos Germany <http://www.lycos.de/>
The German-language edition of the popular search engine.

Yahoo! Deutschland <http://www.yahoo.de/>
The German-language edition of the popular Web directory.

IRELAND

The Wellcome Trust <http://www.wellcome.ac.uk/>
The Trust spends hundreds of millions annually on research in biomedical science and the history of medicine, making it the largest non-governmental source of funds for biomedical research in Europe. Grants are made to researchers in the UK and the Republic of Ireland, and for a variety of purposes, including programmatic, training, travel abroad, and equipment. Loads of information here in two flavors—frames-based and text-only.

ITALY

Vialardi di Sandigliano Foundation
<http://www.gvo.it/VdSF/torrione_atrium.html>
Dedicated to the conservation of the medieval castle complex of Torrione, in northern Italy, and to creating and administering nonprofit activities and collaborative projects that make a significant contribution to preserving history and tradition.

JAPAN

Japan Center for International Exchange (JCIE) <http://www.jcie.or.jp/>
An independent nonprofit organization dedicated to strengthening Japan's role in international networks of policy dialogue and cooperation. Major components of the Center's Web site include Global ThinkNet, a cluster of JCIE-sponsored activities designed to broaden policy research and dialogue on issues pertaining to Japan's relationships with other countries; and CivilNet, which is designed to advance the cause of the nonprofit sector in the Asia Pacific region, with a special emphasis on the development of civil society in Japan. The CivilNet portion of the site is the gateway to information about the Asia Community Trust (ACT), a Japan-based charitable trust committed to financially supporting the grassroots

efforts of NGOs involved in sustainable social and economic development across Asia.

MEXICO

Fundacion Mexico Unido <http://www.m3w3.com.mx/MexicoUnido/>
The United Mexico Foundation promotes the appreciation of Mexico's traditional cultural values through grants, mutual benefit programs, and the efforts of volunteers, with the focus on children, teachers, and women. Visitors to the site will find a mission statement in English and Spanish and contact information.

SPAIN

Fundesco <http://www.fundesco.es/>
A nonprofitmaking institution set up by Telefonica de Espana, promoting research into, and use of, telecommunications and information technologies. Spanish and English versions.

SWEDEN

Lycos Swedenm <http://www.lycos.se/>
The Swedish-language edition of the popular search engine.

UNITED KINGDOM

Scottish Community Foundation <http://www.caledonian.org.uk/>
A non-sectarian, non-political charitable trust in its second year of operation that raises funds around the world to help the work of charities in Scotland.

Charities Aid Foundation <http://www.charitynet.org/index.html>
CAF, a British nonprofit whose aim is to encourage charitable giving in the United Kingdom as well as internationally, sponsors the Charitynet Web site, "a resource centre for the non-profit sector and its contributors." The site includes contact information for thousands of charities and serves as a technical assistance provider to both funders and nonprofits. Of special interest is the site's Corporate Community Involvement Resource Center, an alpha list of links to more than 100 corporate (U.S.-based and multinational) Web sites with charitable giving information.

The Commonwealth Foundation <http://www.oneworld.org/com_fnd/>
Intergovernmental organization supporting exchange, training opportunities, and the sharing of skills, experience, and information in the British non-governmental sector.

Oxfordshire Community Foundation
<http://www.i-way.co.uk/~oxcomm/home.html>
Supports programs in education, disability, poverty, and health within Oxfordshire County.

UK Fundraising <http://www.fundraising.co.uk/>
Comprehensive resource for charities and nonprofit fundraisers in the UK.

The Wellcome Trust <http://www.wellcome.ac.uk/>
The Trust spends hundreds of millions annually on research in biomedical science and the history of medicine, making it the largest non-governmental source of funds for biomedical research in Europe. Grants are made to researchers in the UK and the Republic of Ireland, and for a variety of purposes, including programmatic, training, travel abroad, and equipment. Loads of information here in two flavors—frames-based and text-only.

NONPROFIT FUNDRAISING—GENERAL

Foundations On-Line <http://www.foundations.org/othersites.html>
Links to various foundations and grantmakers, fundraising software vendors and consultants, not-for-profit attorneys, and related sites.

Internet Prospector <http://w3.uwyo.edu/~prospect/>
Internet Prospector is a unique Web site/service that, every month, gathers and presents the efforts of as many as eight researchers from across the country who "mine" the Internet to report on sites useful to prospect researchers. Organized into a number of broad categories (Access, Archives, Corporations, Ethics, Grants, International, News Online, and People), the site offers a wealth of annotated links to news and information resources, online directories, grantmaker Web sites, and search engines. For those who prefer their information in more manageable chunks, the IP crew publishes a monthly e-newsletter that summarizes their most recent finds.

EDUCATION

The Chronicle of Higher Education <http://chronicle.com/>
Published weekly, the online version of the Chronicle is an award-winning source of news and information for college and university faculty and administrators and includes lists of recent gifts and grants to higher education, new software titles, and appointments and promotions in the academic world. "Academe Today," a free online service available to subscribers of the print version of the Chronicle, provides daily updates on federal grant opportunities in addition to other features. Limited grant and award deadline information is available to non-subscribers.

Nonprofit Resources, General

GENERAL

HandsNet on the Web <http://www.igc.apc.org/handsnet/>
A national nonprofit organization that promotes information sharing, cross-sector collaboration, and advocacy among individuals and organizations working on a broad range of public interest issues.

IGC's Activism/Internet Resource Center
<http://www.igc.org:80/igc/issues/activis/index.html>
A comprehensive directory of links to nonprofit resources on the Internet. The "activist toolkit" includes links to a number of e-zines, Web-based publications, and helpful legislative directories.

INDEPENDENT SECTOR <http://www.indepsec.org/>
INDEPENDENT SECTOR, the D.C.-based coalition of corporate, foundation, and voluntary organization members, has developed a site that reflects its wide-ranging outreach efforts. Standard Web site components (e.g., mission statement, contact information) are complemented by the site's program modules: government relations (with information on pending legislation affecting the sector); management/ethics; research (with a searchable database compiled by the National Center for Charitable Statistics); membership; and public information and education.

IUPUI University Special Collections <http://foyt.iupui.edu/special/>
The Special Collections department at the University Library of Indiana University-Purdue University Indianapolis (IUPUI) encompasses the Manuscript Collections, University Archives, and Rare Books—located in the Ruth Lilly Special Collections and Archives—and the Joseph and Matthew Payton Philanthropic Studies Library (PPSL). (The Manuscript Collections' "Philanthropy" section houses the Foundation Center Historical Foundation Collection, 1896–1994.) Special Collections also compiles and maintains the Philanthropic Studies Index, a reference to literature, primarily periodicals and research reports, on voluntarism, nonprofit organizations, fund raising, and charitable giving.

Mining Co. Guide to Nonprofit Charitable Organizations
<http://nonprofit.miningco.com/index.htm>
A mini-Web site within the comprehensive Mining Company site that serves as a useful guide to resources and information about nonprofit organizations, foundations, jobs, educational opportunities, and the latest developments in the field. Visitors can search feature archives as well as the entire Mining Co. site, participate in chats, and receive newsletters via e-mail.

National Center for Charitable Statistics <http://nccs.urban.org/>
NCCS, a program of the Center on Nonprofits and Philanthropy at the Urban Institute, is the national repository of data on the nonprofit sector in the United States. Newly available at the Center's Web site are fact sheets on the number and types of nonprofits in the U.S. circa 1989, 1992, and 1994; and the number of tax-exempt organizations registered with the IRS, 1989-1995. Also available are individual state profiles (i.e., number and basic financial information) taken from NCCS' State Nonprofit Almanac 1997; an introduction to the Center's various databases; examples of various IRS forms (e.g., 990, 990-PF) in Adobe Acrobat (.PDF) format; and a nice collection of links to Internet sites of interest.

Nonprofit Outreach Network, Inc. <http://www.norn.org/>
Organizational site dedicated to helping other nonprofit organizations utilize the power of the Internet and World Wide Web to disseminate information.

Nonprofit Prophets
<http://www.kn.pacbell.com/wired/prophets/prophets.res.topics.html>
A comprehensive index of annotated links to resources for investigating problems/research organized by topic. Categories include the environment/ecology; global conflict/politics; family issues; homelessness, hunger, and poverty; disasters; and major online news sources.

CHARITY-MONITORING ORGANIZATIONS

National Charities Information Bureau <http://www.give.org/>
The mission of NCIB is "to promote informed giving and charitable integrity, to enable more contributors to make sound giving decisions and . . . to encourage giving to charities that need and merit support." In addition to "Tips for Givers" and a bi-weekly report on a "Featured Charity," NCIB's Web site has a number of interesting features, including an online reference guide to more than 300 public charities; a help desk; and an interactive order form that can be used to request e-mail updates on new additions to the site.

E-ZINES/NEWSLETTERS/MAILING LISTS (See Chapter 8 for a full listing of nonprofit journals; see Chapter 9 for more on mailing lists.)

Board Cafe <http://www.supportcenter.org/sf/boardcafe.html>
A monthly electronic newsletter for members of nonprofit boards published by the Support Center for Nonprofit Management. Each issue includes numerous "Little Ideas," as well as one "Big Idea" that can be applied to your board work.

Internet Prospector <http://w3.uwyo.edu/~prospect/>
Internet Prospector is a unique Web site/service that, every month, gathers and presents the efforts of as many as eight researchers from across the country who "mine" the Internet to report on sites useful to prospect researchers. Organized into a number of broad categories (Access, Archives, Corporations, Ethics, Grants, International, News Online, and People), the site offers a wealth of annotated links to news and information resources, online directories, grantmaker Web sites, and search engines. For those who prefer their information in more manageable chunks, the IP crew publishes a monthly e-newsletter that summarizes their most recent finds.

Philanthropy Journal Online <http://www.pj.org/>
The digital version of the Philanthropy Journal of North Carolina is a comprehensive source of nonprofit news, information, and links. Features include Philanthropy Links (formerly Ellen's List), the Meta-Index of Nonprofit Organizations, and Philanthropy Journal Alert, an e-newsletter. Also a good regional source of nonprofit job openings and listings.

Philanthropy News Digest (PND) <http://www.fdncenter.org>
This free weekly online journal is a Web-based electronic publication of the Foundation Center Online. Content includes a compendium, in digest form, of philanthropy-related articles and features gathered from print and electronic media outlets nationwide. Abstracts summarize the content of each original articles, and

include complete citations (to assist in locating the complete original article through a library or document delivery service). Many abstracts include "FCnotes," providing the most current statistical information on mentioned grantmakers from the Foundation Center's database, and "Other Links" connect readers to Web sites adding in-depth coverage on featured topics. Timely pull-out quotes of the week, excerpted from each abstract, begin each journal issue, and there are book, CD-ROM, and philanthropic Web site reviews. Subscribe to the free PND Listserv and receive the journal weekly via e-mail Tuesday evenings, the night before each issue is posted to the Web (instructions available at PND home page < http://fdncenter.org/phil/philmain.html>). The PND home page also lists the eight most recent issues of the journal, in chronological order; the full text of each is just a link away. And prior issues dating back to the first, January 9, 1995, can be accessed through an archives; individual abstracts can be accessed by clicking on a headline in the table of contents, or scrolling through each issue. A search engine allows readers to perform key word searches, or click on name indexes of the foundations or of the donors, officers, and trustees cited in PND.

JOB OPPORTUNITIES

Community Career Center <http://www.nonprofitjobs.org/>
The Career Center provides a place for employers and prospective employees in the nonprofit sector to find each other. Employers can post jobs and candidates can submit their credentials. Also provides information on other services available for nonprofit managers.

Nonprofit Career Network <http://www.nonprofitcareer.com/>
Created to fill the needs of the nonprofit sector, the Nonprofit Career Network is a "one-stop resource center" for job seekers looking for employment within a nonprofit organization and for nonprofits seeking qualified candidates. Visitors can post jobs or resumes, search national job listings, consult a nonprofit organization directory and corporate profiles, and find out about job fairs, conferences, and workshops going on around the country. Internships and volunteer information for a handful of nonprofit organizations is also available.

NEWSGROUP

Nonprofit FAQ <http://www.eskimo.com/~pbarber/npofaq/index.html>
The frequently asked questions file, divided into 21 topics, for the newsgroup soc.org.nonprofit. Categories include start-up and management issues, fundraising, marketing, nonprofit organizations and the Internet, education and training, and general theoretical discussions.

WEB DEVELOPMENT/HOSTING/SOFTWARE

Charity Village <http://www.charityvillage.com/charityvillage/lib8.html>
Created and maintained by the Toronto-based Hilborn Group, publishers of Canadian Fundraiser, the excellent Charity Village site offers a number of directories with information on software for nonprofits. The site's "Software" section lists about a dozen products along with brief product descriptions and appropriate

contact information. From there, jump to the "Professional Building" section of the site for listings of "products and services especially for the nonprofit community" under such categories as donor management, direct mail, fundraising, and grant writing.

Flatiron WebWorks <http://www.flatiron.org/>

A nonprofit organization "dedicated to creating and promoting affordable Internet presence and customized World Wide Web pages for small business and nonprofit organizations." Site offerings include a mission statement, client list, and detailed price sheet.

The Nonprofit Software Index
<http://www.shu.edu/~kleintwi/tnopsi/tnopsi.html>

Hosted by Seton Hall University's Center for Nonprofit Service, this low-graphics, frames-based site lists software packages in a variety of categories, including fundraising, financial, personnel, and volunteer management. Each entry includes a detailed description of the software, system requirements, and company contact information.

Rockefeller Technology Project <http://www.rffund.org/techproj/index.html>

The Technology Project is a collaboration of funders interested in helping grantees learn about, and effectively use, new communication technology. The Project's no-frills Web site provides examples of several nonprofits organizations' innovative sites, as well as links to resources for activists and organizations providing technical assistance.

Technology Tip Sheets for Nonprofits <http://www.coyotecom.com/tips.html>

Tip sheets to help organizations and individuals reap money-saving, program-enhancing benefits from technology. Most of the material is geared to not-for-profit and public sector organizations.

UK Fundraising <http://www.fundraising.co.uk/software.html>

Howard Lake's highly regarded UK Fundraising site has a section on fundraising software that lists more than 20 products. A brief description of the product, links to developers' Web sites, and links to sites with additional information on software for nonprofits are also included.

VOLUNTARISM

Points of Light Foundation <http://www.pointsoflight.org/>

The Washington, D.C.-based foundation was founded in 1990 with a mission to engage more people more effectively in volunteer community service. The Foundation's beautifully-designed Web site offers useful information for volunteers, would-be volunteers, and organizations that employ or train volunteers.

Nonprofit Resources, by Program Area

AGING

Administration on Aging <http://www.aoa.dhhs.gov/>
An exhaustive online resource for senior citizens and issues concerning aging and
senior health.

American Association of Retired Persons <http://www.aarp.org/>
The advocacy voice of older Americans concerned with questions about health
insurance, housing, consumer rights, transportation, crime prevention, and more.

Project on Death in America <http://www.soros.org/death/death.html>
Supports research and innovation surrounding the issues of dying and bereave-
ment. Part of the Soros Foundations Network.

SeniorNet <http://www.seniornet.org/>
A national nonprofit organization dedicated to building a community of computer-using seniors who use their new skills for their own benefit and to benefit
society. The site provides a listing of SeniorNet Learning Centers by state, round
table discussions and e-mail pen pals, information on computer discounts, and
more.

SPRY Foundation <http://www.spry.org/>
Helps older adults plan for a healthy and financially secure future by conducting
research and developing education programs. An information-rich site.

ARTS—GENERAL

Americans for the Arts <http://www.artsusa.org/>
A creation of the American Council for the Arts, Americans for the Arts supports
the arts and culture nationwide through resource, leadership, and public policy
development, information services, and education.

The Artsnet Homepage <http://artsnet.heinz.cmu.edu/>
Offers information on and links to development resources, career services, discussion forums, arts management resources, and art sites on the Internet.

Arts Wire <http://www.artswire.org/>
A comprehensive clearinghouse of cultural resources on the Web. Offers, among a
variety of features, a monthly "curated tour" of Web sites devoted to a specific
cultural topic.

The Estate Project for Artists With AIDS <http://www.artistswithaids.org/>
The Estate Project is part of the Alliance for Arts, a nonprofit arts service organization dedicated to policy research, information services, and advocacy for the
arts in New York State. EP's Web site offers information on arts news, artists'
resources, specific strategies for arts preservation, lists of grants that have been
awarded in the arts, and information and/or links to relevant arts organizations,

many of which are national in scope. The site is geared toward the special needs of artists with AIDS, but provides information useful to others involved with the arts communities and information on how to donate to the project.

Intermedia Arts <http://www.intermediaarts.org/>
The mission of Minneapolis-based Intermedia Arts, a nonprofit multidisciplinary art center, is to help "build understanding among people through art" by providing artist support, programs, and community education in the upper Midwest region. Among other features, visitors to the Web site will find an artist opportunities page that offers guidelines for fiscal sponsorship and a list of funding opportunities nationwide.

National Alliance for Media Arts and Culture <http://www.namac.org/>
Founded in 1980, NAMAC is a nonprofit association of more than 160 organizations whose purpose is to further the media arts in all its forms: film, video, audio, and interactive. The group's Online Support Center provides a central place where media arts organizations and media makers can connect, locate profiles of the nation's major media arts groups, find current news and useful resources, and share their experiences. The site also provides job and event listings, advocacy information of relevance to the field, and an archive of NAMAC's quarterly newsletter.

National Endowment for the Arts <http://arts.endow.gov/>
The NEA's elegant Web site provides information on the endowment's programs and funding guidelines and serves as a comprehensive resource for the arts community and its supporters.

National Gallery of Art <http://www.nga.gov/home.htm>
Created in 1937 for the people of the United States, the National Gallery began with the private art collection of financier and art collector Andrew Mellon, and today houses a growing number of world-class art collections. The NGA's elegant Web site is an outstanding example of the marriage of good design with compelling information. Art scholars can visit the Academic Programs section, which includes the Center for Advanced Study in the Visual Arts and the Conservation Division, to explore available fellowships. A variety of volunteer and internship opportunities are also available.

Nebraska Arts Council <http://www.gps.k12.ne.us/nac_web_site/nac.htm>
The NAC promotes the arts, cultivates resources, and supports excellence in artistic endeavors for all Nebraskans. Still under construction, the NAC Web site provides general information about its grant programs and application requirements; an artists directory; links to other art councils (community and state), state organizations, and art museums on the Web; and contact information.

North Carolina Arts Council <http://www.ncarts.org/>
The mission of the NCAC is to enrich North Carolina's cultural life by supporting the arts. The Council is a catalyst for the development of arts organizations, and awards grants and offers technical guidance statewide. The Council's colorful Web site provides, among other items, program and grant information; links to various arts organizations, government agencies, and regional and national arts

partners; and contact information for 285 North Carolina arts organizations organized by county and by type of art group.

Ohio Arts Council <http://www.oac.ohio.gov/>

Established in 1965 to "foster and encourage the development of the arts and
assist the preservation of Ohio's cultural heritage," the OAC funds programs to
make arts activities available to the public and also supports Ohio artists through
25 different grant programs. The Council's Web site provides information about
all OAC programs, complete grant guidelines, an impressive search engine, links
to both state and national arts resources, and e-mail links to staff members.

Open Studio: The Arts Online <http://www.openstudio.org/home.html>

A joint effort of the Benton Foundation and the National Endowment for the Arts,
Open Studio provides free public Internet access at arts and community institutions and helps nonprofit arts organizations and artists go online by offering training and technical assistance. Links to more than 80 Internet access sites and hundreds of links to arts-related sites and resources.

South Dakota Arts Council
<http://www.state.sd.us/state/executive/deca/sdarts/sdarts.htm>

The SDAC encourages and supports artists, strengthens arts organizations and arts
education programs, and increases South Dakotans awareness of the arts. As a
state agency of the Department of Education & Cultural Affairs, the Council
makes grants to schools, individuals, and arts organizations. Grantseekers will
especially appreciate the Council's online program guide, which includes detailed
grant application guidelines and a handy glossary of terms.

North Dakota Council on the Arts <http://www.state.nd.us/arts/>

Established in 1967 by the state legislature, the NDCA is responsible for the support and development of the arts and artists in North Dakota. In addition to making grants based on recommendations from artists and arts administrators, the
Council administers the Cultural Endowment Fund, through which it secures private and public funds to enhance existing programs. The Council's Web site provides program information, application instructions, grant-writing tips, related
arts resource links, and contact information.

CHILDREN, YOUTH, & FAMILIES

Child Welfare League of America <http://www.cwla.org/>

The Child Welfare League of America is devoted to the well-being of America's
children and their families. In addition to action alerts, statistics, and information
about work the organization is doing, the CWLA Web site offers links to CWLA
member organizations.

Children Now <http://www.childrennow.org/>

This colorful, well-organized site devoted to the nurturing, safety, and rights of
children offers news, job listings, volunteer opportunities, and a wealth of related
links, many of which lead to funding opportunities in children's issues.

Children, Youth and Family Consortium, University of Minnesota
<http://www.cyfc.umn.edu/>
An electronic gateway to information and resources on children, youth, and families.

Children's Defense Fund <http://www.childrensdefense.org/>
Marion Wright Edelman founded CDF in 1973, and the organization has since become a leader in child advocacy, particularly for minority children and those with disabilities. The CDF Web site provides a variety of information, resources, news, and links related to children's well-being.

HandsNet <http://www.handsnet.org>
A national nonprofit organization that promotes information sharing, cross-sector collaboration, and advocacy among individuals and organizations working on a broad range of public interest issues.

KidsHealth.org <http://kidshealth.org/>
This great-looking site devoted to the health of children and teens offers a plethora of up-to-date health and medical information and fun educational features.

Quest International <http://www.quest.edu/>
Quest International strives to "empower and support adults throughout the world to nurture responsibility and caring in young people where they live, learn, work, and play." The organization serves more than two million children in some 30 countries, and its founder, Rick Little, was recently honored by the Council of Foundations with the 1997 Robert W. Scrivner for creativity and risk-taking in grantmaking. Though often slow, the Quest Web site offers extensive information about the organization itself, a collection of articles on and about community-based service-learning, a workshop calendar, a bulletin board for threaded discussions, and links to dozens of relevant Web sites.

COMMUNITY DEVELOPMENT

Coalition for Healthier Cities and Communities
<http://www.healthycommunities.org/>
The Coalition is a network of hundreds of community partnerships working to improve the health and quality of life of the country's communities. Through its Web site, CHCC is compiling a database of people, organizations, and initiatives dedicated to the sustenance of healthy communities around the nation. The site also offers a library of materials, tools, and resources; press releases and a calendar; and a password-restricted area where visitors can contribute and share stories and lessons with others.

Communities and Community Development Corporations
<http://www.pitt.edu/~friendsh/cdc/hotcdc.html>
Listings of the top 20 U.S. and top 20 international economic development Web sites, plus some 90 other sites that didn't make the top 20 U.S. list, as ranked by students in the University of Pittsburgh's Urban and Regional Planning Program. Includes documentation on procedures and criteria. Last updated April 1996.

NeighborWorks Network <http://www.nw.org/>
The NeighborWorks Network site "promotes the creation of healthy communities through affordable housing, home ownership and investments in neighborhood revitalization through local partnerships of residents, nonprofits, lenders, business community and local government." Comprehensive and well-organized, the site includes extensive information about a range of programs, coalitions, and organizations, including the Neighborhood Reinvestment Corp., the Neighborhood Housing Services of America, and the Rural NeighborWorks Alliance. A handy table of contents, site-wide search engine, conference calendar, and library of links organized alphabetically and/or by category round out the features at this very useful site.

ELEMENTARY & SECONDARY EDUCATION

Computers 4 Kids <http://www.c4k.org/>
C4K accepts donated computers, refurbishes them, and donates them to schools and organizations in need. The site has a list of needed equipment, grant information, downloadable application forms, and news of upcoming events.

Education Week <http://www.edweek.org/>
A clearinghouse of information about education reform, schools, and the policies that guide them, brought to you by Editorial Projects in Education Inc., the publishers of Education Week and the monthly Teacher Magazine. Offers online versions of both publications, a Daily News section (access to the best articles written about education in newspapers around the country), a series of special reports, and a great links section.

Eduzone <http://www.eduzone.com/>
Resources, scholarships, grants, education news, and free home pages for teachers and educators.

ERIC: Clearinghouse on Elementary and Early Childhood Education <http://ericeece.org/>
This University of Illinois at Urbana-Champaign site provides access to the Educational Resources Information Center (ERIC), a comprehensive database of education-related literature administered by the National Library of Education. Also includes links to family, technology, and education resources.

National Education Association <http://www.nea.org/>
The NEA is America's oldest and largest organization committed to advancing the cause of public education. The NEA Web site includes links to local and state affiliates and new school sites, notes on school funding and grants for study abroad, pilot programs, TV specials, and information about education in cyberspace.

National Education Service <http://www.nes.org/>
The NES site includes an online teaching journal and newsletter, information about professional development opportunities, links to education resources, and access to a chat network with peers and authors in the field.

The 21st Century Teachers' Network <http://www.21ct.org/>
Comprising leading education organizations, the 21st Century Teachers' Network is a nationwide initiative designed to encourage teachers to work with their colleagues to develop new skills for using technology in their teaching. The Network's Web site offers news, grant and professional development information, links to research findings, and updates on specific events around the country.

The Well-Connected Educator <http://www.gsh.org/wce/>
An interactive publishing forum for the K-12 community where participants can read, write, and talk about educational technology.

THE ENVIRONMENT

**Amazing Environmental Organization WebDirectory
<http://www.webdirectory.com/>**
The name says it all. An enormous searchable directory of environmental organizations on the Web.

Conservation Action Network <http://takeaction.worldwildlife.org/>
A new electronic advocacy network created by the World Wildlife Fund. The network disseminates concise information on issues such as endangered species, global warming, forest protection, and fisheries conservation, and uses emerging communications technologies to facilitate communication between concerned individuals and members of Congress, state legislators, newspaper editors, corporations, foreign government leaders, and international agencies.

Earth Share of Washington <http://www.esw.org/esw/>
A federation of 66 environmental nonprofits working to conserve and protect the environment internationally, nationally, and locally in Washington State. The user-friendly Earth Share Website provides eco tips, information on workplace giving and volunteer opportunities, a speakers' bureau, and links to member organizations.

EcoNet <http://www.igc.org/igc/econet/index.html>
Provides news on environmental issues and timely Action Alerts on opportunities for public involvement.

Environmental Defense Fund <http://www.edf.org/>
Founded in 1967 by volunteer conservationists on Long Island, New York, who wanted to ban the pesticide DDT, the EDF today focuses on a broad range of regional, national, and international environmental issues. An inspired—and inspiring—action-oriented site.

Environmental Grantmaker Association <http://www.ega.org/>
A voluntary association of foundations and giving programs concerned with the protection of the natural environment.

Environmental "NewsLink" <http://www.caprep.com/index.htm>
News service with a comprehensive list of links to government agencies. An excellent place to track environmental legislation.

Environmental News Network <http://www.enn.com/>
Daily news updates on all aspects of environmental activity on the Web.

Goldman Environmental Prize <http://www.goldmanprize.org/goldman/>
A small but elegant site devoted to the world's largest prize program honoring grassroots environmentalists. Founded in 1990 by philanthropists Richard and Rhonda Goldman, the Goldman Environmental Prize and $100,000 is awarded annually to an activist from each of the planet's six inhabited continental regions.

National Audubon Society <http://www.audubon.org/>
The Audobon Society is dedicated to conserving and restoring natural ecosystems for the benefit of humanity and the earth's biological diversity.

The Nature Conservancy <http://www.tnc.org/>
The Nature Conservancy operates the largest private system of nature sanctuaries in the world, and preserves threatened species by buying and putting into trust the habitats they need to survive. A great "green" site.

HEALTH

National Institutes of Health <http://www.nih.gov/grants/>
The federal government's principle biomedical research agency and a terrific online resource for NIH grant and fellowship information.

MedWeb <http://www.gen.emory.edu/medweb/medweb.grants.html>
Created by the folks at Emory University's Health Sciences Center Library, MedWeb is billed as a Biomedical Internet Resource. The site's Grants and Funding area offers a lengthy, well-organized list of links to funding opportunities, newsgroups, libraries, and medical and health organizations, as well as a variety of grantseeking and -writing resources. Many of the grantwriting links are also of interest to general grantseekers.

Office of Minority Health Resource Center <http://www.omhrc.gov/>
Established in 1985 by the U.S. Department of Health and Human Services, OMH-RC exists to promote improved health among American minority groups. The site contains an impressive amount of easily navigable material, including news releases, publications, and a database of funding and grant resources to help support minority health projects. Visitors can also browse OMH-RC's Funding Resource Guide, which was developed with grantseekers in mind.

HIGHER EDUCATION

American Council on Education <http://www.acenet.edu/>
The ACE site features information about training and programs, international initiatives, women and minorities in education, upcoming events, and products and

services. Also offers a clearinghouse on post-secondary education for individuals with disabilities through the HEATH Resource Center.

Beyond Bio 101: The Transformation of Undergraduate Biology Education <http://www.hhmi.org/BeyondBio101/>

A colorful, well-designed report from the Howard Hughes Medical Institute based on the experiences of many of the 220 colleges and universities that, since 1988, have been awarded grants by the Institute's Undergraduate Biological Science Education Program. The 88-page report can be read online, or it can be downloaded to your hard drive and read offline.

EDUCAUSE <http://www.educause.edu/>

EDUCAUSE, a membership organization created by the merger of Colorado-based CAUSE and the Washington, D.C.-based Educom, focuses on "the management and use of computational, network, and information resources in support of higher education's missions of scholarship, instruction, service, and administration." Visitors to the Web site can learn about award and fellowship opportunities, upcoming conferences, and current issues in the field; post appropriate job openings; download extended excerpts from relevant print publications; and join any of a dozen or so online discussion lists.

The Chronicle of Higher Education <http://chronicle.merit.edu/.index.html>

Published weekly, the online version of the Chronicle is an award-winning source of news and information for college and university faculty and administrators and includes lists of recent gifts and grants to higher education, new software titles, and appointments and promotions in the academic world. "Academe Today," a free online service available to subscribers of the print version of the Chronicle, provides daily updates on federal grant opportunities in addition to other features. Limited grant and award deadline information is available to non-subscribers.

Federal Information Exchange, Inc. <http://web.fie.com/fedix/index.html>

FEDIX provides free access to information on government research and education grants, programs, contracts, and more. Supported by selected federal agencies under a cooperative agreement forged by the Department of Energy and the Office of Science Education and Technical Information, the FEDIX Web site is comprehensive and easy to use. Visitors can search by audience or subject and can also receive targeted funding opportunities via E-mail. Other features include news updates and a Grants Keyword Thesaurus, which can be downloaded by eligible nonprofit institutions.

FinAid: The Financial Aid Information Page <http://www.finaid.org/>

The most comprehensive collection of links to information about student financial aid on the Web. Includes name and subject indexes as well as links to mailing lists and newsgroups, financial aid calculators, and FastWEB, a free scholarship search service.

National Science Foundation <http://www.nsf.gov/>

The NSF is dedicated to fostering science and engineering research and education nationwide. As you'd expect from the agency that step-fathered the Internet into adolescence, the NSF Web site is comprehensive, well-organized, and fast. The site includes program and grants and awards info in biology, education, engineering, the geosciences, math and physical sciences, polar research, social and behavioral sciences, and much more.

PEP Directory of Computer Recycling Programs
<http://www.microweb.com/pepsite/Recycle/recycle_index.html>
Sponsored by Children's Software Revue and Custom Computers for Kids, the PEP (Parents, Educators, and Publishers) directory on the Web is a comprehensive guide to organizations that supply low-cost or donated computer equipment to nonprofits and schools. The annotated index is arranged by state, and also includes national and international listings.

Science's Next Wave <http://www.nextwave.org/>
Billed as "an electronic network for the next generation of scientists," the Next Wave site features profiles of and practical career advice for young scientists, as well as links to numerous scientific organizations and funding sources.

HIV/AIDS

Bailey House <http://www.baileyhouse.org/>
A clearinghouse for information on programs and trends in AIDS housing from the second-oldest AIDS organization in New York City.

CDC National AIDS Clearinghouse <http://www.cdcnac.org/>
The National AIDS Clearinghouse, a service of the Centers for Disease Control and Prevention, is "designed to facilitate the sharing of HIV/AIDS and STD resources and information about education and prevention, published materials, and research findings, as well as news about related trends." Among other features, the site offers four searchable databases: a Resources and Services database, with descriptions of more than 19,000 organizations; an AIDS Daily Summary database, with abstracts of HIV/AIDS-related articles from major news outlets; a funding database; and an educational materials database.

The Estate Project for Artists With AIDS <http://www.artistswithaids.org/>
The Estate Project is part of the Alliance for Arts, a nonprofit arts service organization dedicated to policy research, information services, and advocacy for the arts in New York State. EP's Web site offers information on arts news, artists' resources, specific strategies for arts preservation, lists of grants that have been awarded in the arts, and information and/or links to relevant arts organizations, many of which are national in scope. The site is geared toward the special needs of artists with AIDS, but provides information useful to others involved with the arts communities and information on how to donate to the project.

Gay Men's Health Crisis <http://www.gmhc.org/>
Founded by volunteers in 1981, Gay Men's Health Crisis offers AIDS education and political advocacy nationwide and direct services to men, women, and children with AIDS, as well as their families, in New York City. GMHC's Web site is divided into eight areas: HIV Alert, What Can You Do?, Who Can You Talk To?, Stopping HIV, Living with HIV or AIDS, AIDS Library, the Press Room, the

Geffen Center, and Careers and Internships. Each area summarizes the issues specific to it and directs visitors to practical information.

MINORITIES

Foundation Funding Sources for Tribal Libraries
<http://www.u.arizona.edu/~ecubbins/founfund.html>
Provides links to funding sources for North American Indian tribal libraries.

National Association for the Advancement of Colored People
<http://www.naacp.org/>
The largest civil rights organization in the United States is dedicated to ensuring the political, educational, social, and economic equality of minority group citizens.

Office of Minority Health Resource Center <http://www.omhrc.gov/>
Established in 1985 by the U.S. Department of Health and Human Services, OMH-RC exists to promote improved health among American minority groups. The site contains an impressive amount of easily navigable material, including news releases, publications, and a database of funding and grant resources to help support minority health projects. Visitors can also browse OMH-RC's Funding Resource Guide, which was developed with grantseekers in mind.

PUBLIC SAFETY, DISASTER PREPAREDNESS & RELIEF

Disaster Relief.Org <http://www.disasterrelief.org/>
An easy-to-navigate clearinghouse for worldwide disaster aid and information.

SCIENCE & TECHNOLOGY

Beyond Bio 101: The Transformation of Undergraduate Biology Education
<http://www.hhmi.org/BeyondBio101/>
A colorful, well-designed report from the Howard Hughes Medical Institute based on the experiences of many of the 220 colleges and universities that, since 1988, have been awarded grants by the Institute's Undergraduate Biological Science Education Program. The 88-page report can be read online, or it can be downloaded to your hard drive and read offline.

National Science Foundation <http://www.nsf.gov/>
The NSF is dedicated to fostering science and engineering research and education nationwide. As you'd expect from the agency that step-fathered the Internet into adolescence, the NSF Web site is comprehensive, well-organized, and fast. The site includes program and grants and awards info in biology, education, engineering, the geosciences, math and physical sciences, polar research, social and behavioral sciences and much more.

OMB's Nonprofits and Technology Project
<http://www.ombwatch.org/ombwatch/npt/>
The goal of the Nonprofits and Technology Project is to improve communications linkages within the nonprofit sector to strengthen public policy participation. Through the project, OMB Watch will offer grants to nonprofits in the range of $5,000 to $25,000 to help fund innovative and creative applications of technology to the field of public policy participation.

Rockefeller Technology Project <http://www.rffund.org/techproj/index.html>
The Technology Project is a collaboration of funders interested in helping grantees learn about, and effectively use, new communication technology. The Project's no-frills Web site provides examples of several nonprofits organizations' innovative Web sites, as well as links to organizations providing technical assistance, activist resources, and technology news.

Science's Next Wave <http://www.nextwave.org/>
Billed as "an electronic network for the next generation of scientists," the Next Wave site features profiles of and practical career advice for young scientists, as well as links to numerous scientific organizations and funding sources.

SeniorNet <http://www.seniornet.org/>
A national nonprofit organization dedicated to building a community of computer-using seniors who use their new skills for their own benefit and to benefit society. The site provides a listing of SeniorNet Learning Centers by state, round table discussions and e-mail pen pals, information on computer discounts, and more.

Technology Tip Sheets for Nonprofits <http://www.coyotecom.com/tips.html>
Tip sheets to help organizations and individuals reap money-saving, program-enhancing benefits from technology. Most of the material is geared to not-for-profit and public sector organizations.

SUBSTANCE ABUSE

Join Together Online <http://www.jointogether.org/>
Join Together Online works to reduce substance abuse and gun violence across the nation. The JTO Web site provides considerable information in the areas of public policy and community action, as well as funding news, grant announcements, foundation profiles, and link to hundreds of related Internet sites.

National Institute on Alcohol Abuse and Alcoholism
<http://www.niaaa.nih.gov/>
One of 18 agencies that comprise the National Institutes of Health, NIAAA supports and conducts biomedical and behavioral research on the causes, consequences, treatment, and prevention of alcoholism and alcohol-related problems.

Phoenix House <http://www.phoenixhouse.org/>
The nation's leading nonprofit drug abuse service organization has developed a comprehensive Web site loaded with news and links to related resources.

PREVLINE: Prevention Online <http://www.health.org/>
Offers electronic access to searchable databases and substance abuse prevention materials that pertain to alcohol, tobacco, and drugs.

WOMEN & GIRLS

Ann Castle's Home Page <http://www.hamilton.edu/personal/acastle/>
A terrific bibliography and resource list compiled by the woman who researches and edits The Slate 60.

Feminist Internet Gateway <http://www.feminist.org/gateway/master2.html>
A comprehensive list of women's sites.

WomensNet <http://www.igc.org/igc/womensnet>
WomensNet supports women's organizations worldwide by providing and adapting telecommunications technology to enhance their work.

Women's Philanthropy Institute <http://www.women-philanthropy.org/>
The WPI is a nonprofit educational organization that brings together philanthropists and fundraisers to educate, encourage, and empower women as philanthropists.

Women's Wire <http://www.womenswire.com/talk/>
A very nice women's news resource.

Philanthropy Resources

GENERAL

**National Commission on Philanthropy and Civic Renewal
<http://www.ncpcr.org/>**
Chaired by former Tennessee governor and Education secretary Lamar Alexander, the National Commission on Philanthropy and Civic Renewal is dedicated to the proposition that "'less from government, more from ourselves' is a sound basis on which to care for the needy and revitalize communities." Among other items, visitors to the NCPCR Web site will find a copy of the Commission's charter; a full text version of the Commission's report, "Giving Better, Giving Smarter: Renewing Philanthropy in America"; and links to research and Web resources that reflect the Commission's agenda.

National Committee for Responsive Philanthropy <http://www.ncrp.org/>
Convinced that, in "the Age of Newt," nonprofit advocacy groups have been targeted by Congress while mainline philanthropic organizations watch from the sidelines, the National Committee for Responsive Philanthropy is committed "to making philanthropy more responsive to socially, economically and politically disenfranchised people, and to the dynamic needs of increasingly diverse communities nationwide." In addition to information about the Committee's projects and publications, the NCRP Web site, portions of which are under construction, offers

a selection of reports on such topics as "Philanthropy's Responsibilities to the Public and Private Sectors," "10 Powerful Trends That Are Transforming the Media World," and "Corporate Giving for Racial/Ethnic Populations."

Philanthropy Roundtable <http://www.philanthropyroundtable.org/>
The Philanthropy Roundtable is a national association of grantmakers founded on the principle that "voluntary private action offers the best means of addressing many of society's needs, and that a vibrant private sector is critical to creating the wealth that makes philanthropy possible." The Web site features the journal, Philanthropy, which includes hot relevant topics in the philanthropy field, as well as other Roundtable publications and Roundtable-sponsored conferences and events.

Project Involve! <http://www.alfsv.org/involve/>
The mission of the American Leadership Forum's Project Involve! is to build philanthropy, public service, and community in Silicon Valley. Among other features, the Involve! Web site offers the "Resource Guide," an online guide to organizations and resources for companies exploring or expanding their corporate contributions programs, and "Winning Strategies for Corporate Community Involvement," which contains the basics of how to plan, select, and initiate community-oriented programs. Althought the site focuses on Northern California, many of the organizations listed are national in scope.

REGIONAL ASSOCIATIONS OF GRANTMAKERS

Associated Grantmakers of Massachusetts <http://www.agmconnect.org/>
AGM is a statewide association of more than 90 corporate and foundation grantmakers whose mission is to "support and advance effective and responsible philanthropy throughout the Commonwealth." The Association's Janet C.Taylor Library, a Foundation Center Cooperating Collection, maintains an extensive collection of publications that focus on local and national grantmaking, fundraising, and nonprofit management. AGM's Web site offers detailed descriptions of the services it provides to grantmakers and nonprofit organizations in the Bay State, information on events of interest to grantseekers and grantmakers, a catalogue of AGM books and videos for sale, extensive links to online nonprofit and philanthropy resources, and contact information.

Coordinating Council for Foundations <http://www.hartnet.org/~ccf/>
The mission of the CCF, a membership association of Hartford-area grantmaking institutions, is to support and promote effective philanthropy. To that end, CCFF's Web site provides information about its services; news from and about its members (under construction); a downloadable version of its common grant application form; a short list of publications it makes available to the public; and a set of links to other philanthropic organizations on the Internet.

Council of Michigan Foundations <http://www.novagate.net/~cmf/>
The membership of CMF comprises private, community, and corporate foundations and giving programs in Michigan. The Council assists Michigan grantmakers in their work in order to enhance philanthropy through education, networking, technological assistance, information on philanthropic issues and

research, and advocacy. The no-frills CMF site provides information on membership, library services, fax-on-demand service, and grantseeking information.

Delaware Valley Grantmakers <http://www.libertynet.org/dvg/>
DVG, a membership organization comprised of private, trustee managed, corporate and community foundations, charitable trusts, federated funds, and corporate giving programs, promotes philanthropy in the Delaware Valley area, acts as a clearinghouse of information, and educates grantmakers, recipients of grants, and the general public on the role of private philanthropy in improving the quality of life for all persons. In addition to statements of its mission, purposes, and values, DVG's Web site provides visitors with a listing of members and their telephone numbers, a list of DVG-sponsored publications, and links to member organizations that have established Web sites of their own. Visitors to the site can also download DVG's common grant application form and its common report form.

Donors Forum of Chicago <http://www.donorsforum.org/>
The Donors Forum, an association of Chicago-area grantmaking institutions, promotes effective philanthropy through its educational, collaborative, and networking efforts. The main offering at the Forum's no-frills Web site is an updated 1994 version of its foundation grants database, searchable by foundation name, recipient, beneficiary type, support type, and grant purpose. Search results are displayed in plain-vanilla ASCII, but with approximately 7,500 grants made by some 50 Chicago-area funders, the Forum's database is worth exploring.

Indiana Donors Alliance <http://www.indonors.com>
The Indiana Donors Alliance, a membership association serving Indiana's grantmaking community, acts as a catalyst for philanthropic action "by providing information and education, by facilitating communication and collaboration, and by encouraging new opportunities for giving and volunteering." Offerings at its Web site, which is under construction, include a mission statement; a calendar of IDA-sponsored workshops and conferences; information about the Directory of Indiana Foundations, its flagship publication; and links to other sites.

Metropolitan Association for Philanthropy <http://www.mapstl.org/>
MAP, a regional association of grantmakers in metropolitan St. Louis, serves both donors and donees to facilitate more effective philanthropy in the St. Louis region. The Association's Web site offers information about the MAP library (a Foundation Center Cooperating Collection) and various MAP programs; listings of MAP members and publications available from the Association; an interactive "Nonprofit Profile Form"; and a number of links to related sites.

Minnesota Council on Foundations <http://www.mcf.org/>
Founded in 1969, the Minnesota Council on Foundations is a regional membership association of more than 155 public, private, and corporate foundations dedicated to strengthening and increasing participation in philanthropy in Minnesota and neighboring states. The MCF Web site is a good starting point for the latest news and information on grantmaking organizations, people, and trends in Minnesota; general grantseeking resources; listings of nonprofit events and grantmaker job opportunities in the region; and links to other online resources. The site also

offers a downloadable version of the Minnesota Common Grant Application Form.

Minnesota Council of Nonprofits <http://www.mncn.org/>

The Minnesota Council of Nonprofits, a statewide membership organization that shares information, services, and research in order to educate its members and the community, advocates for "the unique role of nonprofits in society." In keeping with its mission, the Council's Web site is chock-full of useful links and resources, including a weekly Minnesota legislative update; a nonprofit job board and a separate nonprofit bulletin board; and links to a number of searchable databases.

Southern California Association for Philanthropy <http://www.scap.org/>

Created in 1973, the Southern California Association for Philanthropy (SCAP) is a nonprofit association of private sector grantmakers committed to increasing the impact of philanthropy in Southern California. SCAP currently has more than 120 member organizations, including corporations, family and independent foundations, community foundations, and other private sector funders. In addition to general organizational info, SCAP's Web site provides a listing of its member organizations and member guidelines, a calendar of SCAP-sponsored workshops and meetings (with an online registration option), a directory of local resources for grantseekers, and a dozen or so links to other sites of interest.

CHAPTER EIGHT

Online Journals

The range of information that is available on the World Wide Web is vast and growing daily. There are publications that simply post their print contents online, and journals and newsletters created specifically for the Web. You'll find foundation-sponsored publications, government-sponsored journals relating to topics on the federal, state, and local levels, and newsletters researched and written by private companies and individuals. No longer do you have to wait for a monthly print newsletter to arrive in your "snail mail" box, or wait until the first of the month for a favorite magazine to appear on the newstand. Some of the online publications are posted daily, some bi-weekly, some monthly, some several times a year. (All should indicate how often the content is updated.) At least one (*The Chronicle of Philanthropy*, http://www.philanthropy.com), had reporters at the spring 1997 Presidents' Summit in Philadelphia, posting daily news updates. More and more frequently these online publications are becoming available as "listservs." This means that if you have an e-mail address, you can subscribe to the publication (directly from the Web site, or by sending your e-mail address to the listed e-mail address of the publication), without logging onto the Internet. (See Chapter 9 for more on joining mailing lists.)

Although some of the publications require a user name and password, most are open for free access. Content ranges from well-researched, in-depth features to abstracts of notable articles and library indexes. Many of the journals include photographs, colorful graphic images, and links to other philanthropy-related Web sites. Some are collections of news notes, grants and program listings, and upcoming events—gathered on a site devoted to user groups, bulletin boards, and online forums.

Below is a listing of some of the philanthropy-related journals now on the Web, with a brief description of each. Specific pages for some of the sites containing these journal are mentioned in other chapters. Here we try to focus on the online journals themselves.

JOURNALS ON THE WEB, LISTED ALPHABETICALLY

Academe This Week <http://chronicle.merit.edu/.events/.edead.html>

This newletter is actually a service of the Ohio-based *The Chronicle of Higher Education*, a weekly publication targeted to university and college faculty members and administrators; if you subscribe to *The Chronicle of Higher Education*, you receive free access to *Academe This Week*, providing information on the Web and via listserv. (If you already are a subscriber and need an *Academe Today* account, instructions are available at the site.) *Academe This Week* offers grant and fellowship listings, as well as research competitions (organized by deadline date, academic categories), news items, daily updates on federal grants, notices of workshops and institutes, calls for papers and job listings from *The Chronicle of Higher Education* (available the Friday before the printed paper is mailed). Daily briefings on developments in higher education are sent via e-mail, with full reports posted on the Web. From the Web, subscribers can access the current issue of *The Chronicle of Higher Education*, fully searchable, each Monday morning, and access an archive filled with six years' worth of issues, all fully searchable. There are also links to other related Web sites.

American Philanthropy Review <http://philanthropy-review.com/>

Based in Rancho Santa Margarita, California, this site features reviews of nonprofit periodicals, books, and software (in the "We Review" section), written by close to 100 volunteers from the fundraising field, and listing the topics covered in each chapter and biographies of the reviewers.

These reviews are also posted regularly to three of the site's free e-mail discussion forums, "Talk-AmPhilRev" (directed to anyone with an interest in the nonprofit world—in the areas of fund development, management, legislation, publishing, software, etc.), "W-AmPhilRev" (the e-mail discussion list of the

"Women and Philanthropy" forum, targeted to those interested in women as donors and/or nonprofit fund development programs focusing on women), and "PG-AmPhilRev" (focusing on everything related to planned giving in the U.S. and Canada). Other Web-based discussion forums on site include "Grants and Foundations Online," "Planned Giving USA!," "Mentoring Forum" (inviting some of the most experienced fund development professionals in the U.S. to mentor their newer colleagues). Through an association with Amazon.com, the site also offers an online bookstore stocked with over 400 books on fundraising (ranging from classics to new releases), listed by title, author, subject, and publisher; most are available at a discount of 10 percent or more and will be delivered within three days.

Aris Funding Reports: Creative Arts and Humanities Report, "Subject Headings" <http://www.lib.msu.edu/harris23/grants/ariscart.htm>

This Web newsletter provides subject indexes (divided by "Art," "Humanities," and "General" subjects, with page numbers), of issues of the San Francisco-based *Creative Arts and Humanities Report (CAHR)*; complete volumes are located at Michigan State University (MSU) Main library, and are available via interlibrary loan. (MSU stuents , faculty, and staff can access the full text of each issue from the Web site.) *CAHR* provides current information on funding opportunities and policies in the humanities (i.e., humanistic and social and community applications), as well as creative arts (i.e., performing and visual arts), agency activities, new programs (i.e., private and public). The indexed bi-monthly issues date back to February 15, 1995. You can subscribe to complete print issues from Aris (415) 558-8133.

**ArtsWire CURRENT <http://www.artswire.org/Artswire/www/current.html>;
archives of past issues**
<http://www.artswire.org/Artswire/www/current/archive.html>
This online journal is a project of Arts Wire, a national computer-based network
which serves the arts community; ArtsWire is a program of the New York Foundation for the Arts (with major support provided by the Masters of Arts Management Program of Carnegie Mellon University).

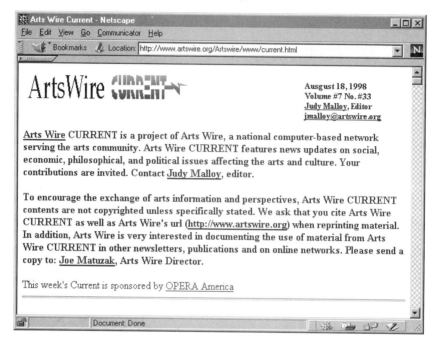

The journal includes news updates on philosophical, political, social, and economic issues which affect the arts and culture. News topics in a 1997 issue ranged
from the resignation of Jane Alexander as chair of the National Endowment for
the Arts to the opening of the new Chicago Symphony Hall. Also featured are
paragraph descriptions of and links to other Web sites of artists and art organizations who are ArtsWire members. And there is a section titled "Conferences,
Symposia, Lectures," with descriptions of events, time, date, place, and contact.
Other pluses are a "Call For Entries" section—requests for articles to be submitted to other journals, "Funding News"—a searchable database of current funding
opportunities for artists and arts groups (with contacts), and "Jobs" (descriptions
and contacts). An "Elsewhere on the Net" section updates readers on Internet
news relating to the arts and film showings. Free subscription is available via e-
mail (instructions available at the site), although membership ($60/year for indi-
viduals; $100/year for organizations) in Arts Wire supports the publication of
ArtsWire Current.

Canadian FundRaiser <http://www.charityvillage.com/charityvillage/cfr.html>
This Toronto-based online "journal of record" for Canada's fundraising professionals actually has space on the server of *Charity Village*, a large and inclusive Web site targeted to the Canadian nonprofit community (see listing, this chapter). The eight-page bi-weekly print edition of *Canadian FundRaiser* is available through subscription ($197 CDN +GST=$210.79 for one year/24 issues); log on to the Charity Village site though, and a large banner ad links you to information for subscriptions for small charities at a 54 percent savings (just $97 Canadian + GST). Subscribers also receive special-topic issues and "Careers and Coming Events Bulletins." Content includes "timely, usable fundraising news, ideas, and information" in the areas of corporate giving, postal matters, accountability, planned giving, media, and public relations, directed to those involved with developing and managing fundraising programs. Tips are targeted toward helping readers remain competitive among the 70,000+ registered charities in Canada—all seeking a share of the $6 billion expected to be donated by Canadians this year. Articles range from the topics of "Charitable Gaming" to "Volunteer Recruitment." Writers are practitioners, consultants, and academics in the Canadian fundraising community, and contributions are welcome. Also included in *Charity Times* is a supplement with content from the now defunct *DONORS* magazine; some *DONORS* articles will be reprinted on the Web at the *DONORS* site <http://www.fundraising.co.uk/mags/donors/html>.

Charity Village Newsweek <http://www.charityvillage.com>
This weekly newsletter appears within Charity Village, the charming Canadian-based site with colorful icons and "main streets" to meander down that remind one that the world is truly a global village. Select the English or French path, and then enjoy the 1,000 pages of news, jobs, information, and resources targeted toward staffers, donors, and volunteers in the nonprofit sector of Canada. *Charity Village NewsWeek* includes a timely, in-depth cover story, five shorter stories, a section of "Newsbytes" or notes about notable persons in the philanthropic field and their achievements, new business standards, and calls for proposals. There is also a Volunteer Bulletin Board, a "People on the Move" section announcing new job titles for those in the philanthropic field, "Career Opportunities" detailing available nonprofit jobs, a "What's Your Opinion" section inviting site-user feedback about a recent statement or event that is relevant to nonprofits, an "Op/Ed Page," a "HelpLink" for in-kind exchanges of goods and services, and a "Coming Events" section. Also within the Charity Village site, you'll find a Library with entertaining and succinct reviews of books from the nonprofit sector, a Research Section containing selected articles in 50 subject areas (ranging from Accounting to Women and Philanthropy) from *Canadian FundRaiser* and *Charity Village NewsWeek*, an online Book Store offering philanthropic titles through Amazon.com (most at a 10 percent discount), lists and links to Online Resources for Nonprofits and Online Publications for Nonprofits.

Charity World <http://www.fundraising.co.uk/mags/chworld/chworld.html>
This url takes you to a Web site that simply describes a two-in-one information service produced by the Surrey, England-based Tolley Publishing Co. Ltd. Tolley publishes the magazines *Charity World* and *Charity World Bulletin*, which provide news, information, and guidance to the charity field on investment, trusteeship, fundraising, and technical subjects.

The Chronicle of Philanthropy <http://www.philanthropy.com>
This is an abbreviated online version of the bi-weekly print publication *The Chronicle of Philanthropy*, considered the "newspaper of the nonprofit world."

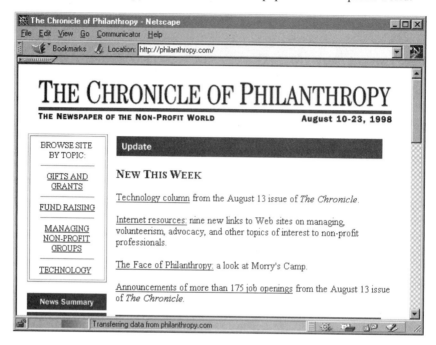

Log onto the Web site and you'll find a tabloid-like newspaper layout, a home page with four-color news photographs, excerpts from stories appearing in the recent print edition of *The Chronicle of Philanthropy*, a search engine which allows you to browse the site by topic (Gifts and Grants, Fundraising, Managing Nonprofit Groups, Technology), a News Summary from the contents of the current issue of *The Chronicle of Philanthropy* (updated every other week at 9 a.m., EST, the Monday preceding each issue date), or from previous issues. You'll also find a listing of upcoming conferences in the field, as well as news of workshops; links lead you to other philanthropic Internet sources. Job postings are updated the Monday following each issue date. Contributions for news articles and letters to the editor/opinion pieces, are welcome. Subscribe online from the site, via e-mail, or snail mail ($67.50/year, 24 issues; $36/six months, 6 issues). And subscribe to *The Chronicle*'s free e-mail list to receive updates on what's new in the newspaper and on the site, plus special bulletins when major philanthropic news stories break (subscription instructions available at the site).

Consumer Information Center <http://www.pueblo.gsa.gov>
This is the Web site of the Consumer Information Center of the U.S. General Services Administration, based in Pueblo, Colorado, and publisher of helpful and service-oriented consumer brochures on everything from safe drinking water to safer sunning. Most relevant to the nonprofit field are links to the financial publications "Establishing a Trust Fund," "IRS Guide to Free Tax Services," "Planning Your Estate," and "Swindlers Are Calling." A search engine will help you navigate the site, and link you to the Web sites of other federal agencies, programs, and resources.

EnetDigest (Government on the Web)
<http://www.enetdigest.com/design.com>
This site includes a bi-monthly electronic guide to Internet resources worldwide
in the areas of the environment, natural resources, and agriculture compiled by
Kathy E. Gill, a public affairs professional in the natural resources sector (food,
agriculture, forest and paper products) with experience as writer, publications
designer, Webmaster. Each issue offers annotated links to sites divided into the
categories of "Agriculture, Environmental and Natural Resources," "General and
Government Resources," "Discussion (e-mail) Lists," Periodicals," "For Fun,"
and "Web Tools." There is an archives of back issues, and the site has a search
engine to assist with navigation. Criteria for sites selected for links include content and browser compatibility. There are also links to government agency Web
sites in the above-mentioned subject areas, organized by continent. The site is also
an associate of Amazon.com, offering books in these subject areas for sale online
(most at a 10 percent discount). Look, too, for a calendar of upcoming environmental conferences, and daily contents pages form the Federal Register for U.S.
Environmental Protection Agency.

ERC Newsbriefs <http://www.lib.msu.edu/harris23/grants/pererc.htm>
This online site offers the complete Tables of Contents of the Washington, D.C.-
based monthly (except in July) newsletter *ERC Newsbriefs*. It is published by
Ecumenical Resource Consultants, Inc., which publishes grant and loan opportunities, news, and information about upcoming conferences and seminars for
church-related social ministry agencies, educational institutions, and community-
based organizations. The Tables of Contents online, dating back to the August 31,
1995, issue, is divided into subject areas including Front Page News, Aging,
Children, Community Development, Drugs and Alcohol, Education, Fundraising,
Health, Housing, Management, Minority Affairs, Parish Life, Rural, Women, and
Youth. Online, there is also a closing feature on a topic of interest to visitors (e.g.,
"Tips for Preparing Proposal Budgets"). Annual subscription fee for the complete
print newsletter is $128; back issues are $8 each. Individual copies are available at
the Michigan State University Main Library and other college and university
libraries.

Foundation News & Commentary
<http://www.cof.org/foundationnews/index.html>

This bi-monthly print publication published by the Washington, D.C.-based Council on Foundations (COF) has an electronic presence on the Web site of COF, offering highlights from the Tables of Contents of the complete print issues, dating back to July/August 1996, and links to the complete text of selected articles. There is also an Author Index, and a Subject Index, as well as a "People" section detailing job changes in the foundation world—compiled from press releases and news media, many previously published in the print version of the publication.

The editorial content of *Foundation News & Commentary* focuses on the grant-making community and includes case studies of foundation programs, round-ups of trends and news in the philanthropic field, and interviews with leaders in the nonprofit area. It also offers news, analysis, commentary and ideas—all conducive to effective grantmaking. The target audience is trustees and staff of donor organizations, but the publication is also read by grantseekers, financial advisors, policy makers, anyone interested in the philanthropic field. You can subscribe to the print publication (annual subscription fee is $48) via the online subscription form on the COF site.

Fund$Raiser Cyberzine <http://www.fundsraiser.com>

This online monthly cyberzine offering "hands-on" fundraising news is available free on the Web and also via listserv subscription.

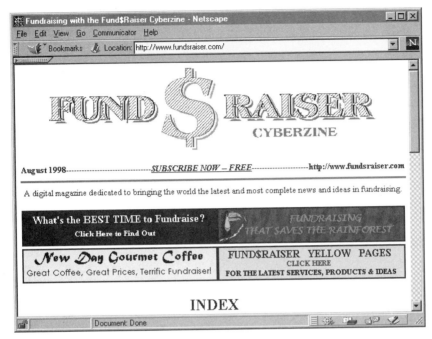

Back issues are available for a fee ($6/issue, with varying fees up to $39/12 issues; all nine 1996 issues on 3.5" disc for $21); view each issue's index from the Web site. Content includes an FAQs section about the cyberzine; a publisher's editorial about a timely issue in the field of philanthropy; excerpts of fundraising chatter taken from usenet newsgroups each month by the publication's editors; news about fundraising raffles; new products, publications, and related Web sites; a *Yellow Pages* section with links to fundraising resources, consultants, and supplies; how-to information on planning fundraisers and organizing a group; and announcements of fundraising event nationwide. The target audience includes small to medium nonprofit groups (ranging from booster clubs and sports teams to church groups) seeking to raise funds.

Funding Digest <http://www.rtipub.demon.co.uk>

This 12-year-old United Kingdom monthly digest, based in Newcastle upon Tyne, is actually considered a fundraising information service—focused on the needs of charities, voluntary organizations, local authorities, public sector agencies, and those who support them (ranging from chief executives and fundraising managers to librarians). The editorial content includes new sources of grant aid (or awards) from companies, trusts, government—for local, regional, and national projections throughout the United Kingdom and for United-Kingdom-based organizations overseas. News items detail total amount of funds available, and for what purpose, and lists contacts, application closing dates, tips on application preparation and approach. Online, you can always link to and download the various sections of the most recent issue (organized under the headings of Funding, European News, National Lottery, Information, Government Watch, and Resources), and review the indexes of the past two issues. To consistently receive complete print or electronic issues, you must subscribe (you can download a subscription form from the site if you also download a Netscape Plug-In), or call for more information. Single-User subscriptions (for small charities and organizations, for internal use), are 108.00 pounds/year. Enhanced Multiple User subscriptions (for large organizations, information services), are 234.00 pounds/year, and may be received on computer disc or via e-mail, allowing recipients to edit and reprint the publication to their own specifications. Multiple User subscribers receive approximately 50 quarterly New Trusts supplements every three months, with news about newly formed charitable trusts.

A Fundraiser's Newsletter from Joyaux Associates
<http://www.lib.msu.edu/harris23/grants/.newsy.htm>

This is a periodic free print bulletin published by the Rhode Island-based nonprofit consulting firm Joyaux Associates. It features news on fundraising, management, and nonprofit organization boards and is available on the "Grants and Related Resources" Web site of Michigan State University Library, compiled by Jon Harrison. Published approximately twice a year, the site location also includes an archives linking to issues dating back to October 1993. The July 1997 newsletter features abstracts from timely stories on philanthropy from related publications (e.g., *The Chronicle of Philanthropy*, *The American Benefactor*), links to Web sites with volunteerism resources, and brief descriptions of helpful books and videos.

The Grant Advisor Plus <http://grantadvisor.com>

This is the new online subscription service for academic faculty and graduate students ("grantspersons") in higher education, including the 14-year-old newsletter *The Grant Advisor*, which reports grant and fellowship opportunities for U.S. institutions of higher education (ranging from federal agencies to foundations).

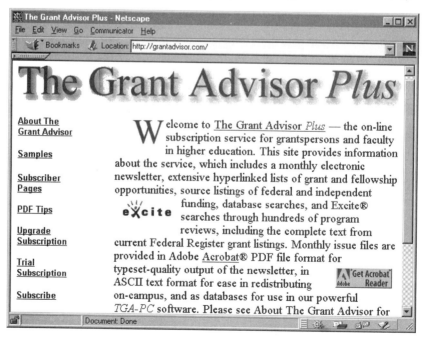

The Virginia-based newsletter is published monthly; each issue reviews 15–20 programs, describing eligibility requirements, criteria, funding amounts, contacts, as well as the "Deadline Memo"—over 300 listings of fellowship and grant programs, divided into eight academic divisions (fine arts, humanities, sciences, social sciences, education, international, health-related, unrestricted/other). Listings include links to Web sites offering funding sources and fellowships, and text from the Federal Register grant listings and National Science Foundation. As a subscriber you can also access the service's database search engines, searching by funding agency, keywords, academic divisions, program listings. Or, access "The Grant Works," hundreds of essays with tips for seeking grant money in higher education. Sign up for a free 30-day trial subscription from the Web site, or subscribe from the site for one year ($385).

Grants and Related Sources
<http://www.lib.msu.edu/harris23/grants/grants.htm#periodicals>
This invaluable section of the Michigan State University Libraries site (www.lib.msu.edu), includes a listing of links divided by subject areas. "Foundation Collection Guides" are listed under "Subject"; "Grants for Individuals"; and "Conferences, Meetings, and Workshops." "Web Resources" (related to funders, financial aid, fundraising) range from "Funding Newsletters" and "Academic Financial Aid" to "Nonprofit Organizations" and "Job Information."

The Grantsmanship Center Magazine
<http://www.tgci.com/publications/magazine.htm>
This quarterly publication (circulation 200,000+) is free to nonprofit and government organizations in print format or electronically via the Web on the site of the Los Angeles-based Grantsmanship Center (TGCI), a 25-year-old source of training and information for the nonprofit sector—in the areas of program planning, grantsmanship, and fundraising.

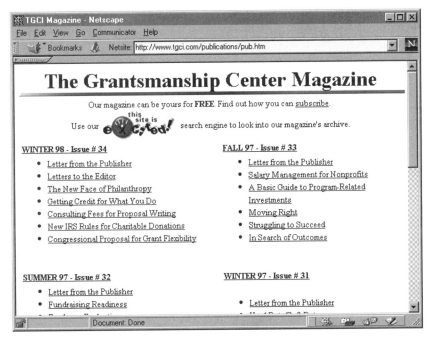

The site offers daily grant announcements and news from the Federal Register and federal government agencies, daily contract solicitations from *Commerce Business Daily*, listings of federal grant programs from the Catalog of Federal Domestic Assistance, and an index of links to grantmaking foundations' Web pages (divided by arts, community, or international foundations; corporate foundations and donors; associations of grantmakers; grantmaking private foundations or public charities). There are also daily funding tips, links to other nonprofit resources in the areas of finance and accounting, legal resouces, online fundraising, nonprofit directories, mailing lists and newsgroups, research and statistics. Soon to come: an online subscription service for TGCI, offering all current grant opportunities on the Internet, cross-referenced and with searchable databases for federal and state funding, daily updates of the Federal Register and *Commerce Business Daily*. Each issue of *The Grantsmanship Center Magazine* includes a publisher's letter and in-depth features on grant-related subjects, nonprofit administration, and resource development, plus listings of TGCI publications and upcoming training events. Back issues accessible on the Web site date back to the Fall 1995. Subscribe to a print edition of the magazine directly from the TGCI Web site.

HandsNet on the Web <http://www.handsnet.com>

This 11-year-old national, nonprofit organization based in Washington, D.C., has a mission of providing leadership in assisting human services organizations to use new information technologies to enhance communication, information sharing, and collaboration and encourage public-interest advocacy. Online, it includes a nationwide network of 5,000+ public interest and human service organizations (clearinghouses, research centers, community-based service providers, foundations, local and state government agencies, public policy advocates, legal services programs, grassroots coalitions). The site includes news notes and features on timely surveys, data, legislation, budget issues, issues ranging from managed care and welfare reform to HIV prevention and neighborhood preservation. There are also links to pertinent federal government Web sites, alerts on pending legislation, position papers, sign-on letters, committee rosters, experts' analysis and recommended actions—complete with contact information and automatic mail forms. Members of HandsNet ($30/month, $300/annual, $180/student, grassroots annual) can post calls for action and access any of the HandsNet Forums in the areas of Budget & Tax Policy, Children, Youth & Families, Comprehensive Strategies, Health Issues, Housing and Community Development, Legal Services, News & Blues (a daily clipping service of national human services news; training and events and job announcements; funding opportunities; directories of congressional, media, national support center contacts), the Federal Register Forum (including abstracts and link to full-text articles). There is a search engine for researching the HandsNet library by keyword, article title, or topic. And members can send or receive e-mail, upload or download documents from the forums. Subscribe from the site, or sign up for a free 30-day trial membership.

Hearts and Minds: Inspiration and Information for Change
<http://www.heartsandminds.org>

This New York City-based nonprofit, nonpartisan, and nonsectarian organization has a mission of increasing the positive impact of individuals on the world through volunteering effectively and building effective organizations and individuals. Their Web site offers photos, graphics, and features written "from the heart and mind"—personal accounts and advice on subjects such as homelessness, the environment, children and poverty, sweatshops, campaign finance reform. There are self-help and nonprofit links, articles on political lobbying and socially responsible food, inspirational quotes, tips on where and how to volunteer effectively, listings of low-cost or free cultural activities in New York City. The group has plans to launch a print publication in 1998.

Horizon <http://www.horizonmag.com>

This is the handsome, newly launched magazine of the Washington, D.C.-based Enterprise Foundation, one of the world's leading community-development organizations, with the goal of bringing community issues and individuals together on the Internet. The publication's mission officially is to "help people learn and chat about challenges and successes in America's communities" and to "expand discussion about community revitalization."

The inaugural issue was launched at the Enterprise Foundation's annual conference during the first week of November 1997, with a "Dear Friends" letter from Vice President Al Gore and a feature on Kweisi Mfume, who left the U.S. House of Represetatives to head the NAACP, plus musings from actor Ed Norton on the community of New York versus Los Angeles. Other features include "On the Street"—real answers from real people on community issues, "Media Cuts"—including short highlights from recent magazine articles that offer insight into community building and action needed, plus book and CD-ROM reviews, links to more resources, letters from viewers, an archives (to come), discussion forums, essays—all illustrated with four-color photos and clever colorful graphics.

Internet Prospector <http://w3.uwyo.edu/~prospect>

A free monthly newsletter appears on the site of this three-year-old nonprofit service to the Prospect Research Fundraising Community, located on the server of the University of Wyoming Web site in Laramie, Wyoming. Internet Prospector is produced by dedicated volunteers nationwide who "mine the Net for prospect research nuggets, targeted to nonprofit fundraisers."

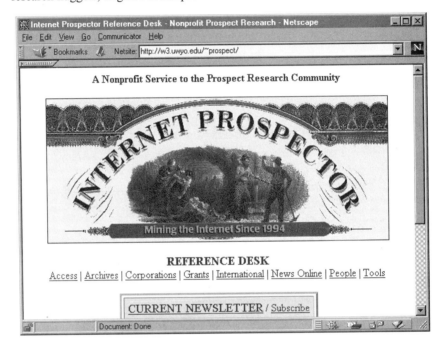

The site is indeed heavy with mining and gold prospecting imagery, color pen-and-ink graphics from the Gold Rush era, and mining puns (e.g., burros transport your prospect "nuggets," and the phrase "Dig It!" is used repeatedly). The newsletter includes news organized under the headings Corporations, Foundations/ Grants (organized by U.S. private funding, grants and sponsored research, nonprofit information links, fundraising news online), International (private and government), People (biographical resources and a Reference Desk), Ethics, News Online, International (i.e., Canadian Nonprofit Annual Reports), Tools, Search Engine Prospecting, and Access. There is also an archives on the site of the past 12 issues of the newsletter. Other exclusive site features include a directory of online U.S. secretary of state incorporation records, test results of leading search engines, tricks of the trade for foundation searches. The newsletter is also available via e-mail subscription (for newsletter only) or PRSPECT-L listserv (including an electronic discussion list); instructions are available on the site <http:// plains.uwyo.edu/~prospect/subscrib.html>.

Join Together: Online <http://www.jointogether.org/jto>
This site is a Boston-based national resource center and meeting place for communities working together with the goal of reducing substance abuse (e.g., illicit drugs, excessive alcohol, tobacco) and gun violence. It is a project of Boston University School of Public Health, offering technical assistance to community groups, public policy panels, a national leadership fellows program, communications, and national surveys. The site contains frequently updated News & Communications, Features & Headlines—short summaries with links to complete articles ranging from a Halloween advertising campaign to Congress's extension of a ban on federal funding for needle exchanges. The editors estimate that each month, users access 200,000 documents concerning substance abuse news, grant announcements, community stories, policy and media information, action alerts. A search engine allows you to browse funding-related news by the week.

Michigan Nonprofit Inter@ctive <http://comnet.org/interactive>
This online newsletter for the nonprofit community in Michigan is located on the Michigan Comnet site, providing Web-based information services since 1994 to nonprofit professionals in Michigan. Michigan Comnet is a free online and information-sharing network for nonprofit public-service organizations. Those actively engaged in public service in the state are urged to register and benefit from guest-access services. There is an archive of past issues dating to September 1996, a director's note, an Inter@ctive Forum, a listing of participating organizations.

News About Nonprofits <http://nonprofit.miningco.com/msubmed.htm>
This informative page is a "Netlink" on the New York City-based Mining Company Web site <http://home.miningco.com>. The Mining Company is an Internet service with over 500 "Guides," in subject areas grouped into 13 categories ranging from arts/entertainment to news/issues, each led by a guide who has either formal training or life experience in his or her particular subject matter. Each guide "mines" the Internet for pertinent information, highlights site that are noteworthy, excerpts information from discussion groups and chats; they present regular features, host special events, discussion groups (in chat rooms) and maintain bulletin boards. The guide for the "News About Nonprofits" section is Stan Hutton, who has been a nonprofit manager, consultant, grant writer, and volunteer. Content includes a valuable listing of online publications in the area of philanthropy with brief descriptions, relevant news headlines and features, an archive of previous features, hand-picked Net links for exploring Nonprofit Charitable Organizations, job listings, and a site-wide search engine.

***Nonprofit Online News*: News of the Online Nonprofit Community**
<http://www.gilbert.org/news>

This compilation of "Current News" in the nonprofit area is a program of the Gilbert Center, with opinions and observations added by Michael Gilbert. News items range from announcements of upcoming conferences and available e-mail newsletters to notes about interesting features on philanthropic sites and links to relevant articles.

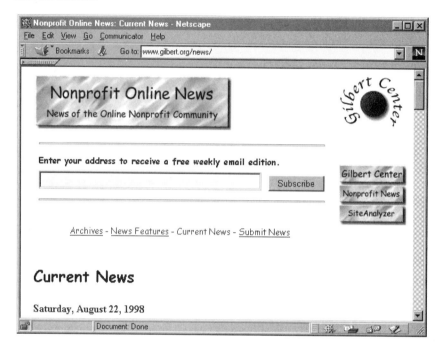

A site archives gives you access to back issues dating to August 1997. And through the feature "Nonprofit Site Analyzer," Gilbert regularly surveys nonprofit Web sites in particular subject areas (e.g., children and youth) to determine average age of site, links, content, and "vitality." News items in the areas of computer-mediated communications, resources for nonprofit organizations, and experiences of nonprofits online are welcome.

The NonProfit Times On-Line **<http://www.nptimes.com>**

This monthly print newsletter presents excerpts from its contents online—"hard-hitting and useful information on the business of managing your nonprofit organization"—first viewed via a newspaper-like home page with highlighted headlines. The target audience is nonprofit executive managers (34,000 subscribers to date).

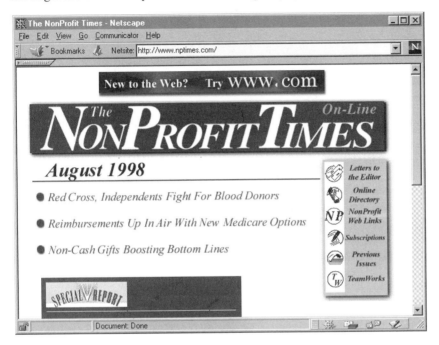

On the Web, you'll have access to lead stories from the current issue and back issues dating to May 1995, letters to the editor, an online advertisor directory, links to other nonprofit sites, classified ads/job listings, a Newsmakers of the month section, the opportunity to ask questions of "Dr. Nonprofit"—a featured nonprofit expert of the month. Although you can view the complete Table of Contents, the entire issue is available only through print subscription (information and subscription form available on-site), $59/16 issues including a "Direct Marketing Edition"; $98/32 issues; $89/year, Canada and Mexico; $129/year, international. As a subscriber, there is also access to TeamWorks, the publication's Interactive News Forums in the areas of Fundraising, Association Member Development, Volunteerism, Nonprofits and Technology, Current Events, Nonprofit Management. Administrative.

Nonprofit World <http://danenet.wicip.org/snpo/newpage2.html>

This is the print journal of the Wisconsin-based Society for Nonprofit Organizations (SNO), published since 1983. Subscription information is available on the SNO site ($79/six issues). You will also find a complete Table of Contents for the current issue, listing article and department topics and authors under publications. Each issue includes features, an editor's page, an "Ask the Experts" section, a "Fundraising Forum," "Creative Fundraising Ideas," a legal section, a section on "People and Technology," a "Resource Center Catalog" (filled with books and other nonprofit resources), a "Directory of Nonprofit Providers" nationwide, "Relevant Reviews" (of books), links connecting you to other nonprofit sources, and "Nonprofit Briefs" on issues facing nonprofit organizations. The SNO site also includes an Index of articles appearing in Nonprofit World since its founding in 1983, organized by topics ranging from Accounting to Volunteers; reprints are available for $1.00/pg. plus $2.00/postage. And, the site offers a "What's New" section with lively news notes and announcements about persons and organizations in the nonprofit sector.

Non-Profit Nuts & Bolts <http://www.nutsbolts.com>

This New Jersey-based monthly print newsletter, presented in quick, digest format, is directed to nonprofit executives and includes "Practical Tips for Building Better Non-Profits." In eight pages it offers the "nuts and bolts," the nonprofit tools, resources, and links to assist in building better organizations. On the Web there is a listing of the complete Tables of Contents for current and back issues, with access to the full text of selected articles. There is also an articles index, as well as classified ads, links to nonprofit publications, listservs, resources, lists of free publications from various nonprofit sources. To gain access to the complete text of each issue, you must subscribe (information available at site, $89/12 issues; 25 percent discount on one-year subscription for Volume Discount Program Partners—to be distributed to members). From the site, nonprofit organizations can also request a free sample issue, and join an "E-mail Updates" list, to receive free notices about what's new in the newsletter and on the nonprofit resources list, as well as nonprofit management tips, news releases, site enhancements.

Oneworld <http://www.oneworld.org>

This site represents a partnership of over 150 organizations working for human rights and sustainable development, and is the Internet "arm" of One World Broadcasting Trust, a charity in the United Kingdom launched in 1995 and a registered charity since 1997. Its mission is to publish information about global issues at low cost.

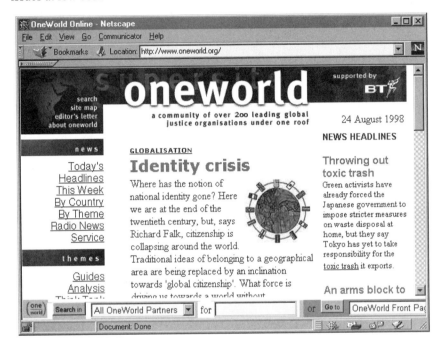

Within the site is a "News" section which functions as a daily newswire; content is focused on global justice issues, and is updated daily and cross-indexed by themes (ranging from Agriculture to Women's Rights), country, and week and is linked to the news sections of all of the sites listed on OneWorld. Also on site is an "Action" section providing facts on the campaigns, appeals, job vacancies, and voluntary work placements of the 88 OneWorld partners. The "Think Tank" and "Guides" are the location for professional debate on issues such as the banning of landmines. The site also offers a Web radio station.

Par' a.digms: The Pursuit of Non-profit Excellence
<http://www.libertynet.org/~rhd/Paradigms/Paradigms2/>

This is a virtual posting board for the nonprofit community, devoted to nonprofit service. In keeping with the title (defined as "a pattern, example, or model"), the site includes an online forum for announcing projects and exchanging strategies, and hosts a searchable directory of project models, as well as discussions on issues important to the nonprofit field. Nonprofit groups are encouraged to post news about innovative projects online; each month two are profiled, detailing mission statements, programs, and expenditures, and illustrated with photos.

Philanthropy in Texas Online
<http://www.philanthropy-texas.com/home.html>

This monthly online magazine is an electronic extension of the Dallas-based print magazine *Philanthropy in Texas*, with the mission of "informing and educating the fundraising executive, development director, volunteer board member, donor, and trust and grant community about charitable giving as it relates to Texas." The online publication makes these goals interactive and more readily accessible. The first members of a "Texas Philanthropy Hall of Fame," sponsored by the publication, were recently induced (in a ceremony to rotate among Texas cities in the future). Each issue there is a Philanthropy Datebook with announcements of upcoming benefits and symposia, organized by city; a publisher's note, and news and features in the areas of Cities, Corporate Giving, Foundations, Fundraising, Familiar Faces; and job listings (under Marketplace). Advertising is accepted in the print and online editions. A downloadable subscription form is available at the site ($57/12 issues).

Philanthropy Journal of North Carolina (Philanthropy Journal Online)
<http://www.pj.org/>

This online newsletter is published by *The Philanthropy Journal*, a North Carolina-based nonprofit print publication founded in 1991 by Todd Cohen, former business editor of *The News & Observer,* who created and writes the Sunday philanthropy column in that newspaper. Cohen is the editor and publisher of *Philanthropy Journal of North Carolina*, which includes "Philanthropy, Fundraising, Foundation and Nonprofit Newsbriefs."

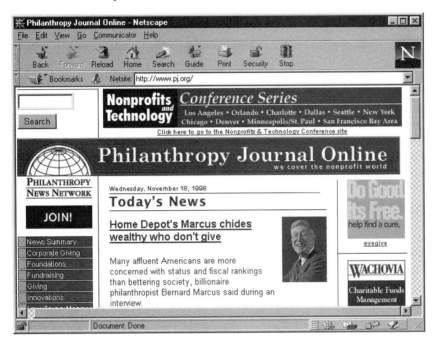

The online journal's home page is designed to resemble the front page of a newspaper, with article leads, a link away from the full text of each piece. A section tells readers what is new that week, and there is a National News Summary. Articles are also organized by topic, under the headings Fundraising, Volunteers, Foundations, Corporate Giving, Technology & Software. There is a classified section listing nonprofit jobs (Nonprofit JobNet), as well as in Index of Nonprofits, links to other philanthropy sites, a Guestbook, and a search engine that allows you to search the site by key word or phrase. An archive allows readers to access back issues dating to February 17, 1997. The "WebTalk" sections includes real-time interviews with professionals and authors in the philanthropic field; transcripts are posted to the site after the event. You can also subscribe to *Philanthropy Journal Alert* (information available at site), a free weekly newsletter for the nonprofit sector delivered via e-mail, with national nonprofit news about grants, fundraising, corporate sponsorships, and updates about issues and trends affecting taxes, volunteers, foundations, technology, and nonprofits; nonprofit job listings; and a programming guide for upcoming guests to appear online, at "Nonprofit Web Talk." The parent publication *The Philanthropy Journal* sponsors an annual conference and seminar, hosts town meetings nationwide in the area of philanthropy, presents the North Carolina Philanthropy Award, and sponsors a fellowship program in philanthropy.

Philanthropy News Digest (PND) **<http://www.fdncenter.org>**

This free weekly online journal is the first Web-based electronic publication of the Foundation Center Online. Content includes a compendium, in digest form, of philanthropy-related articles and features gathered from print and electronic media outlets nationwide. Abstracts summarize the content of each original article, and include complete citations (to assist in locating the original article through a library or document delivery service). Many abstracts include "FCnotes," providing the most current financial information on mentioned grantmakers from the Foundation Center's database, and "Other Links" connect readers to Web sites adding in-depth coverage on featured topics. Timely pull-out quotes of the week, excerpted from each abstract, begin each journal issue, and there are book, CD-ROM, and philanthropic Web site reviews. Subscribe to the free PND Listserv and receive the journal weekly via e-mail Tuesday evenings, the night before each issue is posted to the Web (instructions available at *PND* home page, http://fdncenter.org/phil/philmain.html>.

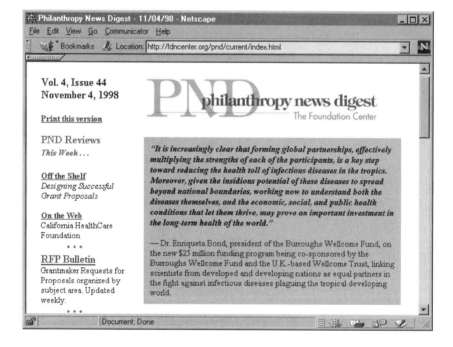

The *PND* home page also lists the eight most recent issues of the journal, in chronological order; the full text of each is just a link away. And prior issues dating back to the first, January 9, 1995, can be accessed through an archives; individual abstracts can be accessed by clicking on a headline in the table of contents or scrolling through each issue. A search engine allows readers to perform keyword searches or click on name indexes of the foundations or of the donors, officers, and trustees cited in *PND*.

Planned Giving T.O.D.A.Y <http://www.pgtoday.com>
Called "The Practical Newsletter for Gift-Planning Professionals," this monthly, Seattle-based, 12-page print newsletter launched in 1990 focuses on planned-giving issues relevant to nonprofit organizations and those who support them and is targeted to gift-planning professionals. Its publisher and editor is G. Roger Schoenhals, former foundation director, college teacher, editorial director, and author. Although the publication now is only available via subscription and first-class mail (to 5,000 readers in 50 states and Canada), it does have an electronic presence on the site of the Seattle Community Network (SCN), part of the Seattle Community Network Association, a public-access computer network run by volunteers and maintaining 32 modem lines for the use of those who would not have access to the Internet otherwise. Community pages on the Network are hosted by neighborhood, environmental, and arts groups, political parties, schools, health care and social advocates, and outdoor clubs. Free registration entitles you to an Internet e-mail account and online forums. Also on-site is a Planned Giving Bookshelf with brief descriptions, a Charitable Sector Video Library, links to other philanthropic sites, and a French-language planned-giving newsletter. Subscription information for *Planned Giving Today* is available from the SCN site <http://www.scn.org>. Content of the newsletter includes how-to articles, reports, reviews, and essays; marketing ideas; interviews; case studies; humorous anecdotes; reprintable material; a training events calendar; surveys, contests, awards; annual index; access to back issues. From the SCN site, you can access ten sample newsletter articles, ranging from ethical issues to tax information.

The Planned Giving Web Letter <http://www.recer.com/news/index.htm>
This monthly cyber-newsletter is produced by Recer Companies, a Washington, D.C.-based for-profit company describing its employees as "planned giving specialists" and offering estate services and American trust marketing. It is described as the Web's first newsletter targeting the planned-giving and estate-planning informational needs of nonprofit executives, and has a credo of "Put Not Your Trust in Money But, Put Your Money in Trust." The content is actually quite clever, with features such as "How to Disinherit Your Son-in-Law . . . and Stiff the IRS," a "National Wills Test," and a monthly drawing to award a copy of a selected book relevant to planned giving. The site also includes an archives of complete newsletter issues dating back to August 1996, information about the company's seminars on identifying potential donors within the community, and an offer to design Web sites to assist nonprofit organizations in publicizing their planned-giving programs for current and future donors.

Prospect Research Online (PRO) <http://www.rpbooks.com>
This is a subscriber-based service for nonprofit agencies seeking new sources of financial support. Complete access to all services is via password only (information on nonprofit and corporate rates at site). Content includes the Newsroom, a listing of the week's most important stories assembled from press releases, annual reports, newspapers, newsletters, and Web sites; company histories and corporate biographies; proxy statements; lists of officers and directors; links to various stock markets; Edgar and SIC codes and links to corporate Web sites; contact names and phone numbers for charitable donation requests; giving guidelines and histories; weekly "What's New" reports with major gift announcements from individuals, corporations, foundations, employee groups, and major U.S.

government agencies. The service is produced by Rainforest Publications, Inc., involved in charitable donations research since 1989. A Canadian version of *PRO* has been available since September 1996. Information for arranging a free ten-minute tour is also available on-site.

Pulse! <http://www.lib.msu.edu/harris23/grants/pulse.htm>

This national online San Francisco-based newsletter is delivered via e-mail bi-weekly, providing readers with a timely summary of what's happening in the non-profit sector and the management-support community.

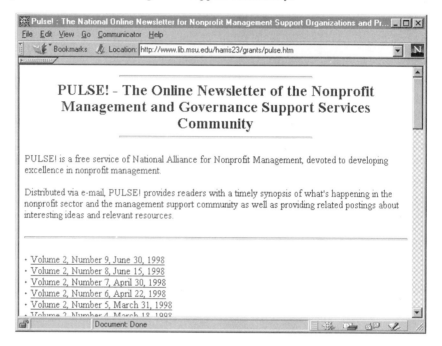

Content includes a brief digest of current happenings within the sector, new ideas, and postings on relevant resources. The newsletter is a free service of Support Centers of America (a network of nonprofit management support organizations and providers founded in 1971 and offering training, consulting, and information resources; see listing, this section) and the Nonprofit Management Association, founded in 1975, a "learning community" with the mission of improving leadership and management skills in the nonprofit sector through the development of management-support professionals. Complete contents of back issues for the past year is accessible through the Michigan State University Libraries site <http://www.lib.msu.edu/harris23/grants/pulse.htm>.

Registered Charities Newsletter
<http://www.revcan.ca/menu/EmenuJAA.html>

This newsletter is located on the site of Revenue Canada, based in Ottawa, Ontario. From the site, you can access complete issues dating back to the Fall of 1991. Contents include in-depth cover stories focusing on topics such as the Canada-United States Income Tax Convention Treaty and its impact on donations and news summaries on issues ranging from the replacement of tobacco sponsors for events to trials and legal issues relevant to the nonprofit community. There are also notes on honors and awards, accounting standards, calls for proposals, a "News Archive," "Coming Events," "People on the Move," a "Volunteer Bulletin Board," a "What's Your Opinion" section, an "Op/Ed Page," "Career Opportunities," and links to other nonprofit resources.

Support Center for Nonprofit Management <http://www.igc.org/sf>

This San Francisco-based consulting and training organization has a regional focus, yet a national reach. It offers consulting, workshops, publications, and management programs for nonprofits, helping them utilize the best management tools and concepts to best serve their communities. The site includes a section of FAQs on nonprofit management questions; "Consultants ONTAP," a searchable database of consultants in the Bay Area; a Library with a nonprofit bookshelf offering reviews of the books which the editors believe should be in the offices of those with 12 different nonprofit management positions. There is also an Online Workshop Catalog for the Bay Area, Technology and Fundraising Forums (in which you can meet the grantmakers for fundraising advice and tips), and a Nonprofit Web Directory with links to 40 sites. You can also subscribe online to receive via e-mail or fax the free bi-weekly newsletter *Food for Thought*, offering news and information about funding opportunities, conferences, opinions, and online resources for the Bay Area's nonprofit organizations. A recent issue included a note about the U.S. government's new Web site for nonprofits, with links to information on grants, taxes, and legislation, as well job openings.

Village Life News Magazine <http://www.villagelife.org/info/contents.html>

This weekly online publication is located on the site of Village Life, created by Kaleidoscope Ministries Ltd. with content "Bringing Hope & Meaning to Today's News." Magazine contents include the "human side" of daily news, a cover story on a current social issue (such as independence for the developmentally disabled or psychologists testifying in child custody suits), a news archives, features, "In the Carousel" (music, movie, and video reviews, plus travel features), an "In the Church" section (highlighting religious news and features and "Christians in the News"), and a "Relief Now Network" (offering up-to-date news of current disaster and recovery efforts and links to related sites). The Village Life site also includes an online bookstore stocked with Christian fiction and nonfiction titles for adults and kids (at a 10-40 percent discount, through Amazon.com), a "Faith News" section, and a "Cafe Chat Forum" offering discussions in the areas of Entertainment, Ministries, and Lifestyles.

CHAPTER NINE

Interactive Services for Grantseekers: Bulletin Boards, Discussion Groups, Mailing Lists

Interactive Communication on the Internet

INTRODUCTION

The rapid growth of the Internet has increased enormously the ability of grantseekers to share information, advice, and techniques with colleagues through electronic mail, newsgroups, forums, and live chats. Like an ongoing mini-conference, participants can learn efficiently from each other about useful directories, books and software, upcoming conferences and meetings, fundraising strategies, job announcements, and more. Electronic mail is currently the most utilized form of interactive communication on the Internet—it's the most universal Internet function, it's easy to use, and it can be used in a variety of ways. When setting out to discuss interactive communication on the Internet, it quite naturally became the primary focus of this chapter.

Grantseekers can communicate with each other on a wide range of nonprofit-related topics by subscribing to key mailing lists. By simply e-mailing a command to the appropriate e-mail address, a grantseeker may join what is really a discussion group and begin to receive automatically any messages posted to that list, as well as respond to messages and inquiries posted by others. There are also several relevant newsletters to which a grantseeker may subscribe electronically, newsletters that are also delivered via e-mail.

DISCUSSION GROUP BASICS

"Mailing list," "listserv," and "discussion group" are all terms used interchangeably to describe a community of subscribers to an electronic mailing list. Mailing list manager software—such as Listserv (actually a brand name), Listproc, Majordomo, Mailbase, or Mailserv—is used by the list owner to set up and administer the list. Subscribers, on the other hand, only need e-mail access to participate. Every mailing list has two e-mail addresses. There is an administrative address for subscribing, unsubscribing, and other useful commands, which will be described below. (When sending an e-mail to an administrative address, keep in mind that it is only being read by a computer. Although the commands are simple, misspellings and even slight deviations from the prescribed format will prevent your message from getting through correctly.) The second address is the one you use to send messages to the entire list of subscribers. Keep this important distinction between the addresses in mind in order to avoid sending an administrative message to all the other subscribers or posting your comments to a computer that won't receive them. If you wish to communicate directly with the person that manages the mailing list—often referred to as the list owner, list manager, or list administrator—you will need to send your message to that individual's personal e-mail address.

Another important distinction in mailing lists is whether the list is unmoderated or moderated. Unless it is stated otherwise, it is safe to assume that a list is unmoderated. This means that there is no filter on what gets posted to the list. This does not, however, mean that anything goes. Most lists have a ban on advertising and other specific rules as to what constitutes suitable subject matter. Violate these rules and you will likely hear from the list manager. You may also be barraged by negative messages from other subscribers, "flamed" in Internet speak. If the violation is particularly egregious or persistent, the list manager can and will "unsubscribe" you.

If you subscribe to a moderated list, your messages are forwarded to the list owner, who then decides whether or not they will be posted. The moderator also reserves the right to edit your material. The moderator is usually an individual, a volunteer, or a group of volunteers. There are various reasons that lists may be moderated. Often, the list owner wants to keep the discourse tightly focused. Another reason might be that a list with heavy volume is receiving too many administrative commands which are being sent mistakenly to the posting address for all subscribers to read. Subscribers may become annoyed and begin leaving the list as a result. A moderated list will introduce a slight delay in receipt of messages, though rarely more than one day.

FINDING LISTS

There are several ways to find suitable mailing lists. Immediately below are directories of mailing lists of interest to grantseekers. Once you are on a mailing list, you are bound to read about other related lists which may interest you. If you are seeking a list on a specific topic and you are already on a related mailing list, it is a legitimate query to post to the rest of the subscribers. There are also several excellent Internet sites, some of which are searchable, that contain directories of lists. The following sites will be helpful:

Liszt Search <http://liszt.com>

Liszt is basically a mailing-list spider; that is, it queries servers from around the world and compiles the results into a single directory. This method ensures that the data Liszt provides is always up-to-date, since it comes directly from the list servers each week. Liszt's main directory contains 71,618 mailing lists.

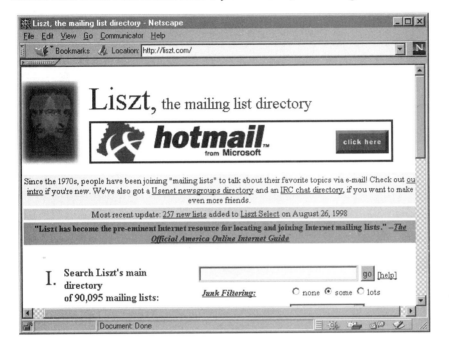

Tile.net <http://www.tile.net>

Tile.net, a Web site by Walter Shelby Ltd., accepts paid advertisements and describes itself as a "Comprehensive Internet Reference to Discussion Lists, Newsgroups, FTP Sites, Computer Product Vendors, and Internet Service and Web Design Companies."

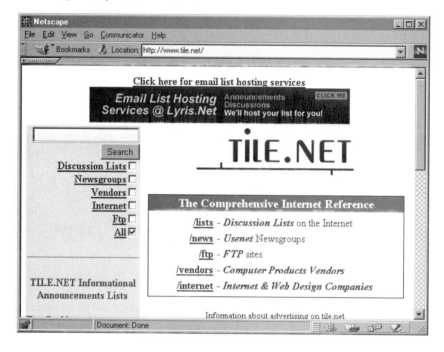

Inter-Links Internet Access
<http://www.alabanza.com/kabacoff/Inter-Links/listserv.html>
This Web area is an Internet navigator, resource locator, and tutorial provided as a
public service by Robert K. Kabacoff. It contains a wide range of reference information, including a search engine for discussion lists.

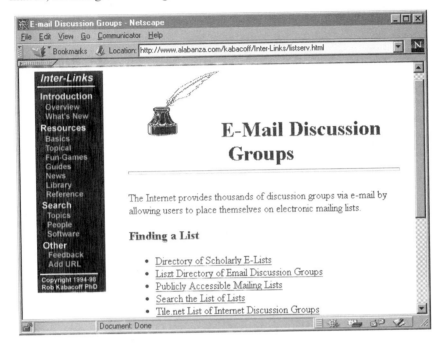

Publicly Accessible Mailing Lists <http://www.Neosoft.com/internet/paml>
The resources section of the Neosoft homepage, developed by Stephanie and
Peter DaSilva, contains a search engine and links to many useful mailing list sites.
Click on the index and then in the index screen that comes up, click on "Subjects"
for an alphabetical index of categories of mailing lists.

There are also several excellent Web sites that contain lists of discussion groups of
interest to the nonprofit sector. These lists include the name of the list, a brief
description, and the subscription and posting addresses for the list. One example
is a page on a Web site operated by Jon Harrison, the Foundation Center Cooperating Collection Supervisor at Michigan State University. His list can be found at
<http://www.lib.msu.edu/harris23/grants/maillist.htm>.

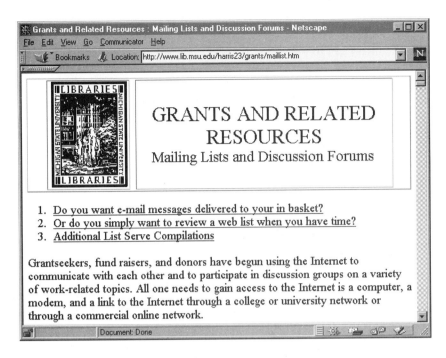

Grants and Related Resources : Mailing Lists and Discussion Forums - Netscape

File Edit View Go Communicator Help

Bookmarks   Location: http://www.lib.msu.edu/harris23/grants/maillist.htm

GRANTS AND RELATED RESOURCES

Mailing Lists and Discussion Forums

1. Do you want e-mail messages delivered to your in basket?
2. Or do you simply want to review a web list when you have time?
3. Additional List Serve Compilations

Grantseekers, fund raisers, and donors have begun using the Internet to communicate with each other and to participate in discussion groups on a variety of work-related topics. All one needs to gain access to the Internet is a computer, a modem, and a link to the Internet through a college or university network or through a commercial online network.

Document: Done

Charity Village, a web site for Canadian Charities and nonprofits, contains a valuable list of discussion groups among its 1,000+ pages of information. The list can be found at <http://www.charityvillage.com/charityvillage/stand.html#list>.

Once you find a specific list of interest to you, you may want to get more information about it to determine if it is really what you want. In most cases you may request information directly from the list by e-mailing the following message to the list administrative address: "info <list name>" (without the brackets or quotes). Leave the subject of your message blank. In addition, many lists have an archive of previous postings, sometimes searchable, in a Gopher file on the Internet or at a World Wide Web site. You may look in the archives to determine the level of activity and the type of discussions that have come before. Finally, you may subscribe to the list and view the messages that you receive to determine if the subject matter is relevant to you. Keep in mind that a subscription address can change.

HOW TO SUBSCRIBE

To subscribe to a list, send an e-mail to the list subscription address (administrative address) and leave the subject or "re:" line blank. In the body of the message, type: "subscribe <list name>" (without the brackets or quotes). Some lists require that you include your first and last name after the list name. The subscribe command varies slightly depending on the mailing list management software used by the list owner. Shortly after sending your subscription request, you will receive an e-mail acknowledging your subscription. You should read the instructions that you receive and *print out and save them in a paper file.* The acknowledgment normally includes a description of the list, appropriate subject matter, rules and additional commands that you may wish to use in the future—especially "unsubscribe."

SENDING A MESSAGE: DO'S AND DON'T'S

Before long you will be ready to post a message. But wait, don't be in a hurry! "Lurk" for a week or so, i.e., listen in for a while. One of the most valuable aspects of discussion groups is the fact that you have time to consider other postings and your own comments. Therefore, try to focus on sending concise, productive, and relevant comments or questions, not emotional ones. Be sure that your contribution is on target. Consider going to the list's archive, if it exists, to see if your topic has already been covered. Long-time subscribers can become impatient with novices that ask questions that have been repeated over and over in the past. If you are in a hurry, apologize up front before posting what could be an "old" topic and ask for advice about where to find the prior discussion.

Before responding to any posting to a list, think about whether you want to respond to an individual directly or post your response to the whole list. Hitting the reply button will normally mean that you are responding to the entire list. A typical mistake that a beginner makes is posting a private comment to the whole list. This can prove embarrassing. You can avoid embarrassment by making it a rule to keep personal comments or confidential information out of any e-mail. It may be unwise, for example, to send your resume over the Internet. Job announcements are frequently posted to mailing lists. We've seen people attach their resume and respond with the reply button, sending it to the entire list.

You should name the subject of your message carefully. Some lists have specific subject categories that you should use. These will be included in the initial instructions you receive upon acknowledgment of your subscription. Follow the rules. It will make it a lot easier for other subscribers to delete unwanted messages.

There is also the issue of advertising. Most lists specifically forbid advertising, although some lists actually invite it. Don't delude yourself into thinking that you are simply supplying information to a community of subscribers. An advertisement will always be recognized for what it is. If you are still unsure about how your communication will be construed, you can e-mail a message to the list owner and ask if your message would be acceptable.

A few other tips that will help you to be a productive member of your new list community include:

- If you ask a broad question, invite other subscribers to send their messages directly to you and offer to provide feedback to the list in the form of a summary.
- Be careful with humor, subjective comments, insults, etc. It is very easy to be misunderstood in this medium. You also risk being unsubscribed or censured by the other subscribers.
- Don't post irrelevant, whimsical, pick-me-ups. Many subscribers will resent receiving unwanted messages in their e-mail box.

SOME LISTS TO INVESTIGATE

Below is a compilation of mailing lists of interest to development professionals, prospect researchers, and grantseekers. Each example includes the name of the mailing list, a brief summary, subscription and posting addresses, archive address (if one exists), and other useful information, where available, such as whether the list is moderated and the volume of its "traffic." When subscribing to a mailing list, always leave the "subject" line blank. Remember, too, that a subscription address can change.

ALUMNI-L

This unmoderated list is dedicated to the interchange of ideas and information among alumni relations professionals at colleges, universities, and independent schools. Topics include alumni education, working with boards and volunteers, alumni training and workshop programs, activities of the Council for Advancement and Support of Education, cooperation with one's development office, and more. Traffic is fairly heavy on this list. It is not unusual to receive five to ten messages per day.

To subscribe to Alumni-L, send an e-mail message to listserv@ brownvm.brown.edu. In the body of your message type: subscribe alumni-l <firstname lastname>. To post a message to the list, send your e-mail to alumni-l@brownvm.brown.edu. The list managers are Paul Chewning (chewning@ ns.case.org) and Andy Shaindlin (shain@umich.edu). The address of the archive is <http://www.pacificgroup.com/html/alumni.htm>.

CFRNET

Cfrnet is an unmoderated discussion group for people involved in building partnerships among educational institutions and corporations and foundations. Issues may include solicitation strategies, stewardship programs, proposal writing, prospect tracking, corporate giving, gift-in-kind programs, and student recruitment by companies.

To subscribe to cfrnet, send an e-mail message to listproc@medicine.wustl.edu. In the body of your message type: subscribe CFRNET <firstname lastname>. To post a message to the list, send your e-mail to cfrnet@medicine.wustl.edu. The list manager is Patricia Gregory (cfrnet-mgr@medicine.wustl.edu). The address of the archive is <http://www.pacificgroup.com/html/cfrnet>.

CONSULT-L

An electronic discussion group established in 1997, consult-l was created for fundraising consultants or those people interested in consulting. The purpose of the list is to discuss issues related to philanthropy and its associated services. Points of discussion may include such business aspects of consulting to nonprofit organizations as marketing, client/consultant relations, fees and collection, ethics, strategies, and resources.

To subscribe to consult-l, send an e-mail message to listserv@jtsa.edu. In the body of your message type: subscribe consult-l. To post a message to the list, send your e-mail to consult-l@jtsa.edu.

The list owner is Andrew Grant (angrant@jtsa.edu).

FUNDLIST

This list is primarily for fundraising professionals with an emphasis on education. Fundlist is heavily used, with a wide range of topics in the areas of annual campaigns, planned giving, development, and many others. The list often generates five to ten messages per day.

To subscribe to fundlist, send an e-mail message to listproc@ listproc.hcf.jhu.edu. In the body of your message type: sub fundlist <firstname lastname>. To post a message to the list, send your e-mail to fundlist@ listproc.hcf.jhu.edu. The list manager is Stephen A. Hirby (Stephen.A.Hirby@ lawrence.edu). The address of the archives is <http://www.pacificgroup.com/ html/fundlist.htm>.

FUNDSVCS

This list is for those interested in the more technical aspects of fundraising ser-vices. It is designed as a companion to, and not a replacement for, fundlist. Fundsvcs is a "nuts & bolts" oriented discussion.

To subscribe to fundsvcs, send an e-mail message to majordomo@ acpub.duke.edu. In the body of your message type: sub fundsvcs <firstname lastname>. To post a message to the list, send your e-mail to fundsvcs@ acpub.duke.edu. The list manager is John H. Taylor <fundsvcs-owner@ duke.edu>. The address of the archives is <http://www.pacificgroup.com/html/ fundsvcs.htm>.

GIFT-PL

Gift-pl is the electronic mail forum for gift planners that involves the development and dissemination of information in the field of gift planning. This forum is pro-vided by the National Committee on Planned Giving (NCPG).

To subscribe to gift-pl, send an e-mail message to listserv@iupui.edu. In the body of your message type: sub gift-l <firstname lastname>. To post a message to the list, send your e-mail to gift-pl@iupui.edu. The list manager is Barbara Yeager (byeager@indyunix.iupui.edu).

GRANTS

Introduced by *American Philanthropy Review* in November 1997, Grants focuses on all aspects of grants and foundations. Grantseeking in any field, foundation formation, foundation funding, and foundation administration are all suitable top-ics. As soon as it was launched, the list quickly gained in popularity all over the United States across many nonprofit fields. With the support of the users, the list editors decided to lightly moderate the list on an experimental basis in order to maintain the quality of the postings.

To subscribe to grants, send an e-mail message to listserv@Philanthropy-Review.com. In the body of your message type: subscribe grants <firstname lastname>. To post a message to the list, send your e-mail to grants@Philan-thropy-Review.com. The list owner is *American Philanthropy Review* (List-Editors@Philanthropy-Review.com).

HEPID-D

One of many lists from the Higher Education Processes (HEPROC) Network Group, hepid-d is focused on institutional advancement, including fundraising, publications, media relations, and the wide range of related topics. For more information about this list, HEPROC, and other HEPROC lists, visit HEPROC's Web site at http://heproc.org.

To subscribe to hepid-d, send an e-mail message to listserv@heproc.org. In the body of your message type: subscribe hepid-d <firstname lastname>. To post a message to the list, send e-mail to hepid-d@heproc.org. The list owner is Carl Reimann (educ@heproc.org).

HILAROS

The purpose of hilaros is to provide a forum for discussion among Christians in fundraising. The list complements other development lists. Topics include a Christian perspective in fundraising, sharing ideas and information to help one another in this work, asking for suggestions from others on the list, and prayer requests.

To subscribe to hilaros, send an e-mail message to majordomo@ mark.geneva.edu. In the body of your message type: subscribe hilaros. To post a message to the list, send your e-mail to hilaros@mark.geneva.edu. The listowner is Cliff Glovier (hilaros-owner@mark.geneva.edu).

IGRANTS-L

This list is one of many discussion groups moderated by Carl Reimann, owner of the Higher Education Processes (HEPROC) Network Group, who administers several lists of interest to higher education administrators. This list focuses on funding, grant development requirements, and other aspects of developing projects within institutions of higher education around the world. The list provides a forum for sharing experience, ideas, thoughts, comments and sources of information on the preparation and administration of contracts and grants. Employment requests or announcements are not accepted. For more information about HEPROC and their other lists, visit their Web site at http://heproc.org.

To subscribe to igrants-l, send an e-mail message to listserv@heproc.org. In the body of your message type: subscribe igrants-l <firstname lastname>. To post a message to the list, send your e-mail to igrants-l@heproc.org. The listowner is Carl Reimann (educ@heproc.org).

NIHGDE-L

The *NIH Guide to Grants and Contracts* mailing list provides updates on research funding policy and program information for the National Institutes of Health. Individuals can use this list to share information on related NIH research opportunities.

To subscribe to nihgde-l, send an e-mail message to listserv@list.nih.gov. In the body of your message type: sub nihgde-l <firstname lastname>. To post a message to the list, send your e-mail to nihgde-l@list.nih.gov. The list owner is the National Institutes of Health (nihgde-l-request@list.nih.gov).

PG-AMPHILREV

This list was established in March 1997 by the *American Philanthropy Review.* It focuses mainly on issues of planned giving in the U.S. and Canada. It is much broader in scope than gift-pl, a forum provided by the National Committee on Planned Giving.

To subscribe to pg-amphilrev, send an e-mail message to listserv@Philan-thropy-Review.com. In the body of your message type: subscribe pg-usa<your e-mail address>. To post a message to the list, send your e-mail to pg-USA@Philan-thropy-Review.com. The list owner is *American Philanthropy Review* (List-Editors@Philanthropy-Review.com). The address of the archive is <http:// www.pacificgroup.com/html/amphil.html>.

PRSPCT-L

Prspct-l is a discussion list for prospect researchers and development professionals in education and service organizations. Participants share resources and techniques for a wide range of topics, including rating prospects, ethics, job
announcements, and foundations. This is a busy list, full of research leads.

To subscribe to prspct-l, send an e-mail message to listserv@bucknell.edu. In
the body of the message type: subscribe prspct-l <firstname lastname>. To post a
message to the list, send your e-mail to: prspct-l@bucknell.edu. The list owner is
Joe Boeke (boeke@bucknell.edu). The address of the archive is <gopher://
gopher.bucknell.edu:70/11/services/listserv/prspct-l>.

ROOTS-L <http://www.rootsweb.com>

Roots-l is the first and largest mailing list for people who are interested in genealogy. In 1997 there were over 8,000 subscribers. Roots-l is a heavy volume list and
messages are pre-screened due to a recent poll of subscribers who overwhelm-
ingly supported the move after too many listserv commands were sent to the posting address. The Rootsweb homepage contains more information about this list as
well as links to several genealogical databases.

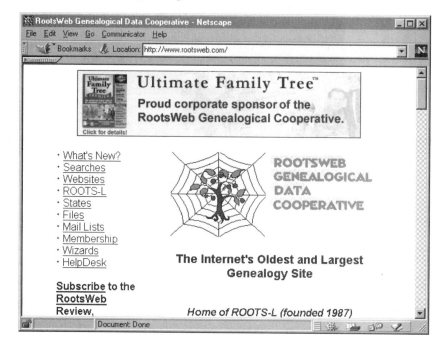

To subscribe to roots-l, send an e-mail message to roots-l-request@
rootsweb.com. In the body of your message type: subscribe. To post a message to
the list, send your e-mail to roots-l@rootsweb.com. The list owner is Rootsweb
(roots-l-request@rootsweb.com).

TALK-AMPHILREV

This popular list, established in 1994, is for those who are interested in hearing
from people outside of their particular area. It invites people from almost every
segment of the nonprofit sector to participate. Fund development professionals,
nonprofit CEOs, college presidents, consultants, accountants, and academics are

all encouraged to contribute their expertise to a wide range of topics. It is not unusual to receive five to ten messages in a single day from this list. Brief, "tasteful" commercial messages are permitted. The list is sponsored by *American Philanthropy Review*.

To subscribe to talk-amphilrev, send an e-mail message to listserv@ Philanthropy-Review.com. In the body of your message type: subscribe talk <your name>. To post a message to the list, send your e-mail to talk@ Philanthropy-Review.com. The list owner is *American Philanthropy Review* (list-editors@Philanthropy-Review.com). The address of the archive is <http:// www.pacificgroup.com/html/amphil.html>.

World_USA

This forum was launched in late 1997. It focuses on the challenges on non-U.S. charities raising funds from individuals, foundations, and corporations in the U.S.

To subscribe to World_USA, send an e-mail message to listserv@Philanthropy-Review.com. In the body of your message type: subscribe world_usa <your real name>.

To post a message to the list, send your e-mail to world_usa@Philanthropy-Review.com. The list owner is *American Philanthropy Review* (lists-editors@Philanthropy-Review.com). The address of the archive is <http:// www.pacificgroup.com/html/amphil.html>.

MANAGING YOUR MAIL

You need to know several commands to keep your electronic mailbox from overflowing, to find previous postings on a subject, and even to conceal your subscription to a list. When you subscribe to a mailing list, your subscription is usually acknowledged. With the acknowledgment, you will receive a message containing the basic commands that you need. If that information is not sufficient, more information on list commands can be found by sending a message to the administrative address of the list and typing "help" in the body of your message.

Since there are five major mailing list manager software packages in use, there are variations in the commands used. For an easy-to-follow chart of the basic mailing list commands for the various list management software programs, see the Case Western University Law Library Web site page maintained by James Milles <http://lawwww.cwru.edu/cwrulaw/faculty/milles/mailser.html#commands>. There is a handy chart there that you can print out in its entirety.

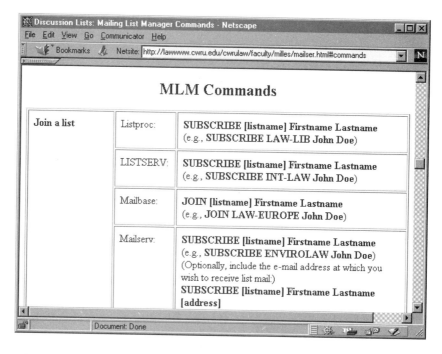

A quick overview here of the most common commands will include digest, postpone, index, and conceal. If you have subscribed to a list with fairly heavy volume, such as prspct-l, you may send an e-mail to the administrative address (listserv@bucknell.edu) and in the body of the message type in "set prspct-l mail digest." This will allow you to receive batches of messages periodically rather than individually. The list manager determines the interval at which the digest will be sent—often daily or weekly. To undo this command, send a message to the administrative address again and type the following in the body of your message, "set <listname> nodigest or set <listname> mail." The digest command, usually included in your initial instructions after you sign on, is available for mailing lists that are managed by Listproc, Listserv, and Majordomo, but not Mailbase or Mailserv.

Lists that are handled by Listproc, Listserv, and Mailbase (but not Mailserv or Majordomo) also offer the option of postponing your mail if you will be away for a period of time. Send an e-mail to the administrative address with the following words in the body of your message: "Set <listname> mail postpone" (for Listproc lists); or "set <listname> nomail" (for Listserv lists); or Suspend mail <listname> (for Mailbase lists). When you wish to receive messages once again, you must send a new command to the administrative address. The command for Listserv-managed lists is "set <listname> mail." For Mailbase it is "resume mail <listname>." Since Listproc has at least three different commands for resuming receipt of messages, you may need to send a "help" message ahead of time to the administrative address of the list, in order to get the correct command.

The index command, available from all list manager software, allows you to obtain a list of archived files for the list. The command is the same for all lists. Send an e-mail to the administrative address of the list with the word "index" in the body of the message.

"Conceal" is another useful command. All mailing lists have a command whereby others may request that a list of the subscribers be sent to them via e-mail. In most cases this includes the e-mail address and first and last name of the person (i.e., no more than the information you provide when subscribing). With Listproc and Listserv, you have the option of sending a "set <listname> conceal yes" or "set <listname> conceal" command in order to conceal your address, so that it will not be included in any subscriber lists that are requested by others.

E-MAIL NEWSLETTERS, DIGESTS, AND OTHER PUBLICATIONS

Another use of the term "mailing lists," refers to one-way communications, such as newsletters, digests, journals and other periodicals to which you may subscribe to receive on a regular basis via e-mail. We will review some examples of philanthropy-related electronic publications that are available for free. Many publications are available in World Wide Web versions (see Chapter 8). These usually have more graphics and links but lack the convenience of automatic delivery to your e-mailbox.

The Chronicle of Philanthropy and *The Philanthropy Journal* are examples of well-established, leading print publications in the nonprofit sector that now offer free electronic subscriptions to abridged news alerts. Free updates of the *Chronicle*, announcements about what's new in the paper or at the *Chronicle*'s Web site, and special bulletins when major news breaks are available through a mailing list. To sign up, send a message to chronicle-request@philanthropy.com. In the body of your message include "subscribe chronicle <your name and organization>."

Philanthropy Journal Alert, a weekly newsletter, is the electronic offshoot of the printed magazine, *Philanthropy Journal of North Carolina.* This popular online publication can be accessed in its Web version, *Philanthropy Journal Online* at <http://philanthropy-journal.org> or received by e-mail. To subscribe, send an e-mail message to pjalert-on@mail-list.com. In the body of the message type "subscribe." To cancel your subscription, send a message to the same address with the word "unsubscribe" in the body of the message. Archives going back approximately one year can be found at <http://www.lib.msu.edu/harris23/grants/pja.htm>.

Some other electronic newsletters of interest to grantseekers include, the *Internet Prospector, Philanthropy News Digest,* and *Pulse! The National Online Newsletter for Nonprofit Management Support Organizations.* The *Internet Prospector* is a monthly electronic newsletter that publishes information on Internet resources for prospect researchers. To subscribe send an e-mail to chlowe@uci.edu. In the body of the message type "subscribe Internet prospector." The newsletter is also delivered monthly to the entire prspct-l mailing list. The current newsletter, archives, and additional information are available on the Internet Prospector site on the World Wide Web: <http://w3.uwyo.edu/~prospect/>.

Philanthropy News Digest's PND-L is an e-mail version of a Web-based publication produced by the Foundation Center. It is a weekly digest of nonprofit-related developments culled from national and regional media. Many of the articles include "FC Notes," which provide information from the Foundation Center's database regarding grantmakers mentioned in the original article. The current issue as well as archives of issues dating back to 1995 are available at the Center's Web Site at <http://fdncenter.org>. To subscribe to the *Philanthropy News Digest*, send an e-mail message to listserv@lists.fdncenter.org with the words "subscribe

PND-L <your name>" in the body of your message. You may also subscribe directly from the Center's Web site.

PULSE!, a free service of Support Centers of America and the Nonprofit Management Association, has been distributed twice a month since Spring 1997. *PULSE!* provides readers with a timely synopsis of what's happening in the nonprofit sector and the management support community as well as providing related postings about interesting ideas and relevant resources. You can subscribe directly from the Support Centers Internet site and find archives, at <http://www.igc.org/sca/pulse.html>.

A new development that has enhanced the interactive potential of read-only newsletters is the use of hotlinks in newsletters. The latest versions of Web browsers will allow you to receive your e-mail, open it, and read it in your browser. In this way, the publishers of newsletter can now provide links to related Web sites.

NEWSGROUPS, ON-LINE FORUMS, AND LIVE CHATS

Newsgroups, on-line forums, and live chats are more examples of interactive communication available to the grantseeker on the Internet. In Usenet newsgroups, people with similar interests can chat about their favorite topic, exchange ideas, and so on, as they would on a mailing list. Newsgroups, however, do not operate by e-mail and are not moderated or owned by anyone. To access a newsgroup, you need to have a "Newsreader"—software that is usually included with your ISP software. You then go to the Usenet site where you can view previously posted messages, which you will find organized by topic. To participate, you post a message, technically referred to as an "article," of your own. Before starting a new thread (topic), you are advised to read the newsgroup's FAQs to see if the topic has already been thoroughly covered.

Each newsgroup has a name that signifies the subject matter covered. For example, newsgroups of interest to the nonprofit sector include, soc.org.nonprofit, alt.activism., alt.society.civil-liberties, to name just a few. Usenet newsgroups are hosted by a wide range of organizations from government agencies and large universities to high schools and businesses. Among the periodic postings in newsgroups, you will find listings of active newsgroups. An official Usenet primer is available from *Deja News* on the Web at <http://dejanews.com/info/primer1.shtml>. This document also contains a "Newsgroup Directory" link. Or you can visit <http://tile.net>, the Web site discussed earlier, which will allow you to search for newsgroups.

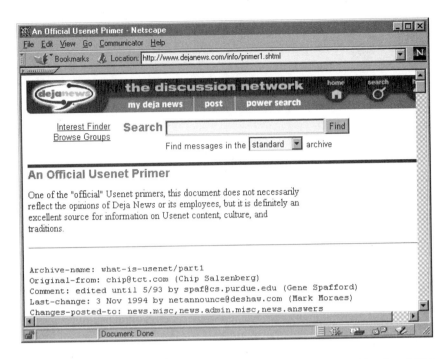

Like newsgroups, the online forums available at many nonprofit-related Web sites allow you to review ongoing discussions organized by topic. It is not necessary to have any additional software besides your Internet browser to participate in such forums. Web-based forums can be very convenient because your e-mail box won't fill up with messages that are not of interest to you. If you are seeking information or a dialog on a specific subject, you can start your own "thread" (topic), or go to the appropriate forum to see if it has been covered.

For a forum to be successful, however, its existence must be well publicized in print and through mailing lists, or the Web site must be compelling enough to attract repeat visitors. The *American Philanthropy Review* Web site <http://philanthropy-review.com> is particularly active in this area and offers several forums, such as one on Internet discussions and another on nonprofit-sector book reviews. In late 1997, this site successfully introduced "Grants and Foundations Online" for anyone interested in the grants and foundation field of fund development.

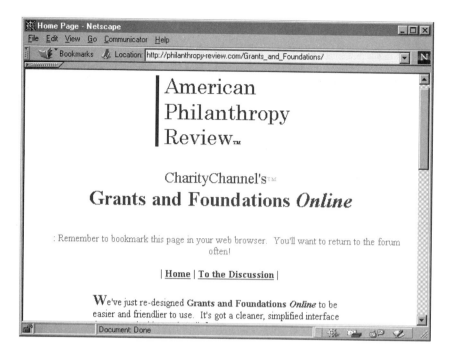

Another example of a successful Web-based forum can be found at the Interaction Web site.

Interaction: American Council for Voluntary International Action is a coalition of 150+ nonprofit organizations worldwide. It has an active forum of interest at their Web site <http://www.interaction.org>.

The forum on this site is called "Global Connections: A National On-line Conversation About the Changing World." It is necessary to register to use the forum, as is usually the case. A password is required. Instructions for getting a password are available at the site.

Live chats are yet another opportunity to get together online with colleagues to discuss topics of mutual interest. Chats are usually hosted at a Web site and, even more than forums, require a good deal of pre-publicity in order to be a success. Participants must come to a certain site at a specified date and time to engage in a "real time" conversation on a specific topic. Special guests are sometimes available to answer questions on the topic. Live chats have been especially popular on large commercial providers of Internet services, such as America Online, where the content is highly organized. In the nonprofit sector, this medium is particularly effective in membership-based organizations, where a structure exists to get the word out to potential participants.

Conclusion

Clearly, grantseekers can take advantage of a number of methods to interact electronically. Primarily e-mail based at this time, these interactions can be productive, inexpensive, and very convenient. Some of the other interactive capabilities (e.g., live chat and real-time conferencing) require more planning and organizing and may therefore be more suitable for specialty uses. However, many grantseekers and fundraisers have found that an easy way to get started communicating with one's colleagues is to subscribe to a mailing list and then "listen in" on the conversation for a time. If you are not interested, you can unsubscribe and try another. Once you are involved in a mailing list or a newsgroup, you will find frequent postings covering technical advice and pointing the way to the growing resources available over the Internet.

CHAPTER TEN

A Guided Tour of the Foundation Center's Web Site

The Role of the Web Site in Fulfilling the Mission of the Foundation Center

The Foundation Center's mission is to foster public understanding of the foundation field by collecting, organizing, analyzing, and disseminating information on foundations, corporate giving, and related subjects for use by grantseekers, grantmakers, researchers, policy makers, the media, and the general public. The Center uses various media, increasingly electronic, to achieve its mission. The Center's Web site opens virtual doors to Foundation Center libraries for audiences not reached in the past, and makes foundation information more accessible to audiences already familiar with the Center.

Technology Used on the Center's Web Site

In order to reach the widest possible audience, the Foundation Center's Web site was designed for almost everyone, from high-level computer users to novices, including those using older, slower computer equipment. The file size of the home page is just 30 K, and major directory pages range from 40–42 K, allowing them to download quickly on most platforms. If you are using a 14.4 Kbps or slower connection and/or Netscape 1.1, Internet Explorer 2.0, or another browser with limited graphical capabilities, you may want to bookmark the text-only versions of the home page, the four main directory pages, and the five home pages for the Foundation Center libraries in New York; Washington, D.C.; Atlanta; Cleveland;

and San Francisco. Overall, the site design uses frames, to allow for easier navigation and the incorporation of large volumes of varied information into the confined area of the computer screen; JavaScript, to generate floating windows, graphical effects, and to enhance site navigation; and interactive features such as specialized search engines, listserv automatic subscription forms, and a secure form for online credit card purchases and seminar registration.

An Overview of the Foundation Center's Web Site

First go to the home page of the Foundation Center. In the location window of your browser, enter the URL (Uniform Resource Locator) or Web address <http://www.fdncenter.org> for the Center's Web site. (Most browsers will allow you to omit the "http://" preceding all Web site addresses.)

The Foundation Center's Web site greets you with an attractive and informative home page that will quickly guide you to the information you seek, living up to its tag line, "Your gateway to philanthropy on the World Wide Web." Links to the four main directories of the site—Grantmaker Information, Online Library, Marketplace, and About Us—and a link to the *Digest* (abbreviated from *Philanthropy New Digest)* are located just below our logo.

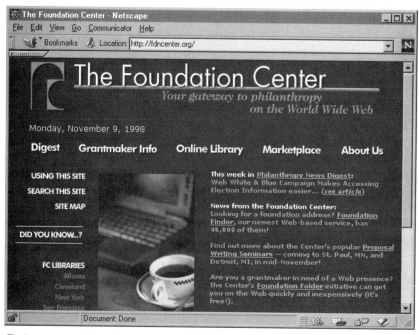

The home page of the Foundation Center's Web site.

From the left column of the home page, you will find a link to an overall introduction entitled "Using This Site," which first-time visitors will find especially valuable. The left column also provides links to "Search This Site," a site-wide search engine for broad keyword searches of the site; and the "Site Map," an image map of the directory structure of the site that can deliver you directly to your destination when you click on the map's individual elements.

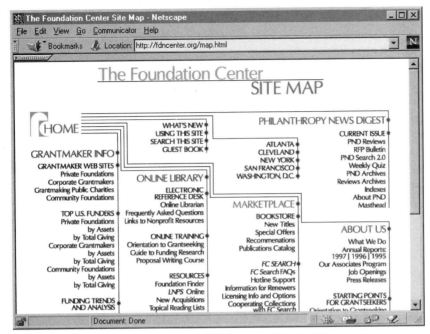

The Site Map is an important area of the Foundation Center's Web site. It is a visual guide to the site and a good tool for reorienting yourself if you're not sure where to go next.

From the left column of the home page, you also can link directly to customized home pages for each of the five Foundation Center field office libraries.

Click on the words "Did you know" to access a pop-up window with a fascinating fact about philanthropy which includes links to sites that expand on the topic covered. An archive of these facts, searchable by keyword or date, can be reached from the pop-up window.

The right column of the home page offers "news notes" about current features on the site and events and news from the Center, and an excerpt from a *Philanthropy News Digest* (*PND*) abstract. New items are posted here daily.

The center of the home page offers a window with "Quick Links" to the most interactive and frequently accessed features of the site: What's New, Foundation Finder, Online Librarian, *Literature of the Nonprofit Sector* Online, Training & Seminars, Foundation Folders, Cooperating Collections, Top U.S. Funders, Trends & Analysis, Guide to Funding Research, Proposal Writing Short Course, and Publications Catalog.

If you have an immediate fundraising question, you can link directly from the bottom of the home page to the Online Librarian, 24 hours a day, seven days a week, and expect a response within 48 hours. And, if you are a first-time visitor to the site or have an observation to share with the Center's Online Services staff, click on Guest Book and fill out the interactive form.

The Web site's four main directories are designed to aid grantseekers and grantmakers by providing specific tools and directed information according to the needs of each visitor. Clicking on the name of each directory on the top navigation bar will take you to the main page of that directory, which provides an index of links for the content within the directory.

On the main page of each directory, you will find a paragraph summarizing the overall content within, as well as direct links to Using This Site, Site Map, and

Search. The main navigation bar at the top of each directory page will take you to any of the other main directory pages, to the *Digest*, or back to the home page. The four main directory pages (as well as the individual library home pages) also offer the same Quick Links provided on the home page. In the deeper levels of the site, almost every page provides a common navigation bar to take you to the main directories, the *Digest,* the home page, the site map, or the site-wide search engine.

| The Foundation Center | | | Site Map | Search | Home |
| Grantmaker Info | Online Library | Marketplace | About Us | Digest |

At the top of almost every page of the Center's Web site, a navigation bar will quickly deliver you to the main directories, the home page, site map, or search engine.

Let's briefly go through the four main areas of the Web site.

ABOUT US

It is the nature of the Web that there are no real beginning, middle, or end points, but About Us is a good place to start if you are new to the Foundation Center and its services. As its title suggests, the "What We Do" area found here provides basic information about the Foundation Center, its mission, and services. Within About Us you will find also annual reports for the past three years, contact information, and a complete description of the benefits and services offered by the Center's Associates Program, a membership program offered by the Center for a fee to professional grantseekers. And you will find listings of current job openings at the Center, recent press releases about new products or upcoming events, and a general FC Calendar of Events. There are also links to the Orientation to Grant-seeking and the *User-Friendly Guide to Funding Research and Resources* (two key starting points for grantseekers), and to grantmaker services such as the Foundation Folders project (a service for grantmakers without a previous presence on the Web). You can also link to both fee-based and free workshop information, and to each of the individual library home pages.

About Us also provides information on the Center's "Electronic Grant-Reporting Initiative." Although it likely sounds intriguing to grantseekers and will ultimately benefit them, it is, in fact, a vehicle for grantmakers to report their grants to the Foundation Center electronically, to facilitate putting this information into the Center's publishing database. There is also a link to the Internet Edition of the *Grants Classification System Indexing Manual*, which details how the Center adds value to database information through its grants-indexing procedures.

You can also link directly from the left column to information about the Center's 200+ Cooperating Collections—public or special libraries holding the core set of Foundation Center publications in their collections. (You should be sure to find out if there is a Center Library or Cooperating Collection located near you.)

ONLINE LIBRARY

The Online Library holds a wealth of information for anyone new to the Foundation Center or the novice grantseeker. The Electronic Reference Desk, like the reference desk in an actual library, answers questions and refers visitors to specific resources. The Electronic Reference Desk directs visitors to the answers of frequently asked questions about the Center and the grantseeking process, allows visitors to ask questions of an Online Librarian via e-mail, and provides annotated links to hundreds of Web sites providing nonprofit resources, categorized as they would be if found in a Foundation Center Library.

Within the Online Library are two resources that new grantseekers will find particularly useful. These are the Orientation to Grantseeking and the Guide to Funding Research, formally known as *The Foundation Center's User-Friendly Guide to Funding Research and Resources*. The Orientation is a step-by-step guide to the grantseeking process for true beginners to grantseeking and the Internet. The Orientation is designed in a linear fashion to guide grantseekers through each step of the process. For those who want to jump right into the fundraising process, the *User-Friendly Guide* is the Internet version of a book by the same name. The online version has a hyperlinked table of contents and is presented in frames for quick navigation directly to the questions you need answered. The entire guide can also be downloaded as one file for future reference. Both the Orientation and the *User-Friendly Guide* offer an introduction to proposal writing, which is elaborated on in the Proposal Writing Short Course, also found in the Online Library. A prospect worksheet, which can be printed and copied, is available to keep track of potential funders as you progress with your research.

More experienced researchers will find the *Literature of the Nonprofit Sector* (LNPS) Online a useful tool. The LNPS Online is a searchable database of the literature of philanthropy, incorporating the contents of the Center's five libraries. A supplementary list of new acquisitions is updated on a bimonthly basis.

The Online Library also houses Topical Reading Lists, User Aids for specific categories of individuals and nonprofits, the answer to a weekly reference question, an interactive news quiz (based on the current issue of *Philanthropy News Digest*), and a series of common grant application forms.

Finally, the Online Library provides links directly to the home pages of the Center's five libraries and to information about Cooperating Collections—those libraries throughout the country that make the core titles of the Center's collection of directories available to the public. The Collections are listed by state and provide the name of the library, address, phone number, whether or not the library has a copy of *FC Search: The Foundation Center's Database on CD-ROM*, and whether or not the library holds private foundation information returns (IRS Forms 990-PF) for their state and/or neighboring states. Links are provided to Cooperating Collections that have Web sites.

GRANTMAKER INFORMATION

The Center's Grantmaker Information directory provides you with the most current and accessible information about grantmakers who have a presence on the World Wide Web. While not every foundation or grantmaker has a Web site, the list is growing rapidly. To make your job easier, Foundation Center staff explore grantmaker and other nonprofit Web sites and provide links with annotations to hundreds of them.

The information culled from grantmaker Web sites is presented in several formats—approximately 600 hot links, alphabetized links with annotations, and the ability to search annotated links by geography or subject keyword—to provide you with the most direct route to information about prospective grant sources. These 600 links can truly serve as "your gateway to philanthropy on the World Wide Web." These grantmakers are organized within four areas: private foundations, corporate grantmakers, grantmaking public charities, and community foundations.

You will find also in Grantmaker Information a description of the Center's Foundation Folder initiative. It is the Center's goal to encourage more foundations to develop a Web presence and to put more foundation information before a wider audience. Any domestic independent, community, or company-sponsored foundation can have a folder—that is, a virtual Web site—on the Center's Web server at no charge. The Foundation Center has created folders for more than 40 foundations, a few of which have used their folders as stepping stones to creating and maintaining Web sites of their own. Foundation Folders are listed here separately by total giving category and by geographic location, but folders are pulled up just like any home pages by people using various search engines, whether those used on the Center's site or those used to search the Web at large.

Grantmaker Web site annotations and Foundation Folders are updated at regular intervals and dated individually, providing you with a sense of how current the information is. Keep in mind, however, that in addition to checking the date that information was updated on the Foundation Center's Web site, it is important that you attempt to ascertain the currency of information posted on a particular grantmaker's Web site.

Grantmaker Information also links you to lists of the nation's top funders and to the Funding Trends and Analysis section of the site. If you are new to this sort of research, you may find this area instructive in becoming more familiar with the foundation world and giving trends. The Center lists the top U.S. funders by assets and total giving, using the most current audited financial information received from the foundations themselves.

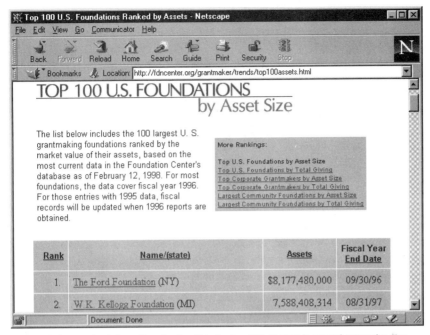

The site's Grantmaker Information directory lists the top U.S. funders in several categories at a glance.

The highlights and excerpts from Foundation Center publications provided in Funding Trends and Analysis will put some of this data into a useful context and give you some sense of how, why, and to whom foundations are giving grants. Adobe .PDF files of selected research materials from this area of the site can be ordered or downloaded.

MARKETPLACE

In addition to operating libraries that provide directories of grantmaker information, nonprofit literature collections, and other tools to aid grantseekers, the Foundation Center publishes and sells many books about foundations and fundraising.

The Marketplace directory offers the Center's Publications Catalog in its entirety, and revolving book titles are conveniently featured within New Titles, Special Offers, and Recommendations (for beginners, individuals, or international grantseekers). Grantseekers can read detailed descriptions about the Center's directories of grantmakers, grants, and subject areas of grantmaking, as well as descriptions of books about nonprofit management, fundraising, and philanthropy. The books in the catalog can be ordered online, using either an interactive form or a form that can be printed and then faxed or mailed. The catalog is updated three times a year, in conjunction with the Center's print catalog.

The Publications Catalog also offers information about ordering *FC Search: The Foundation Center's Database on CD-ROM,* or subscribing to DIALOG, a service through which Foundation Center databases can be accessed on the Internet.

From the Marketplace main directory page, you can access the *FC Search* area, which includes FAQs, information on our toll-free support hotline, information for *FC Search* renewers and on licensing options, and a list of those Cooperating Collections that have *FC Search* available.

You'll also find information on the Center's Fax-on-Demand service, available 24 hours a day, seven days a week, through which you can order profiles of the top 100 foundations included in the print work *The Foundation 1000.*

Finally, under Seminars and Training Registration you will find links to detailed information on the Center's fee-based seminars and training, which include Proposal Writing Seminars, *FC Search* training programs, Grantseeking on the Web training programs, and Meet the Grantmakers programs. Online registration is available for selected programs. In the left column of the Marketplace directory main page, you will find a link to Free Workshops, which include Library Orientations, weekly introductions to library resources providing an overview of the funding research process; Beyond the Basics, a series of seminars for nonprofit grantseekers who are acquainted with the Center's resources and want to enhance their understanding of specific aspects of funding research; Electronic Resources Overview, a weekly introduction to the Center's electronic research tools; and other workshops on special topics.

PHILANTHROPY NEWS DIGEST

Philanthropy News Digest (PND) is a weekly online news service of the Foundation Center. You will find it by clicking "Digest" from almost any page on the site. *PND* is a compendium, in digest form, of philanthropy-related articles and features culled from print and electronic media outlets nationwide. The most recent issue of *PND* is posted to the Web site every Wednesday afternoon. It is also available by listserv, a free e-mail subscription service called PND-L, on Tuesday evening.

The front page of each issue of *PND* features a quote of the week and lists news headlines. Clicking on a headline takes you to a page with one abstracted news story, as well as links to the other stories in the issue, PND Search, and the Front Page.

Besides keeping grantseekers and others abreast of the recent and significant developments in the world of philanthropy, the abstracts in *PND* are accompanied by FCNotes, information from the Center's database regarding grantmakers mentioned in each article. This is the most current information available and may not yet be published in print form. Indexes of abstracts (with accompanying FCNotes) by Foundation and by Donor, Officer, and Trustee are continually updated on the Web site. Each abstract has an indexing number. Each index lists the names of foundations and individuals alphabetically, and each entry is followed by the index number of the abstract including a mention of the foundation or individual. The index numbers link directly to their corresponding abstracts.

From the left column of the *PND* Front Page, you can also link to PND Reviews—Off the Shelf (book reviews) and On the Web (Web site reviews). From each sub-level page, you can link to an archive of previously posted reviews. You can also link from the Front Page to the RFP Bulletin, a listing by category of active grantmaker "requests for proposals," complete with posting dates and deadlines. And from the Front Page you can visit Other Links, Web sites of interest related to the current week's stories, and to the Weekly Quiz, an interactive test of what you've learned from *PND.*

All issues of *PND* from January 1995 to the present are archived on the Web site, and can be found by going to the *PND* Archives and selecting the issue date. Past issues can also be searched by entering a keyword in the search form on *PND*'s Front Page. Results of your search will list the titles of abstracts, in date order, in which your search terms appear.

If you would like *PND* delivered to your e-mail box every Tuesday evening, just enter your e-mail address into the subscription box on the Front Page and click "Add me!"

Grantseeker Research Using the Center's Web Site

With its ever-growing sources of information the Web is an excellent place for you to begin your fundraising research. Once you are generally acquainted with the Foundation Center's Web site, you will want to explore the tools specifically designed to aid grantseekers with their research. Bear in mind that the Foundation Center is not going to find grants for you. However, the Web site will prove to be an invaluable resource in your research.

LEARNING THE PROCESS

A logical place to start your research on the Web is in our Online Library. The Online Library offers excellent guides to grantseeking and proposal writing, and it is the place to find answers to questions that will crop up as you proceed with your research. In the Online Library, you will also find a prospect worksheet and common grant application forms.

Online Orientation

For new grantseekers with little experience on the Web, the Online Orientation is the ideal resource. The Orientation to the Grantseeking Process introduces you to grantseeking from private foundations step by step, as you will see if you choose this as a starting place. One of the most exciting aspects of the Web is its non-linear design, allowing you to see an interesting link and jump to it in an instant, within one Web site or among the myriad Web sites that exist. However, the somewhat chaotic nature of the Web can be overwhelming. Unlike other resources on the Web that offer a jumble of links to choose from, the Orientation is designed in a linear format with a clear beginning and end with links that guide you through it page by page.

From the home page, click on the Online Library tab. This will take you to the table of contents of that directory. From this page, you can view all that the Online Library comprises. You will find the link called Orientation to Grantseeking that will take you there. The Orientation will acquaint you with the following topics:

- What the Foundation Center is and the services we offer.
- What a foundation is, and how foundations typically operate.
- Three approaches to funding research.
- Who gets foundation grants.
- What funders look for in a grantee.
- What types of support grantmakers typically give.
- How to establish a nonprofit organization.

- How to find support available to individuals.
- Effective tools for funding research.
- Hints on proposal writing.

After a general introduction, the Orientation follows two main paths: grantseeking for individuals and grantseeking for nonprofit organizations. Within those paths, it branches further into specific tools, skills, and topics of interest. The Orientation provides several resources for further research on the Internet, but the bulk of its listings for additional resources are printed materials. Other areas of the Web site, which we discuss later in this chapter, have extensive lists of links to Internet resources.

The Foundation Center's User-Friendly Guide to Funding Research and Resources

If you are familiar with the Web and the grantseeking process or have completed the Center's orientation, the Internet edition of *The Foundation Center's User-Friendly Guide to Funding Research and Resources* is a good refresher and reference as you conduct your research. Also a link within the Online Library (click on Guide to Funding Research), the *User-Friendly Guide* contains much of the same information as the Orientation but offers it in more standard Web format. From its table of contents and navigation frames, you can choose just the subjects you want to review and jump around if you like, without going through the material in linear fashion.

The *User-Friendly Guide* also has a glossary of common terms you will likely encounter in your research. You might want to print it out or bookmark it in your browser. As you conduct your research on the Web, it is a good idea to bookmark pages that you think you will return to again. If you are using Netscape, you will find the heading Bookmarks at the top of the screen. When you find a page you'd like to bookmark, click on Bookmarks and then select Add Bookmark from the pull-down menu. (Internet Explorer uses the heading Favorites, but you use the same procedure to mark the page.)

In the table of contents of the *User-Friendly Guide*, you will see that you can print or save to your computer a single text file of the entire *Guide*. If you don't have regular access to a computer, you may want to consider printing the file for future reference.

Electronic Reference Desk

Although you will find a wealth of information about the grantseeking process in the Orientation and the *User-Friendly Guide*, you will certainly have additional questions. And if you don't have questions now, you are like to once you have begun your research. At that time you will want to go to the Electronic Reference Desk in the Online Library. Here you will find the answers to frequently asked questions—FAQs, in Web parlance. If you have gone through the FAQs and still don't have an answer, you can pose your question to the Online Librarian by e-mail. There are links to the Online Librarian from the home page, the Online Library, and other strategic locations throughout the Web site. The Online Librarian will respond to your question within 48 hours.

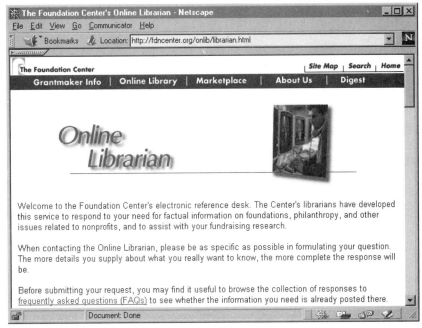

If you can't find an answer to a question in the FAQs (frequently asked questions) section of the Online Library, you can send your question to the Online Librarian.

Philanthropy News Digest (PND)

While you are conducting your grantseeking research, read the Center's online newsletter weekly, or subscribe to PND-L, to have the newsletter e-mailed to you every Tuesday. *PND* will keep you abreast of major developments in philanthropy, and provide you with information that will help you with your research.

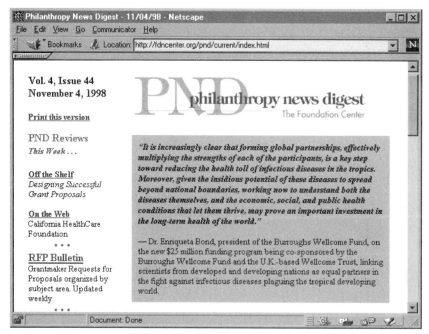

Philanthropy News Digest will keep you abreast of major news in the world of philanthropy. Subscribe to the free digest by entering your e-mail address in the box on the Front Page. Use PND Search and the Indexes of Foundations and their Donors, Officers, and Trustees to find information on prospective funders.

GETTING TO WORK

Now that you know what you need to do to begin researching and applying for grants to fund your project, the Web is a good place to start your research. However, since there are many foundations and grantmakers without a presence on the World Wide Web, assume that you will also have to explore some of the printed directories and guides the Center and other organizations publish about fundraising. The fundraising research you will conduct on the Web primarily will involve exploring the Web sites of grantmakers.

The Foundation Center has incorporated into its broader mission the collection of information about grantmakers' Web sites. Because the information on the Web is not organized, you could easily spend a great deal of time just finding out whether or not various grantmakers have Web sites at all. The Center has done this legwork for you by providing links to virtually every grantmaker with a Web presence. But the Center's Web site does not just provide you with blind links. The grantmaker Web sites are organized by type of grantmaker. Each Web site has been individually explored and annotated, and those annotations can be searched by subject or geographic keyword (a keyword is a descriptive term, e.g. "health" or "Southeast," entered into a search program).

Before beginning your research, you can become familiar with the Prospect Worksheet found within the Online Library.

Prospect Worksheet

This is a simple form to print out and copy before starting your research. It will help keep your research organized and focused. As you locate funders whose priorities closely match your project, fill out a prospect worksheet for each funder. The prospect worksheet will help you match the properties and needs of your project with the properties and interests of funders. Use this simple tool to record financial data; subject focus; geographic limits; types of support; populations served; foundation officers, donors, trustees, and staff; application information; sources from which you gathered information about the foundation; notes; and follow-up communications.

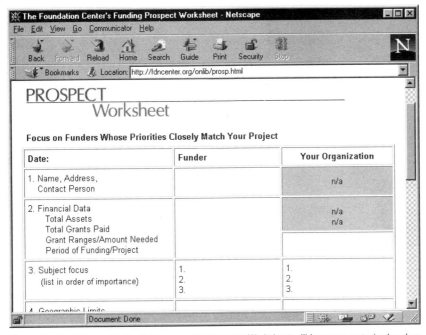

As you begin to research potential funders, the Prospect Worksheet will keep you organized and on track.

Grantmaker Information

With your prospect worksheet in hand, click on Grantmaker Information (a link provided at the top of almost every page on the site, including the Prospect Worksheet). The links to grantmaker Web sites fall into four categories: private foundations, corporate grantmakers, grantmaking public charities, and community foundations. (You can select "no-frames" versions of the first three to assist your navigation if you have a browser that doesn't support frames.)

The directories for the Web sites of private foundations, corporate grantmakers, and grantmaking public charities are organized in a similar fashion. The main page for each of these directories contains a list of hot links, a program to search the annotations, links to keyword lists to help you focus your search, and links to the alphabetized annotated links.

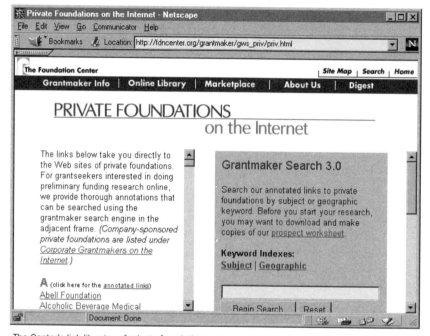

The Center's link libraries of private foundations, corporate grantmakers, and grantmaking public charities on the Web share the same elements: hot links to grantmaker Web sites, searching of Web site annotations, and alphabetical lists of annotated links.

There are three ways to use these directories. If you are familiar with a grantmaker and would like to go directly to the grantmaker's Web site, the list on the left side of the screen provides direct links to those grantmakers' Web sites. If you have heard of a grantmaker, but would like some preliminary information before visiting its Web site, find the grantmaker in the list on the left side of the screen. Instead of selecting the name of the grantmaker, select "annotated links" for the letter of the alphabet under which the grantmaker falls. You will find a list of grantmakers, links to their Web sites, and descriptions of what you will find at each Web site.

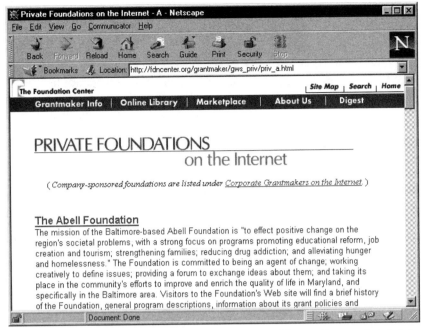

The Center provides descriptions of grantmaker Web sites to provide you with a snapshot of what you will find at each site. Annotations about grantmaker Web sites are listed alphabetically. These annotations are prepared in a consistent format so they can be searched online by subject terms or geographic locations.

If you are looking for funders focusing in a particular subject area or geographic location, you will find the Grantmaker Search the most helpful. Go to the right side of the screen. In the box enter a word or words that describe the type of project you are trying to fund, or enter the geographic location of the project. To make your search more successful, click on Subject or Geographic to retrieve the lists of known words the search engine will find. Find the word or words that fit your project and enter them in the box. Now click Begin Search. You will receive a list of grantmakers for which the Center has annotated links. When you click on a grantmaker name in the search results list, you will find a description of the grantmaker and its Web site. There will also be a link to that Web site. The Grantmaker Search searches only one directory of grantmakers (private, corporate, or public) at a time. Grantmakers are broken into these categories to provide more information about them and how they operate—private foundations operate quite differently than corporate grantmakers—and this will help grantseekers to better understand prospective funders.

The directory for community foundations is not searchable in the same fashion; rather, the foundations are organized by state. You should be able to identify easily those foundations in your geographic location.

If you know the grantmakers you'd like information about or you've compiled a list of prospects by performing searches across the text of the annotations, you can visit those Web sites by clicking on the name of the grantmaker, either on the main page of the directory or the page on which its annotation appears. You will look for the following things when you visit a grantmakers Web site:

Does the grantmaker fund projects similar to yours? Most Web sites state explicitly the sort of projects that are funded, or if the foundation gives grants at all. Go through the Web site thoroughly to get a sense of its mission, founders, and history.

Does the Web site offer a listing of grants that have been awarded? If such a list is not apparent, see if the grantmaker has posted its annual report on the Web site. Often annual reports will contain grants lists. Some Web sites provide links to the Web sites of their grantees. Exploring these Web sites will also provide you with additional information about the kinds of projects and organizations funded by the grantmaker.

Does the grantmaker accept applications? Some grantmakers consider projects by invitation only.

What are the application guidelines? This area, provided on most grantmaker Web sites, will tell you in the clearest terms whether or not a project such as yours would be considered for funding. The application guidelines will provide you with application procedures and deadlines, and whether you should apply directly or first send a letter of inquiry. Some grantmaker Web sites have application forms, which you can download or print from the screen. A few will allow you to apply online.

Look through the annual report. If there is one available, it should contain financial data on the grantmaker.

Look for funding restrictions. These are usually stated explicitly, often in the application guidelines.

Locate the contact information for the grantmaker. Note the correct address, phone number, and e-mail address. Before you contact a grantmaker, become familiar with that grantmaker's application guidelines. Some accept e-mail inquiries and online applications, but the majority will require that you send a formal letter or proposal by post.

Find out the names of officers, trustees, and staff. If this information is available, when you contact the grantmaker, you will be able to address your inquiry to the correct person, not the foundation at large.

A word of warning about information found at grantmaker Web sites: as mentioned earlier, it is important to try to ascertain how recently the information was posted to the Web site. If the information is vague or not dated, you will need to confirm the information you have gathered from another source or directly from the grantmaker.

Fill out a prospect worksheet for each grantmaker Web site you visit. You will have concrete results from your research on the Web, and you will know what information you must find from other sources.

If you really want to do your homework, search for more information about funders you've identified in the *Philanthropy News Digest* indexes. Information from the Foundation Center's database about foundations and their officers, trustees, and donors is joined with news items about them going back to 1995.

Links to Nonprofit Resources

To complement your research on the Web, the Center has a great many links, also annotated, to other nonprofit resources. Links to Nonprofit Resources is located in the Online Library. You may want to look through sites listed here for information from organizations doing work related to philanthropy or the Internet. You will find scores of links in the following categories:

- General Resources (Business & Industry, the Internet, Library Links, Policy Institutes, and Reference)
- Nonprofit Resources, General (Charity-Monitoring Organizations, E-Zines/ Newsletters/ Mailing Lists, Job Opportunities, Membership Organizations, Newsgroups, Web Development/Hosting/Software)
- Nonprofit Resources, by Program Area
- International Resources
- Philanthropy Resources
- Nonprofit Management Resources
- Nonprofit Fundraising Resources
- Government Resources

Other Valuable Online Resources

If you are searching for quick contact information for a particular foundation, you can access the Foundation Finder from the Quick Links on the Center's home page, or from the Online Library directory page. The Foundation Finder is a free look-up tool that allows users to search for a foundation by name (or partial name), further narrowing by city or state, and then receive the address, phone number, contact information, and basic financial information for that grantmaker.

If you are searching for a particular book or publication, enter the *Literature of the Nonprofit Sector* (LNPS) Online. This is a searchable database of the literature of philanthropy, incorporating the unique contents of the Center's five libraries, containing tens of thousands of full bibliographic citations, many of which have descriptive abstracts. It is updated on a regular basis.

To further assist you in your research, there are New Acquisitions lists—including books, articles, and other resources recently added to LNPS Online. You'll also find Topical Reading Lists—annotated bibliographies in the areas of Fundraising Ethics, State and Local Funding Directories, and Working in Nonprofits. And finally, you can access the Center's User Aids—created by Center librarians to guide visitors (individuals or nonprofit organizations) with particular interests (e.g., artists, students, job seekers) to use effectively the resources in the Center's library collection.

Foundation Center Publications

If you need to conduct more research to complete your fundraising search, whether to fill in gaps of information about grantmakers, or to locate information about grantmakers who haven't yet developed a Web presence, the Center's Web site has yet more information for you. Using Quick Links from the home page or a main directory page, or directly from the site map, go to Cooperating Collections. Here you can find out if there is a Cooperating Collection nearby where you can continue your research. As you may recall, Cooperating Collections are libraries that house the core collection of Foundation Center publications as well as *FC Search: The Foundation Center's Database on CD-ROM*. So, our materials may be available to you even if you do not have access to one of the Center-operated libraries located in New York, Washington, D.C., Atlanta, Cleveland, or San Francisco.

If you are not near a library or Cooperating Collection, or if you are a professional grantseeker, you may want to purchase Center publications or our CD-ROM to continue your research. To review detailed descriptions of titles published by the Foundation Center, go to the Publications Catalog in the Marketplace directory. As mentioned earlier, you can order all Foundation Center publications online.

If you live in the geographical region where a Foundation Center field office library is located, you may want to visit that library's own home page to find out about library hours, local services, and upcoming events, including training seminars and workshops. At these five field office libraries, the Foundation Center offers educational programs on the fundraising process, proposal writing, grantmakers and their giving, and related topics.

The individual home pages of Center-operated libraries can be accessed from the Center's home page, the Online Library, and About Us.

FINISHING THE JOB

Once your research is complete, and you've identified grantmakers to whom you would like to apply for your grant, you will begin the process of writing your proposal. The Center's Web site will guide you through this process.

A Proposal Writing Short Course

Both the Online Orientation and the *User-Friendly Guide* will give you an over-view of the key elements of proposal writing, but the Center's Web site also has a Proposal Writing Short Course, which will give you more detailed instruction in writing a proposal. You will find links to this tutorial from the home page, the Online Library, the Orientation, and the *User-Friendly Guide.* Use this tutorial to get you through what can be a daunting process, and consider bookmarking it so that you can refer to it each time you have to write a new proposal. Remember: even though far more time should be spent developing your program or project and researching and cultivating appropriate funders than on actual proposal prepa-ration, you do want to approach the proposal process with care.

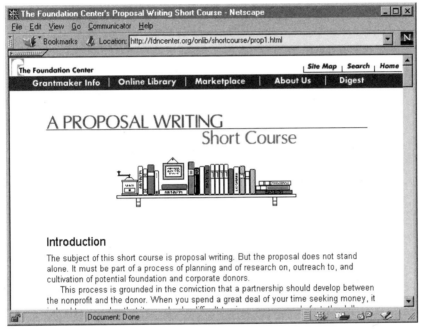

The Center's Web site provides a short course in grant proposal writing. This is a good introduction if you've never written a grant proposal, or a refresher if it has been a while.

Common Grant Application Forms

The common grant application format has been adopted by groups of grantmakers to allow grant applicants to produce a single proposal for a specific community of funders, thereby saving time. Before applying to any funder that accepts a common grant application form, be sure to check that your project matches the funder's stated interests, and ascertain whether the funder would prefer a letter of inquiry in advance of receiving a proposal. Also be sure to check whether the funder has a deadline for proposals, as well as whether it requires multiple copies of your proposal.

The following common grant applications and guideline are available in the Online Library:

- Association of Baltimore Area Grantmakers
- Coordinating Council for Foundations (CT) (hosted by CCF)
- Delaware Valley Grantmakers (DE) (hosted by DVG)
- Grantmakers of Western Pennsylvania (hosted by Carnegie Mellon University)
- Minnesota Council on Foundations
- National Network of Grantmakers
- New York/New Jersey Area Common Application Form
- Rochester Grantmakers Forum
- Washington Regional Association of Grantmakers
- Wisconsin Common Application Form (hosted by Marquette University)

Conclusion

The Foundation Center's Web site, like the Foundation Center itself, is a gateway to the foundations and other grantmakers who share your interest in a common cause, and you should leave the Center's Web site closer to your goal of finding the funds you seek to carry out your work. The Center's site also, through its information resources and organized Web link libraries, will inform a variety of audiences about the philanthropic field generally. Before you leave the Center's Web site, remember to bookmark the pages you will likely return to the next time you visit. And please sign our Guest Book and share your impressions of the Foundation Center's Web site and its many features and functions.

APPENDIX A

A Brief History of Internet Time

If you never thought your life would be affected by something called "packet switching," think again.

In 1962, in helping the Department of Defense figure out how to safeguard its ability to communicate after a nuclear war, in a Rand Corporation study Paul Baran proposed a computer system with no central authority, a system with no individual computers upon which all the other computers would depend. In this system there would be no key parts easily targeted for attack. Mr. Baran also proposed that the system would send messages broken into smaller pieces of data called packets. Each packet would have its own destination address and could travel by itself through any route available on the system, even at a different time, and rejoin other packets at a common destination point. In this way, the system would deliver a coherent, complete message, no matter what damage may have occurred to various parts of the overall computer system in the meantime.

In a relatively short time, this basic concept—a radical egalitarianism of computers and data—has evolved in unforeseen ways to give all of us the opportunity of finding any information that someone, in any part of the world, chooses to make available. This basic concept spawned the Internet and the World Wide Web.

This appendix will present a very brief history of this evolution simply because it is fascinating: the very nature of Mr. Baran's concept made accurate prediction of its consequences and impact impossible, and still does.

so that scientists around the world could use each other's computer systems. As it turned out, these scientists began communicating with each other, not just with each other's computers. This new system had facilitated person-to-person communication.

In the seventies, standards were developed that would let different kinds of computers make use of ARPANET. Robert Kahn and Vinton Cerf were central to this effort. (The accepted lore has it that Mr. Cerf diagrammed key aspects of the new system architecture on the back of an envelope in the lobby of a San Francisco hotel.) The details of the packet-switching concept were worked out and standardized into what is known as TCP/IP (Transmission Control Protocol/Internet Protocol). The TCP/IP protocols created the information packets and handled the addressing necessary to route them to the right place on a decentralized computer network. By the early eighties, TCP and IP were firmly established as the protocols used by the ARPANET. Any computer that used TCP/IP could join what began to be known as the "internet." No one owned TCP/IP and so more people were able to participate. They couldn't be kept out.

In the mid-eighties, the National Science Foundation (NSF) created NSFNET, basically connecting more powerful computers to what now became known as "the Internet." The system's overall capacity grew quickly, and the original ARPANET section of the Internet disappeared. This now beefier Internet accommodated a growing number of connections, called nodes, particularly at universities, where there were lots of computers and people who knew how to use them. For a time NSF was the primary backbone of the whole Internet (a particular segment of the overall Internet network is called a "backbone"). Now there are many. Also in the eighties, the different Internet "domains" were created along with the "domain names" that contain the suffixes denoting different types of institutions: ".gov" (government), ".mil" (military), ".edu" (education), ".com" (commercial), ".org" (nonprofit), ".int" (international), and ".net" (computers set up specifically to connect people to the Internet at large).

ADDRESSING THE INTERNET

With all this democracy of computers and access, one of the things that makes the Internet possible is the organized assigning and maintaining of IP addresses. IP addressing can be complex because of the number of computers and files involved. To simplify the way people could contact another computer, the first name server was developed at the University of Wisconsin in 1983, around the time TCP/IP became the standard protocol suite for the Internet.

The first domain name server was introduced in 1984, when there were 1,000 computer hosts on the Internet. The name server simplifies the addressing process by providing for the translation between the common-language domain names and the numerical computer addresses. Within the Internet, this means translating from a name such as "fdncenter.org" to an IP address such as "204.5.210.11." Now the end-user no longer had to know the exact path to another computer in order to contact that computer.

Over the next decade, use of the Internet got more sophisticated. The network population was changing in both number and character. By 1993 there were 1,000,000 host computers on the Internet. This kind of growth required that the Internet, though unregulated in a strict sense, maintained integrity of services central to its continued operation and growth. In 1993, the National Science

Over the next decade, use of the Internet got more sophisticated. The network population was changing in both number and character. By 1993 there were 1,000,000 host computers on the Internet. This kind of growth required that the Internet, though unregulated in a strict sense, maintained integrity of services central to its continued operation and growth. In 1993, the National Science Foundation sponsored the creation of InterNIC to provide specific Internet services, which included a complete Domain Name System (DNS). InterNIC defined the DNS as:

> A distributed database of information that is used to translate domain names, which are easy for humans to remember and use, into Internet Protocol (IP) numbers, which are what computers need to find each other on the Internet. People working on computers around the globe maintain their specific portion of this database, and the data held in each portion of the database is made available to all computers and users on the Internet. The DNS comprises computers, data files, software, and people working together.

The Evolution of Essential Internet Services

Before establishment of the DNS, the hostname-to-address mappings had been maintained by the NIC (Network Information Center) in a single file, which was downloaded by all the hosts on the Internet. Local organizations were administering their own names and addresses, but had to wait for the NIC to make changes in the central file to make the changes visible to the Internet at large. Created to address limitations, the DNS is a set of protocols and distributed databases. Like the Internet itself, there is no dependence on a central computer. The DNS provided standard formats for resource data, standard methods for querying the database, and standard methods for name servers to refresh local data from other name servers.

In addition to translating names to addresses for hosts that are on the Internet, the DNS provides for registering DNS-style names for other hosts reachable (via electronic mail) through gateways or mail relays. The records for such name registrations point to an Internet host (one with an IP address) that acts as a mail forwarder for the registered host. This gives electronic mail users a uniform mail addressing syntax and avoids making users aware of the underlying network boundaries.

InterNIC Registration Services, located at Network Solutions, Inc. (NSI), was created by a cooperative agreement from the National Science Foundation to provide registration services for the Internet community via telephone, electronic mail, and U.S. postal mail. InterNIC Registration Services worked closely with domain administrators, network coordinators, Internet service providers, and other various users in its registration activities.

The IP allocation functions had been subsidized by domain name registration fees. The U. S. government also provided funding to InterNIC for handling IP allocation functions. In 1997, after more than a year of Internet infrastructure meetings and various discussions in the Internet community, there was agreement that the management of domain names and of IP numbers should be separate activities. As a result, the American Registry for Internet Numbers (ARIN), a nonprofit organization, was established for the purpose of administration and registration of Internet Protocol (IP) numbers to the geographical areas formerly managed by InterNIC.

In December 1997, ARIN assumed responsibility for IP address allocation and network registration functions previously performed by InterNIC. NSI, through InterNIC, cooperated in the launch of ARIN in initiating discussions and proposals to bring IP numbering in the Americas under a model like that of the Reseaux IP Europeens (RIPE) and the Asia Pacific Network Information Center (APNIC). These organizations are also supported by their respective members. ARIN is an independent, nonprofit organization responding to its membership.

ARIN officially opened for operation on December 22, 1997, through the authorization of the National Science Foundation and the transfer by the Internet Assigned Numbers Authority (IANA) of authority of IP number administration from Network Solutions, Inc./InterNIC to ARIN. Imposition of fees is required because the U.S. government no longer funds IP number administration, an activity becoming increasingly more cost-intensive and commercial. The fee schedule of ARIN is in line with the other two IP Registries, RIPE in Europe and APNIC in the Asia Pacific region. With the addition of ARIN, there now are three geographically aligned IP Registries which have coordinated management activities and are supported by user funding.

This change in how IP numbers are administered won't be visible to most end users. IP addresses are mostly registered by ISPs (Internet Service Providers) and then distributed to end users. This description of the evolution in the provision of essential Internet services is included to show that, although available to all and owned by no one, maintaining the Internet is not costless and depends on the cooperation, commitment, and expertise of many people around the world.

INTERNET FUNCTIONALITY

The original Internet (pre-World Wide Web) provided a number of different capabilities, briefly described below. (Many of these were subsequently incorporated into the Web environment, working seamlessly within popular Web browsers, see Chapter 1.)

E-mail
Personal messaging was from the outset, the most widely used Internet function. Practically everyone could have a use for it. All it required was a computer, a little facility with it, and someone else with these two things.

Usenet
Usenet is a world-wide distributed discussion system. It consists of a set of "newsgroups" with names that are classified hierarchically by subject. "Articles" or "messages" are "posted" to these newsgroups by people on computers with the appropriate software—these articles are then broadcast to other interconnected computer systems via a wide variety of networks. Some newsgroups are "moderated." In moderated newsgroups, the articles are first sent to a moderator for approval before appearing in the newsgroup.

Because of the nature of Usenet, there is no way for any user to enforce the results of a newsgroup vote (or any other decision, for that matter). Therefore, for your new newsgroup to be propagated widely, you must not only follow the letter of the guidelines; you must also follow its spirit.

If you want to start a newsgroup idea, read the "news.groups" newsgroup for a while, at least six months, to find out how things work. A new newsgroup is unlikely to be widely distributed unless its sponsor follows the newsgroup creation guidelines. (Guidelines require that a new newsgroup pass an open vote run by neutral volunteer votetakers).

Telnet

Telnet is the generic name for logging onto a remote computer and making use of programs that reside there, as if you were actually using that computer.

File Transfer Protocol (FTP)

FTP was and still is one of the most useful of Internet functions. It lets a person download computer files from (and, less often, upload computer files to) any Internet host that is set up to allow this. FTP can require a password, but many FTP sites allow files to be downloaded by anyone. (This kind of "open season" FTP is known as Anonymous FTP.) The downloading of free software programs is probably the most well-known FTP practice. This ability was particularly important in the early days of the Internet when it was put together and operated by a smaller number of knowledgeable computer users, who basically built the Internet by sharing their experience and knowledge as they used it. A tremendous amount of information, both computer programs and text, was originally made available on the Internet via FTP for anyone with the equipment and ability to access it. FTP sites were searchable by using a program generically referred to as Archie, a nickname for Archive Server.

Gopher

In 1991 a team at the University of Minnesota developed a system whereby files were made available on the Internet and a menu system allowed users to locate information they wanted wherever it was on the Internet. The term "Gopher" referred to the state animal of Minnesota, as well as the University of Minnesota (whose teams are called the "Golden Gophers"), and euphoniously referred to the term "gofer," someone who fetches. Various locations established Gopher servers containing various files they wished to make available. Client software treated these many Gopher servers as connected. Gopher menus grew and users were able to "bookmark" those sites and files they were to visit regularly. Following on the name "Archie," in 1992 a program called "Veronica" was created that was able to search the growing "Gopherspace" for specific words appearing on Gopher menus. The results of Veronica searches looked themselves like Gopher menus and so Gopherspace became even more transparent to the user. As Gopherspace continued to grow, it became a practical necessity to search only parts of it. Veronica searches looked across the whole array of Gopher servers and the results could be unwieldy. As a result, a program called "Jughead" was developed at the Computer Center at University of Utah and released in 1993. Because Jughead generally searched higher level menus, rather than looking for words in all Gopher menus, it was good for doing more general research.

Wide Area Information Service (WAIS)

In 1991, another development appeared which extended a person's ability to search through material being made available on the Internet. Unlike the Archie software that searched for FTP archive files, or the Gopher/Veronica/Jughead software which searched through the growing number of Gopher menus, the Wide Area Information Service (WAIS) employed software that would search the entire text of all the articles, papers, etc. that were placed on WAIS servers. Initially the material made available was from the technical and scientific community around the world. In light of what was to happen to Internet functionality a short time later, it's fair to say that the WAIS search capabilities brought before a more general audience some new concepts for searching archived material: relevancy rankings and Boolean searching.

A WAIS search looked for keywords wherever they appeared in text, and the results of these keyword searches could include things out of context, things that fell outside of the intentions of the searcher. So the software tried to rank the items in results lists according to how well the items matched up with the keywords. The user could then pick and choose among the results list items based on how "relevant" they seemed relative to each other. Boolean searching allows the user to combine search terms in different ways when a search is performed, so that a search could be made more general or more specific, depending on the user's needs and the nature of the material. Boolean searching was already well known to experienced computer users, but the Internet was distributing this concept more broadly, along with information.

Getting good results from WAIS searches involved a higher level of conceptualization from the user for a number of reasons. The software did the picking and choosing by looking at text hidden from the user, rather than presenting various levels of menus (as in Gopherspace) for user review and selection. This in turn required that the user have more familiarity with the material being searched; one had to understand in advance the nature of the text to be searched in order to choose appropriate search terms. The system also depended on having enough different information sets which shared common concepts and issues. This made it particularly useful for the technical and scientific communities, where this condition pertained.

World Wide Web: The Internet Takes Off

The World Wide Web was developed by Tim Berners-Lee in Switzerland at CERN (European Laboratory for Particle Physics) in 1991. The key capability that created this new-thing-unto-itself, was a fairly simple implementation of "hypertext," a function which lets you jump from one document or file on the Internet to another, one that presumably is related to the first. Documents could now be created which included hypertext "links" that took users directly to other documents. Below we reproduce a version of the original World Wide Web vision of Berners-Lee, written around 1992. This prophetic synopsis was taken from the Web site of the World Wide Web Consortium (W3C) <http://www.w3.org>, another organization dedicated to allowing the Web not only to keep going and growing, but developing in more sophisticated and useful ways.

This is an interesting presentation because it describes the Web specifically from the "viewer" (or "client") side and from the "information provider" (or "server") side. Concurrent developments on both sides would continue to spur the Web's rapid growth. In fact, the Web has exhibited "client-server" architecture to the world at large. That is, at least for those without previous experience of being connected to a network at an office, corporation, university, etc., the World Wide Web exemplified the oft-quoted adage, "The network is the computer."

WORLD WIDE WEB—EXECUTIVE SUMMARY OF THE ORIGINAL VISION <HTTP://WWW.W3.ORG/SUMMARY.HTML>

The WWW project merges the techniques of networked information and hypertext to make an easy but powerful global information system. The project represents any information accessible over the network as part of a seamless hypertext information space.

The WWW was originally developed to allow information sharing within internationally dispersed teams, and the dissemination of information by support groups. Originally aimed at the High Energy Physics community, it has spread to other areas and attracted much interest in user support, resource discovery and collaborative work areas. It is currently the most advanced information system deployed on the Internet, and embraces within its data model most information in previous networked information systems.

In fact, the web is an architecture which will also embrace any future advances in technology, including new networks, protocols, object types and data formats. Clients and servers exist for many platforms and are under continual development.

Reader view

The WWW world consists of documents, and links. Indexes are special documents which, rather than being read, may be searched. The result of such a search is another ("virtual") document containing links to the documents found. A simple protocol ("HTTP") is used to allow a browser program to request a keyword search by a remote information server.

The web contains documents in many formats. Those documents, which are hypertext (real or virtual), contain links to other documents, or places within documents. All documents, whether real, virtual or indexes, look similar to the reader and are contained within the same addressing scheme.

To follow a link, a reader clicks with a mouse (or types in a number if he or she has no mouse). To search an index, a reader gives keywords (or other search criteria). These are the only operations necessary to access the entire world of data.

Information Provider View

The WWW browsers can access many existing data systems via existing protocols (FTP, NNTP) or via HTTP and a gateway. In this way, the critical mass of data is quickly exceeded, and the increasing use of the system by readers and information suppliers encourage each other.

Providing information is as simple as running the WWW server and pointing it at an existing directory structure. The server automatically generates the hypertext view of your files to guide the user around.

To personalize it, you can write a few SGML hypertext files to give an even more friendly view. Also, any file available by anonymous FTP, or any internet newsgroup can be immediately linked into the web. The very small start-up effort is designed to allow small contributions. At the other end of the scale, large information providers may provide an HTTP server with full text or keyword indexing. This may allow access to a large existing database without changing the way that database is managed. Such gateways have already been made into Oracle, WAIS, and Digital's VMS/Help systems, to name but a few.

The WWW model gets over the frustrating incompatibilities of data format between suppliers and reader by allowing negotiation of format between a smart browser and a smart server. This should provide a basis for extension into multimedia, and allow those who share application standards to make full use of them across the web.

This summary does not describe the many exciting possibilities opened up by the WWW project, such as efficient document caching, the reduction of redundant out-of-date copies, and the use of knowledge daemons. . . .

In many ways the hypertext function, which spawned the World Wide Web, was the natural extension of the "classic" Internet capabilities described briefly earlier. But it also marked a clean break with this past (which is also still present), allowing a true quantum leap in global interconnectivity and communication. But a couple of things had to happen to bring about this accelerated evolution.

Hypertext was a marvellous development. Now people could zoom through the chutes and ladders of a growing World Wide Web by jumping from link to link. The question immediately became, link to what? In the beginning, adding hypertext links to documents was a painstaking process. Further growth of the Web would depend both on the ease with which people could make hypertext information available and the ease with which people could access it. From this point forward, the development of both hypertext authoring and viewing capabilities became intertwined in an upward-leading spiral. Authoring would become a simpler process and allow a tremendous proliferation of content available on the Web, and viewers would become more point-and-click oriented to make viewing that content easier. By the mid-90s, the ability to "surf" the Web, a term first heard in 1992, was within the grasp of considerably more people.

HYPERTEXT MARKUP LANGUAGE (HTML)

At the heart of Tim Berners-Lee idea for a network of hypertext documents was the development of the tagging system required to create the hypertext documents and the links that would knit them together. He looked to the already existing Standard Generalized Markup Language (SGML), an international standard (ISO 8879) for tagging electronic text that allows another user or machine to know how the text should look, how it should be presented. This standard formatting language (a "metalanguage") could be used across all computer networks and systems.

By consistently using standard format tags for document elements, not only could electronic text be presented consistently on any device, but the documents could be "structured" using SGML tags. For instance, tables of contents could be automatically generated by presenting just the different levels of headings from a long text document. With SGML, information about the document was sent along with the text of the document so that machines could read and present the material consistently.

Berners-Lee used a small piece of the full SGML to create the original Hypertext Markup Language. HTML is really just one "Document Type Definition" (DTD), any number of which can be created using SGML. Restricting the Web markup language basically to one document type helped get it adopted rapidly, when people were primarily posting only very simple text documents to the Internet.

The system was beguilingly simple. Cross-platform capability was key, with standard format tags allowing consistent presentation of documents. The system also needed to include an addressing scheme that would allow creation of hypertext pointers, so the Internet addresses were incorporated into the tagging system. Also required was a transport mechanism that would let documents move across networks. This was developed to become the HyperText Transport Protocol (aka "http"), and "http" became the most common prefix used in Internet addresses. All these requirements were met by the "language" that became known as HTML. Similar to the adoption of TCP/IP, in which an "open" system can be open only if standards are developed and then accepted by a majority of users, HTML became the standard language of content generation on the Web. To become available to the widest group of users, the various Web viewing programs (known as "browsers") being developed needed to support the HTML standard, that is, they had to recognize HTML tagging in order to present documents appropriately.

THE WORLD WIDE WEB CONSORTIUM AND THE DEVELOPMENT OF STANDARDS

The World Wide Web Consortium (W3C) was founded in 1994 to develop common protocols for the evolution of the World Wide Web. It is an international industry consortium, jointly hosted by the Massachusetts Institute of Technology Laboratory for Computer Science [MIT/LCS] in the United States; the Institut National de Recherche en Informatique et en Automatique [INRIA] in Europe; and the Keio University Shonan Fujisawa Campus in Asia. Initially, the W3C was established in collaboration with CERN, where the Web originated, with support from DARPA and the European Commission.

The Consortium is led by Tim Berners-Lee, Director of the W3C and creator of the World Wide Web, and Jean-François Abramatic, Chairman of the W3C. It is funded by Member organizations. The W3C is vendor-neutral, working with the global community to produce specifications and software that is made freely available throughout the world.

HTML was an important area of activity for the W3C when it began in 1994. Tim Berners-Lee's original HTML (now known as HTML 1) was extremely simple. However, by 1994 there were many "extensions" to HTML and the language was becoming complex and unwieldy. More to the point, Netscape, Microsoft, and other browser vendors had begun implementing different HTML features. In 1994, under the auspices of the Internet Engineering Task Force (IETF), HTML 2 was developed to specify the commonly used HTML tags and extensions. Going further, the Consortium felt it necessary to address the resulting incompatibilities, and in 1995 formed the HTML ERB (Editorial Review Board) to bring vendors together to prepare a common standard for HTML.

The original HTML was a simple subset of SGML. The same simplicity that had aided its rapid adoption as a standard quickly began to feel like a limitation. As Web publishing became so widespread, and people started talking about "Web design," there was great interest in restoring the full capabilities of a complete SGML-like system to the Web environment through the development and standardization of an expanded markup language. The W3C created a working committee of a variety of industry groups and vendors to develop a new system. In February 1998, the W3C released the specification for XML 1.0, the first version of an enhanced system for "defining, validating, and sharing document formats on the Web." XML stands for Extensible Markup Language.

XML—BACK TO SGML ROOTS

HTML had proved too simple for the more complex Web applications people wanted to develop. However, SGML was very complex and therefore hard to learn completely. XML is an attempt to strike the right balance between those two extremes. The excerpts below from a W3C press release <http://www.w3.org/Press/1998/XML10-REC> hint at the potential for XML to further advance the capabilities and scope of the World Wide Web. Many different DTDs can be created within XML (e.g., specific industries can create complex applications of interest only to their industry group). Existing HTML tagging can still be used as long as it is "well formed," that is, it meets some standards for consistency. We reproduce these far-ranging excerpts as a reminder that technological advances and the development of standards are both continuous processes. (In fact, technology advances seem inevitable, whereas the acceptance of standards can be difficult, especially if it affects industry economics.)

> XML 1.0 is a subset of an existing, widely used international text-processing standard (Standard Generalized Markup Language, ISO 8879:1986 as amended and corrected) intended for use on the World Wide Web. XML retains ISO 8879's basic features—vendor independence, user extensibility, complex structures, validation, and human readability—in a form that is much easier to implement and understand. XML can be processed by existing commercial tools and a rapidly growing number of free ones. . . . XML is primarily intended to meet the requirements of large-scale Web content providers for industry-specific markup, vendor-neutral data exchange, media-independent publishing, one-on-one marketing, workflow management in collaborative authoring environments, and the processing of Web documents by intelligent clients. It is also expected to find use in metadata applications. XML is fully internationalized for both European and Asian languages, with all conforming processors required to support the Unicode character set. The language is designed for the quickest possible client-side processing consistent with its primary purpose as an electronic publishing and data interchange format.
>
> *Copyright © 1997 World Wide Web Consortium, (Massachusetts Institute of Technology, Institut National de Recherche en Informatique et en Automatique, Keio University). All Rights Reserved.*

This discussion of the development of HTML and XML displays once again the rapidly expanding potential of the Web for serving a diverse global audience. Already, various DTDs (Document Type Definitions) are being developed using XML, but for some time to come, most Web surfers will be using their browsers to look at documents created using HTML tags.

What's Next

The software language known as Java made its first appearance on the Internet timeline in 1995. Created by Sun Microsystems, Java represents a significant development whose outcome is still unclear, but Java at least holds the potential to revolutionize life on the Web. A description of Java (published by Jones Digital Century in 1997) explains its potentially revolutionary aspects:

> Because Java is platform-neutral, it facilitates the building of software that can run seamlessly across all computers on the Internet, and on private intranets. Java allows developers to embed small software applications, called applets, into HTML documents that can be sent to, and used by, users on any operating system. . . . It is possible that in the future, Java-enabled sites will be able to perform the functions of most home and business software, and even to serve as telephones or VCRs. Early proponents have therefore suggested that Java applications could some day replace the larger applications on computer hard drives, essentially establishing the Internet as a universal operating system.

Widespread acceptance of Java may depend on technology advances in the World Wide Web generally, but it could potentially revolutionize the way people use computers over the Web.

APPENDIX B

How to Connect to the Internet

This material was contributed by the Fund for the City of New York <http://www.fcny.org>. It is based on material presented in Internet instruction offered through the Fund's Internet Academy. The full range of offerings of the Internet Academy can be viewed at <http://www.fcny.org/tech/acad-cal.htm>.

Access

Two of the more common ways to access the Internet are through Direct Phone Line Access and High Speed Dedicated Access

DIRECT PHONE LINE ACCESS: SHELL VS. SLIP/PPP ACCOUNTS

The most common form of Internet access is direct phone line access or "POTS" (Plain Old Telephone Service). It generally involves a regular dial-up line with a standard modem (which is not connected all the time), but can involve a dedicated phone line that provides a dedicated connection.

Theoretical modem speeds are up to 33.6 kbps, though the actual performance is usually slower. While this type of Internet access is the most commonly used, and fine for mail, Newsgroups, chat and most web browsing. It can prove to be slow for downloading large files and graphics. Within direct phone line access, there are two types of accounts commonly used: Shell and SLIP/PPP.

Shell Account

A shell account calls up the host computer that is on the Internet. Your own computer is only used as a terminal. In most cases, the computer you are connecting to will run a version of UNIX.

The advantages to a shell account are:

- Minimal equipment needed: a shell account does not require a fast computer processor, Windows/Mac graphical environment, or Internet software;
- low cost; and
- simple setup

The disadvantages to a shell account are:

- may be more difficult to use as it requires some UNIX knowledge;
- there is no Graphical User Interface;
- there are extra steps in downloading files as all files must be FTPed to the host computer and then downloaded from there.

SLIP/PPP Accounts

SLIP (Serial Line Internet Protocol) and PPP (Point to Point Protocol) are two types of protocols, though PPP is the more commonly used at this point. A SLIP/PPP connection is similar to a shell account. It allows you to call up an Internet Service Provider who is really connected to the Internet. However, in this case both computers are running a TCP/IP software application. TCP/IP stands for Transmission Control Protocol/Internet Protocol, which defines how computers on the Internet exchange information. The TCP/IP software will establish a connection to your Internet provider and transmit data back and forth according to the Internet protocol. It also temporarily gives your own computer a direct connection to other Internet computers, using a graphical user interface such as Windows. A direct advantage of this is that it allows FTP sessions to be handled directly between your computer and the remote FTP site without going through your service provider's computer.

Terms to Know When Using a SLIP/PPP Account

Important terms to know about when using SLIP/PPP accounts are:

IP Address: a network address expressed in numbers. Note: both your computer and the host computer will have an IP Address.

Name Server: A computer that manages Internet names and numeric addresses.

Domain Suffix: the DNS of your service provider

Hardware and Software Requirements to Use a SLIP/PPP Account

SLIP/PPP Requirements Include:

- Computer: 386 DX minimum (the faster the better), Mac 68030 processor minimum
- Modem: 9600 bps minimum (the faster the better)
- Software to perform various Internet functions (i.e., Web browsing software, FTP software, Newsreader software, etc.)

Access Through Your Office PBX (Private Branch Exchange)

Your office may be using a PBX for its telecommunications. Here are a few things to consider.

- Desktop jacks may not support modems
- Some modem PBX systems use digital signaling which is incompatible with modem output check with your PBX vendor
- Test thoroughly before committing
- You may need to install a direct phone line, bypassing the pbx.

HIGH SPEED DEDICATED ACCESS

Access is provided from the Local Area Network (LAN) through a gateway or router to the service provider to the backbone and over the Internet. The Service Provider leases a dedicated telephone line at a speed of your choosing. This is ultimately the most flexible connection. Each computer has TCP/IP software and consequently all Internet Services (FTP, E-Mail, Telnet, WWW, IRC, etc.) and is a full-fledged member of the Internet. It is most appropriate for a group setting, and completely impractical for home use, due to its cost. However, its costs are prohibitive to many organizations as well (see: "Costs").

ISDN (Integrated Services Digital Network):

ISDN uses digital telephone lines (twisted-pair copper wires) between home/office and telephone switching offices. It is a dedicated digital connection available in Basic (3 Channels) and Primary Rate Interface (24 Channels). It uses multiple channels for voice, data and video at transmission speeds of 56 kbps, 64 kpbs or 128 kpbs.

T1 & T3 Lines

T1 and T3 lines are bandwidth conduits. A T1 line is a "bundle" of 24 64 kbs dedicated lines (1.54 mbps) A T3 line consists of 24 T1 lines (45 mbps). Some communications companies may also offer fractional T1 & T3 lines. You can operate the T1 & T3 lines as channelized (i.e., voice and data-dedicated) or free (data or voice), each solution requiring the appropriate DSU/CSU converter.

Modems

Connection to the Internet is facilitated by modems. MODEMs (an acronym for MOdulator-DEModulator) convert digital data supplied by your computer to a modulated analog waveform that can be transmitted over the phoneline. Similarly, they accept modulated analog waveforms from the phoneline and convert them to digital information comprehensible to your local PC.

MODEM SPEEDS

2400 bps

Very slow. Only usable for text (i.e., e-mail).

9600 bps, 14.4 kpbs, 28.8, 33.6 kpbs
Minimum speed for accessing graphics, Web browsing, FTPing, etc. is 9600. Obviously, the faster the better.

Theoretically, 28.8/33.6 kpbs modems will transmit data at 28,8000 or 33,600 bits per second under ideal phone line conditions, and by using data compression they can achieve an even higher rate on compressible files. This, however, is never the case.

INTERNAL VS. EXTERNAL MODEMS

Internal modems are on a card that plugs into your PC's bus, contain their own serial port onboard, and use your PC's power supply.

Internal Modems
- Install in slot, and can therefore be more difficult to install and configure
- Are generally less expensive due to no case or power supply
- No cables to get knocked loose
- Require no desktop space
- Do not require a 16550A serial card and serial cable

External modems
External modems are normally self-contained in their own case, have a separate power supply, and connect to your computer via a serial cable to one of the serial ports on the back of your PC.
- Easy installation
- Easy to switch to another computer
- Generally incorporate panel of lights, LEDs or an LCD to display information about the current session
- Require external power supply with transformer which is bulky and clumsy
- Requires checking the UART chip

MODEM TERMINOLOGY

BPS, Baud, CPS
Baud. named after the 19th century French inventor Baudot, it originally referred to the speed a telegrapher could send Morse Code. It later came to mean the number of times per second that a signal changes state. Bits per second and Baud are not the same thing. Phase shifting and other modulation and data handling techniques allow more than one bit to be transmitted with each baud in high speed modems—that is 28,800 bits per second can be transmitted using a substantially lower baud rate (most modems use a baud rate of about 1800 to 2000—roughly the middle of the telephone system bandwidth).

BPS. Bits per second. A bit is a single binary piece of information represented by a 0 or a 1. A normal byte or character contains 8 bits. Start and Stop bits (required for asynchronous data stream) are sent and received by the corresponding serial port's UARTs. Note however, that implementation of certain types of error control send information synchronously, removing the start and stop bits.

CPS. Characters per second

Data Compression and DTE Speed

DCE Speed (Data Communications Equipment Speed). The line speed at which your modem talks to another modem.

DTE Speed (Data Terminal Equipment Speed). The speed at which your modem communicates with your PC.

Modern high-speed modems have the ability to compress the data they transmit. Consequently, uncompressed data should be fed from your PC to your modem at a higher rate than the modem can send the compressed data over the phone line. It is recommended that you set your computer-to-modem DTE speed higher than the maximum connect rate you expect your modem to achieve. Note: High speed modems generally are not able to further compress files which are already compressed (i.e., .zip, .jpg, and .gif files)

Modem Initialization Strings

Modem init. strings are commands that are sent to the modem. A very common Dial command is : "ATDT". It breaks down as follows: "AT" is a required command prefix that begins all commands, "D" dials the specified phone number. If "D" is followed by a "P" that signifies pulse or rotary dial. If it is followed by a "T" that signifies Tone dial. You may note that your hangup command is "+++ATH". The command "+++" escapes to an online-command mode. "AT" is the required command prefix and "H" controls the On/Off hook. A "0" after the "H" would signify Hang up (go on hook). A "1" after the "H" signifies "go off hook". In this case there is no number following "H". If you do not type a number, "0" is assumed.

The manual which comes with your modem generally has a default setting, or specifies what type of modem string you should type in. For instance, your modem manual may tell you to enter "AT&F1" ("AT" being the command prefix, "&F1" loading a read-only (non-programmable) factory configuration of hardware flow control, which includes a fixed serial port rate and full result codes).

These are very basic commands. Your manual should also list a complete Command Summary list. If you have trouble connecting, contact your Internet Service Provider, prepared with your modem commands. They might suggest adding or removing commands from the initialization.

In the meantime, note that your maximum command length is 60 characters. The modem will not count the AT prefix, carriage returns or spaces. Your commands can be typed in either upper or lower case, but not in a combination.

Hardware

Another consideration in connecting to the Internet is the Hardware to use.

PROCESSORS

80286

These processors are too slow to run Windows software, and consequently cannot use Windows PPP software such as Netscape, Eudora, Free Agent, WSFTP, etc. Non-windows applications can be run (i.e., Pine, Lynx, gopher, etc.)

80386SX

Windows software can run (hence Windows ppp software can be used), but it is extremely slow.

80486 or Pentium

Ideal performance for all Internet services.

Note: on the Macintosh platform, the minimum processor recommended is 68030.

DISK SPACE

Some Internet activities require a significant amount of disk storage. If you plan to FTP applications and files, download graphics, sound clips and video, or subscribe to a high volume of lists, you will want to have a significant amount of available disk space. Internet software itself tends to require very little disk space.

SERIAL COMMUNICATIONS

Check the communications chip (UART—Universal Asynchronous Receiver—Transmitter) in your computer. All serial devices, such as serial modems, use a UART interface chip or emulate a UART, to communicate with your pc. External modems connect to your PC using a serial cable hooked to one of your PC's UART-based serial ports, while internal modems have a UART-based serial port (or emulator) on board.

8250

Too slow to be running Windows Internet Software.

16550

Can run Windows software, however on many systems Windows may not be able to fetch characters from the UART fast enough to prevent the next incoming character from overwriting the single-character buffer, resulting in a "comm overrun" or "CRC" error.

16550A, 16550AF or 16550AFN

Ideal for Windows Internet software (external modems will not run faster than 9600bps if your UART is less than 16550A.)

Note: To determine if you have a 16550 UART, run MSD.EXE, the Microsoft diagnostic program which comes with current releases of both DOS and Windows. Purchasing a new serial card which contains a 16550 UART will cost roughly $30.

COM PORTS

The Windows control panel allows you to set COM port speeds. However, virtually all communication programs ignore those settings. The "Advanced" settings controlling port addresses and IRQs are important. Be careful if/when making changes to those.

Whether you have an external or internal modem, many will suggest that you put your modem on COM2 if possible (as opposed to COM1) because COM2 has a higher interrupt priority than COM1. This can be of significance if you have a slower system or use a serial mouse. Many modems come with a factory default configuration of COM2. You can choose whichever port you wish.

Software

There are a variety of software packages that are necessary for working on the Internet. These packages will vary, depending on the platform you are working in (DOS, Windows, and Macintosh).

ANTIVIRUS SOFTWARE

The Internet is largely unprotected from viruses. It is necessary to use up-to-date software that can guard against the latest viruses. Especially, if you are downloading files. Commonly used packages include:
- Norton Anti-Virus
- Intel VirusProtect (for LANS)
- SAM (for Macintosh)

BACKUP SOFTWARE

Restoring files may be a necessary procedure following a virus attack, or in the event that you accidentally overwrite files. Commonly used packages include:
- Norton Backup
- FastBack

COMMUNICATIONS SOFTWARE

Communications software will allow you to configure your modem, store phone numbers for various service providers/BBS, handles dialing, and handles the transmission of data back and forth. There are many terminal programs available. Commonly used packages include:
- BCOM (DOS/Windows)
- Terminal (Windows)
- Zterm (Macintosh)

INTERNET SOFTWARE

Many Internet programs are freeware or shareware. They can be obtained directly from your Internet Service Provider, either by downloading or on a floppy. Generally, you receive a self-extracting bundle of files, which automatically configures your system with the appropriate IP Addresses and phone numbers, as well as configuring optimal settings for MTU (Maximum Transport Unit, or the number of packets that can be sent at a time), TCP RWIN (which determines the number of receivable packets), etc. This bundle generally includes a variety of Internet programs (i.e., a web browser, e-mail, ftp and news programs, etc.)

These bundles, however, often do not include the latest version of these applications. Consequently, it is recommended that once you are online you check some of the FTP sites, which provide reviews and evaluations of the software as well as links to FTP sites to automatically download the programs to your computer.

Recommended FTP Sites for Internet Software:

- Tucows: http://www.tucows.com/index.html
- C|Net Shareware: http://www.shareware.com
- Strouds: http://cws.wilmington.net

More complete versions of many of these applications can be purchased.

TCP/IP

For a slip/ppp connection you will need a TCP/IP software program.

- Trumpet Winsock (Windows)
- Config PPP/Mac TCP (Macintosh)

E-Mail Programs

- Pine (Text-based—UNIX)
- Eudora (Windows/Macintosh)
- Pegasus (DOS or Windows)
- E-Mail on an office LAN (DOS or Windows)
- Windows base: Gateway Software available for most networks

Web Browsers

- Lynx (DOS)
- Netscape (Windows/Macintosh)
- NCSA Mosaic (Windows/Macintosh)

Newsreaders

- Netscape (WWW Browser)
- Free Agent (graphical)
- NetXpress (graphical)
- Tin (text)
- Nn (text)
- Newswatcher (Macintosh)

Telnet

- NetTerm (Windows)
- Ewan Telnet (Windows)
- NCSA Telnet (Macintosh)
- TN3270 (Macintosh)

FTP

- WSFTP (Windows)
- Fetch (Macintosh)
- Anarchie (Macintosh)

CONFIGURING YOUR HELPER APPLICATIONS

As multi-media and other types of files and procedures become more prevalent on the World Wide Web, it is necessary to have an understanding of Helper Applications. Helper Applications are programs that are configured to be launched from your Web Browser. When you click on a specific type of file (video, audio, Real Audio, etc.) to play (or download), the appropriate application is launched to run the file or program. All the FTP sites listed above under Internet Software allow you to download a variety of applications.

To download an application, go to the FTP site and look under the category you wish. Read the reviews. Make sure that they are compatible with your web browser and note the type of files they run. For example, to run video files, you generally need a viewer that can play QuickTime movies. Some applications can play both QuickTime and MPEG files (these files can have the following extensions: .mov, .qt, .vid, .mpeg, .mpe, .mpg).

When you click on the file to download it your browser will request a disk and directory to which it should store the file. It is a good idea to create a separate directory to which downloaded files can be stored.

Downloaded files are generally compressed and must be extracted. Compressed files on the IBM will have either an .exe or a .zip extension. If it has an extension of .exe it is executable or self-extracting. Double-click on the file in the File Manager or simply enter the filename at the DOS prompt. It will automatically extract itself.

If it has a .zip extension you must run PKUnzip to open it. (Note: If you do not have PKZip/PKUnzip you can download it from any of the FTP sites. It will download as a self-extracting file.) To open the zipped file, simply type "pkunzip <filename.zip>" at the DOS prompt. If you would like for it to unzip into another directory, you can type "pkunzip <filename.zip> Disk:\directory."

Compressed files on the Macintosh generally have the following extensions: .hqx, .sit, sea. A file with a ".sea" extension is a self-extracting file. Simply double-click on it and specify the disk and folder to which it should be uncompressed. ".sit" and "hqx" files with need a program like Stuff It Expander for decompression. Simply drag and drop the compressed file onto Stuff It.

Once the application has been decompressed, open your Web Browser. Locate your browser's preferences and locate the controls for Helper Applications. Select the Mime Type and appropriate Extensions for the files you wish to run from your browser. (For example, for Video, select Mime Type: "Video/QuickTime." It will have the extensions .qt, .vid, and .mov listed). Click on the Browse button and locate the player you downloaded. Turn "Launch Application" on and click on "Okay."

Access Providers

One of the most important decisions you will make in connecting to the Internet is who should be your provider.

COMMERCIAL ONLINE SERVICES

Commercial Online Services such as CompuServe, Prodigy, America Online, etc. were the primary destination of the modem user who wanted to tap into extensive text databases, make computerized airline reservations, retrieve stock quotes, or join worldwide discussion groups before the Internet became a viable option. When you dial into a commercial online service you generally connect directly to their mainframe, using whatever features are made available to its members. Until recently, these commercial services were a world unto themselves. This, however, is changing as the idea of Internet access increases in popularity. All of the commercial services have set up gateways of one kind or another to the Internet, and many allow you access to the World Wide Web.

Note: The connect rates of Commercial Online Services tend to be quite high, so they are not necessarily a cost-efficient way of getting on the Internet. In many respects, they are easier to set up (with a single quick installation procedure that installs all software and also establishes a login name and password). However, you may not have much flexibility in terms of the software you wish to run. Major Commercial services currently include: America Online, CompuServe, Prodigy, Microsoft Network and Delphi.

INTERNET SERVICE PROVIDERS

In general, Internet Service Providers provide access to the internet directly, without many of the "frills" of a commercial service, and are consequently less expensive (for instance, it is unlikely that you will find forums and chat rooms with many ISPs). Still, many Internet Service Providers attempt to make getting started on the Internet easy, by sending you (or providing through FTP/Download) the software which may automatically set your system up for you. Because of the Internet's explosion in terms of popularity, many ISPs are having trouble keeping up with the growth, and are being accused of promising more than they can deliver. Some good providers include: Interport, IGC, AlterNet, NYSERNet, Panix, Echo.

Technical Support

There are many ways to locate the technical support you need to work on the Internet. These include:
- Look for and use FAQs
- Subscribe to a support Newsgroup or Mailing List
- Explore the Web for sites with helpful, up-to-date information
- Your Internet Provider's help desk or bulletin board
- Your computer or LAN maintenance consultant
- knowledgeable friends and colleagues
- Hand-On training at the Internet Center for Nonprofits of the Fund for the City of New York

Costs

DIRECT PHONE LINE ACCESS

Commercial Online Services
- AOL: $19.95 for unlimited access
- Compuserve: $8.95 for first 5 hours/month, additional hourly rates depend on the premium service accessed
- Handsnet: $35/month plus $5–$10/hour after 2 hours

Internet Service Providers: PPP Account
- Generally between $20–$30/month.
- Usually includes Internet software packages (i.e., Netscape, Eudora, Free Agent, etc.)
- Usually includes 5 MB of hard disk space (sometimes less, sometimes up to 10 MB)
- Number of hours varies: some provide 40 hours of primetime usage, unlimited usage during non-prime hours, etc.

Line Costs/Local Usage Charges
- Single Phone Line Installation fee: $200
- Average Monthly Usage: $50–$75/month

Modem
- One Time purchase: $75–$200

Software
- Communications Software: $0–$125
- Virus Protection Software: $0–$150
- Internet Software: $0–$100

DEDICATED INTERNET CONNECTIONS

One-Time Costs for Equipment (depending on Provider)
- Router from LAN to Internet Provider: $4,000–$7,000
- High-speed digital modem device (connects the Telco channel to router): $2,000

Telephone Company provider of line to network connection (cost varies based on type of line):
- 56K Line: $400–$800/Month
- T1 Line (1.45mbps): $1,000/Month
- T3 Line (45 mbps): $9,000/Month

APPENDIX C

Bibliography: Grantseeking on the Internet

The following reading list was selected from the Foundation Center's bibliographic database, available to search on our Web site as the *Literature of the Nonprofit Sector Online.* Be sure to check *LNPS Online* <http://www.fdncenter.org/onlib/lnps/index.html> regularly to keep abreast of new publications. Simply input the term "internet" from the subject list.

Allen, Nick, Mal Warwick, and Michael Stein, eds. *Fundraising on the Internet: Recruiting and Renewing Donors Online.* Berkeley, CA.: Strathmoor Press, 1996.
> Focuses on how nonprofits can acquire new donors through the Internet. Topics discussed include online tools, translating direct mail and telephone fundraising techniques to an electronic medium, fundraising opportunities online, and useful Web sites for fundraisers. Provides a glossary of Internet terms.

Corson-Finnerty, Adam and Laura Blanchard. *Fundraising and Friend-Raising on the Web.* Chicago, IL: American Library Association, 1998.
> Intended for library administrators, but with approaches that will succeed for any nonprofit, the book offers advice on such topics as developing and measuring the impact of a Web site; creating donor recognition in cyberspace; delivering your site directly to potential donors on disk or CD-ROM; fundraising with digital cash. Throughout, examples currently on the Web are provided. A CD-ROM disk is included.

Bergan, Helen. *Where the Information Is: A Guide to Electronic Research for Nonprofit Organizations.* Alexandria, VA: BioGuide Press, 1996.
    Bergan explains in nontechnical language how electronic resources can help nonprofit organizations identify and cultivate potential donors, find grant funding, and manage daily operations. Chapters cover CD-ROMs, DIALOG, CompuServe, America Online, e-mail, using the Internet, and Internet resources of interest for nonprofits. Provides sections that list the names and addresses of vendors and groups that are involved in making electronic technology available for use by nonprofit organizations. Includes bibliography and index.

Council on Foundations. *Grantmakers Technology Report.* Washington, DC: Council on Foundations, 1997.
    Presents data from the first survey of grantmakers by the Council on Foundations regarding the communications and computing technologies used by the 771 respondents. Information is organized by grantmaker type. Within each grantmaker type, data answers questions related to staffing, technology usage, technology planning, hardware and operating/network software, applications software, Internet access, and fax and voice systems.

DeAngelis, James, ed. *The Grantseeker's Handbook of Essential Internet Sites.* 2nd ed. Alexandria, VA: Capitol Publications, 1997.
    Contains descriptions of more than 500 Internet sites of interest to grantseekers. Each description includes the resource's address and login or subscription instructions where applicable. Sites are arranged in the following categories: corporations, foundations and associations, government, research, and resources. Includes indexes by site name, type of program, and major giving category for corporations and foundations.

Demko, Paul. "Free Space in Cyberspace." Chronicle of Philanthropy 9 (12 June 1997): 47–9.
    Discusses the new ways that charities benefit from increased online exposure as for-profit World Wide Web publishers donate advertising space.

Demko, Paul, and Domenica Marchetti. "High-Tech Fundraising: Boon or Bane?" Chronicle of Philanthropy 8 (25 January 1996): 21, 23.
    Describes how electronic pledge cards, automated telephone systems, and benefit concerts on the Internet are transforming the way employee fundraising campaigns are conducted.

Demko, Paul. "On-Line Solicitors: Tangled Web". *Chronicle of Philanthropy* 10 (29 January 1998) p. 23–4.
    Discusses the Web sites that are raising money for charities through the Internet, and the subsequent questions about whether they should be regulated.

Dickey, Marilyn. "E-mailing for Dollars". *Chronicle of Philanthropy* 10 (10 September 1998). p. 23–4.

    Recounts successful fundraising efforts accomplished through various uses of e-mail.

Dickey, Marilyn. "Charities' World-Wide Wait." Chronicle of Philanthropy 9 (7 August 1997): 23–5.

    Charities using Web sites to attract donations remain optimistic about the fundraising potential of cyberspace, even though hitherto only small sums have been collected online. It appears the public does not yet feel that giving out credit card information online is safe. Another explanation might be that donating on the Web presumes a self-motivated surfer, who seeks out a charity and volunteers a pledge. Charities have learned that direct and simple language works better online, that surfers dislike scrolling down multiple screens, that site design needs to encourage participation, that site content ought to be changed often.

Dickey, Marilyn. "Fund Raisers Turn to the Internet: They Find Quick, Up-to-Date Access to Information That Helps Them Locate Potential Grant Makers." Chronicle of Philanthropy 9 (1 May 1997): 23–4.

    Includes a list with URLs and descriptions of Internet resources for grantseekers.

Eckstein, Richard M., ed. *Directory of Computer and High Technology Grants*. 3rd ed. Loxahatchee, FL:Research Grant Guides, 1996.

    Provides information on more than 500 foundations and corporations that grant funds or donate equipment to nonprofit organizations seeking computers, software, and related technology. Includes four essays: "A Grant Seeker's Guide to the Internet: Revised and Revisited" by Andrew J. Grant and Suzy D. Sonenberg; "Proposal Writing Basics" by Andrew J. Grant; "Computers and the Nonprofit Organizations" by Jon Rosen; and "Take Nothing for Granted" by Chris Petersen. Indexed by name and subject.

Ensman, Richard G., Jr. "Turn Small Shops into Big Shops Via the Internet." Fund Raising Management 28 (June 1997): 18–9.

Foundation Center. *National Guide to Funding for Information Technology*. Edited by Elizabeth H. Rich and Rebecca MacLean. New York , NY: Foundation Center, 1997.

    Provides information on 320 grantmaking foundations, thirty-six direct corporate giving programs, and forty-nine public charities that have shown a substantial interest in information technology, either as part of their stated fields of interest or through actual grants of $10,000 or more reported in the last year of record. Selected grants for information technology are listed for 307 of the entries.

Frenza, JP. and Leslie Hoffman. "Organizing Your Web Site Content." Nonprofit World 15 (November–December 1997): 14–6.
    Provides tips on how to arrange Web site content in a way that will make sense for users' needs.

Frenza, JP, and Leslie Hoffman. "So You Want a Web Site, Now What: There Is One Big Decision That Will Set the Stage for Everything Else." Nonprofit World 15 (September–October 1997): 21–4.
    Provides advice for choosing the most important aspect of Web page design - content.

Green, Marc. "Fundraising in Cyberspace." Grantsmanship Center Magazine (Fall 1995): 21–6.
    Describes innovative ways that several nonprofits are using the Internet for fundraising purposes. Identifies Web sites about fundraising.

Grobman, Gary M. and Gary B. Grant. *The Non-Profit Internet Handbook.* Harrisburg, PA: White Hat Communications, 1998.
    Comprehensive information about the uses of the Internet for nonprofits, devoting one chapter to fundraising. Includes case studies, issues to consider, and citations and reviews of numerous Web sites.

King, Karen N. and Julia K. Nims. "Yes, the Internet Sounds Great, But is it Really for Us?" *Nonprofit World* 16 (March–April 1998) p. 5–8.
    Details the value of the Internet, specifically for small nonprofits. Lists URLs for Web sites specifically geared to the interests of nonprofits.

Lake, Howard. *Direct Connection's Guide to Fundraising on the Internet.* UK: Aurelain Information Ltd. 1996.
    British guide to fundraising on the Internet. Covers such topics as how to get on the Internet, Internet demographics, building a fundraising World Wide Web site, and finding fundraising information on the Internet. Provides a directory of Internet resources for fundraisers. Includes a glossary, bibliography, and index.

Lane, Carole A. Naked in Cyberspace: *How to Find Personal Information Online.* Edited by Helen Burwell and Owen B. Davies. Somerville, MA: Pemberton Press Books, 1997.
    One chapter on prospect research indicates how to use public records, telephone directory databases, motor vehicle records, news and biographical database to search for wealthy prospects.

Moore, Jennifer. "Donor Details on the Net: The Internet Has a Wealth of Information about Potential Contributors, But Finding the Data Is Not Easy." Chronicle of Philanthropy 7 (10 August 1995): 29, 31.
    Lists sources of information on the Internet for prospect researchers. A side article gives the sources' uniform resource locators (URLs).

Moran, Amanda M., ed.*CyberHound's Guide to Associations and Nonprofit Organizations on the Internet*. Detroit, MI: Gale Research, 1997.
  Provides entries for 2,500 Web sites of associations and other nonprofit organizations. Entries contain the Uniform Resource Locator (URL); site description; updating frequency; site establishment date; geographic area and time span covered; language; target audience; contact information; and ratings of site content, design, and technical merit. Includes bibliography, glossary of Internet terms, and indexes of organization name, contact person, and subject.

Needleman, Ted. "Untangling the Web: A Consultant in Your Personal Computer." NonProfit Times 11 (November 1997): 60, 63.

Notess, Greg R. *Government Information on the Internet*. Lanham, MD: Bernan Press, 1997.
  Covers more than 1,200 U.S. government Internet resources. Organized into eighteen subject categories, and indexed by primary and alternative access URLs, Superintendent of Documents number, publication title, agency, and subject.

Pascolutti, Claire. "Born Again on the Internet." Charity 14 (September 1997): 34–5.
  Established by the Charities Aid Foundation (CAF) in 1995 and still funded by it, CharityNet continues to promote use of the World Wide Web by charities. CharityNet's Web site design, programs and aims are discussed.

Reisner, Neil. "Prospecting for On-Line Gold: Donor Research in Cyberspace." NonProfit Times 10 (October 1996): 1, 8, 11.
  Discusses how to conduct donor research on the Internet.

"Researching Funding Sources on the Web". *Grassroots Fundraising Journal* 17 (August 1998) p. 12–3.
  Provides Web addresses for foundation, corporate giving, government, individual donor, and business Internet sites.

Ryan, Ellen. "Making the Most of the World Wide Web: How the Internet Is Helping Prospect Researchers Find New Information and Share It with Colleagues." Currents 22 (June 1996): 50–1.
  Lists several World Wide Web sites that would be of use to prospect researchers.

Vimuktanon, Atisaya. "Non-Profits and the Internet." Fund Raising Management 28 (October 1997): 25–8.
  Explores the use of the Internet to increase visibility and fundraising for nonprofit organizations.

Zeff, Robbin Lee. *The Nonprofit Guide to the Internet*. Nonprofit Law, Finance and Management Series. New York, NY: John Wiley & Sons, 1996.

> Surveys the hardware and software needed to get online. Explores and gives examples of fundraising online. Discusses Internet legal issues for nonprofits. Includes a bibliography, glossary, and directory of nonprofit related Web sites and addresses.

APPENDIX D

Internet Glossary

ILC Glossary of Internet Terms

AND   (Advanced Digital Network)—Usually refers to a 56Kbps leased-line.

ADSL   (Asymmetric Digital Subscriber Line)—A method for moving data over regular phone lines. An ADSL circuit is much faster than a regular phone connection, and the wires coming into the subscriber's premises are the same (copper) wires used for regular phone service. An ADSL circuit must be configured to connect two specific locations, similar to a leased line.

   A commonly discussed configuration of ADSL would allow a subscriber to receive data (download) at speeds of up to 1.544 megabits (not megabytes) per second, and to send (upload) data at speeds of 128 kilobits per second. Thus the "Asymmetric" part of the acronym.

Another commonly discussed configuration would be symmetrical: 384 Kilobits per second in both directions. In theory ADSL allows download speeds of up to 9 megabits per second and upload speeds of up to 640 kilobits per second.

ADSL is often discussed as an alternative to ISDN, allowing higher speeds in cases where the connection is always to the same place.

See also: bit, bps, ISDN

Anonymous FTP　　*See:* FTP

Applet　　A small Java program that can be embedded in an HTML page. Applets differ from full-fledged Java applications in that they are not allowed to access certain resources on the local computer, such as files and serial devices (modems, printers, etc.), and are prohibited from communicating with most other computers across a network. The current rule is that an applet can only make an Internet connection to the computer from which the applet was sent.

See also: HTML, Java

Archie　　A tool (software) for finding files stored on anonymous FTP sites. You need to know the exact file name or a substring of it.

ARPANet　　(Advanced Research Projects Agency Network)—The precursor to the Internet. Developed in the late 60's and early 70's by the US Department of Defense as an experiment in wide-area-networking that would survive a nuclear war.

See also: Internet

ASCII　　(American Standard Code for Information Interchange)—This is the de facto world-wide standard for the code numbers used by computers to represent all the upper and lower-case Latin letters, numbers, punctuation, etc. There are 128 standard ASCII codes each of which can be represented by a 7 digit binary number: 0000000 through 1111111.

Backbone　　A high-speed line or series of connections that forms a major pathway within a network. The term is relative as a backbone in a small network will likely be much smaller than many non-backbone lines in a large network.

See also: Network

Bandwidth　　How much stuff you can send through a connection. Usually measured in bits-per-second. A full page of English text is about 16,000 bits. A fast modem can move about 15,000 bits in one second. Full-motion full-screen video would require roughly 10,000,000 bits-per-second, depending on compression.

See also: Bps, Bit, T-1

Baud   In common usage the baud rate of a modem is how many bits it can send or receive per second. Technically, baud is the number of times per second that the carrier signal shifts value—for example a 1200 bit-per-second modem actually runs at 300 baud, but it moves 4 bits per baud (4 x 300 = 1200 bits per second).
See also: Bit, Modem

BBS   (Bulletin Board System)—A computerized meeting and announcement system that allows people to carry on discussions, upload and download files, and make announcements without the people being connected to the computer at the same time. There are many thousands (millions?) of BBS's around the world, most are very small, running on a single IBM clone PC with 1 or 2 phone lines. Some are very large and the line between a BBS and a system like CompuServe gets crossed at some point, but it is not clearly drawn.

Binhex   (BINary HEXadecimal)—A method for converting non-text files (non-ASCII) into ASCII. This is needed because Internet e-mail can only handle ASCII.
See also: ASCII, MIME, UUENCODE Bit
(Binary DigIT)—A single digit number in base-2, in other words, either a 1 or a zero. The smallest unit of computerized data. Bandwidth is usually measured in bits-per-second.
See also: Bandwidth, Bps, Byte, Kilobyte, Megabyte

BITNET   (Because It's Time NETwork (or Because It's There NETwork))—A network of educational sites separate from the Internet, but e-mail is freely exchanged between BITNET and the Internet. Listservs, the most popular form of e-mail discussion groups, originated on BITNET. BITNET machines are usually mainframes running the VMS operating system, and the network is probably the only international network that is shrinking.

Bps   (Bits-Per-Second)—A measurement of how fast data is moved from one place to another. A 28.8 modem can move 28,800 bits per second.
See also: Bandwidth, Bit

Browser   A Client program (software) that is used to look at various kinds of Internet resources.
See also: Client, URL, WWW, Netscape, Mosaic, Home Page (or Homepage)

BTW   (By The Way)—A shorthand appended to a comment written in an online forum.
See also: IMHO, TTFN

Byte   A set of Bits that represent a single character. Usually there are 8 Bits in a Byte, sometimes more, depending on how the measurement is being made.
See also: Bit

Certificate   An issuer of Security Certificates used in SSL connections.
Authority   *See also:* Security Certificate, SSL

CGI   (Common Gateway Interface)—A set of rules that describe how a Web Server communicates with another piece of software on the same machine, and how the other piece of software (the "CGI program") talks to the web server. Any piece of software can be a CGI program if it handles input and output according to the CGI standard.

    Usually a CGI program is a small program that takes data from a web server and does something with it, like putting the content of a form into an e-mail message, or turning the data into a database query.

    You can often see that a CGI program is being used by seeing "cgi-bin" in a URL, but not always.
See also: cgi-bin, Web

cgi-bin   The most common name of a directory on a web server in which CGI programs are stored. The "bin" part of "cgi-bin" is a shorthand version of "binary," because once upon a time, most programs were refered to as "binaries." In real life, most programs found in cgi-bin directories are text files—scripts that are executed by binaries located elsewhere on the same machine.
See also: CGI

Client   A software program that is used to contact and obtain data from a Server software program on another computer, often across a great distance. Each Client program is designed to work with one or more specific kinds of Server programs, and each Server requires a specific kind of Client. A Web Browser is a specific kind of Client.
See also: Browser, Server

co-location   Most often used to refer to having a server that belongs to one person or group physically located on an Internet-connected network that belongs to another person or group. Usually this is done because the server owner wants their machine to be on a high-speed Internet connection and/or they do not want the security risks of having the server on thier own network.
See also: Internet, Server, Network

Cookie   The most common meaning of "Cookie" on the Internet refers to a piece of information sent by a Web Server to a Web Browser that the Browser software is expected to save and to send back to the Server whenever the browser makes additional requests from the Server.

Depending on the type of Cookie used, and the Browser's settings, the Browser may accept or not accept the Cookie, and may save the Cookie for either a short time or a long time. Cookies might contain information such as login or registration information, online "shopping cart" information, user preferences, etc.

When a Server receives a request from a Browser that includes a Cookie, the Server is able to use the information stored in the Cookie. For example, the Server might customize what is sent back to the user, or keep a log of particular user's requests.

Cookies are usually set to expire after a predetermined amount of time and are usually saved in memory until the Browser software is closed down, at which time they may be saved to disk if their "expire time" has not been reached.

Cookies do not read your hard drive and send your life story to the CIA, but they can be used to gather more information about a user than would be possible without them.

See also: Browser, Server

Cyberpunk Cyberpunk was originally a cultural sub-genre of science fiction taking place in a not-so-distant, dystopian, over-industrialized society. The term grew out of the work of William Gibson and Bruce Sterling and has evolved into a cultural label encompassing many different kinds of human, machine, and punk attitudes. It includes clothing and lifestyle choices as well.

See also: Cyberspace

Cyberspace Term originated by author William Gibson in his novel Neuromancer the word Cyberspace is currently used to describe the whole range of information resources available through computer networks.

Digerati The digital version of literati, it is a reference to a vague cloud of people seen to be knowledgeable, hip, or otherwise in-the-know in regards to the digital revolution.

Domain Name The unique name that identifies an Internet site. Domain Names always have 2 or more parts, separated by dots. The part on the left is the most specific, and the part on the right is the most general. A given machine may have more than one Domain Name but a given Domain Name points to only one machine. For example, the domain names: matisse.net, mail.matisse.net, and workshop.matisse.net can all refer to the same machine, but each domain name can refer to no more than one machine.

Usually, all of the machines on a given Network will have the same thing as the right-hand portion of their Domain Names (matisse.net in the examples above). It is also possible for a Domain Name to exist but not be connected to an actual machine. This is often done so that a group or business can have an Internet e-mail address without having to establish a real Internet site. In

these cases, some real Internet machine must handle the mail on behalf of the listed Domain Name.
See also: IP Number

E-mail   (Electronic Mail)—Messages, usually text, sent from one person to another via computer. E-mail can also be sent automatically to a large number of addresses (Mailing List).
See also: Listserv, Maillist

Ethernet   A very common method of networking computers in a LAN. Ethernet will handle about 10,000,000 bits-per-second and can be used with almost any kind of computer.
See also: Bandwidth, LAN

FAQ   (Frequently Asked Questions)—FAQs are documents that list and answer the most common questions on a particular subject. There are hundreds of FAQs on subjects as diverse as Pet Grooming and Cryptography. FAQs are usually written by people who have tired of answering the same question over and over.

FDDI   (Fiber Distributed Data Interface)—A standard for transmitting data on optical fiber cables at a rate of around 100,000,000 bits-per-second (10 times as fast as Ethernet, about twice as fast as T-3).
See also: Bandwidth, Ethernet, T-1, T-3

Finger   An Internet software tool for locating people on other Internet sites. Finger is also sometimes used to give access to non-personal information, but the most common use is to see if a person has an account at a particular Internet site. Many sites do not allow incoming Finger requests, but many do.

Fire Wall   A combination of hardware and software that separates a LAN into two or more parts for security purposes.
See also: Network, LAN

Flame   Originally, flame meant to carry forth in a passionate manner in the spirit of honorable debate. Flames most often involved the use of flowery language and flaming well was an art form. More recently flame has come to refer to any kind of derogatory comment no matter how witless or crude.
See also: Flame War

Flame War   When an online discussion degenerates into a series of personal attacks against the debators, rather than discussion of their positions. A heated exchange.
See also: Flame

FTP   (File Transfer Protocol)—A very common method of moving files between two Internet sites. FTP is a special way to login to another

Internet site for the purposes of retrieving and/or sending files. There are many Internet sites that have established publicly accessible repositories of material that can be obtained using FTP, by logging in using the account name anonymous, thus these sites are called anonymous ftp servers.

Gateway   The technical meaning is a hardware or software set-up that translates between two dissimilar protocols, for example Prodigy has a gateway that translates between its internal, proprietary e-mail format and Internet e-mail format. Another, sloppier meaning of gateway is to describe any mechanism for providing access to another system, e.g., AOL might be called a gateway to the Internet.

GIF   (Graphic Interchange Format)—A common format for image files, especially suitable for images containing large areas of the same color. GIF format files of simple images are often smaller than the same file would be if stored in JPEG format, but GIF format does not store photographic images as well as JPEG.
See also: JPEG

Gigabyte   1000 or 1024 Megabytes, depending on who is measuring.
See also: Byte, Megabyte

Gopher   A widely successful method of making menus of material available over the Internet. Gopher is a Client and Server style program, which requires that the user have a Gopher Client program. Although Gopher spread rapidly across the globe in only a couple of years, it has been largely supplanted by Hypertext, also known as WWW (World Wide Web). There are still thousands of Gopher Servers on the Internet and we can expect they will remain for a while.
See also: Client, Server, WWW, Hypertext

hit   As used in reference to the World Wide Web, hit means a single request from a web browser for a single item from a web server; thus in order for a web browser to display a page that contains 3 graphics, 4 "hits" would occur at the server: 1 for the HTML page, and one for each of the 3 graphics.

"Hits" are often used as a very rough measure of load on a server, e.g., "Our server has been getting 300,000 hits per month." Because each hit can represent anything from a request for a tiny document (or even a request for a missing document) all the way to a request that requires some significant extra processing (such as a complex search request), the actual load on a machine from 1 hit is almost impossible to define.

Home Page (or Homepage)   Several meanings. Originally, the web page that your browser is set to use when it starts up. The more common meaning refers to the main web page for a business, organization, person or simply the main page out of a collection of web pages, e.g., "Check out so-and-so's new Home Page."

Another sloppier use of the term refers to practically any web page as a "homepage," e.g., "That web site has 65 homepages and none of them are interesting."
See also: Browser, Web

Host   Any computer on a network that is a repository for services available to other computers on the network. It is quite common to have one host machine provide several services, such as WWW and USENET.
See also: Node, Network

HTML   (HyperText Markup Language)—The coding language used to create Hypertext documents for use on the World Wide Web. HTML looks a lot like old-fashioned typesetting code, where you surround a block of text with codes that indicate how it should appear, additionally, in HTML you can specify that a block of text, or a word, is linked to another file on the Internet. HTML files are meant to be viewed using a World Wide Web Client Program, such as Netscape or Mosaic.
See also: Client, Server, WWW

HTTP   (HyperText Transport Protocol)—The protocol for moving hypertext files across the Internet. Requires a HTTP client program on one end, and an HTTP server program on the other end. HTTP is the most important protocol used in the World Wide Web (WWW).
See also: Client, Server, WWW

Hypertext   Generally, any text that contains links to other documents—words or phrases in the document that can be chosen by a reader and which cause another document to be retrieved and displayed.

IMHO   (In My Humble Opinion)—A shorthand appended to a comment written in an online forum, IMHO indicates that the writer is aware that they are expressing a debatable view, probably on a subject already under discussion. One of may such shorthands in common use online, especially in discussion forums.
See also: TTFN, BTW

Internet   (Upper case I) The vast collection of inter-connected networks that all use the TCP/IP protocols and that evolved from the ARPANET of the late 60's and early 70's. As of July 1995 he Internet connected roughly 60,000 independent networks into a vast global internet.
See also: internet

internet (Lower case i) Any time you connect 2 or more networks together, you have an internet—as in inter-national or inter-state.
See also: Internet, Network

Intranet A private network inside a company or organization that uses the same kinds of software that you would find on the public Internet, but that is only for internal use.

As the Internet has become more popular many of the tools used on the Internet are being used in private networks, for example, many companies have web servers that are available only to employees.

Note that an Intranet may not actually be an internet—it may simply be a network.
See also: internet, Internet, Network

IP Number (Internet Protocol Number)—Sometimes called a dotted quad. A unique number consisting of 4 parts separated by dots, e.g., 165.113.245.2

Every machine that is on the Internet has a unique IP number—if a machine does not have an IP number, it is not really on the Internet. Most machines also have one or more Domain Names that are easier for people to remember.
See also: Domain Name, Internet, TCP/IP

IRC (Internet Relay Chat)—Basically a huge multi-user live chat facility. There are a number of major IRC servers around the world which are linked to each other. Anyone can create a channel and anything that anyone types in a given channel is seen by all others in the channel. Private channels can (and are) created for multi-person conference calls.

ISDN (Integrated Services Digital Network)—Basically a way to move more data over existing regular phone lines. ISDN is rapidly becoming available to much of the USA and in most markets it is priced very comparably to standard analog phone circuits. It can provide speeds of roughly 128,000 bits-per-second over regular phone lines. In practice, most people will be limited to 56,000 or 64,000 bits-per-second.

ISP (Internet Service Provider)—An institution that provides access to the Internet in some form, usually for money.
See also: Internet

Java Java is a network-oriented programming language invented by Sun Microsystems that is specifically designed for writing programs that can be safely downloaded to your computer through the Internet and immediately run without fear of viruses or other harm to your computer or files. Using small Java programs (called "Applets"), Web pages can include functions such as animations, calculators, and other fancy tricks.

We can expect to see a huge variety of features added to the Web using Java, since you can write a Java program to do almost anything a regular computer program can do, and then include that Java program in a Web page.
See also: Applet

JDK   (Java Development Kit)—A software development package from Sun Microsystems that implements the basic set of tools needed to write, test and debug Java applications and applets.
See also: Applet, Java

JPEG   (Joint Photographic Experts Group)—JPEG is most commonly mentioned as a format for image files. JPEG format is preferred to the GIF format for photographic images as opposed to line art or simple logo art.
See also: GIF

Kilobyte   A thousand bytes. Actually, usually 1024 (2^{10}) bytes.
See also: Byte, Bit

LAN   (Local Area Network)—A computer network limited to the immediate area, usually the same building or floor of a building.
See also: Ethernet

Leased-line   Refers to a phone line that is rented for exclusive 24-hour, 7-days-a-week use from your location to another location. The highest speed data connections require a leased line.
See also: T-1, T-3

Listserv®   The most common kind of maillist, "Listserv" is a registered trademark of L-Soft International, Inc. Listservs originated on BITNET but they are now common on the Internet.
See also: BITNET, E-mail, Maillist

Login   Noun or a verb. Noun: The account name used to gain access to a computer system. Not a secret (contrast with Password). Verb: The act of entering into a computer system, e.g., Login to the WELL and then go to the GBN conference.
See also: Password

Maillist   (or Mailing List) A (usually automated) system that allows people to send e-mail to one address, whereupon their message is copied and sent to all of the other subscribers to the maillist. In this way, people who have many different kinds of e-mail access can participate in discussions together.

Megabyte   A million bytes. Actually, technically, 1024 kilobytes.
See also: Byte, Bit, Kilobyte

MIME   (Multipurpose Internet Mail Extensions)—The standard for attaching non-text files to standard Internet mail messages. Non-text files include graphics, spreadsheets, formatted word-processor documents, sound files, etc.

An email program is said to be MIME Compliant if it can both send and receive files using the MIME standard.

When non-text files are sent using the MIME standard they are converted (encoded) into text—although the resulting text is not really readable.

Generally speaking the MIME standard is a way of specifying both the type of file being sent (e.g., a QuicktimeÖ video file), and the method that should be used to turn it back into its original form. Besides email software, the MIME standard is also universally used by Web Servers to identify the files they are sending to Web Clients, in this way new file formats can be accommodated simply by updating the Browsers' list of pairs of MIME-Types and appropriate software for handling each type.
See also: Browser, Client, Server, Binhex, UUENCODE

Mirror   Generally speaking, "to mirror" is to maintain an exact copy of something. Probably the most common use of the term on the Internet refers to ômirror sitesö which are web sites, or FTP sites that maintain exact copies of material originated at another location, usually in order to provide more widespread access to the resource.

Another common use of the term "mirror" refers to an arrangement where information is written to more than one hard disk simultaneously, so that if one disk fails, the computer keeps on working without losing anything.
See also: FTP, Web

Modem   (Modulator, DEModulator)—A device that you connect to your computer and to a phone line, that allows the computer to talk to other computers through the phone system. Basically, modems do for computers what a telephone does for humans.

MOO   (Mud, Object Oriented)—One of several kinds of multi-user role-playing environments, so far only text-based.
See also: MUD, MUSE

Mosaic   The first WWW browser that was available for the Macintosh, Windows, and UNIX all with the same interface. Mosaic really started the popularity of the Web. The source-code to Mosaic has been licensed by several companies and there are several other pieces of software as good or better than Mosaic, most notably, Netscape.
See also: Browser, Client, WWW

MUD   (Multi-User Dungeon or Dimension)—A (usually text-based) multi-user simulation environment. Some are purely for fun and

flirting, others are used for serious software development, or education purposes and all that lies in between. A significant feature of most MUDs is that users can create things that stay after they leave and which other users can interact with in their absence, thus allowing a world to be built gradually and collectively.
See also: MOO, MUSE

MUSE (Multi-User Simulated Environment)—One kind of MUD—usually with little or no violence.
See also: MOO, MUD

Netiquette The etiquette on the Internet.
See also: Internet

Netizen Derived from the term citizen, referring to a citizen of the Internet, or someone who uses networked resources. The term connotes civic responsibility and participation.
See also: Internet

Netscape A WWW Browser and the name of a company. The Netscape (tm) browser was originally based on the Mosaic program developed at the National Center for Supercomputing Applications (NCSA).

Netscape has grown in features rapidly and is widely recognized as the best and most popular web browser. Netscape corporation also produces web server software. Netscape provided major improvements in speed and interface over other browsers, and has also engendered debate by creating new elements for the HTML language used by Web pages—but the Netscape extensions to HTML are not universally supported.

The main author of Netscape, Mark Andreessen, was hired away from the NCSA by Jim Clark, and they founded a company called Mosaic Communications and soon changed the name to Netscape Communications Corporation.
See also: Browser, Mosaic, Server, WWW

Network Any time you connect 2 or more computers together so that they can share resources, you have a computer network. Connect 2 or more networks together and you have an internet.
See also: internet, Internet, Intranet

Newsgroup The name for discussion groups on USENET.
See also: USENET

NIC (Networked Information Center)—Generally, any office that handles information for a network. The most famous of these on the Internet is the InterNIC, which is where new domain names are registered.

Another definition: NIC also refers to Network Interface Card which plugs into a computer and dapts the network interface to the

appropriate standard. ISA, PCI, and PCMCIA cards are all
examples of NICs.

NNTP   (Network News Transport Protocol)—The protocol used by client
and server software to carry USENET postings back and forth over
a TCP/IP network. If you are using any of the more common
software such as Netscape, Nuntius, Internet Explorer, etc. to
participate in newsgroups then you are benefiting from an NNTP
connection.
See also: Newsgroup, TCP/IP, USENET

Node   Any single computer connected to a network.
See also: Network, Internet, internet

Packet   The method used to move data around on the Internet. In packet
Switching   switching, all the data coming out of a machine is broken up into
chunks, each chunk has the address of where it came from and
where it is going. This enables chunks of data from many different
sources to co-mingle on the same lines, and be sorted and directed
to different routes by special machines along the way. This way
many people can use the same lines at the same time.

Password   A code used to gain access to a locked system. Good passwords
contain letters and non-letters and are not simple combinations
such as virtue7. A good password might be: Hot$1-6.
See also: Login

Plug-in   A (usually small) piece of software that adds features to a larger
piece of software. Common examples are plug-ins for the Netscape
browser and web server. Adobe Photoshop also uses plug-ins.
     The idea behind plug-in's is that a small piece of software is
loaded into memory by the larger program, adding a new feature,
and that users need only install the few plug-ins that they need, out
of a much larger pool of possibilities. Plug-ins are usually created
by people other than the publishers of the software the plug-in
works with.

POP   (Point of Presence, also Post Office Protocol)—Two commonly
used meanings: Point of Presence and Post Office Protocol. A
Point of Presence usually means a city or location where a network
can be connected to, often with dial up phone lines. So if an
Internet company says they will soon have a POP in Belgrade, it
means that they will soon have a local phone number in Belgrade
and/or a place where leased lines can connect to their network.
     A second meaning, Post Office Protocol refers to the way e-mail
software such as Eudora gets mail from a mail server. When you
obtain a SLIP, PPP, or shell account you almost always get a POP
account with it, and it is this POP account that you tell your e-mail
software to use to get your mail.
See also: SLIP, PPP

Port

3 meanings. First and most generally, a place where information goes into or out of a computer, or both. E.g., the serial port on a personal computer is where a modem would be connected.

On the Internet port often refers to a number that is part of a URL, appearing after a colon (:) right after the domain name. Every service on an Internet server listens on a particular port number on that server. Most services have standard port numbers, e.g., Web servers normally listen on port 80. Services can also listen on non-standard ports, in which case the port number must be specified in a URL when accessing the server, so you might see a URL of the form: gopher://peg.cwis.uci.edu:7000/ shows a gopher server running on a non-standard port (the standard gopher port is 70).

Finally, port also refers to translating a piece of software to bring it from one type of computer system to another, e.g., to translate a Windows program so that is will run on a Macintosh.
See also: Domain Name, Server, URL

Posting

A single message entered into a network communications system. E.g., A single message posted to a newsgroup or message board.
See also: Newsgroup

PPP

(Point to Point Protocol)—Most well known as a protocol that allows a computer to use a regular telephone line and a modem to make TCP/IP connections and thus be really and truly on the Internet.
See also: IP Number, Internet, SLIP, TCP/IP

PSTN

(Public Switched Telephone Network)—The regular old-fashioned telephone system.

RFC

(Request For Comments)—The name of the result and the process for creating a standard on the Internet. New standards are proposed and published on line, as a Request For Comments. The Internet Engineering Task Force is a consensus-building body that facilitates discussion, and eventually a new standard is established, but the reference number/name for the standard retains the acronym RFC, e.g., the official standard for e-mail is RFC 822.

Router

A special-purpose computer (or software package) that handles the connection between 2 or more networks. Routers spend all their time looking at the destination addresses of the packets passing through them and deciding which route to send them on.
See also: Network, Packet Switching

Security Certificate

A chunk of information (often stored as a text file) that is used by the SSL protocol to establish a secure connection.

Security Certificates contain information about who it belongs to, who it was issued by, a unique serial number or other unique identification, valid dates, and an encrypted "fingerprint" that can be used to verify the contents of the certificate.

In order for an SSL connection to be created both sides must have a valid Security Certificate.

See also: Certificate Authority, SSL

Server
A computer, or a software package, that provides a specific kind of service to client software running on other computers. The term can refer to a particular piece of software, such as a WWW server, or to the machine on which the software is running, e.g., "Our mail server is down today, that's why e-mail isn't getting out." A single server machine could have several different server software packages running on it, thus providing many different servers to clients on the network.

See also: Client, Network

SLIP
(Serial Line Internet Protocol)—A standard for using a regular telephone line (a serial line) and a modem to connect a computer as a real Internet site. SLIP is gradually being replaced by PPP.

See also: Internet, PPP

SMDS
(Switched Multimegabit Data Service)—A new standard for very high-speed data transfer.

SMTP
(Simple Mail Transport Protocol)—The main protocol used to send electronic mail on the Internet.

SMTP consists of a set of rules for how a program sending mail and a program receiving mail should interact.

Almost all Internet email is sent and received by clients and servers using SMTP, thus if one wanted to set up an email server on the Internet one would look for email server software that supports SMTP.

See also: Client, Server

SNMP
(Simple Network Management Protocol)—A set of standards for communication with devices connected to a TCP/IP network. Examples of these devices include routers, hubs, and switches.

A device is said to be "SNMP compatible" if it can be monitored and/or controlled using SNMP messages. SNMP messages are known as "PDU's"—Protocol Data Units.

Devices that are SNMP compatible contain SNMP "agent" software to receive, send, and act upon SNMP messages.

Software for managing devices via SNMP are available for every kind of commonly used computer and are often bundled along with the device they are designed to manage. Some SNMP software is designed to handle a wide variety of devices.

See also: Network, Router

Spam (or Spamming)
An inappropriate attempt to use a mailing list, or USENET or other networked communications facility as if it was a broadcast medium

(which it is not) by sending the same message to a large number of people who didnÆt ask for it. The term probably comes from a famous Monty Python skit which featured the word spam repeated over and over.

The term may also have come from someone's low opinion of the food product with the same name, which is generally perceived as a generic content-free waste of resources. (Spam is a registered trademark of Hormel Corporation, for its processed meat product.) E.g., Mary spammed 50 USENET groups by posting the same message to each.

See also: Maillist, USENET

SQL (Structured Query Language)—A specialized programming language for sending queries to databases. Most industrial-strength and many smaller database applications can be addressed using SQL. Each specific application will have its own version of SQL implementing features unique to that application, but all SQL-capable databases support a common subset of SQL.

SSL (Secure Sockets Layer)—A protocol designed by Netscape Communications to enable encrypted, authenticated communications across the Internet.

SSL is used mostly (but not exclusively) in communications between web browsers and web servers. URL's that begin with "https" indicate that an SSL connection will be used. SSL provides 3 important things: Privacy, Authentication, and Message Integrity.

In an SSL connection each side of the connection must have a Security Certificate, which each side's software sends to the other. Each side then encrypts what it sends using information from both its own and the other side's Certificate, ensuring that only the intended recipient can de-crypt it, and that the other side can be sure the data came from the place it claims to have come from, and that the message has not been tampered with.

See also: Browser, Server, Security Certificate, URL

Sysop (System Operator)—Anyone responsible for the physical operations of a computer system or network resource. A System Administrator decides how often backups and maintenance should be performed and the System Operator performs those tasks.

T-1 A leased-line connection capable of carrying data at 1,544,000 bits-per-second. At maximum theoretical capacity, a T-1 line could move a megabyte in less than 10 seconds. That is still not fast enough for full-screen, full-motion video, for which you need at least 10,000,000 bits-per-second. T-1 is the fastest speed commonly used to connect networks to the Internet.

See also: Bandwidth, Bit, Byte, Ethernet, T-3

T-3   A leased-line connection capable of carrying data at 44,736,000 bits-per-second. This is more than enough to do full-screen, full-motion video.
See also: Bandwidth, Bit, Byte, Ethernet, T-1

TCP/IP   (Transmission Control Protocol/Internet Protocol)—This is the suite of protocols that defines the Internet. Originally designed for the UNIX operating system, TCP/IP software is now available for every major kind of computer operating system. To be truly on the Internet, your computer must have TCP/IP software.
See also: IP Number, Internet, UNIX

Telnet   The command and program used to login from one Internet site to another. The telnet command/program gets you to the login: prompt of another host.

Terabyte   1000 gigabytes.
See also: Byte, Kilobyte

Terminal   A device that allows you to send commands to a computer somewhere else. At a minimum, this usually means a keyboard and a display screen and some simple circuitry. Usually you will use terminal software in a personal computer—the software pretends to be (emulates) a physical terminal and allows you to type commands to a computer somewhere else.

Terminal Server   A special purpose computer that has places to plug in many modems on one side, and a connection to a LAN or host machine on the other side. Thus the terminal server does the work of answering the calls and passes the connections on to the appropriate node. Most terminal servers can provide PPP or SLIP services if connected to the Internet.
See also: LAN, Modem, Host, Node, PPP, SLIP

UDP   (User Datagram Protocol)—One of the protocols for data transfer that is part of the TCP/IP suite of protocols. UDP is a "stateless" protocol in that UDP makes no provision for acknowledgement of packets received.
See also: TCP/IP

UNIX   A computer operating system (the basic software running on a computer, underneath things like word processors and spreadsheets). UNIX is designed to be used by many people at the same time (it is multi-user) and has TCP/IP built-in. It is the most common operating system for servers on the Internet.

URL   (Uniform Resource Locator)—The standard way to give the address of any resource on the Internet that is part of the World Wide Web (WWW). A URL looks like this: http://

www.matisse.net/seminars.html; or: telnet://well.sf.ca.us; or: news:new.newusers.questions, etc.

The most common way to use a URL is to enter into a WWW browser program, such as Netscape, or Lynx.
See also: Browser, WWW

USENET   A world-wide system of discussion groups, with comments passed among hundreds of thousands of machines. Not all USENET machines are on the Internet, maybe half. USENET is completely decentralized, with over 10,000 discussion areas, called newsgroups.
See also: Newsgroup

UUENCODE   (Unix to Unix Encoding)—A method for converting files from Binary to ASCII (text) so that they can be sent across the Internet via e-mail.
See also: Binhex, MIME

Veronica   (Very Easy Rodent Oriented Net-wide Index to Computerized Archives)—Developed at the University of Nevada, Veronica is a constantly updated database of the names of almost every menu item on thousands of gopher servers. The Veronica database can be searched from most major gopher menus.
See also: Gopher

WAIS   (Wide Area Information Servers)—A commercial software package that allows the indexing of huge quantities of information, and then making those indices searchable across networks such as the Internet. A prominent feature of WAIS is that the search results are ranked (scored) according to how relevant the hits are, and that subsequent searches can find more stuff like that last batch and thus refine the search process.

WAN   (Wide Area Network)—Any internet or network that covers an area larger than a single building or campus.
See also: Internet, internet, LAN, Network

Web   *See:* WWW

WWW   (World Wide Web)—Two meanings—First, loosely used: the whole constellation of resources that can be accessed using Gopher, FTP, HTTP, telnet, USENET, WAIS and some other tools. Second, the universe of hypertext servers (HTTP servers) which are the servers that allow text, graphics, sound files, etc. to be mixed together.
See also: Browser, FTP, Gopher, HTTP, Telnet, URL, WAIS